WITHDRAWN

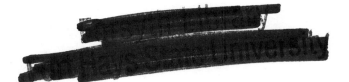

Landmark Essays

Landmark Essays

on
Aristotelian Rhetoric

Edited by
Richard Leo Enos and Lois Peters Agnew
Texas Christian University

LAWRENCE ERLBAUM ASSOCIATES, PUBLISHERS
1998   **Mahwah, New Jersey**   **London**

Landmark Essays Volume Fourteen

Cover design by Kathi Zamminer

Lawrence Erlbaum Associates, Inc., Publishers
10 Industrial Avenue
Mahwah, New Jersey 07430

Library of Congress Cataloging-in-Publication-Data

Landmark essays on Aristotelian rhetoric / edited by Richard Leo Enos and
Lois Peters Agnew
        p. cm. — (Landmark essays : v. 14)
   ISBN 1-880393-32-8 (pbk. : alk. paper)
   1. Aristotle. Rhetoric. I. Enos, Richard Leo. II. Agnew, Lois Peters.
   III. Series.
PN173.L36   1998
808.5–dc21   97-49447
                                           CIP

Printed in the United States of America
10 9 8 7 6 5 4 3 2 1

In Memoriam

The Reverend
William M. A. Grimaldi, S.J.

Born: October 24, 1917

Ordained: June 22, 1947

Died: October 9, 1991

Dominius vobiscum, Father Bill . . .

About the Editors

Richard Leo Enos is Professor and Holder of the Lillian Radford Chair of Rhetoric and Composition at Texas Christian University. Lois Peters Agnew is a doctoral candidate in the Department of English at Texas Christian University with a concentration in the history of rhetoric.

Acknowledgments

We gratefully appreciate the help and cooperation of the following individuals and organizations who assisted in securing reprint permissions and in the preparation of this volume: Ted Spencer and the Speech Communication Association, Jan Wilson and The Pennsylvania State University Press, Mona Wilson and the Southern Illinois University Press, Stephanie Clay and the *American Journal of Philology*, and members of the Editorial Board for *Hermes: Zeitschrift fuer Klassische Philologie*. We also wish to express our appreciation to those who offered suggestions and advice that greatly aided in the completion of this project: Mary Schulte, Editor of Fordham University Press, and Landmark Essays Series Editor James J. Murphy. We also thank Sally Helppie for her advice and observations on international copyright procedures and protocol. Finally, the unfailingly cooperative people at Lawrence Erlbaum Associates, especially our editors, Kathleen O'Malley and Linda Bathgate.

The works in this volume originally appeared as follows:

Bitzer, Lloyd. "Aristotle's Enthymeme Revisited." *Quarterly Journal of Speech* 45 (December 1959): 399-408.

Brandes, Paul D. "Printings of Aristotle's *Rhetoric* During the Fifteenth and Sixteenth Centuries." *Communication Monographs* 52 (December 1985): 368-76.

Enos, Richard Leo and Janice M. Lauer. "The Meaning of *Heuristic* in Aristotle's *Rhetoric* and Its Implications for Contemporary Rhetorical Theory." *A Rhetoric of Doing: Essays on Written Discourse in Honor of James L. Kinneavy.* Eds. Stephen Witte, Neil Nakadate, and Roger D. Cherry. Carbondale: Southern Illinois University Press, 1992: 79-87.

Erickson, Keith V. "The Lost Rhetorics of Aristotle." *Speech Monographs* [now *Communication Monographs*] 43 (August 1976): 229-37.

Grimaldi, William M.A., S.J. "Studies in the Philosophy of Aristotle's Rhetoric." *Hermes* 25. Wiesbaden: Franz Steiner, 1972: 1-151.

Kinneavy, James. "William Grimaldi—Reinterpreting Aristotle." *Philosophy and Rhetoric* 20 (1987): 183-200.

Nadeau, Raymond. "Some Aristotelian and Stoic Influences on the Theory of Stases." *Speech Monographs* [now *Communication Monographs*] 26 (1959): 248-54.

Solmsen, Friedrich. "The Aristotelian Tradition in Ancient Rhetoric." *American Journal of Philology* 62 (1941): 35-50 and 169-90.

Table of Contents

Historical Perspectives:

Introduction

There is little doubt that Aristotle's *Rhetoric* has made a major impact on our field. This impact has not only been chronicled throughout the history of rhetoric but has more recently been contested as contemporary rhetoricians re-examine Aristotelian rhetoric and its potential for facilitating contemporary oral and written expression. This re-examination has led to rival interpretations that have fueled considerable controversy. Some scholars claim that Aristotelian rhetoric has constrained rival paradigms–such as sophistic rhetoric–and has thereby limited our understanding of the relationship between thought and expression. Other scholars think the opposite, maintaining that we are only now at the stage of beginning to understand the wealth of insights offered by Aristotle's *Rhetoric*. For both camps, and for all of us, a resource that provides readers with the best and most influential scholarship on Aristotelian rhetoric is welcome. We believe that current arguments concerning Aristotelian rhetoric will be more fruitful and authoritative when advanced from thorough knowledge of this scholarship.

The issues and complexities of Aristotelian rhetoric are important not only for those who do research in the history of rhetoric but for all engaged in rhetorical studies. A recent survey by Thomas Miller and published in *Rhetoric Review* (Fall 1993) reveals that the vast majority of doctoral programs in rhetoric offer at least one course in the history of rhetoric; this survey does not even begin to account for the numerous undergraduate courses offered throughout the country and abroad. There is little doubt that this collection will be valuable for both teachers and students. Our belief, as stated earlier, is that the essays provided in this volume will make readers better participants in today's deliberations about the merits of Aristotelian rhetoric in contemporary teaching and research.

Lastly, and perhaps most important of all, this collection provides teachers and students with major works on Aristotelian rhetoric that are difficult to acquire elsewhere. One example illustrates our point. The Table of Contents makes it apparent that this collection is centered around William M. A. Grimaldi's monograph, "Studies in the Philosophy of Aristotle's Rhetoric."Written in English but published in the German classical journal *Hermes* in 1972, this work is commonly acknowledged as one of this century's major contributions to Aristotelian rhetoric but is virtually inaccessible. Making available the scholarship of Father Grimaldi would, by itself, warrant a volume. To a lesser degree, this situation is true of many of the other essays in this collection. The last major collection of scholarship on Aristotle's *Rhetoric* was edited by Keith V. Erickson, *Aristotle: The Classical Heritage of Rhetoric*. Published by The Scarecrow Press in 1974, this collection is no longer readily available and, of course, does not account for the research of the last two decades.

Our rationale for the order and selection of the essays is to provide a context for Aristotelian rhetoric through three sections. First, a section that offers an understanding of the history and philosophical orientation of Aristotle's *Rhetoric*. Second, a section that emphasizes theoretical scholarship on concepts and issues central to understanding Aristotelian rhetoric. Third, a section that offers essays that examine the historical impact and consequences of Aristotelian rhetoric. The works selected under these rubrics were taken from a review of thirty-three possible entries. The essays of this final selection offer readers a coherent collection of scholarship on Aristotelian rhetoric and provide a firm foundation for advancing observations about Aristotelian rhetoric.

Orientations to Aristotle's Rhetoric

The Lost Rhetorics of Aristotle

Keith V. Erickson

The literature of antiquity in our possession represents a fraction of the works generated by ancient authors. This is true of Aristotle's works. Numerous scholars have attempted to reconstruct the "lost" works of Aristotle and to correct extant texts.[1] Philological interpretation and correction of the extant *Rhetoric* has clarified greatly Aristotlelian rhetorical theory,[2] yet the content and philosophy of his lost rhetorics remain largely unknown. This is unfortunate as these rhetorics constitute Aristotle's earliest thinking on the subject and likely represent the nascent origins of his rhetorical theory as developed in the *Rhetoric*.[3] The purpose of this article is to review philological research attempting to reconstruct and interpret Aristotle's lost rhetorics and to show, where possible, their influence upon his mature philosophy of rhetorical discourse.

Primary evidence confirms the ancient existence of Aristotle's "lost" rhetorics, although it is unclear why they disappeared and the *Rhetoric* remains.[4] According to the testimony of ancient catalogers Aristotle authored numerous tracts on rhetoric. Diogenes[5] lists eight titles while other catalogues list as many as nine.[6] The lists of these catalogues are something of a mystery as little is known of their sources of information. Moreover, many of the entries appear spurious, their philological status ordinarily established by cross-referencing to primary sources. Modern scholarship recognizes four works from these lists as dealing with rhetoric; the extant *Rhetoric*, *On Rhetoric* or *Gryllus*, *Synagōgē technōn*, and *Theodectea*.

Gryllus

The *Gryllus* has attracted considerable scholarly attention.[7] The text, however, is wholly lost (various passages of Quintilian's *Institutio oratoria*,[8] though, are considered by Thillet and Chroust to be fragments or paraphrases of the *Gryllus*).

Secondary sources offer a rich base of philological evidence, however. Significantly, both Diogenes and the *Vita Aristotelis Hesychii* consider it an authentic work. Modern critics, with the exception of Valentini Rose[9] who entertained the possibility of the *Rhetoric* being a pseudo-Aristotelian work, likewise attribute the work to the Stagirite, with Jaeger and others[10] believing it to be the first literary or exoteric publication of Aristotle, authored approximately 360-359 B.C.[11]

The *Gryllus* is philologically interesting on several counts, including its atypical title, Aristotle's motivation for composing it, and its relationship to the *Rhetoric*. The title of the work, it is generally agreed, emanates from Gryllus, the son of Xenophon who was killed at the battle of Mantinea in 362 B.C. Scholars suggest Aristotle dedicated this work to Gryllus, supposedly a close friend, and hence the title.[12] No evidence exists, however, to suggest Aristotle was even an acquaintance of Xenophon's son, making it unlikely that he wished to honor or commemorate him. Because Diogenes mentions "Aristotle had insisted that a great many people had composed epitaphs and encomia upon Gryllus, largely for the purpose of ingratiating themselves with his father Xenophon,"[13] Thillet and Solmsen believe he may have been considerably annoyed by the behavior of these orators.[14] There is little doubt that much false praise was heaped upon Gryllus by people only remotely familiar with him. Aristotle no doubt was irked by the participation of prominent rhetoricians in this favor seeking display. "This is the only possible connection between the title of this dialogue and its real subject matter—between Gryllus and rhetoric."[15] Thus the excesses of orators in composing false and inartistic eulogies to Gryllus prompted Aristotle's rejoinder, apparently an anti-rhetorical position, aimed at rebuking the substance and manner of their addresses. A key to interpreting this work, therefore, lies in determining whom Aristotle was charging with the inartistic employment of rhetoric. Chroust (and others) suggest the *Gryllus*' arguments were directed principally at Isocrates.[16] Chroust reasons that Isocrates might well have written one of these eulogies—reason enough to kindle Aristotle's attack as Isocrates was a long standing competitor and antagonist of the Academy.

Thillet and Solmsen, in determining the content of the *Gryllus*, reason that the work was polemical rather than doctrinal, taking the position that not all forms of rhetoric constitute art. They argue that Aristotle contrasted inartistic rhetoric with true or ideal rhetoric. Evidence in support of this thesis is found in Quintilian who reviews what appear to be Aristotelian arguments (some may be those of Critolaus and Athenodorus, also mentioned by Quintilian) concerning the relationship of rhetoric to art, and it is obvious from Quintilian's remarks that he was impressed by their strength. Hill translates the passage as: "Aristotle in his *Gryllus* produces some tentative arguments to the contrary which are marked by characteristic ingenuity. On the other hand he also wrote three books on the art of rhetoric, in the first of which he not merely admits rhetoric is an art but treats it as a department of politics and also of logic."[17] Chroust further theorizes that "Aristotle must have alleged that proper rhetoric, and not every form of rhetoric, has always been considered an art, and not merely a natural faculty or talent; that no one had ever seriously disputed this; and that the several arguments which attempted to deny that true rhetoric was an art, despite their acumen, may not be taken seriously in that they were purely dialectical performances or devices without any real merit—an intellectual veneer invented to enliven and dramatize the whole discussion."[18] Chroust implies by his remarks that Aristotle, the youthful Platonist, distinguished true from sophistic rhetoric as envisioned in the *Phaedrus*. However, in concert with the majority of scholars, Chroust sees the *Gorgias* as the source of Aristotle's arguments. This is an intriguing issue as Plato's attack upon the sophists not only would have served Aristotle's purposes but would have reflected the Master as well: "Hence, it is not surprising that Aristotle, the disciple of Plato, should object to such contemptible practices as well as to the ultimate philosophic outlook underlying them. In rejecting and denouncing this type of rhetoric, Aristotle acts in full accordance with the spirit and tenets of Plato's basic philosophic teachings."[19]

The *Gryllus*, therefore, Platonically railed against the value of rhetoric as interpreted by Isocrates and his associates rather than explicating its techniques.

Quintilian's remark that Aristotle advanced many arguments of his own making in the *Gryllus* led modern critics to theorize that he tested a new form of dialogue. Jaeger sees the *Gryllus* imitating the *Gorgias* in an "expository" rather than "dramatic" format,[20] although little philological evidence supports such speculation. Moreover, the *Gryllus* was to launch Aristotle's career, as here was the perfect opportunity for him to attack a long standing enemy of the Academy, employ his mentor's work, and to simultaneously advance and test arguments of his own making. In so doing, he likely secured the support of the enemies of Isocrates, made himself known to Plato, and tested his own powers of intellect. Chroust sees Aristotle's opportunity to teach rhetoric arising directly from the strength of this work. He argues that the *Gryllus* probably became the occasion for Aristotle being permitted to offer this course in the Academy, since in this dialogue he seems to have demonstrated not only his qualifications as a teacher of rhetoric, but also his ability to stand up to Isocrates, a man much disliked by the members of the Academy.[21]

The *Gryllus* represents the young Aristotle responsive primarily to the philosophical considerations of Platonism, while the *Rhetoric* evidences the genetically developed thinking of a mature philosopher. Although the *Rhetoric* develops the rhetorical method, the *Gryllus* may have influenced the *Rhetoric*. As an apparently anti-rhetorical work in the tradition of the *Gorgias*, the *Gryllus* probably argued that inartistic rhetoric arouses the emotions and passions. "This argument loosely resembles Socrates' proof that it is not an art because it can give no rational account of using the *pathe* of the hearers. The idea that there can be no *techne* of using the *pathe* clearly dictated the standard of *Rhetoric* I i, which banishes them from among the artistic proof."[22] Further, this passage suggests that the criticism of Isocrates enunciated in the *Gryllus* was considered by Aristotle still viable some thirty years later upon the "publication" of the *Rhetoric*. "It would mean that in the preparatory period for the first stage of the *Rhetoric*, Aristotle's thought was dominated by the quarrel with Isocrates."[23] Kennedy observes, however, that several passages citing Isocrates are mellow, if not complimentary.[24] This inconsistency, one among many, highlights the fact that Aristotle did not have a single theory of rhetoric. Aristotle, for example, had two theories of artistic and inartistic rhetorical devices, as Hill suggests "they were products of different environments, and they were never completely knit together."[25] Moreover, though, subject specific content of the *Gryllus* probably did not find its way into our *Rhetoric*, although early drafts may have evidenced its reasoning. I. Düring, for instance, believes that major portions of the *Rhetoric* belong to the late fifties of the fourth century, or shortly after the *Gryllus'* appearance.

Synagōgē technōn

Little is known of the actual content and thrust of the *Synagōgē technōn*, thought to be composed between 360 and 355 B.C. Spengel attempted to reconstruct portions of the work,[26] but much of his evidence is secondary and his conclusions speculative. Cicero is our chief source of evidence having cited and described briefly its contents in three of his works.[27] He tells us: "I read. . . that book of his, setting forth the rhetorical theories of all his forerunners, and those other works containing sundry observations of his own on the same art. . . ."[28] Primary sources, passages thought to be fragments of the lost work, are evident in Dionysius of Halicarnassus and Cicero.[29] Basically, the work constituted a history of rhetoric and rhetoricians as found in early rhetorical handbooks. Prior to Aristotle, efforts to preserve these handbooks were minimal, and following his treatment of them in the *Synagōgē technōn*, few survived beyond the fourth century. Aristotle openly belittles the shallowness of these handbooks in the *Rhetoric* (1354a12-15); can we infer, then, that he collected these works not for their historical value but for research or teaching purposes? This, of course, would be in keeping with Aristotle's tradition of observing and cataloging relevant data when investigating a topic. "Presumably he was gathering material in preparation for his own works on rhetoric in the way that he gathered information on constitutions as part of his study of politics."[30]

Aristotle began the compendium with Corax and Tisias and brought it forward to Plato and Isocrates' Technē.[31] The work may have resembled an anthology suitable for lecturing on rhetoric. Whether Aristotle employed it when he lectured on rhetoric in the Academy or much later in the Lyceum is uncertain. In any event, the theories of ancient and contemporary rhetoricians apparently were outlined in detail. The *De inventione* informs us that:

Aristotle collected the early books on rhetoric, even going back as far as Tisias, well known as the originator and inventor of the art; he made a careful examination of the rules of each author and wrote them out in plain language, giving the author's name, and finally gave a painstaking explanation of the difficult parts. And he so surpassed the original authorities in charm and brevity that no one becomes acquainted with their ideas from their own books, but everyone who wishes to know what their doctrines are, turns to Aristotle, believing him to give a much more convenient exposition.[32]

Douglas, contrary to the glowing accolade bestowed upon Aristotle by Cicero, suggests that the *Synagōgē technōn*'s account of history was forced and tendentious. Cicero's *Brutus* 46-48 recounts the now famous introduction of rhetoric by Tisias and Corax and contrasts Lysias and Isocrates. Douglas examines various contradictions and fallacies in the passage and concludes that "to any reader not hypnotized by the claim of Aristotle's authority, the malice of the passage is obvious, and the schematic contrast of Lysias and Isocrates suspicious . . . Our choice is to recognize either that . . . Aristotle's approach was less than fully scientific, or that the work was entrusted to a student who lacked the urbanity and mastery of the head of the school."[33]

While purely speculative, the ancient existence of this work may account for the *Rhetoric*'s infrequent references to contemporary rhetoricians known to Aristotle. Chroust, though, sees evidence of the *Synagōgē technōn* in the *Rhetoric*,[34] and George Kennedy, perhaps overstating the case, believes the *Rhetoric* "made much use of all of them [sources and techniques catalogued in the *Synagōgē technōn*]."[35] The *Synagōgē technōn*'s impact upon the *Rhetoric* is difficult to assess, the collection probably serving both a teaching and resource function. Aristotle's familiarity with numerous treatises on rhetoric enabled him to glean and winnow principles suited to his philosophy. The work surely provided Aristotle with the pragmatics of rhetoric, techniques inherited from his sophistic predecessors. Aristotle obviously did not devise each of the *Rhetoric*'s precepts, but probably refined and altered many techniques catalogued in the *Synagōgē technōn*. The *Synagōgē technōn* may have served, therefore, as a major resource in the genetic development of the *Rhetoric*. Another important contribution of this work was its preservation of classical rhetoric. Numerous historians and rhetoricians of antiquity owed their understanding of early rhetoric to first hand or filtered interpretations of the *Synagōgē technōn*'s contents.

Theodectea

Considerable controversy engulfs the *Theodectea* as it may not have been an Aristotelian composition. Aristotle may have commissioned it, or Theodectes, the dramatist, may have authored or edited the work. Even the ancients were divided on this question. Quintilian and Dionysius of Halicarnassus believe the work to be Aristotle's while Cicero favors Theodectes.[36] There is reference in the *Rhetoric*[37] to the *Theodectea* but no confirmation of the author's identity. The *Rhetorica ad Alexandrum* also refers to the work but is noncommittal as to whether the work was edited by or addressed to Theodectes.[38]

Several modern critics investigating the authenticity of the *Theodectea* hold differing interpretations. Richard Shute[39] is emphatic in his belief that Aristotle authored no such work. Rose,[40] however, is certain no "art" of Theodectes existed, while Heitz[41] argues it is a genuine Aristotelian composition. Diels,[42] elaborates the most interesting account of the work, drawing much of his information from the speculations of Valerius Maximus. In essence, Diels believes that upon Plato's death in 348-347 B.C. Aristotle left the Academy, leaving behind him his lecture notes or *florilegium* on rhetoric. Theodectes, formerly a student of Isocrates and recently a close friend of Aristotle, chose to remain in Athens. Assuming the vacated position of instructor in rhetoric he began to teach from, and in the process revise and enlarge, Aristotle's notes. Sometime during these intervening years he or one of his associates published the work. It appeared bearing the name of Theodectes. Diels reasons that Aristotle, upon returning to Athens in 335 B.C., made no attempt to rectify this compromising situation. Rather, upon Theodectes' death he resumed lecturing on rhetoric. Finally, perhaps sensing the need for a clearer edition, Aristotle may have revised and enlarged the *Theodectea* which ultimately culminated in the *Rhetoric*. The "publication" date of the *Theodectea* is placed at approximately 335 B.C. and the *Rhetoric* near 330 B.C.

Friedrich Solmsen presents a more reasoned and widely accepted interpretation of the *Theodectea*.[43] Solmsen theorizes that Aristotle authored a résumé of Theodectes' original work on rhetoric. Thus, two works were in circulation bearing similar titles but having different authors, which would account for the confusion and inconsistency of early catalogers. This would appear to satisfy both the arguments of those insisting Theodectes wrote such a work and those favoring Aristotle's hand. The *Theodectea* and *Rhetoric* must surely have been similar in philosophy, if not content. It seems unlikely that Aristotle would have prepared a résumé of a work abhorent to him. Solmsen's explanation likewise refutes the arguments of those who assert the *Theodectea* was written during Aristotle's stay in Asia Minor.[44]

The content and subject matter of the *Theodectea* generate numerous hypotheses. Basically, one's view of the work depends upon the acceptance or rejection of Diels' or Solmsen's account. Diels' explanation suggests Aristotle's lecture notes on rhetoric made up the work, which Blass dates at 355 B.C. (shortly after the writing of the *Gryllus*), during his first residency in the Academy.[45] He further contends that these lecture notes represent the genesis of the *Rhetoric*, a view shared by Düring. Blass contends that Plato's *Phaedrus* significantly influenced Aristotle's lectures, and thus the *Theodectea*. Chroust agrees: "The Platonic *Phaedrus* and the notions about the proper use of rhetoric and dialectic expressed there probably furnished the general program of how rhetoric ought to be taught."[46]

Gohlke, of a similar opinion, suggests that the *Theodectea* resembled a manual or collection of useful materials for the instruction of rhetoric.[47] He also argues against Solmsen's treatment which concludes that the *Theodectea* is a paraphrase or model of Theodectes' work, fragments of which, Gohlke claims, appear in the *Rhetoric*. Judging by the few surviving fragments of Theodectes' work, however, his rhetorical theories differed from Aristotle's.

In book three of the *Rhetoric* Aristotle contrasts his views of style with Theodectes'. According to Cicero,[48] Theodectes enunciated the qualities of prose rhythm, paeans, and developed five virtues of narration (three adapted from Isocrates to which he added *hedû* and *megaloprepeia*). Kennedy notes that Theodectes also assigned objectives to the various parts of speech, although he observes that "neither the five virtues nor the special objects of the various parts of a speech are specifically stated in Aristotle, though the latter might be said to be implied in the discussion. This seems to indicate that the *Theodectea* and its contents did not constitute a major part of book three of the *Rhetoric* as we now have it except for the discussion of periodicity and rhythm, where Aristotle specifically mentions it."[49] *Rhetoric*, 1410b2, (dealing with the beginnings of periods) is considered by several scholars to be an artifact of Aristotle's earlier theory of style, presumably dating to the *Theodectea*.[50] This passage, though, is considered a scholium by Rose and Heitz. Diels considers the *Theodectea* to be a rough "draft" of the *Rhetoric*, and A. Kentelhardt[51] identifies passages 1354 11-1354b23 (expanded by Solmsen to include 1354a1-1354a10) as dating to Aristotle's lectures on rhetoric (and perhaps the *Theodectea*). Solmsen and Kennedy assign the origin of the introduction to book I and the *topoi* in book II to the *Theodectea*.[52]

Conclusion

During all three periods of his life (residency in the Academy, sojourn to Asia Minor, and term as *scholarchatē* of the Lyceum) Aristotle composed rhetorical tracts. Hill sees the lost rhetorics (and other works) as stages in Aristotle's process of "refining current notions, seeking that which could be founded on scientific deductions, discarding the cruder notions, advancing step by step toward his *telos*, a perfect system at which he knew he would never arrive."[53] Philological conclusions regarding the content, philosophy and authenticity of Aristotle's lost rhetorics are several and divergent. Evidence concerning the influence of the lost rhetorics upon the extant *Rhetoric* is not overwhelming. The urge to speculate upon the origins of each passage in the *Rhetoric* must be tempered by available *Aristotelicum* and *testimonium*, which are neither extensive nor conclusive; we must make choices among several competing judgments. Nonetheless the considerable scholarship supporting the various arguments has greatly enlarged our understanding of these works.

The function of the *Gryllus*, besides assailing Isocrates, amounted to philosophically establishing the value parameters of rhetoric. Certainly the arguments of the *Gryllus*, abstracted from the *Gorgias*, asserted that rhetoric (or at least ubiquitous encomium) is inartistic. "This conclusion almost surely is established by Quintilian's *testimonium*. And it is a point well worth making, for in the *Rhetoric*, I. 1, Aristotle dismisses the arguments about the value of rhetoric quite briefly."[54] While subject specific arguments of the *Gryllus* (arguments against Isocrates) do not surface in the *Rhetoric*, nowhere is the genetic development of the *Rhetoric* more apparent than when it is juxtaposed against the *Gryllus*. The extraordinary differences in philosophy, content, and scope distinguish the mature philosopher from the young scholar subservient to Platonic idealism. The *Synagōgē technōn* collected the numerous rhetorics of antiquity together with succinct analyses of their historical and practical worth. It is much more than an anthology of ancient rhetorical wisdom, however. Used as lecture notes in the Academy, Aristotle drew from this *florilegium* usable rhetorical techniques of early sophistic *technes* and integrated them into the *Rhetoric*. Evidence of the *Theodectea* likewise exists in the *Rhetoric*. Diels and Gohlke contend the *Theodectea* was an initial draft of the *Rhetoric*, whereas Solmsen, sensing the work to be a résumé of Theodectes' *techne*, credits it with less of an impact. Solsmen, however, does assign the *topoi* and the introduction to Book I to the *Theodectea*.

We have reviewed research reconstructing and interpreting Aristotle's lost rhetorics, and demonstrated, where possible, their influence on the *Rhetoric*. Aristotle's lost rhetorics document his life long attraction to rhetoric and the evolutionary development of the *Rhetoric*. The interface of philological fact and conjecture is difficult to assess, however, and until by some good fortune one or more of these works surface, caution is advised in estimating their content and significance. Chroust places in perspective the philologist's attempts at reconstructing the lost works of Aristotle.

> Despite all learned discussion and conjectures of the past fifty years, the main problem still confronting modern Aristotelian scholarship is simply this: although in recent times much valuable material has been gathered and collated by a host of competent and enterprising scholars, and although on the whole, this was done with much care, much effort and astounding acumen, we can never be certain whether this material may in fact be credited to Aristotle in general or to definite Aristotelian lost works in particular.[55]

Recovery of any of the lost rhetorics in whole or part is not impossible, but extremely improbable. It could come only by the discovery of hitherto unknown medieval manuscripts or of new, large-scale papyrus finds, neither of which is very likely. In sum, while the recovery of any of the lost rhetorics would provide a fascinating contrast of Aristotle's early and late theories of rhetoric, philological and textual limitations drastically reduce the chance of fully knowing these works.

Notes

[1] Historically, fragments of Aristotle's lost works have generated considerable discussion concerning their authenticity. Scholars both admit and reject fragments from the accepted *Corpus Aristotelicum*. Valentini Rose held that all "so-called" Aristotelian fragments and doxographical reports are apocryphal, his *De Aristotelis librorum ordine et auctoritate commentatio* (Berlin, 1854) regretting only the loss of the *Problemata*, dismissing as spurious the Stagirite's rhetorics. Rose published a collection of these fragments and reports in his *Aristoteles Pseudepigraphus* (Leipzig, 1863). The *Corpus Aristotelicum* of Immanuel Bekker and the Berlin Academy included Rose's much improved and expanded *Aristotelis qui ferebantur librorum fragmenta* (1870), while a third edition, *Bibliotheca Teubneriana*, was published at Leipzig in 1886. Each work maintained the pseudo-Aristotelian status of the fragments and reports. Interestingly, Rose did not adhere to a systematic schema as he considered the fragments to be spurious, adopting Diogenes Laertius' list as a means of distribution; neither did he attempt to justify the inclusion or ascription of each item.

Philological research documents the inadequacy of Rose's methodology. Among those disagreeing with Rose is Jacob Bernays, *Die Dialoge des Aristoteles in ihrem Verhältniss zu seinen übrigen Werken* (Berlin, 1863), who sees no reason to dispute the genuineness of the dialogues. Moreover, the evidence in support of the dialogues led to Werner Jaeger's thesis that the works of Aristotle evolved genetically, the dialogues representing his early philosophy (*Aristoteles. Grundlegung einer Geschichte seiner Entwicklung*, Berlin, 1923). With the increase of studies in Aristotelian remains, however, the fragments and doxographical reports of Rose are more and more looked upon as genuine. A re-examination and careful qualification of Rose's inclusions is critical lest readers of these works be misled by Rose's assignments and judgments.

Additionally, Aristotle's lost works are examined by: Anton-Hermann Chroust, "The Problem of the *Aristotelis Librorum Fragmenta*," *Classical Journal*, 62 (1966), 71-74; "Werner Jaeger and the Reconstruction of Aristotle's Lost Works," *Symbolae Osloenses*, 42 (1967), 7-43; *Aristotle: New Light on His Life and on Some of His Lost Works* (Notre Dame: Univ. of Notre Dame Press, 1973), 2 vols; Edward M. Cope, "The Lost Rhetorics," in *An Introduction to Aristotle's Rhetoric; with Analysis Notes and Appendices* (London, 1867); W. Gerson Rabinowitz, *Aristotle's Protrepticus and the Sources of its Reconstruction* (Univ. of California Publications in Classical Philology, vol. 16, No. 1, 1957); Mario Untersteiner, *Aristotele: Della Filosofia* (Rome, 1963); Paul Wilpert, "The Fragments of Aristotle's Lost Writings," in *Aristotle and Plato in the Mid-Fourth Century*, ed. I. Düring and G. E. L. Owen (Göteborg, 1960), pp. 257-64.

[2] See, for example, a recent collection of readings explicating the *Rhetoric*: Keith V. Erickson, ed., *Aristotle: The Classical Heritage of Rhetoric* (Metuchen, N.J.: The Scarecrow Press, 1974). Philological research investigating the *Rhetoric* is compiled in bibliographic form by Keith V. Erickson, *Aristotle's Rhetoric: Five Centuries of Philological Research* (Metuchen, N.J.: The Scarecrow Press, 1975).

[3] The *Rhetoric*, as is generally thought, was neither written in one "inspired seizure" nor formally published. Scholarship leans to a genetic explanation, that the *Rhetoric* is a product of several years refinement and alteration. Moreover, the *Rhetoric* may not have been formally "published" but existed in a lecture-note format. Arguments in support of the genetic development of the *Rhetoric* are well known and need not be reiterated here. While these arguments may be criticized for certain controversial emendations, the thesis itself appears certain.

[4] Several scholars have attempted to trace the works of Aristotle, including: Paul D. Brandes, "The Composition and Preservation of Aristotle's *Rhetoric*," *SM*, 35 (1968), 482-91; Anton-Hermann Chroust, "The Miraculous Disappearance and Recovery of the *corpus Aristotelicum*,"

Classica et Mediaevalia, 23 (1962), 50-67; James J. Murphy, "Aristotle's *Rhetoric* in the Middle Ages," *QJS,* 52 (1966), 109-15; Richard Shute, *On the History of the Process by which the Aristotelian Writings Arrived at Their Present Form* (Oxford, 1888); Herman Jean de Vleeschauwer, *L'Odyssée de la Bibliothèque d'Aristote et ses Répercussions Philosophiques* (Pretoria, 1957); Edward Zeller, "Aristotle, Die *Rhetorik,*" *Die Philosophie der Griechen in ihrer geschichtlichen Entwicklung* (Leipzig, 1879), pp. 147-52.

[5]Diogenes Laertius v. i 22, 24.

[6]Hesychius of Smyrna, *Vita Aristotelis Hesychii,* 10; Ptolemy (-el-Garib), "Catalogue"; Ingemar Düring, *Aristotle in the Ancient Biographical Tradition* (Studia Graeca et Latina, vol. 5, Gothoburgensia, Göteborg, 1957); Paul Moraux, *Les Listes Anciennes des Ouvrages d'Aristote* (Louvain, 1951).

[7]Anton-Hermann Chroust, "Aristotle's First Literary Effort: The *Gryllus,* A Lost Dialogue on the Nature of Rhetoric," *Revue des Études Grecques,* 78 (1965), 576-91; Felix Grayeff, "The Problem of the Genesis of Aristotle's Text," *Phronesis,* 1 (1956), 105-22; Forbes Iverson Hill, "The Genetic Method in Recent Criticism of the *Rhetoric of Aristotle,*" Diss. Cornell 1963; Paul Thillet, "Note sur le *Gryllos,* Ouvrage de jeunesse d'Aristote," *Revue Philosophique de France et de l'Etranger,* 147 (1957), 352- 54.

[8]*Institutio oratoria* II. 17.17; II. 17.18; II. 17.22; II. 17.26; II.17.30.

[9]Rose, *Pseudepigraphus,* p. 167.

[10]Jaeger; Chroust, "Aristotle's First," p. 591.

[11]Anton-Hermann Chroust, "The Probable Dates of Some of Aristotle's Lost Works," *Rivista Critica di Storia della Filosofia,* 23 (1967), 3-23.

[12]Ernst Heitz, *Die Verlorenen Schriften des Aristoteles* (Leipzig, 1865), pp. 166-67.

[13]Diogenes Laertius II.55.

[14]Thillet, p. 353; Friedrich Solmsen, *Die Entwicklung der aristotelischen Logik und Rhetorik* (Berlin, 1929), p. 200.

[15]Chroust, *Aristotle,* II, 33.

[16]Chroust, "Aristotle's First," p. 585; Hill, p. 137; Thillet, p. 353.

[17]Hill, p. 132.

[18]Chroust, *Aristotle,* II, 32.

[19]Chroust, "Aristotle's First," p. 583.

[20]Jaeger, pp. 30ff.

[21]Chroust, "Aristotle's First," p. 591.

[22]Hill, p. 136.

[23]Ibid.

[24]George Kennedy, *The Art of Persuasion in Greece* (Princeton, N.J.: Princeton Univ. Press, 1963), p. 72.

[25]Hill, p. 194.

[26]Leonard Spengel, ΣΥΝΑΓΩΓΗ ΤΕΧΝΩΝ *sive Artium Scriptores ab initiis usque ad editors Aristotelis de Rhetorica libros* (Stuttgart, 1828).

[27]*De inventione* II. 2.6; *De oratore* II.38.160; *Brutus* 12.

[28]*De oratore* II. 38.160.

[29]Dionysius of Halicarnassus, *De isocrate* 18; *Brutus* 46-48.

[30]Kennedy, p. 58.

[31]An anonymous *Life of Isocrates* credits Aristotle with including in his *Synagōgē technōn* a rhetorical handbook by Isocrates. The existence of a *Techne* by Isocrates has been widely debated by philologists. It is curious that Aristotle, an antagonist of Isocrates, would have included his work unless, as was his bent, for purposes of thoroughness or in order to irk Isocrates by publicly displaying what must have been a private or even secret work. In addition, Syrianus' "fragment" on style, which he attributes to Isocrates, may have been gleaned from

the *Synagōgē technōn* . See Georg Thiele, "Das Lehrbuch des Isocrates," *Hermes*, 27 (1892), 11ff. and Michael Sheehan, *De fide artis rhetoricae Isocrati tributae* (Bonn, 1901).

[32] *De inventione* II. 2.6.

[33] A. E. Douglas, "The Aristotelian *Synagōgē technōn* After Cicero *Brutus*, 46-48," *Latomus*, 14, (1955), 536, 539.

[34] Chroust, "Aristotle's First," p. 588.

[35] Kennedy, p. 80.

[36] *Institutio oratoria* II. 15.10; IV.2.31; *Orator* LI. 172; LVIII. 194.

[37] *Rhetorica* 1410b2.

[38] *Rhetorica ad Alexandrum* 1421a38; see also Paul Wendland, *Anaximenes von Lampsakos* (Berlin, 1905), who believes the *Rhetorica ad Alexandrum* and the *Rhetoric* have common ties to the *Theodectea*, and Adalbert Ipfelkopfer, *Die Rhetorik des Anaximenes* (Würzburg, 1889), who does not accept this relationship.

[39] Shute, pp. 100-101.

[40] Rose, p. 137.

[41] Heitz, pp. 85-87.

[42] Hermann Diels, "Über das dritte Buch der aristotelischen Rhetorik," *Abhandlungen der Königlichen Akademie der Wissenschaften zu Berlin*, Philologisch-historische Klasse, 4 (1886), 11-16.

[43] Friedrich Solmsen, "Drei Rekonstruktionne zur antiken Rhetorik and Poetik, II: *Theodektes*", *Hermes*, 67 (1932), 144-51.

[44] Eduard Zeller, *Aristotle and the Earlier Peripatetics: Being a Translation from Zeller's 'Philosophy of the Greeks'*, trans. B.F.C. Costelloe and J. H. Muirhead (New York, 1897), p. 73.

[45] Friedrich Blass, *Die Attische Beredsamkeit* (Leipzig, 1892), II, 64-65.

[46] Anton-Hermann Chroust, "Aristotle's Earliest Course of Lectures on Rhetoric," *L'Antiquité Classique*, 33 (1964), 71. See also Keith V. Erickson, *Plato: True and Sophistic Rhetoric* (Amsterdam, The Netherlands, forthcoming).

[47] Paul Gohlke, "Die Entstehung der Aristotelischen Ethik, Politik, Rhetorik," *Sitzungsberichte Österreichischen der Akademie der Wissenschaften in Wien*, Philologisch-historische Klasse, 223 (1944), 111-141.

[48] *Orator* 173.

[49] Kennedy, p. 81.

[50] Ibid., p. 80.

[51] Adolphus Kantelhardt, *De Aristotelis Rhetoris* Diss., Gottingale 1911.

[52] Kennedy, p. 81; Solmsen, *Die Entwicklung*, pp. 213f.

[53] Hill, p. 194.

[54] Hill, p. 141.

[55] Chroust, *Aristotle*, II, xiv.

STUDIES IN THE PHILOSOPHY OF ARISTOTLE'S RHETORIC

William M. A. Grimaldi, S. J.

INTRODUCTION

Despite the extensive use of Aristotle's *Rhetoric* as a critical document in the study of literature and literary composition a common judgment of the work is fairly well represented in the observation that "Advertising . . . is perhaps the best example of an activity that practices what Aristotle preached".[1] If one were to argue that, on the contrary, the object of Aristotle's treatise on rhetoric is ultimately an analysis of the nature of human discourse in all areas of knowledge, the argument would be received with suspicion. For as an academic discipline rhetoric has long been identified exclusively with the facile manipulation of language. We find this view reflected in every phase of contemporary critical activity. Prose, poetry, painting, politics and philosophy are dismissed as "rhetorical" when the criticism is to underscore concentration on form with little or no reference to content. It should be more than obvious that when the form of language is cultivated without regard to the content of the statement we have the misuse of language. We do not, however, have "rhetoric", and to describe this misuse by the words "rhetoric" or "rhetorical" is at the very least to misunderstand the art of rhetoric as it was developed by the Greeks who gave it their attention. Aristotle, Plato and Isocrates when they spoke of rhetoric and rhetorical study were speaking of the intimate articulation of matter and form in discourse.

This stance on the part of these men becomes more readily understandable when we realize that for the Greeks rhetorical study was a method of education and consequently a responsible activity. To equate this *paideusis*, as has been done, with public relations, advertising, or even with college textbooks on English composition is an admission that we have little or no idea of what the Greeks were about. Certainly Plato in works like the *Phaedrus, Gorgias, Protagoras*, Isocrates in his *Antidosis, Panegyricus, Against the Sophists*, and Aristotle in the *Rhetoric* and *Poetics*, give no indication that they are concerned with the mere surface techniques of speaking and writing. Their attention is centered on the character, nature, and use of language as the vehicle of communication. Isocrates aptly expresses the idea: "the proper use of language is the most substantial index of sound thinking" (*Antidosis* 255; *Nicocles, or the Cyprians* 7). Plato speaks of one who "plants and sows words grounded in knowledge. . .words which are fruitful and carry a seed from which other words are implanted in other minds" (*Phaedrus* 276e). The study of rhetoric occupied itself with the way in which language was used and it realized quite early that the content of discourse is substantially conditioned by the way in which it is expressed. The only reasonable way to explain the genesis of the study (even if we accept the traditional account of Tisias-Corax and the Sicilian law courts) is a realization on the part of the Greeks that content is inextricably bound in with the medium, that the "what" of one's statement is eminently qualified by the "way-in-which" or "way-by-which" one expresses the statement. Aristotle's *Rhetoric*, for example, occupies itself essentially with the principles which are necessary if one is to make significant statements on any subject in a way which communicates this significance most effectively. This is the simple object of the whole exercise: "Rhetoric is valuable because truth and justice are naturally superior to their opposites; and so, if incorrect judgments are made, truth and justice are worsted through their own fault" (*A* 1, 55a 21-23). At the same time it should be clear that a formal treatise, such as the *Rhetoric* is, will be specified, as any intelligent analysis will, by the concrete historical and cultural context in which the author is working as well as by the commonly accepted understanding of the subject which he is analyzing. One cannot dismiss the background from which it arose. It is not surprising, then, that the dominant tenor of the *Rhetoric* is oral discourse in the field of deliberative, judicial, and epideictic oratory. On the other hand, without attributing to the analysis more than its due, one should not emasculate the work by a reading narrowly limited to its surface statement. For the character of the analysis is a substantially critical study of discourse as men employ it to communicate with their fellow men whether the subject be philosophy, history, literature, political science. In its essential character Aristotle's analysis has much in common with Plato's study of rhetoric in the *Phaedrus* as expressed in the thematic statement at 261a ff.

Herein Aristotle's work reflects its antecedents since the Greeks were of the opinion that when men use language to speak to each other they need rhetoric, for this was the *techne* whose concern is the structure of language as the mode of human communication.[2] For Aristotle, the rhetorical *techne* includes within its ambience any subject which is open to discussion and deliberation. Further, it attends to all the aspects of that subject which admit of verbal presentation and which are necessary to make the subject understandable and acceptable to an other. Dialectic, for example, considers the same general kind of subject for the purpose of rational investigation and speculative discussion. Rhetoric, its counterpart for Aristotle,[3] approaches the subject under the formality of communication, that is to say with the intention of presenting the matter to an other in such a way as to make accessible to the other the possibility of reasonable judgment. As the art of language among the Greeks rhetoric recognized the fact that language originates from people and is destined for persons. Consequently it was the study of discourse in order to discover the most effective way in which to present the problematic so that an other person may reach an intelligent decision.

The more common way of saying this when one speaks of rhetoric is to say that "rhetoric effects persuasion", a phrase attributed to Gorgias by Plato (*Gorgias* 453a) and frequently repeated in discussions on rhetoric. This kind of statement certainly does not describe Aristotelian rhetoric. He certainly does not speak of "effecting persuasion", but rather of discovering in the subject those things which are suasive to an other. It is unfortunate that the word "persuasion" somehow or other prejudices the whole undertaking insofar as it has long carried with it an acquired pejorative connotation. To many "persuasion" has always implied the coercion of reason and the distortion of evidence under the pressure of careless or false reasoning and a strong appeal to the emotions. Since both can falsify the truth "persuasion" has been looked upon as unbecoming a man of reason.[4] Persuasion *qua* persuasion was not interpreted in such an exclusive manner by the Greeks. Furthermore such an attitude of mind is erroneous in itself because of its refusal to acknowledge that persuasion is at the heart of all communication be it in discourse with the self or the other. As soon as man comes into contact with the world of reality (contingent or absolute) and wishes to make a judgment, he puts before himself or others those reasons which not only represent the real facts or real situation insofar as he can apprehend them, but which are also the more convincing to himself or to his auditors. When we say "more convincing", or as Aristotle would say "suasive", we are simply accepting the inescapable fact that in all areas of human living there are large complexes of pre-existing convictions and assumptions within which we must attempt to speak to the other. There is first of all the large area of common-sense judgments in which it is taken for granted that normal, intelligent persons would maintain, for example, that justice is better than injustice. Again there are assumptions made by people as members of a particular kind of society; for example, those who live in a democracy ordinarily assume that it is a better form of government. Then there are the series of convictions developed by diverse sub-cultures such as professional training or the academic disciplines. Each milieu has a way of establishing its own set of convictions, assumptions, basic understandings, out of which the individual works. There is not only a rational foundation for discourse but also a psychological and sociological foundation. Aristotle himself recognizes this when he comments that "With regard to winning credence it is a matter of much importance that the speaker appear to be of a certain character and that the hearers assume that he be somehow disposed toward them, and further, too, that the audience be somehow disposed" (*B* 1, 77b 25-29). Discourse is meant to convey meaning, but meaning has both a logical and psychological aspect. Discourse occurs within a social and cultural context in which knowledge, belief, attitude, qualify statement. To accept this, as one must, and to work within it is to admit that one speaks to others in different ways in the effort to speak to them with meaning on a problem of common concern. One of the most obvious instances of this in the field of philosophical discourse are the Socratic dialogues. Their dramatic setting is a factor which actually specifies and constructs their argumentation, and it represents Plato's effort to use the cultural and social context in articulating critical philosophical problems: "truth is essentially communicable, and it is the first task of the lover, as is emphasized in the *Phaedrus*, to arouse an answering or requiting love in the object of his affection".[5] As M. POLANYI remarks (Personal Knowledge, Univ. of Chicago, 1958, p. 3): "For as human beings, we must inevitably see the universe from a centre lying within ourselves and speak about it in terms of a human knowledge shaped by the exigencies of human intercourse. Any attempt rigorously to eliminate our human perspective from our picture of the world must lead to absurdity".

Aristotle understood this, and to call his *Rhetoric* a "rhetoric of persuasion" with the understanding of "persuasion at any cost" is wrong. He was aware of the fact that person speaks to person, to the "other" in whom resides the tension between self-possession and its possible loss which may be incurred in any decision made toward further growth in understanding. In this matter of "persuasion" Aristotle's thesis is simply that good rhetoric effectively places before the other person all the means necessary for such decision making. At this point the person must exercise his own freedom.

Men are always engaged in converse with the self and with others in an effort to grasp meaning in the world of reality. This is particularly true of all educational effort where one is quite conscious that the burden of language is to express and communicate meaning. In view of the fact that rhetoric held a prominent position in the educational effort of the Greeks, to the extent, indeed, that it was seriously argued over in the fourth century B.C., one may legitimately question whether this prominence resulted from a simple interest in the tricks of persuasion or an interest in the more substantial question of the nature of human discourse.

It is usual to attribute the interest in, and the study of the spoken and written word to very practical and hard-headed motives: power and security. In the emerging development of political structures, particularly democracy, facility with the practical skills of using language was, we are assured, a talisman for self-defense in the courts of law and self-advancement in the body politic. Certainly this interpretation is reasonable and a partial explanation. Yet the nature of Greek education and the place of rhetoric within it would seem to indicate that the purpose of rhetorical study was something more substantial than the study of ways and means to gain one's way in the world.

The purpose of these introductory remarks is to suggest that the study of rhetoric among the Greeks was of a more serious character than is frequently suggested, and that Aristotle's *Rhetoric* echoes this original concern and gives it new form. The remarks are somewhat partial in that they do not attend to the "schools" of practical rhetoric, to the technographers of rhetorical handbooks, nor to the criticisms of practical rhetoric found in the major writers. Certainly there were treatises in circulation on what appears to be practical rhetoric (cf. Plato, *Phaedrus* 271c. 266c-269c; Isocrates *Against the Sophists* 19; Aristotle, *Rhetoric A* 1, 54a 12), and there were also teachers of rhetoric usually identified with the Sophists, as is quite clear from Plato, or earlier, Aristophanes. All of this material, however, can be found in any history of Greek rhetoric. Furthermore there is no intent here to dismiss the fact that there were probably rhetoricians who devoted their time exclusively to the practical aspects of technique and verbal expertise. This would be foolish, particularly in view of the fact that one senses the development of such an approach in the strong antagonism in the fourth century between philosophy and rhetoric as the true instrument of education.

It is difficult, however, to accept the study of rhetoric in the schools as vocational training in persuasive speaking when we find the study and the teachers so obviously concentrating on literature and academic subjects. If anything, the evidence supports a concern on their part with language and its structure and its relation to the knowing mind. It is not surprising, then, when we come to the fourth century to find that the men who gave their attention to the problem of rhetoric present us with critiques reflecting the same concern with language and its structure in conjunction with knowledge and understanding. Plato, Isocrates and Aristotle were manifestly exposed to a developing tension between "rhetoric" and "philosophy" as educational methods. But it is certainly an over-simplification to speak, as is done, about "rhetorical education" and the "teachers of rhetoric" in either the fifth or the fourth century, and to describe without qualification the latter (and so the former) as "interested only in the art of persuasion, in rhetorical tricks to arouse the emotions of an audience . . .without regard for morality or truth". If this is true we must conclude that the Greeks, aside from selecting a rather strange method to educate their young people, succeeded in producing a remarkable literature which reveals no significant signs of such an influence, as well as such notable students as Euripides, Pericles, Thucydides, Plato. A side of the coin which is rarely alluded to is the fact that the formal study of rhetoric began and flourished in Greece at a time when there was confidence in the human intellect and in man's ability to formulate his problems. When one examines in this light most of what is dismissed as tricks of the rhetoricians' trade, the common stock dispensed by the teachers of rhetoric, another explanation emerges. Very common techniques, to cite but two, from the teaching of the Sophists, were probability argumentation and the use of antithesis. And yet in the final analysis both are logical methods to open up a question or a problem to all of its implications. They are in fact forms of critical analysis. When we meet the apparent confrontation of rhetorical versus philosophical education in Isocrates and Plato there is still no question of mere verbal expertise and the mechanics of language. Enough has been written on the subject to indicate that neither man would accept rhetoric as a study of the techniques of language manipulation in order to make one's point at any cost and so obtain one's way without regard for fact or truth. The primary concern of these men, and in this they repeat the earlier tradition and were followed by Aristotle, was the ability of the mind to know and to apprehend meaning in the world of reality and to interpret this knowledge to others. Their comments, both formal and informal, on the nature of rhetoric come from within the structure of their philosophical convictions.[6] Aristotle's *Rhetoric*, for example, can be understood correctly, as shall be seen, only when we place it within the context of his philosophy. Plato makes the point well when, speaking in the *Phaedrus* about rhetorical discourse, he asks the aid of those arguments which will prove to Phaedrus that "unless he gets on with his philosophy he will never get on as a speaker on any subject" (269e). Earlier he had remarked that "good discourse demands that the speaker know the truth about the subject of his discourse" (259e), a view reflected in Isocrates' comment that the power of discourse is grounded in the study of philosophy (*Antidosis* 48). It is difficult to escape the conclusion that the interest of these men in rhetoric is with language and its importance as the vehicle of meaning, indeed with form as expressive of meaning.[7] No one questions the fact that the Greeks in their poetry understood the importance of form to convey meaning, although the same understanding of their prose has been, and continues to be identified with sophistry and charlatanism.

Yet the heart of the problem of rhetorical study as seen in Aristotle is that all significant human discourse is structured language, an organic whole, which communicates effectively man's reflection on, and articulation of, reality. In this he reflects the concern of early rhetorical study for structure, Plato's sense of the power of the *logos* in its capacity to engender in the person an awareness of the self and of the world of the real, and Isocrates' theory that rhetoric as the "source of civilization, of law, and the arts" is a creative entity: ποιητικὸν πρᾶγμα (*Against the Sophists* 12). This phrase, interesting in its recognition that language transforms experience, makes rhetoric the analogue in language of the other arts.[8] Rhetoric is the art which presents man with the structure for language, and, by way of structure, enables language to become an effective medium whereby man apprehends reality.

This is a different view of the art of rhetoric than that which is commonly put forward. While it is certainly true of Aristotle's *Rhetoric* there is reason to believe that the *Rhetoric*, in this respect, gives expression to what was substantially the Greek view. For when we turn to the men who are considered to be the exponents of practical rhetoric, the Sophists, we find sufficient evidence to challenge the view that their interest was confined to the superficial tricks of language expression in order to achieve one's principle aims. In the first place the Sophists were educators and MARROU correctly calls the First Sophistic the movement which "produced the great revolution in teaching which was to put Greek education on the road to maturity".[9] As educators their primary interest was with literature and consequently with the study of language. Their studies, and in particular the kind of literary study found in the *Protagoras* 339a-347a, imply that they were alert to the fact that as a cultural instrument the potential of language is realized in the care with which it is used. As FÉNELON remarked "Chez les grecs tout dépendait du peuple et le peuple dépendait de la parole", and language was the instrument the Sophists exploited in their effort to educate. While their curriculum was catholic in its subject-matter, (e.g. philosophy, music, astronomy, mathematics, dialectic, science, semantics), their education followed the traditional pattern in which literature played a prominent role and in which the common denominator was language.[10] Education for them was a matter of the intellect with emphasis on the study of language as the medium whereby man interpreted reality to himself and to others. The concentration of this education on literature, e.g. Protagoras' comment that the study of poetry is the most important part of all education (*Protag.* 338e), developed a sensitivity to the logos, an awareness of the intimate relation between thought and language.[11] Only someone concerned with language and its use could remark as Gorgias did of the logos: "The word is a mighty power. . .it can end fear, abolish pain, instil joy, increase pity".[12] Within this context one can only conclude that rhetorical study as a form of education for the Sophists employed various areas of learning but worked primarily with literature. This apparently continued into the fourth century if the statement of Isocrates (*Panathenaicus* 16-19 with 26) makes any sense.

As a consequence of such an educational process it becomes more easy to comprehend why the Greeks responded readily to language and its effective use, or language in oral and written discourse. When we have an audience educated to be alert to the verbal medium we can understand the large body of distinguished literature which came from them,[13] literature, moreover, which demands sensitivity to language as, for example, the plays of Aristophanes with their literary parody, allusion, and criticism. A minimal enjoyment of such a parody (which we find also in Plato) requires some knowledge in the audience of the literary manner, form, and substance of the object of the sport.

Doubts about the desire of the Sophists to educate and their use of rhetoric as the method are dispelled by dialogues such as the *Gorgias* and *Protagoras* of Plato. What might remain open to question is how they related the two. For example, Protagoras' solicitude for correctness in diction and in linguistic construction, or Prodicus' attention to the semantics of language (e.g. *Protag.* 340b ff.) can readily read as an interest in the mere mechanics of language, or even in mental gymnastics (as is implied in *Protag.* 339a). It can also represent an interest in language meaning, the philosophy of language, which is usually the role of semantics. Since the Sophists, however, have been so consistently identified with attention to the structure and the artistic use of language it is more likely that their primary concern is with man's ability to express meaning for himself and for others by way of language structure rather than with the mere ability to verbalize with a certain panache. This likelihood is further increased when we recall the variety of academic subjects which they taught as well as their attention to philosophical problems in epistemology, ontology, ethics. The same understanding of rhetoric appears to be at work here as has already been mentioned in the case of Plato, Isocrates, and Aristotle, namely, that rhetoric as the study of the intelligent and artistic use of language in discourse requires knowledge.[14]

Gorgias,[15] for example, illustrates both the character and the results of such study in his attempt to construct a theory of the *logos*. A recent account of his work in the area of rhetoric concludes: "The *logos* is no longer only the directive tool of the whole society, the indispensable instrument of communication of the Periclean statesman, but a means of reaching the individual psyche. The emotional conception of the *logos* in Gorgias, moreover, stands in the greatest contrast to the rationalist reaction of Socrates; and the whole system of Plato rests upon the rational force of the *logos* as the antithesis of emotion. . .Thus although Gorgias may not himself have worked out the systematic consequences, psychological and ethical, of his *techne*, nevertheless his rationalistic approach to an area of human activity that did not admit of easy systematization, namely the emotional reaction to art, suggested and stimulated a line of development which proves highly fruitful in the fifth century and culminates as a full-blown 'scientific' theory in the *Poetics* of Aristotle".[16] Whether or not we could confine this effort to Gorgias alone can be argued. For the work of Hippias on the relation between language and music (*Hippias Maior* 285d; *H. Minor* 368d) implies the same acute perception of the character of the verbal medium. Further, we can add that if these studies reached fulfilment in the fourth century they did so most substantially in Aristotle's *Rhetoric*, his study of language as discourse.

In view of the long tradition on the question, however, it would be difficult to deny that the study of rhetoric, even with the Sophists, did on occasion degenerate into training in verbal skill, or what has been called a rhetoric of "verbal surface". To acknowledge this, however, is not at all to accept the usual thesis that their work in rhetoric and education was rigidly confined to such activity. PFEIFFER'S comment, even in the light of the evidence he himself adduces, is far too stringent: "If scholarship were a mere artifice they (the Sophists) would indeed have been its pioneers; for they invented and taught a number of very useful tricks and believed that such technical devices could do everything. . .Still less should they be termed 'humanists'; Sophists concerned themselves not with the values that imbue man's conduct with 'humanitas', but with the usefulness of their doctrine or technique for the individual man, especially in political life".[17] This appears to be tendentious and to be occasioned by the conviction that the educational effort of the Sophists was utilitarian and pragmatic. This kind of criticism is also directed without justification against Isocrates, possibly one of the most distinguished pupils of the Sophistic movement. In this regard one can reasonably question whether the effort of the Sophists was as exclusively utilitarian as it is constantly made out to be.[18] The presence of a practical aspect to their education should neither be surprising nor a cause for condemnation. We must recognize the possibility that the practical aspect of Sophistic teaching was part, as it was with Isocrates, of a larger whole which was humanistic, namely, to make men better. When Isocrates in the *Antidosis* 261-305 (or Protagoras in the *Protagoras* 320d-328d) sets forth his program of study with emphasis on its object to make men who are responsible and of use to the *polis* he is only stating what is, by and large, the general object of any educational effort. Indeed, Plato notwithstanding, one might justifiably ask whether or not the Greeks of the fifth century did not expect this of the arts, particularly literature. Faced with the strictures thrust upon him by Aristophanes, Euripides instructively responds that he makes men better and teaches them to live better (*Frogs* 1009 f.; 971-977).[19] The Sophists and Isocrates in this matter can be more correctly understood from the viewpoint set forth by E. CARR which reflects indeed the tenor of Isocrates' argument in the *Panathenaicus* 30 ff.: "Educators at all levels are nowadays more and more consciously concerned to make their contribution to the shaping of society in a particular mould, and to inculcate in the rising generation the attitudes, loyalties, and opinions appropriate to that type of society; educational policy is an integral part of any rationally planned social policy. The primary function of reason, as applied to man in society, is no longer merely to investigate but to transform; and this heightened consciousness of the power of man to improve the management of his social, economic, and political affairs by the application of rational processes seems to me one of the major aspects of the twentieth century revolution" (What is History?, N. Y. 1962, p. 190). This seems to be an insight as accessible to a Greek of the fifth and fourth century as to men of the twentieth.

On this question of the study of rhetoric Isocrates in many ways is an appropriate summation of the work of the Sophists, and an introduction to that of Aristotle. The program of this student of the Sophists shows rather well what was meant by rhetorical study as a method of education. Quite clearly it was not the commonly understood training in verbal and linguistic skills. Isocrates dismisses such study as false education (*Against the Sophists* 9), adding for good measure that no expositors of prose composition will teach anyone to speak intelligently and with meaning.[20] He continually describes his own manner of educating as ἡ τῶν λόγων παιδεία (*Antidosis* 180) and it is this which he calls his philosophy (*Antidosis* 175 ff.). This stress on philology (love of the word) to specify his philosophy (love of wisdom) points to the fact that Isocrates did not view language as the instrument which simply expressed man's thinking, but that he looked upon thinking itself as a function of language. Thus we find the *logos* placed at the center of man's culture in so far as culture is the expression of the thinking man. This union of *logos* and *nous* is strengthened in the *Panegyricus* 47-50.[21] What at first appears to be a distinction between *logos* and philosophy fuses here into a statement whose main theme is the importance of the *logos* to the cultivated mind. This idea is similar to that expressed in the *Charmides* of Plato (157a) where we read that *kaloi logoi* "engender *sophrosyne* in the soul".

Education for Isocrates is always an education engaged with language, e. g. τὴν περὶ τοὺς λόγους παίδευσιν (*Busiris* 49).[22] The phrase has been interpreted as "rhetorical education". If that is understood in the large sense as the study of language for significant discourse it describes both the endeavor of Isocrates and of rhetorical study in general. If it is understood in the more usual and restricted sense of training in public speaking it does not conform to Isocrates' usage. For him the word "rhetorical" is a rare occurence, and, when it appears, he means by it "public speaking".[23] The word he uses for his work is "logos" in various phrases, and it denotes his concern with rhetoric as the study and use of language in discourse, e. g. *Nicocles, or the Cyprians* 5-10. This interest in the study of language as rational discourse reveals itself in a number of ways. In the first place it appears to be the point of the close connection he maintains between discourse and philosophy in *NC* 1: "there are people who are ill-disposed toward discourse (λόγους) and find great fault with those who pursue knowledge (φιλοσοφοῦντας)". Secondly, he informs us that he welcomes discourse in all branches of learning (NC 10; *Against the Soph.* 16), and, as a background for such work, he tells us that his *paideusis* requires of the student knowledge and understanding in literature and philosophy and is also open to eristics, geometry, astronomy, grammar (*Nicocles* 13; *Antid.* 261).[24] He admits that the types of discourse are quite varied and recognizes specifically theological, philosophical, and historical discourse as well as critical studies of the poets (*Antid.* 45-46). At the same time he finds that his own particular preferences incline him to discourse upon ethics, political science, international affairs (*Antid.* 46-50; *Panath.* 1-11; *NC* 10; *Against the Soph.* 21). From his criticism of those who train men solely in the techniques of eloquence and in the making of speeches (*Helen* 7 ff.; *Against the Soph.* 9-10) it is clear that his kind of education used language study in a much more substantial manner. The goal of his effort in education, as he tells us in the *Panathenaicus* (30 ff.), is the cultivated, informed and responsible mind, or, as he calls it in the *Antidosis* (272): *phronesis*. This is a far remove from mere technical skill and facility with language (Plato's "verbal sport", *Rep.* 539b; *Euthyd.* 271c-272a) and Isocrates makes this obvious when he sums up his educational effort: "I would clearly be found to be more happy with my students who are held in esteem for their lives and their deeds than for those reputed to be excellent speakers" (*Panathenaicus* 87).[25]

In general, then, this is the background out of which Aristotle's *Rhetoric* came, and in terms of which it should be evaluated. The work must obviously speak for itself. It is uncritical, however, to assay its statement apart from its provenance, as well as apart from Aristotle's other works. The treatise has run the gamut of appraisals. It has been described as a mishmash of half-baked logic, psychology, and ethics. Aristotle unquestionably speaks on occasion and at sufficient length in a manner to justify at times the judgment that his critique is nothing but a collection of handbook techniques on practical speaking and writing. Yet others, among whom was Voltaire (who certainly possessed a fine sense of the role of language in discourse), have called it an excellent exposition of the art, "a remarkable product", as RHYS ROBERTS says (Dionysius of Halicarnassus on Literary Composition, London 1910, p. xi), "of its great author's maturity, in reading which constant reference should be made to Aristotle's other works, to the writings of his predecessors, and to those later Greek and Roman critics who illustrate it in so many ways . . . Aristotle . . . looks at rhetoric with the breadth of a lover of wisdom".

The cause of the highly divergent interpretation of the *Rhetoric* is frequently the stance the interpreter takes in the presence of a work which is more complex than it appears to be. When Aristotle studied the art of rhetoric he did not one, but two things. As the first to engage in a formal analysis of the nature of discourse he directed his attention, as Isocrates and Plato did not, to the principles involved as well as to their application. Thus he attempted to found the art on a set of solid and reasonable principles rooted in his philosophical convictions. He also made a serious effort to spell out in some detail the practical applications of these general principles. In reading the treatise the conflict which arises between the philosophy of rhetoric (*theoria*) and applied methodology (*praxis*) has been sufficient to cause careful students of the text to question the unity of the work, the authenticity of the third book, the arrangement of the material in the books, and the consistency of Aristotle's thinking on major themes of his work like the *enthymeme, ethos, pathos.* Each of these problems will be considered in the chapters which follow. To understand them, however, we must recognize that Aristotle is trying to establish a theory of discourse and to give it a ground in philosophy. Relatively little, for example, is said in the pages which follow of the third book of the *Rhetoric*. Yet, if Aristotle's analysis of the organic character of discourse in the first two books is valid, the third book despite its technical character is obviously an integral part of the work. For his study there of the various technical aspects of *lexis* (language) and *taxis* (arrangement) clearly recognizes that language itself and its organization substantially contribute to the organic character of discourse. It is difficult to see that his view in the third book differs from that of COLERIDGE: "Be it observed, however, that I include in the *meaning* of a word not only its correspondent object, but likewise all the associations which it recalls. For language is framed to convey not the object alone, but likewise the character, mood and intentions of the person who is representing it".[26]

The most obvious area in which Aristotle has introduced a theory of discourse to rhetorical study is with the enthymeme, the syllogism of rhetoric. He calls the enthymeme the center of the rhetorical art and the following pages develop entirely about the effort to understand the enthymeme. Among other things the enthymeme introduces Aristotelian logic to rhetoric, i.e. the ways of inference and the axiomatic principles which for Aristotle are the tools enabling the mind to apprehend the true. It makes rhetoric, among other things, the study of reasoned statement. Furthermore in bringing the syllogism into rhetoric Aristotle acknowledges that there is an epistemology of the probable, namely, that the mind can know and use the probable as well as the unconditioned in its attempt to understand the world of reality. At the same time Aristotle also displays a sharp awareness that reason alone does not necessarily speak to the other, something which discourse in its effort to communicate must do. Reason does not possess the power of persuasion. Thus Aristotle introduces into the syllogism, the instrument of reason, his psychology of human action. The enthymeme as the main instrument of rhetorical argument incorporates the interplay of reason and emotion in discourse.

When we see the enthymeme as the integrating structure of rhetorical discourse the *Rhetoric* is found to be a unified whole and to be developed in a sequential manner which can be readily explained. The enthymeme now ceases to be the instrument of reason alone, or "rational proof" as it has been so consistently interpreted by the commentators who strictly separate it from proof by *ethos*, and proof by *pathos*. On the contrary enthymeme is the syllogism of rhetoric precisely because, as the form of deductive demonstration, it incorporates in its argument all of the elements demanded by language as the vehicle of discourse with another: *reason, ethos, pathos*.[27] The enthymeme brings together the logical and psychological reasons which convey meaning to an auditor, and thus Aristotle recognizes that person speaks to person not only with the mind but with the emotions and feelings as well.

At the heart of Aristotle's theory of rhetoric the enthymeme brings meaning to the assumed conflict in the *Rhetoric* between reason and *ethos-pathos*. The enthymeme also serves as the integrating factor whereby Aristotle is able to introduce his *Dialectics* to the art of rhetoric. For the enthymeme explains the methodology of the topics as we find it in the *Rhetoric*. The topics are the source material for argumentation by enthymeme, e.g., (a) the particular topics provide material for intelligent and significant presentation of the subject of discourse as well as a presentation relevant to the auditor; (b) the general topics are axiomatic in character and provide modes of inference, i.e. forms of deductive reasoning which the enthymeme can assume in its effort to speak most convincingly to a particular audience. Finally the enthymeme as the instrument for reasoned discourse makes the third book a perfectly logical conclusion to the work. An analysis which emphasizes the organic nature of discourse must obviously study the medium which articulates such discourse and is also constitutive of it. Like the metaphor in poetry the enthymeme in rhetoric fuses knowing in the person, makes the act of knowing a total perception of intellect, emotion, feelings.

In his *Rhetoric* Aristotle developed the work of the Sophists and Isocrates into an analysis of the underlying principles of discourse bringing about the one thing of concern to Plato: a union of rhetoric and philosophy. He worked out a theory of discourse which is far removed from the activities of advertising or the simple techniques of language composition. As his treatise reveals he perceived that at the center of discourse, as discourse is used when person speaks to person, is a use of the verbal medium in a manner which brings together reason and emotion.

Notes

[1] E. P. J. Corbett, *Classical Rhetoric for the Modern Student*, Oxford University Press 1965, p. 31.

[2] How critically necessary it is to understand this is illustrated by interpretations which criticize the *Rhetoric* for what it is not. To see the work as concerned with a "superficial political science", or "a conventional ethics" (see E. L. Hunt, "Plato and Aristotle on Rhetoric and Rhetoricians", pp. 57 ff., in Historical Studies of Rhetoric and Rhetoricians, ed. R. F. Howes (Ithaca 1961) is to misunderstand it. It is none of these things. Ethics, politics, logic, epistemology, etc. offer the material with which rhetoric works. Rhetoric, like dialectic, is for Aristotle a methodology. But it is a methodology for discourse with others; as a *dynamis* its function is to aid in discovering that structure in discourse on any subject (v. *A* 2, 55b 25-34) which will lead to conviction and belief.

[3] Isocrates, in a way, joins the two when he describes his rhetoric as the faculty whereby "we argue with others on matters open to dispute and investigate for ourselves things unknown" (*Antidosis* 256).

[4] It would be interesting to know how much of this distrust of the art of rhetoric was occasioned by the fact that the 17th century philosophers who developed and strongly influenced modern thought were mainly mathematicians (e.g. Hobbes, Descartes, Spinoza, Leibniz), interested in a language modeled on the symbolism of mathematics: "words often impede me and I am almost deceived by the terms of ordinary language" (Descartes). As a general attitude of mind, prescinding from philosophical distinctions such as we find in the *Gorgias* of Plato, there was no fundamentally intrinsic opposition between persuasion and truth for the Greeks. As a matter of fact the two could be closely related as we see in Cassandra who was a prophetess of truth, ἀληθόμαντις *Agam.* 1241), not given to deceiving (1195); but after violating her oath her words had no effect on anyone: ἔπειθον οὐδέν˙ οὐδέν *persuaded* no one). There is the same close relation five centuries later in Longinus, *On the Sublime* 15.10-11 between factual demonstration and persuasion. Indeed this passage should be compared with BACON's observation: "The duty and office of rhetoric is to apply reason to the imagination for the better moving of the will" (Advancement of Learning, Book II). M. DÉTIENNE says well: "Au même titre que *Pistis*, Peithô est un aspect nécessaire de l'Alétheia. . ." (Les Maîtres de vérité dans la Grèce archaïque, Paris 1967, p. 62). This is the maieutic character of language well used; we see its effect in *Laches* (188 c-d): "When I hear a man discourse on *arete*, or on wisdom, one who is truly a man. . .I am deeply delighted as I behold how both the speaker and his words become each other and are suited to each other". B. MUNTÉANO, "Constantes humaines en littérature" in Stil und Formprobleme in der Literatur, (Heidelberg 1959) after rejecting the idea of Aristotle's *Rhetoric* as a mere collection of tricks and commonplaces (p. 69), continues: "C'est que la structure rhétorique du discours n'est autre chose que la cristallisation en principes et préceptes des données foncières de la nature humaine. . .Au centre

du système fonctionne le principe moteur de la persuasion, où je crois qu'il convient de voir l'expression même de l'instinct qui engage l'individu à communiquer avec ses semblables. . . C'est à *persuader autrui*, c'est à *communiquer* et même, de quelque manière, à *communier* avec lui. . ."

[5]Plato accepts the fact that to teach one must use persuasion, e.g. *Gorg.* 453d; *Crito* 51b-c; *Protag.* 352e; *Apol.* 35c; and this extends to the sciences as well as the humanities, *Gorg.* 454a; see also R. CUSHMAN, Therapeia, Chapel Hill 1958, pp. 219 ff.

[6]If we look at Isocrates from Plato's position then Isocrates' "philosophy" was no philosophy since for Plato philosophy was concerned with infallible knowledge. Isocrates was quite satisfied with "right opinion" on reality (cf. *Panathenaicus* 9). Yet in Isocrates the word "philosophy" both denotes and connotes the exercise of mind and reason in the effort to grasp the world as experience. It is a serious effort toward the truth insofar as the truth can be known by the mind; it is an effort that accepts a kind of total human understanding from knowledge and experience without demanding a metaphysics. On this matter of the relation of rhetorical theory to philosophical convictions P. A. DUHAMEL notes: "There were as many conceptions of rhetoric in the period usually called 'Classical' as there were philosophies, and the rhetoric can be understood only within the commensurable terms of the philosophy. In every observable instance the rhetoric is dependent for its content and orientation upon the more fundamental concepts which are the burden of epistemological or metaphysical discussion. The complete understanding of a system of rhetoric not only entails a scrutiny of the underlying philosophy but the elucidation of those implications is the task of any future historian of the concept of effective expression." ("The Function of Rhetoric as Effective Expression" *JHI* 10, 1949, p. 356).

[7]We find the same concern in the later literary theorists, Dionysius of Halicarnassus and Longinus, in their effort to relate the study of rhetoric to a firm background in literature, philosophy, and the varied branches of learning. They were quite conscious of structure and their work, in the view of W. RHYS ROBERTS, illustrates in many ways the *Rhetoric* of Aristotle (see his Dionysius of Halicarnassus on Literary Composition, London 1910, p. xi).

[8]Oddly enough his teacher Gorgias uses the word *poiesis* of both *logos* and sculpture (*Helen* 9, 18); H. DIELS, Die Fragmente der Vorsokratiker[10], Berlin 1960, 82 B 11 (8 of the *Helen*). In many ways it is difficult to see how the rhetorician is not, as far as Aristotle is concerned, as much a maker as the poet. The rhetorician is making something according to certain definite rules for a definite purpose. In both instances language is the medium; the goal is different in that the object of the poet is knowledge directed toward contemplation, that of the rhetorician knowledge directed toward action. Both arts have to do with the *logos* and H. LAUSBERG (Handbuch der literarischen Rhetorik, Munich 1960, p. 42) is certainly not alone in his judgment of the close relationship of poetic and rhetoric when he writes: "beide. . .sind ja poietische Künste im Bereich der Sprache."

[9]H. I. MARROU, A History of Education in Antiquity (transl. G. LAMB), London 1956, p. 47; A. KOYRÉ, Discovering Plato (transl. L. C. ROSENFIELD), N.Y. 1946, p. 28, n. 12: "Literary criticism, interpretation of classical poets, was one of the main bases of the teaching given by the sophists." R. PFEIFFER, History of Classical Scholarship, Oxford 1968, pp. 16-32, "the sophists. . .were the first to influence by their theories not only prose writing, rhetoric, and dialectic above all, but also contemporary and later poetry. . ." (p. 16).

G. M. A. GRUBE, A Greek Critic: Demetrius on Style, Toronto 1961, speaking of the new sophists, e.g. Gorgias, etc., notes that "as the first *theorists* of the art of language, the Sophists did have a very great influence on the development of Greek style" (p. 4). It surely does not seem an over simplification to ask from where precisely came the impetus to the vast amount of competent work in dramatic literature, historiography, philosophy, and political discourse of the fifth and fourth century if we equate the rhetorical studies of the sophists with mere techniques of writing.

[10]As for the specifically utilitarian character of these studies in the mind of the Sophists the comment of Isocrates merits serious consideration and is quite relevant. Speaking of many of these same subjects he remarks that all of them are of no immediate practical aid (*Antidosis* 262) but do help the student (267) and, like grammar and literature (266), prepare the mind for philosophy, i.e. for an informed and intelligent mind on the critical problems of existence.

[11]MARROU, A History of Education, p. 134 speaking of rhetoric and words has this to say: "These, we said, are inseparable; and this is so because the effort to find the right expression demands and develops a sensitivity of thought, a sense of different shades of meaning, which it is difficult to express in conceptual ideas. . ." There can be little question from the many statements of Isocrates that JAEGER is quite correct in saying that his ideal of culture was *logos* as the union of speech and reason (*Paideia* vol. III, p. 79). E. ARNOLD, Roman Stoicism, Cambridge 1911, pp. 128-154 in setting forth the Stoic doctrine on reason and speech reveals this same idea at work in Stoic concern for the union of language and thought. From the work of the Sophists in the study of the artistic use of language it does not seem correct to attribute the development of literary theory exclusively to the work of Plato and Aristotle as GRUBE does (A Greek Critic, p. 10). Quite clearly the work in rhetoric of Gorgias, Prodicus, Hippias, to mention but three of the Sophists, indicates a body of informed thinking on literary theory. Rhetorical study was directed to the art of language and GRUBE (p. 12) makes the point rather well when he writes: "For we should never forget that *rhêtorikê* was the art of expression as a whole, even if oratory was the art of expression par excellence". The evidence such as it is on "textbooks of rhetoric" and their character ("technical and immoral") is not sufficient to permit firm judgments on their occupation with verbal agility and trickery to the exclusion of substantial theory.

[12]*Helen* 8.

[13]In view of the existence of written works, e.g. *Gorgias* 462b, c, this language study may have been more detailed and precise than we have been accustomed to accept; see also the *Protagoras* 3 25e ff., and PFEIFFER, History of Classical Scholarship, pp. 14-32.

[14]Protagoras' concept of the *dissoi logoi*, the two opposing views which exist with respect to any aspect of the real, can easily suggest debate topics which exhaust themselves in shallow eristics. Considered, however, as a methodology for educating, it appears to be simply an effort to discriminate and determine where the truth may lie on any problem. For example in the *Dissoi Logoi* (Die Vorsokratiker[10, 90]) at the end of the first antinomy the writer remarks (17) that he is not saying what "good" is but attempting to show that it is not the same as "bad". Of this A. E. TAYLOR (Varia Socratica, Oxford 1911, p. 101) notes: "This is precisely the sort of conclusion we get in many of the Platonic dialogues."

[15]Both H. DIELS, Gorgias und Empedokles, Sitzungsberichte der Akademie der Wissenschaften zu Berlin, 1884, pp. 343-368, and O. GIGON, Gorgias über das Nichtssein, Hermes 71, 1936, pp. 186-213, while disagreeing with the place of science, eleatic philosophy, and rhetoric in the development of Gorgias accept the fact that he worked in each area.

[16]C.P. SEGAL, Gorgias and the Psychology of the Logos, Harvard Studies in Classical Philology 66, 1962, pp. 133-134. See also, R. KASSEL, Untersuchungen zur griechischen und römischen Konsolationsliteratur, Munich 1958, on Gorgias (pp. 7 ff.) and the question of the correlation between the effect of *logos* on the psyche and medicine on the body, and H. KOLLER, Die Mimesis in der Antike, Bern 1954, pp. 157-162 on Gorgias' use of the Pythagorean theory of music in his rhetorical study. A passage like the *Theaetetus* (167a) indicates that the *logos* is not simply a logical system and implies that it is polysemantic in character.

[17]History of Classical Scholarship, p. 17, in which he takes issue with the judgments of JAEGER, Paideia and FORBES, 'Greek Pioneers in Philology and Grammar', Classical Review 47

(1933). The difficulty in a judgment like PFEIFFER's is brought into focus by the kind of statement found in Segal ("Gorgias"): "It is again not necessary to assume that Gorgias ever wrote a full-blown treatise systematizing ontology, epistemology, and aesthetics into a unified theory; but the *Helen*, after all, contains an encomium on the *logos* which seems to present at least the basis of a theory of *poiesis*, and other fragments, too, seem to fit into a framework consistent with that theory. . ." (109), "Thus his rhetoric, though concerned primarily with a technique of verbal elaboration, rests ultimately upon a psychology of literary experience."(110).

[18]Some scepticism of the ordinary value judgments in these areas seems in place, or the consequences of these judgments must be accepted. For example one is puzzled when one reads this not untypical judgment of Isocrates' work: "the total effect. . .is one of deadly monotony. His contemporary influence, however, was very great (greater than that of the Academy or Lyceum); his posthumous influence was no less. . ." (GRUBE, A Greek Critic, p. 11). One is constrained to ask: were so many Greeks completely impervious to the stultifying? is there any evidence that his oral style as a teacher (PFEIFFER calls him a pedagogical genius comparable with Melanchthon) differed vastly from his written style on which the judgment is made? do not Isocrates' comments imply that if there was a difference it would be in favor of his written style (e.g. *Panath.* 9, 10 (I was born lacking an adequate voice and self-assurance), *Phil.* 81, *Epp.* 1.9; 8.7). When we also read that "He was the teacher of most of the great Athenians of his day" we must agree that the Athenians were eminently able to transcend their educational experience or that the content of their education distinctly differed from the corpus of Isocrates' work. While the former is possible there is no adequate evidence for the latter.

[19]W. H. THOMPSON, The Gorgias of Plato, London 1871, commenting on 502b has this to say: "The censure which follows is too sweeping even from Plato's point of view, for Euripides at any rate aimed at a moral purpose of one sort or another. . .As a criticism of Sophocles and Aeschylus it is, to modern comprehension, still more deplorable".

[20]From his work Isocrates was clearly concerned with both writing and speaking; he says in *Against the Sophists* 15-16 that his instruction includes writing as well as speaking.

[21]See also *Antid.* 244; *NC* 5-9. It is the task of educators and philosophers to impart the ability to bring the two together.

[22]*Ep. 5 To Alexander* 4-5 explains this τὴν παιδείαν τὴν περὶ τοὺς λόγους in the ideas of *Panegyricus* (47-50) and *NC* (5-9).

[23]ῥητορικός used at *Antid.* 256 in a passage repeated again at *NC* 8; ῥητορεία: *Against the Soph.* 21, *Philip* 26, *Panath.* 2, *Nicocles* 5-9.

[24]Clearly he accepts as valid criticism of any discourse the observation of Socrates that the first discourse of Lysias was poorly written since Lysias does not know what he is speaking about (*Phaedrus* 234-235).

[25]"The things that Isocrates tried to foster in his disciples were—ability to make decisions, an intuitive grasp of the complexity of human affairs, and a perception of all the imponderable factors which help to direct one's "opinion" and make it a just one. Literature—the art (not the science) of speech—is the best instrument for sharpening the faculty of judgment" MARROU, A History of Education, p. 134.

[26]Biographia Literaria c. xxii (vol. 2, p. 115 in 1967 ed. of J. SHAWCROSS, Oxford). C. FRANKENA, "Some Aspects of Language" in Language, Thought and Culture, ed. P. HENLE, Ann Arbor 1958, pp. 121-172, after setting up nine aspects found in linguistic utterance among which are "emotions and conative attitude", "emotional tone", "propositional attitudes" goes on to remark (p. 139): "It would seem, then, that we are justified in holding that all kinds of sentence-utterances, with the relatively trivial exceptions just noted (e.g. hurrah, damn etc.) involve the nine factors we have distinguished". Aristotle's concern with

simile, metaphor, rhythm, choice of language, types of style, etc. in the third book would clearly define his awareness that the verbal medium cannot be simply referential or stenographic but contains within itself organizations of meaning which it communicates to the whole person: mind, emotions, feelings.

[27] Although this point is the subject of an extended argument in c. 2 a preliminary note of a more general character seems in order. Those who accept that Aristotle gave us three distinct modes of rhetorical proof, i.e. *enthymeme* (rational), *ethos* (ethical), *pathos* (emotional) never ask why Aristotle gave his attention to a formal discussion of the misuse of rational proof, namely his discussion of apparent enthymeme in book *B*, but never bothered to discuss formally or informally the misuse of ethical proof or emotional proof. There is certainly an equal demand for such a discussion, particularly in view of the extended discussion of *pathos* in book *B*. It is difficult to understand on what grounds the omission can be justified.

I

THE UNITY OF THE RHETORIC

Any effort to understand Aristotle's *Art of Rhetoric* must begin with its place within his philosophy. For rhetoric functions as a method of communication, spoken or written, between people as they seek to determine truth or fallacy in real situations. To engage in a critical analysis of such communication implicates one's convictions about the nature of reality, the ability of the mind to know it, the nature of language, and in particular the nature of the human persons who use the method. Thus the meaning of "rhetoric" is very largely dependent upon the epistemology, psychology, and metaphysics of the philosophical system in which it occurs.[1] This would seem to be a natural conclusion when rhetoric is subjected to critical analysis as an activity of reasoning man and as an art, and is not considered as a mere collection of technological tricks with which to overwhelm an opponent.

In the cultural context of the Platonic and Isocratean tradition it would have been difficult for Aristotle to dismiss rhetoric as a serious discipline. That he does not do so is obvious from the opening words of his study in which he relates rhetoric to his theory of dialectic and from the substantial study he devotes to the subject. To underline, as it were, the significance of this discipline Aristotle insists from the outset upon showing the relation of his comments to his work on dialectic, epistemology, ethics, and even metaphysics. Thus it is that the relation of rhetoric to its own philosophical system is nowhere more evident than in the *Rhetoric*. Throughout the analysis his constant explicit and implicit reference to his philosophical works clearly reveals that he was working with his own philosophical system in mind, and yet this has been consistently overlooked in much Aristotelian criticism. Here the tendency has been to characterize his analysis as exclusively logical with the result that we have a misreading of his work to say nothing of misunderstanding. Once we subscribe to the common belief that Aristotle committed himself to a purely intellectual theory of rhetoric in which reason and the tools of reason were presumably to play a dominant, indeed an exclusive, role, we meet with the problem that has faced many commentators: open contradiction in the opening statement of his study and inconsistency in the subsequent analysis. For Aristotle's ready acceptance and careful study of the psychological aspect of rhetoric, specifically *ethos* and *pathos*, after an apparently absolute rejection of these elements, seems inexplicable.[2] Even his more sympathetic readers, convinced as they are that Aristotle had in mind a theory of rhetoric which was essentially intellectual, would reason away this study of *ethos* and *pathos* in the *Rhetoric* as sheer accommodation on Aristotle's part to the very real exigencies of a fourth-century audience: a sacrifice, in brief, of theory to expediency.[3]

Thus we find that the character of most interpretation of the *Rhetoric* is a concentrated effort on the role of the mind and reason in human discourse. In this reading of our text Aristotle is concerned exclusively with rhetoric as a purely intellectual discipline. His effort, in other words, was to free rhetoric from what is called the demagoguery of the Sophists with their crude appeal to the emotional (and irrational) in man and to dignify it as a discipline of the mind which is so much more becoming to the rational man. Aristotle would thus carry to substantial fulfilment part of the promise of the Platonic *Phaedrus*. As a partial interpretation this is correct but it falls short of the full answer and in doing so it creates further problems. Placing Aristotle's analysis of rhetoric in the neat category of the thinking, rational mind with its concern for logic and order, and setting it apart from man's emotive life and the whole range of his emotional drives and dynamic energies creates a problem which rightly offends many of his commentators. It creates a division within the psyche which is absolute in character and which neither Aristotle nor Plato would recognize. More disturbing still, as has been said, it condemns this admittedly rather careful thinker to an inescapable contradiction in the very opening chapters of his treatise.

As soon as we accept the common interpretation that Aristotle was committed to a purely intellectual theory of rhetoric in which the rational mind plays a dominant, indeed exclusive, role, we are confronted with the contradiction which has troubled his commentators: after an apparent rejection of the psychological and emotional elements of rhetoric Aristotle engages quite readily in a careful study of these very factors in his extensive analysis of *ethos* and *pathos* in books *A* and *B*.

Those commentators who are rather concerned about this obvious *volteface* attempt to explain it away. Since they remain convinced that Aristotle definitely intended a theory of rhetoric essentially intellectualistic they argue that the study of *ethos* and *pathos* in the *Rhetoric* is either the result of a careless combination of various stages of Aristotle's study of rhetoric, or a ready accommodation on his part to the practical requirements of the concrete human situation in which the art of rhetoric takes place. In the latter instance Aristotle quickly discovered that his theory was not commensurate with human nature or with the practice of rhetoric. This, of course, would be an example of notoriously lax and careless writing and thinking by Aristotle on a substantial point of doctrine in a treatise. No advocates of this thesis advance by way of confirmation other examples of such carelessness on his part and this should give one pause. With respect to the combination of earlier and later theories of rhetoric and a consequent confusion of materials the position is possible but not at all a necessary or convincing solution. It is not necessary since Aristotle's analysis can be shown to be consistent as it stands; it is not convincing since, as we shall see, it demands radical revisions in a text which can be read as an intelligently consistent and consecutive development of a theory of rhetoric.

Such interpretation glosses two rather significant facts. In the first place when Aristotle presumably refuses to situate the art of rhetoric within anything remotely resembling a non-logical environment he is engaged in an obvious polemic. The polemic character of the chapters has never been denied. In his first chapter (*A* 1, 54a 11-55a 3) he takes preceding technographers to task for their exclusive concern with extraneous emotional appeals and for the fact that they are totally unconcerned with the logical demonstration of the subject under discussion. Actually the criticism is directed against a theory of rhetoric which had become somewhat current and was frequently identified, as is familiar to any reader of the *Gorgias* and *Protagoras* of Plato, with the Sophists.[4] Indeed it was a theory which was growing in strength, and the constant criticism of it has conferred upon the word "rhetoric" in all its forms the pejorative meaning so constantly met in critical literature. Against this position Aristotle urges the need for the logical demonstration of the subject-matter and connects this demonstration with the syllogism of rhetoric which he calls the enthymeme (*A* 2, 56b 4-5). In so doing he conveys the impression that the art of rhetoric for him pertains exclusively to the intellect and concerns itself quite simply with merely the logical proof of the subject under discussion.[5] Any polemic tends toward emphatic statement, but particularly does it do so when the subject concerns a strongly felt issue. Consequently when immediately following upon the first chapter Aristotle admits *ethos* and *pathos* as elements co-equal with reason in the art of rhetoric (*A* 2, 56a 1 ff.) it would seem that we would more reasonably inquire whether or not this position is possible for him.

To accuse him of contradicting himself and thus compromising his presumed intention to present a theory of rhetoric grounded exclusively in the intellect and reason is to give too much weight to a brief passage of arms in the opening chapter and to ignore the rest of his study. The opening remarks are obviously directed against an existing situation. Of far more importance is the fact that they must be viewed within the context of the whole *Rhetoric*.

Rather than assume that the rest of the study is at odds with the programmatic statement of the opening chapters it would appear more correct, on the part of those who would interpret the *Rhetoric*, to ask whether or not the opening chapters (which, in fact, encapsulate all of Aristotle's major theoretic statements on rhetoric) are consonant with his general thinking. Certainly the work cannot be studied in isolation when there is in it a frequent cross-reference in the first three chapters alone to his other writings, and when major ideas are introduced for whose full solution assistance must be sought outside the *Rhetoric* itself. It is not a matter of seeking or not seeking this assistance, of asking or not asking the questions of the *Rhetoric* and the other treatises. The *Rhetoric* forces one to ask the questions and to seek the assistance. Because the questions have not been asked the work finds itself saddled with charges of inconsistency and incoherence, e. g. "a curious jumble of literary criticism and second-rate logic".

No one challenges the fact that Aristotle is attempting a scientific analysis of rhetoric similar to the effort of Plato in the *Phaedrus*.[6] The fairly common references within the *Rhetoric* to the *Organon* and the *Ethics* make manifest that he is doing the analysis within the context of philosophical ideas and principles which he considers himself to have established and to be important to his present analysis (e. g. *A* 1, 55b 8-9, *A* 2, 56b 6-11, *A* 11, 72a 1-2). It is in the light of these principles that he makes his major break with Plato. Both men considered rhetoric to be an art (*techne*) in every sense of the word, and an art which played an important role in the life of the *polis*. The major difference between the two was the subject-matter of the art, certainly not the constituent elements of the art. After the extended exposition (257b-279c) in the *Phaedrus* it would be difficult to deny that Plato recognized the role of *pathos* and *ethos* (cf. 270b-272b) as well as the intellect in the rhetorical art. The *logos* at every level of communication is the expression of the whole person. However, Plato (even with his acceptance of ὀρθὴ δόξα in the *Meno*) did not recognize the area of contingent reality and probable knowledge as absolutely valid ground for real knowledge. Consequently, while it is impossible to escape the fact that Plato admits the legitimacy of an art of language in the *Phaedrus* the burden of his argument would appear to restrict its legitimate exercise to the object of the speculative intellect: the knowledge of ultimate, unchanging reality. There can be no art of rhetoric without *episteme*. The fact remains, however, that even the speculative intellect, as any perceptive reading of a Platonic dialogue will reveal, works closely with the emotional and psychological structure of those engaged in such discourse of the mind.[7] This rather enigmatic divorce in Plato between theory and practice was even recognized in antiquity: "*cuius tum Athenis cum Charmada diligentius legi Gorgiam; quo in libro hoc maxime admirabar Platonem, quod mihi [in] oratoribus inridendis ipse esse orator summus videbatur*" (Cicero, *de orat.* 1.47).

Aristotle admitted the fact of contingent reality and, consequently, probable knowledge.[8] Obviously this is an area of reality which is at a level definitely below Plato's world of forms and Aristotle's metaphysics. In this area of reality the human person is faced not with incontrovertible and unchanged absolutes but with factual problems, questions, situations which are subject to change and which while grounded in reality are yet limited by the very nature of this reality. The constitutive elements of this environment admit neither absolute knowledge nor absolute assertion since their very contingency asserts that change is possible and that this very fact of change may very well condition what can be known or said about them. Such factual evidence and such contingent situations admit a probable knowledge about themselves, and they demand deliberation and considered discussion consequent upon which we are able to assent to their probable truth.

Quite clearly this is the area in which the intelligent and prudential course of responsible action (i. e. action most conformable to the existential reality and to truth) will be determined in each instance by the specific evidence which carries the greatest validity. It is primarily and almost exclusively at this level that Aristotle makes his analysis of the rhetorical art. Writing so clearly in terms of his own philosophical commitments Aristotle causes a series of questions to arise in the mind of anyone who would interpret the *Rhetoric*, questions occasioned by the text and its statements. When we find him saying (*A* 1, 55a 24-25): "not even if we should possess the most precise knowledge would it be easy to win conviction with its help" (i. e. the idea of the *De Anima* 433a 1 ff. that intellect alone is not sufficient for action), we ask whether or not in the area of the probable, and in a discipline directed toward winning judgment, he could divorce intellect from the emotions or the appetitive element in man. Indeed even in the quest for truth about absolute and unchanging reality it would be difficult to demonstrate such divorce much less tolerate it. Plato's insight in the *Phaedrus* was to perceive that the complex of intellect, emotions, and psychological attitudes must be put to work in the search for absolute, unchanging truth. There is nothing to indicate that Aristotle would not concur entirely. And strictly speaking there is no evidence in the *Rhetoric* that Aristotle could permit such a separation in the realm of contingent reality.

Thus our immediate concern is this: considering that Aristotle located the primary activity of rhetoric in the area of the contingent and probable is it possible, from what he says in the *Rhetoric* and elsewhere, that he dismissed the whole psychological complex of human action in his study of the art of rhetoric? The answer is that it is not possible. A series of statements in his introduction (*A* 1, 55a 1-*A* 3, 59a 29) make it more than apparent that for Aristotle the very essence of the rhetorical art is constituted by an intimate fusion of the intellectual and appetitive elements in man. *Pathos* and *ethos* are by no means expedient additions or a feeble retreat from a purely intellectualistic position. On the contrary they form with the intellect (*nous*) the integrated act which is the exercise of the art of rhetoric. *Ethos* and *pathos* are not accidental nor epiphenomenal, they are substantial components of the art.

Let us begin where Aristotle begins and follow somewhat carefully the import of his comments. A study of the introduction reveals that Aristotle in rather rapid shorthand sets down what he considers to be the critical elements of the art. Each of his statements implicates the concurring presence of intellect, *ethos* and *pathos* in the use of the art. First of all he posits as the general object of the art of rhetoric the whole area of human activity.[9] Here no absolute certitude is possible since we are working with contingent reality, reality which is subject to change. Such changeable and generally non-predictable subject-matter obviously requires study and deliberation before one is able to make any assertion about it with security. Aristotle indeed makes this more emphatically clear by declaring that the proper activity (*ergon*) of rhetoric is directed to subject-matter which requires deliberation (*A* 2, 57a 1-7; 23 ff.). And lest there be any doubt he follows this with an analysis of the nature of rhetoric and the kinds of rhetoric[10] in which the dominant idea is the role of the audience as judge (*krites*). As judge the hearer must first deliberate and then exercise an act of judgment on the evidence as presented.[11] It might be well to note that the concept of the audience as judge is underlined throughout the *Rhetoric* by frequent references to the fact that all rhetoric is directed toward *krisis*, or judgment, as its final goal.[12]

Reflection upon these statements and their inescapable implication in terms of Aristotle's philosophy clearly reveals that Aristotle could not have devised a rhetoric whose primary and proper nature would be the mere logical demonstration of one's proposition. The moment Aristotle decided that the art of rhetoric directs its major effort upon the world of contingent reality and the area of the probable, and calls into play deliberation and judgment he places it under the domain of what he calls the practical intellect rather than the speculative intellect.[13]

This is an essential point insofar as the difference between the activity of the two intellects is crucial. The difference is specified by the different object of each intellect. The speculative intellect moves toward Being, or ultimate reality, in itself whereas the practical intellect moves toward Being, or reality, insofar as this Being is to issue in human action.[14] Owing to this difference one might say that the role of the appetitive (i. e. *ethos* and *pathos*) is comparatively negligible in, but not absent from, the activity of the speculative intellect compared with its role in the action of the practical intellect. There can be no question that in the effort to grasp and comprehend the nature of ontological reality (or what Aristotle would call the subject-matter of first philosophy, and Plato the world of Forms), the speculative intellect must receive an initial assist from the appetite. Indeed we could go further, although it is neither to the point nor necessary to the argument, and maintain that in any effort to reason to, and understand the nature of, ontological reality the appetitive element works concomitantly with the rational. The practical intellect, however, *demands* the appetitive element in the psyche as an essential component for its activity: ". . . the intellect taken in itself tends uniquely to grasp Being; and it is only as permeated in one way or another by the movement of the appetite towards its own ends that the intellect concerns itself not with Being to be grasped, but with action to be brought about".[15]

In the *EN* 1109b 30-1115a 3 Aristotle attempts to determine the nature of voluntary action, that which man does responsibly and deliberately. It is to this kind of action that the practical intellect directs itself. The important factors in his effort are *proairesis* (choice) 1111b 4-1112a 16, and *bouleusis* (deliberation) 1112a 17-1113a 14. The passage on deliberation, which explains at much greater length Aristotle's brief comments in the *Rhetoric* (A 2, 57a 1-7), definitely establishes that deliberation involves the area of the contingent, of practical action (i. e. things man can do), and it further indicates that with respect to the things about which man deliberates reason alone is not adequate. This last is implicit in the denial that there is any deliberation about the unchangeable, or absolutely regular, and becomes more explicit in the statement on the role of *proairesis* in deliberation at 1113a 2-14. When men deliberate and decide (1113a 4, 12-3) as a result of deliberation, then they desire (ὀρεγόμεθα) in accord with the deliberation (12). But the thing they desire after deliberation is the *proaireton* (9-10). Thus deliberation completes itself by the act of *proairesis* e. g. 9-11: the *proaireton* is one of the things within our power which is desired after deliberation. Deliberation is not complete without *proairesis*. But *proairesis*, or the act of choosing, is only effected in the human person by the activity of both reason (1112a 15-16: μετὰ λόγου καὶ διανοίας) and appetition. In 1111b 4-1112a 17 the place of the appetitive element is expressed negatively when we are told that *proairesis* is *not simply* ἐπιθυμία, θυμός or βούλησις. In 1113a 9-13 we find that *proairesis* is βουλευτικὴ ὄρεξις, a deliberate desire, and the word *orexis*, of course, introduces into the notion of *proairesis* the appetitive element in the soul. At 1139 a 3-b 13 we are presented with a more detailed account of this activity. In a rather succinct summary at 1139b 4 we are told that *proairesis* is either "desireful reason" or "reasonable desire". This phrase would seem to leave no doubt about Aristotle's mind on the unified and integrated action of the two faculties. As a matter of fact Aristotle leads up to this statement by demonstrating that the appetitive element must enter into *proairesis* since choice has its origin in both desire and reason (1139a 32-33), for reason by itself will not cause action (1139a 35-36).

When Aristotle, then, in his introductory analysis of the nature of rhetoric finds that its primary object is discourse about the contingent, changing reality of human existence wherein man must exercise both deliberation and judgment he automatically locates the art under the activity of the practical intellect. Rhetoric becomes an activity of what he calls the "logistic" soul. In other words rhetoric by its nature is an activity of the *nous logistikos*, or the intellect working together with the appetitive element in the soul as man moves toward a judgment, *krisis*. Thus rhetoric for Aristotle must give careful and detailed consideration to rational demonstration and to *ethos* and *pathos*. In effect we have here the very *psychagogia*, or appeal to the whole person in his intellectual and emotional life, which Plato discussed in his *Phaedrus*.

To overlook this fact is to study the *Rhetoric* in a rather strange vacuum and to neglect in the whole process some fundamental Aristotelian ideas on the dianoetic (i. e. reasoning) activity in its relation to human action.

By way of final confirmation of the author's intent in his introductory analysis of rhetoric let us look at his comments on the reason why men engage in this art. He points out that the ultimate goal of rhetorical activity is the effort to perceive in a given subject, or problem, or situation, those elements in it which may effect persuasion. The act of rhetoric seeks out those factors which lead a reasonable mind to accept the subject or the problem (*A* 2, 55b 8-14). This is the proper activity of rhetoric and there it rests.[16] It does not effect persuasion as some of the technographers said (*A* 1, 55b 10; *Topics* 101b 5-10), nor does it, as far as Aristotle is concerned, make persuasion in the same sense as the artist makes his object. Rather it creates an attitude in another's mind, a sense of the reasonableness of the position proposed, whereby the auditor may make his own decision. The art, or technique, of rhetoric is the ability to perceive and to present evidence which makes decision, and a definite decision, possible; but to stop with the presentation. "Its purpose is not to persuade but to discern the possibly suasive in a subject" (*A* 1, 55b 10-11), at which point the auditor must step forward to accept or reject, to make his particular judgment to act or not to act.

Rhetoric, then, is preparatory for judgment and action. To understand the character of the preparation it does help, somewhat, to look at his analysis of the human person in action as seen in the *Poetics*. For there is an inner coherence between his study of rhetoric and drama: the movement of rhetoric is to dispose the person for action (*praxis*), the movement of drama ordinarily is the person-in-act.[17] In the *Poetics* human action is the act of the whole person, the intellectual and appetitive part of man engages totally in the specific human act.[18] It should not, then, appear strange that when Aristotle studies the art which is directed to pre-disposing the person to action he would consider the art as affecting the whole person: *intellect, ethos, pathos.*

Philosophically no other approach would seem possible for Aristotle. Rhetoric incorporated as integral components *reason, ethos* and *pathos* and addressed itself to the whole man. There could be no division nor separation between reason and purely logical demonstration on one side and the emotions and appetitive dynamism on the other. If rhetoric is to work within the terms of Aristotle's philosophical commitments reason and appetite must cooperate.

Within the framework of this commitment the preceding analysis can stand by itself. If we re-examine the structure of the three books of the *Rhetoric*, however, we discover that there is a highly developed coherence within the work which independently confirms the position taken here. Yet this unity has been consistently challenged even though the most convinced critics do not question Aristotelian authorship of the substantials, as well as most of the accidentals, of the rhetorical theory contained within the work. Insofar as it is correct to say that most of the difficulties on the unity of the treatise ultimately arise in the apparent contradiction which has just been discussed, namely the presumed accommodation by Aristotle of his new theory of rhetoric to an older theory grounded in the play upon the emotions and feelings of the audience, it seems appropriate to consider this problem of unity now.

The logical coherence of the treatise as it has come down to us, and indeed in places actual Aristotelian authorship, has been denied for a number of reasons: the seemingly obvious accommodation just mentioned, textual inconsistencies, repetitions, contradictions, obscurity of statement, as well as the apparent failure of the author to follow out in detail programmatic statements which give the organization of the work. It would be foolish not to admit that difficulties are present within the text. It is hardly folly to inquire whether these difficulties require the radical surgery on the text which has been proposed. Certainly many of the difficulties introduced as supporting evidence for the disorganization of the work from Aristotle's original composition are not convincing. If one adds to this the fact that frequently a difficult text passage gives rise to an interpretation (for example the polemic against *pathos* as indicative of an accommodation of two theories of rhetoric) which interpretation is then the source for finding problems with other text passages, it is possible to understand the confusion which can arise. Furthermore some of the problems proposed demand from Aristotle a highly systematized and remarkably detailed organization which is never justified on critical grounds by parallel references to precisely such organization in other works of the *corpus*. It is encouraging to know that Aristotle is held in such high esteem, but it is not particularly helpful to be told rather frequently that a textual statement is "entirely unthinkable", "totally impossible"[19] for Aristotle, or to read:[20] "Scriptorem diligentissimum qualem novimus Aristotelem, hoc modo promisso suo stetisse num cuiquam credibile est? Minime! Ergo haec omnia, quae hic promisit Aristoteles, tractaverat, at deleta sunt et sublata a librario vel redactore minime religioso . . ." Yet the evidence offered, detailed and intricate as it frequently is, does not constrain one to agree.[21]

To argue for unity is neither to deny development in Aristotle's thought nor the possibility of contradictory statements in the text. It would be simple-minded to say that there are no real problems in the text, particularly in view of the fact that difficulties have been perceived since the time of VICTORIUS. In more recent times SPENGEL and VAHLEN[22] called attention to a number of them. ROEMER picked these up and enlarged upon them in his introduction to the Teubner edition of the *Rhetoric*. He concluded that our text results from the efforts of one or two *librarii* working with two copies of the treatise, one of which was in an abbreviated form. MARX in his attempt to further the work of ROEMER created a new series of problems, the most substantial of which is that we are asked to accept our present *Rhetoric* as the result of an unknown editor's reorganization of a student's notes ("Schulheft", pp. 295, 313 f.) of Aristotle's original work. Solmsen developed the twofold enthymeme idea mentioned by MARX, and MAIER (Die Syllogistik des Aristoteles, Tübingen 1900), into an earlier and later *Rhetoric* which are united in our present work.

It is pointless to attempt here a detailed reply to the criticisms proposed by these men. If it can be shown that a correct understanding of the enthymeme, which is so clearly central to Aristotle's theory and admitted by all of them to be such, permits the treatise in its traditional form to evolve as an integral and rational whole, then, at the very least, a re-consideration of the individual arguments against unity is demanded. Since the demonstration here and throughout this study eventually involves many, if not all, of the passages discussed by these scholars it is in its own way a reply to the attack on the unity.

In view of the fact that the whole thrust of most scholarship on this problem is such that the mildest criticism leveled against the *Rhetoric* is that it surely represents an amalgam of earlier and later Aristotelian views of rhetoric it may seem rather temerarious to move in the opposite direction toward a judgment such as that of BRANDIS[23]: "Among all the writings of Aristotle preserved for us there has been none more completely, harmoniously and consistently executed than the *Rhetoric*, none in which thought and expression correspond better with each other. It is a perfect whole". On the other hand the alternatives are unsatisfying. The kind of freedom represented by the following rather typical comments does not encourage one to dismiss unity in the work too readily.[24]

Transcripsit autem, quisquis erat, vel idem vel alter librarius in exemplar brevius et decurtatum supplementa sua, ut supra demonstrare conati sumus, parum ratione habita aut textus iam ex breviore exemplari exarati aut loci, quibus additamentaadnectenda erant . . .   (ROEMER)

Daß Aristoteles jenen Satz so nicht geschrieben haben kann, bedarf keines Beweises.
                                                           (MARX)

Es ist nun wohl dem Leser klargeworden, warum wir nicht die gekennzeichneten Einschübe einem Redaktor zutrauen können, warum wir mit so großer Sicherheit behaupten, sie stammten von Aristoteles selbst: weil sie nur aus seiner Entwicklung heraus verständlich werden.   (GOHLKE)

A slight uneasiness is experienced when we further learn that one such study would suggest a re-organization of the following character: start the treatise with *A* 15, and then follow with *B* 12-17, 1-11, 20-21, *A* 3, 2, 4 etc.[25]. This uneasiness remains even though we apparently have a remarkably facile and subtle editor of Aristotle's original work as is revealed by the clever piece of re-writing done at *B* 26, 03a 34-*Γ* 1, b 23.[26] This disquiet is intensified by a number of further problems:

a) SPENGEL suspects his own suggested order (i.e. *A* 4-15, *B* 18- 26, *B* 1-17) because he believes that *B* 26, 03a 35-b 1 is genuine; and so he admits (p. 494 of Über die Rhetorik. . .") that we could have: *A* 4-15, *B* 1-17, 18-26. BARWICK'S comment on this is that it demonstrates how difficult it is to show that the present arrangement of the text does not go back to Aristotle.[27]
b) Everyone argues for a reorganization by a *librarius* or an editor, but no one has yet explained why any editor experienced the need for, or freely undertook, such a radical reorganization of three books.

The problem on the unity of the *Rhetoric* may be outlined in general in the following manner:

1. the work is fundamentally unified and from the hand of Aristotle,
2. the work is a conflation made by Aristotle of an earlier and later study in which he did not resolve these conflicting theories of rhetoric,

3. the work is a conflation but possesses a unified structure which is Aristotelian in origin,

4. the work, while Aristotelian in character, has been so changed by others that it is not unified, nor intelligible as it stands.

The argument here is for (1). There is no convincing evidence either external or internal for (4). The argument here can accept (3) without difficulty; but the evidence for an Aristotelian conflation is neither firm nor convincing. This last, together with the evidence which will be discussed in what follows, makes (2) unacceptable. For once we locate the importance of the enthymeme in the *Rhetoric* there is a coherent and convincing unity in the treatise.

Resolving the problem of unity at this point is necessary to an intelligent understanding of the following chapters in this book. Unfortunately it also assumes a knowledge of the material discussed in those chapters, for example, the centrality of the enthymeme to the *Rhetoric* (c. 2) and the meaning of "topics", both particular and general, in the *Rhetoric* (c. 4). For the purpose of analyzing what the text says, however, there does not appear to be a more satisfying solution. The attacks on the unified structure of the *Rhetoric* weaken in a very effective way every attempt to understand the statement of the text itself.

Of the passages offered in evidence for the disunity of the *Rhetoric* the largest and most critical involves the section between cc. 18 and 22 in book *B*. This section was first challenged by Spengel who argued that *B* 18-26 should follow immediately after *A* 4-15 because of its study of the enthymeme as syllogism. In actual fact this is really an interpretation determined by the conviction that the *"enthymeme"* is really the third *pistis* from among the three *pisteis* of *A* 2, 56a 1-20, namely, the logical proof of one's thesis. In turn *B* 18- 26 should be followed by *B* 1-17 which discussed the other two *pisteis, ethos* and *pathos*: e.g. *A* 4-15, *B* 18-26, 1-17. VAHLEN agreed with this, as did MARX. ROEMER took up the matter with some qualifications, and SOLMSEN, while he disagreed, has used this section as a further confirmation of his argument for a double enthymeme theory.[28]

Chapters 18-22 are a critical passage but they appear perfectly placed in Aristotle's total exposition. They can be read not only quite reasonably and correctly here without any need for a radical shift, but they also provide an important bridge to cc. 23-26. Aristotle's study is centered on the enthymeme. By book *B* 17 (9lb 7) Aristotle has finished the presentation of the particular aspects of the theory. The general aspects of the theory, however, remain to be considered. At *B* 17 we are clearly at the end of one phase of the development and Aristotle is about to proceed to another. A reading of *B* 18 makes it difficult to understand how this can be overlooked, or with what justification MARX can say: "Aber die größte Unklarheit und Verwirrung herrscht in den darauf folgenden Kapiteln 18-22, welche zu der Darlegung der τόποι überführen". Chapters 18-22 are transitional; before going on to discuss the general aspects of his theory of the enthymeme

Aristotle makes a summation at cc. 18-22. They are in great part parallel to, and a restatement of, many of the ideas in the programmatic statement in *A*, cc. 1-3.

At the end of c. 17 of book *B* Aristotle has come to the conclusion of his analysis of the way whereby one can obtain relevant and specific material for enthymematic statement in rhetorical discourse. Such material demands a knowledge of the subject of discourse in each kind of rhetoric, and a consideration of *pathos* and *ethos* so that this knowledge can be conveyed to others in a meaningful and persuasive way. It was the burden of *A* 4-*B* 17 to place this material before the student. As he tells us at the beginning of book *B* (77b 16 ff.) where he will begin the analysis of *pathos* and *ethos* and their place in discourse: "These, then, are the materials from which one must exhort and dissuade, praise and blame, accuse and defend, and these are the general probabilities and premises useful for the proofs in each case. For the enthymeme implicates these elements and comes from them if we take, so to speak, each kind of discourse by itself. But since rhetoric is directed to judgment . . . it is necessary for the speaker not only to look to the discourse that it be probative and convincing, but also to develop a certain character in himself and in the one deciding. . ." This close co-relation of *A* 4-14 with *B* 1-17, in Aristotle's mind, is further revealed by remarks such as those in book *A* 10 at 69a 28-31, and b 14-15 where he says that *ethos* and *pathos* will be separately discussed later on in the treatise. Moreover we can see the importance of *ethos* and *pathos* for judgment and decision as far as Aristotle is concerned at *A* 10, 68b 3-4. In brief, from *A* 4 to *B* 17 the particular aspects of argument by rhetorical syllogism were presented as promised at *A* 3, 59a 27-28: διαιρετέον ἰδίᾳ περὶ ἑκάστου τούτων.

Then at c. 18 of book *B* we are told (91b 28) that περὶ τούτων διώρισται, namely, that he has discussed: (b 24-28) the particular materials for each kind of rhetoric as well as *ethos*.[29] He continues: there remains to be discussed the *koina*; when these have been defined there remains the discussion of enthymeme in general and example in order that "we may fulfil our initial proposal" (92 a 4). This study of enthymeme in general (i.e. its general topics c. 23, the apparent enthymeme c. 24, refutation c. 25) is made almost exclusively in terms of the enthymeme as an inferential form.

However, before turning to this presentation of the enthymeme as inference Aristotle makes a resumé of a number of the major concepts of his theory of rhetoric which he first presented in cc. 1-3 of book *A*. Pedagogically the summary is quite wise here for it recalls these ideas which were first broached in *A* and which being important to his theory are naturally necessary for an understanding of the discussion on general argumentation by enthymeme. It may be of help here to show how *B* 18-22 repeat the major thematic statements of *A* 1-3.[30]

c. 18	91 b 8-23 relation of persuasive speech to *krisis*	*c. 3*	58a 36-b 7
b 24-29	doxai and *protaseis* for *telos* of each genre	*c. 3*	59a 6-10 *protaseis*
		c. 3	58b 20-30 *telos*

b 29-92al	the *koina* (explained in B 19 and in text below)	*c. 3*	59a 11-27
92a 1-4	the program for cc. 18-26 (this should be compared with:	*c. 3*	59a 27-29)
92a 4-7	introduction to c.19. (preferably it should be the beginning of 19 and not the end of 18)		
c. 19	92a 8-b14 possible-impossible	c. 3	59a 11-27
b 15-93a8	past-future	"	"
93a 9-18	more-less	"	"
a 19-21	conclusion to above		
c. 20	93a 22-27 the two common proofs of rhetoric. (compare 93a 24-25 with 56b 6-7) (*gnome* mentioned here *as part of* enthymeme.)	*c. 2* ––-	56a 35-b 27 — —
	93a 28-94a 19 *paradeigma* (example)	*c. 2*	57b 26-36
c. 21	94a 19-95b 20 *gnome* (which is very closely related to enthymeme: 94a 26-29)		nothing
c. 22	95b 20-96a 4 enthymeme as syllogism	*c. 2*	56b 3-21 57a 7-12; 22-33
	96a 4-b 19 particular topics (a more detailed statement of 58a 17-28 and a recapitulation of *A* 4-14, not of *B* 1-17, but see below: 96b 28-97a 6)	*c. 2*	58a 17-28
	96b 20-22 transition to *stoicheia* of enthymemes, i.e. general topics.	—	——
b 22-28	two kinds of enthymeme: demonstrative, refutative	*c. 1*	no mention formally of such a distinction save indirectly, 55a 30-33
	96b 28-97a 6 summary statement on work done on particular methodology for enthymeme, i.e. both *A* 4-14 and *B* 1-17; followed by a transition to general methodology;	*c. 2*	58a 2-35

concluding with statement
on rest of program:
apparent enthymeme (c. 24)   *c. 2*   56b 2-4
and refutation (c. 25)   nothing, but see
                                                      above under 96
                                                      22-28

In addition to the above there are two critical passages which confirm the fact
that in 18-22 we have a general summation of the work thus far achieved and a
bridge between the study of the particular sources of the enthymeme (*A* 4-*B* 17)
and the study of the enthymeme in general and its general sources. A correct
understanding of what Aristotle is saying in these two passages would appear to
remove the need for radically changing the text about. The two passages are at 91b
29 (c. 18) and 96b 29 (c. 22). Both passages are among the major cruces for those
who argue against the unity of the work.

The first passage involves the meaning of κοινῶν. MARX was so troubled with
it (op. cit.284-295) that he concluded that the passage is another proof "daß wir nur
ein Schulheft . . . nicht ein Originalwerk des Philosophen in der *Rhetorik* erhalten
haben" (295). The second passage which is concerned with the exact meaning of
εἰδῶν makes it quite obvious, when we see the meaning of the word, that these
chapters are a recapitulation of the work thus far achieved in the treatise, a
recapitulation in the form of a transition to the final part of the analysis of the
enthymeme.

We will begin with the passage at 91b 29: λοιπὸν ἡμῖν διελθεῖν περὶ τῶν
κοινῶν; from SPENGEL'S comment the phrase obviously demands elucidation.[31]
Although the word κοινῶν stands by itself Aristotle does indicate at once its
referents: "the possible and impossible, the past and future, the great and small" (b
30-33). In the usual interpretation of the word, however, such a limited meaning is
not attributed to it. It is much more common to accept it in a very large sense, but
one which causes confusion. In this broad sense the word is understood to include
not merely the possible and impossible, past and future, great and small, but also
the κοιναὶ πίστεις and the κοινοὶ τόποι. In the edition of JEBB-SANDYS
(Cambridge 1909) we read, for example, this translation of our passage: "it remains
for us to discuss the *general* appliances", to which the note is appended: "κοινῶν
i. e. both the κοινοὶ τόποι and the κοιναὶ πίστεις.

In terms of our text, however, when Aristotle uses the word here he apparently
means to refer to the possible and impossible, past and future, great and small, and
in doing this he is speaking about concepts which are well-known to the reader (e.
g. *A* 1, 54 a 26-30, b 13-15; *A* 2, 57a 4-7; *A* 3, 58b 2-20, 59a 11-26; *A* 6, 62a 15-16,
37-b 2; *A* 7, 63b 5-65b 21; *A* 8, 66a 17-18; *A* 12, 72a 9-10,etc.) by the time he has
reached *B* 18 of the treatise. Consequently it does not seem correct, and SPENGEL
would appear to agree, to extend the meaning to include the κοιναὶ πίστεις of

B 20, *93a* 23.[32] These are, as a matter of fact, clearly identified in the *Rhetoric* as enthymeme and example.[33]

Further, the word as Aristotle is using it here cannot mean τόποι or κοινοὶ τόποι as VAHLEN and COPE suggest,[34] and as it is often interpreted. Speaking of the great and small at *B* 26, 03a 20-25 Aristotle explicitly denies to this phrase any title to the term τόπος as he understands this term in the *Rhetoric*. And if this is so for the great and small it is also true of the possible and impossible, and the past and future. As he well says: the great and small, the good, the just, etc. are those aspects of a subject *with which* rhetorical argumentation is concerned (*B* 26, 03a 23). But the τόποι are always that from which rhetorical argumentation is derived: τοὺς τόπους ἐξ ὧν at *A* 2, 58a 30 is the common phrase.[35]

To understand what Aristotle may have in mind when he uses κοινῶν of the possible and impossible, past and future, great and small, we must turn to *A* 3, 59a 11-29 and *B* 18, 91b 24-*B* 19, 93a 21. These passages present a formal study of the part played in the rhetorical *techne* by the possible and impossible, past and future, great and small; and the second passage is, in fact, a restatement and explanation of the first.

An analysis of both passages reveals the following (I anticipate my conclusion by using the form κοινά):

1. Aristotle does not use the word τόποι of these κοινά. In no place where they are mentioned are they so termed. Nor is COPE (Comm. II, p. 173) correct in attributing such an identification to SPENGEL in his "Über die Rhetorik des Aristoteles".

2. These κοινά are first introduced in connection with the three ἴδια τέλη of the three kinds of rhetoric (*A* 3, 58a 36-59a 5), and are then specified in both of our passages as *common to* these three ends: e.g. *A* 3, 59a 16-21 and *B* 18, 91b 24-92a 1.

3. We are told that the τέλη are the three specific goals of rhetoric, some one of which an orator must have in mind as he attempts to bring about a judgment on the part of his audience: *A* 3, 58b 2-5 and *B* 18, 91b 8-23. The κοινά are necessary to the orator for achieving this goal: *A* 3, 59a 11-26 and *B* 18, 91b 29-92a 1. (n.b. *A* 3, 58b 2-5 mentions only "past and future" but the whole discussion of the τέλη leads right into the κοινά.)

4. Finally, in the two passages of a more general character in which Aristotle gives a summary presentation of what he means by enthymeme, by example, by the particular topics, and by the general topics, he also discusses the κοινά as part of these structural blocks of his rhetorical theory, e.g. *A* 2, 56a 35-58a 35 (the programmatic statement at the beginning of the work) and *B* 19, 92a 8-*B* 22, 96b 19 (the recapitulation of the major ideas before the concluding section on the enthymeme in general). These two passages present us with

general synopses of a series of key concepts of his rhetoric as we possess it in the first two books. The κοινά are included in each section.

From a study of these passages it appears that what has been missed in the discussion of these κοινά is their particular character and the place which they occupy in Aristotle's rhetorical analysis. From the passages cited above (particularly if we read *A* 2, 57 together with *A* 3, 59) it becomes quite clear that in Aristotle's mind men engage in the practice of rhetoric[36] when faced with a problem which calls for thoughtful consideration. Or as he expresses it himself (*A* 2, 57a 1) rhetoric is concerned with matters about which men usually deliberate since a judgment is required. In the real situation it is obvious that such matters range over a wide area of contingencies and circumstances. But the fact remains that the scope within which the art of rhetoric operates is that wherein there is both the possibility and necessity for deliberation. By the same token, however, men initiate the whole activity of rhetorical discussion only when there is question of a possible matter (δυνατόν) past, present, future (γεγονός — ἐσόμενον) that is of significance to them (μέγεθος — μικρότης). And their deliberation is ordinarily directed toward establishing a subject which is thus qualified as expedient or injurious (deliberative rhetoric), just or unjust (judicial), or honorable or dishonorable (epideictic), that is, one or other of the three ἴδια τέλη τοῦ λόγου.

These κοινά, then, qualify the ends, which is to say that the three special ends of rhetoric can only be such under one or all of these common aspects.[37] Aristotle in both of our passages says as much when he states quite absolutely that it is necessary (ἀναγκαῖον *A* 3, 59a 14, *B* 18, 91b 30) for every speaker to know whether the matter of his discussion is possible or impossible, whether it has happened, is happening, or will take place, and what is its relative importance. From a reading of the text in both passages it is clear that this necessity does not arise from the fact that this is what speakers usually do. Rather it is discovered that this necessity derives from the actual character of the rhetorical *techne* as Aristotle has analyzed it. In this analysis Aristotle has determined the nature of rhetoric in terms of the speaker and the audience as an art concerned with deliberation and directed toward specific judgment in three general areas of human endeavor. When he has established this, namely that there are three kinds of rhetoric, each with its own particular end and each calling for deliberation and judgment, he goes on to make the final determination with respect to the general nature of rhetoric. This last determination sets forth those elements which are ultimately demanded before the whole rhetorical process can begin. These elements are the κοινά, which, in short, represent the common and basic requisites postulated with respect to any subject in order that it may become an object of the rhetorical *techne*. They represent categories within which a subject must fall before it can be used by the orator. Prior to the attempt to demonstrate any one of the three peculiar ends for any subject the orator must know and be able to show for that subject its possibility (or impossibility), its actuality (present-past) or potential actuality (future), and its general significance (great-small). This is clearly set forth at *A* 3, 59a 11-29; it is restated at *B* 18-19, 91b 24-93a 21 as a part of a general summation of what has been thus far achieved in the *Rhetoric* before Aristotle moves on to his discussion of the κοινοὶ τόποι. And not only is this true, but this meaning and use of the κοινά has been employed throughout the first book in the analysis of the three kinds of rhetoric (cf. *supra* pp. 36-37).

The κοινά are in many ways analogous to the concept of the four *organa* in the *Topics* (I. cc. 13-18) but they are more sharply delineated and explained. The *koina* are as critical to the process of rhetorical discourse as the *organa* are to topical methodology for without each there can presumably be neither rhetorical discourse nor topical investigation. It would be satisfying to determine these *koina* more definitely by having the noun to which they apply,[38] but Aristotle apparently felt no need for one since he never suggests one. His failure to do so, however, hardly gives us the right to reduce them to an amorphous concept capable of any extension in its referents.

The passage at *B* 22, 96b 28-97a 1, "multum vexatus a viris doctis", and one which in GOHLKE'S words "schon viel Kopfzerbrechen gemacht hat," contains the phrase (96b 29): τῶν εἰδῶν τῶν χρησίμων καὶ ἀναγκαίων. Most, if not all, of the interpretations of these words are quite attractive and seemingly correct.

It does not appear, however, in the light of the text and context, that ἐιδῶν here can be interpreted as "special topics" or "special subjects"[39] as practically all understand it.[40] Up to this point in the *Rhetoric* it is true that the meaning "special topics" is both acceptable to Aristotle and has received some prominence.[41] Furthermore the word here occurs in a chapter (22) which forms a transition from the discussion of these particular topics (εἴδη) to a discussion of the general topics (κοινοὶ τόποι). It may well be that the confusion has arisen from these circumstances.

And yet εἰδῶν here would appear to refer to the three kinds (γένη) of rhetoric: deliberative, judicial, and epideictic, and not to any such thing as "special topics", or "special subjects."

First of all the use of εἶδος for γένος need occasion no difficulty since Aristotle has already used εἶδος a number of times for "type" or "kind" where we might have expected him to use γένος.[42] Indeed the use here of εἴδη rather than of the more usual γένη (for which compare *A* 2, 58a 33 τὰ γένη τῆς ῥητορικῆς and *A* 3, 58b 7 τρία γένη) should not be too surprising in the light of *A* 3, 58a 36 ἔστιν δὲ τῆς ῥητορικῆς εἴδη τρία. SPENGEL in a note on this passage, although he brackets τῆς ῥητορικῆς εἴδη remarks: "Commutantur haec verba [namely εἴδη and γένη saepius apud auctorem nostrum." And ROEMER in defense of his reading at *A* 3, 58a 36, which I have just cited, comments: "nihil tamen mutare audeo cum et alibi et 1396b, 29 περὶ ἕκαστον τῶν εἰδῶν i. e. γενῶν nisi fallor, dicatur".

Furthermore, both the general context of the passage and the specific text of *B* 22, 96b 28-33 appear to indicate that εἰδῶν refers to the three types of rhetorical discourse and not to "special topics".

The general context of c. 22: In this chapter we have a transitional chapter in which Aristotle is preparing the ground for his discussion (c. 23) of the rhetorical syllogism in terms of the general topics (κοινοὶ τόποι). Before doing so he restates a number of general principles: 1) he reviews briefly the nature of the syllogism or enthymeme (95b 20-96a 4), the mode of demonstration common to each kind of rhetoric; 2) he recalls to our attention that it is the use of the particular topics (εἴδη) proper to one's subject that makes the orator's rhetorical syllogisms pertinent and apposite to the *telos* of the type of rhetoric in which he is engaged.[43] And he exemplifies his meaning at once for *each of the three* genres (96a 4-b 19); 3) he notes further that the use of these particular topics as a source of enthymemes is one way in which to develop rhetorical syllogisms (96b 20), and he continues with the remark (at 96b 28-34) that at this point in the treatise he has given the topics for the *subject-matter, ethos* and *pathos* which fill this role. If we stop and ask what *topoi* (96b 30), what sources from which to form enthymemes (b31-2), we possess at this juncture in the treatise (i. e. from *A* 4, 59b 19 to *B* 17, 91b 7) we discover without much search that we have only the particular topics for *the three kinds* of rhetoric, for *ethos*, and *pathos*.[44]

Aristotle then goes on at 96b 34-97a 6 to say that there is another method, a general method: ἔτι δὲ ἄλλον τρόπον καθόλου περὶ ἁπάντων for obtaining enthymemes, and that he now proposes to consider it. This general method is something different from the particular method of the particular topics which has been the major subject of the study up to *B* 17 (91 b 7). In Aristotle's words we are told at 97a 1 that there is an ἄλλος τρόπος καθόλου; obviously this "method" is being set in contrast to 96b 20: εἰς μὲν οὖν τρόπος τῆς ἐκλογῆς πρῶτος.

Like the first method which is "topical" (96b 20) the second method is also a "topical" method as was promised at 95b 21: μετὰ ταῦτα τοὺς τόπους, and as is eminently clear from c. 23 which immediately follows and begins: ἔστι δὲ εἷς μὲν τόπος. The first topical method is particular and specific to each of the three genres as far as the subject-matter is concerned, and specific to the audience and speaker (*ethos* and *pathos*) depending upon the circumstances. The second topical method is obviously general (97a 1: καθόλου περὶ ἁπάντων) and, as a method, provides ways which enable one to argue by rhetorical syllogism, and ways which also are not restricted *to any one kind* of rhetoric but are equally valid for rhetorical argumentation in *any of the three* genres (cf. the analysis of 96b 28 ff. which follows). From the context, then, it is obvious that Aristotle is speaking throughout the whole passage (i.e. from 96a 4 to b 19) with the three kinds of rhetoric continually in mind.

The text: 96b 28-33: Here we are told that at this point in the treatise we have the topics περὶ ἕκαστον τῶν εἰδῶν (29).[45] It is difficult to understand what else the phrase could mean other than: each of the three kinds of rhetoric. First of all a reason which partly repeats our phrase is immediately given by Aristotle to explain his statement ἐξειλεγμέναι γὰρ αἱ προτάσεις περὶ ἕκαστον (b 30-31).[46] And in answer to the query: Each what? Aristotle replies at once: each of the three γένη (b 31-33).[47] The close logical correlation of the whole statement would seem almost inescapable. And a reading of *B* 18, 91b 24-29 and *B* 1, 77b 16-20 which are parallel to our passage strengthens this meaning.

Our passage, then, would be translated: "Now, then, practically all the topics concerning each of the kinds of rhetoric which are useful or (and) necessary are in our possession; for propositions with respect to each kind have been selected so that now we have the topics from which one is to present enthymemes[48] on good or evil, the honorable or dishonorable, the just or unjust. . ."

On this interpretation the transitional sentence to the discussion of the general topics (97a 1) takes on new meaning. For ἁπάντων in this line must mean the three kinds of rhetoric,[49] and since it also clearly appears to refer back to εἰδῶν at 96b 29 we would seem to have further confirmation that εἰδῶν must mean the three kinds of rhetoric.

We would then translate the whole passage: "Now then practically all the topics concerning each of the kinds of rhetoric which are useful or (and) necessary are in our possession . . . But further let us now take up another method, a general one, with respect to all three kinds of rhetoric."

And with this general summation of his achievement thus far he starts upon his presentation of the general topics which brings to a logical conclusion the program proposed in the opening chapters. Actually this parallelism in subject-matter between *B* 18-22 and *A* 1-3 inclines one to accept our present disposition of the text. Chapters 18-22 restate in more detail a number of the fundamentally new concepts which Aristotle introduced into the study of rhetoric in the opening chapters. Further, they make this restatement at a place in the study which is rather critical. Aristotle has just finished an extended analysis of the particular elements essential to deliberative, judicial, and epideictic oratory (*A* 4 to *B* 17), and he is about to pass on to an analysis of the general elements common to all oratory. Before doing so he recapitulates what has thus far been achieved in his work, and at the same time recalls to the reader's attention the key ideas of his analysis of rhetoric (the role of judgment, the kinds of rhetorical discourse, the *koina*, enthymeme, and example). With this done he is prepared to pass from the analysis of the method of rhetorical argumentation in particular to an analysis of it in general.

If we now move back to the beginning of the *Rhetoric* and take an overview of the work we find an intelligently organized presentation of Aristotle's theory of rhetoric. Chapters 1-3 contain the programmatic statement for the work incorporating the new ideas which Aristotle wishes to introduce to the study of rhetoric.

Chapter 1: 1354a 1-1355b 24: The very first assertion correlates rhetoric with dialectic (54a 1) which at once makes the art of the *logos* a rational and reasonable endeavor, an activity of the intellect. This correlation (which runs through the second chapter also) is underlined a number of times in this first chapter at 55a 8-10, 28, 34-35, b 8-10, 16. The relation between rhetoric and reason is strengthened at once by calling rhetoric a *techne* and so subject to the direction of reason (54a 10-11). The most obvious instance of its *techne* quality, we are told, are the *pisteis*, a word which is itself explained by the word *enthymeme*, 54a 13-15: "the *pisteis* alone come within the province of *techne* . . . but they [the technographers] say nothing about enthymemes which are the body of *pistis*". Aristotle makes this statement more specific at 54b 21-22 where he speaks of the *pisteis entechnoi*, the use of which makes one "master of the *enthymeme*", or, (from what he will eventually say) "master of the way of reasoning in rhetorical discourse". For, as we are told at 55a 3-8, a rhetorical methodology which is subject to reason and rules (ἔντεχνος μέθοδος) involves the *pisteis* and the rhetorical *pistis*, *par excellence*, is the *enthymeme*: the syllogism of rhetoric. With this specification of the *enthymeme* as a form of syllogism Aristotle at once takes the opportunity to repeat again the rational and reasoned aspect of rhetoric by commenting that to know the *enthymeme* one must know the syllogism which, of course, is the proper study of the *Analytics* (55a 8-14; this is picked up a number of times in c. 2, e. g. 57a 28-31, b 24-25). This last statement is followed at once (55a 14-18 and 21-24) by two others which make a close connection between truth and rhetoric; they, in turn, repeat a statement at 54b 10 which implicitly connects rhetoric with truth. All of these introductory statements with reference to dialectic, *techne*, the *Analytics*, truth, emphasize Aristotle's intention to stress from the beginning that rhetoric is an activity of the mind concerned with communicating in a reasoned way to an other the truth in so far as it can be known.

Running as a counter motif to this proposition, and thereby accentuating the thematic announcement of rhetoric as reasoned activity, is the polemic against an emotional rhetoric (54a 15-55a 3) which Aristotle finds in the current handbooks. Although I can accept this statement for what it obviously is, namely, an attack on the ill-conceived use of emotion, an attack, however, in no way at odds with his later statements on the place of *pathos* and *ethos* in rhetoric, some corrective remarks seem in place in view of the way in which the polemic is usually read. As we have already seen these statements of Aristotle in c. 1 are taken as his rejection of *pathos* and *ethos* in rhetoric and consequently in direct conflict with c. 2 (it can only be c. 2 since the question does not arise in c. 3).

The very first statement by Aristotle on the subject at 54a 11-13 acknowledges in its very criticism of the misuse of emotion by the technographers that *pathos* is a part of the rhetorical *techne*: αὐτῆς μόριον (54a 13). It is the non-organic and restricted view of emotion that Aristotle is criticizing when he says that these technographers have "constructed a small portion of the art". Indeed Aristotle is directing his remarks here to something which is usually never noticed, namely, the *practice in judicial rhetoric*: 54b 26-28, 55a 19-20. Obviously, from what he says, the emotions in this branch of rhetoric can be orchestrated for or against the litigant without any regard at all for the real situation at issue. He indicates at 54b 22-33 precisely what he is thinking about. When he speaks of the attention of these technographers to τὰ ἔξω τοῦ πράγματος (54a 15-16) the only correct interpretation of the phrase from the explanation which he gives in the text is "irrelevancies". Certainly one cannot claim that Aristotle is arguing simply for the logical and rational proof of the case. The statement at 55a 24-26 should raise doubts about that: ἔτι δὲ πρὸς ἐνίους οὐδ᾽ εἰ τὴν ἀκριβεστάτην ἔχοιμεν ἐπιστήμην, ῥᾴδιον ἀπ᾽ ἐκείνης πεῖσαι λέγοντας. The point he is making is that the technographers treat of matters that are in no way directed to stating the case (54b 30-31) but to awakening a response in the audience (54a 16-18). I believe that RADERMACHER puts the target of these comments in sight for us in an observation he makes on a text of Anaximenes (Artium Scriptores, Wien 1951, p. 216): "Vereor autem, ne antiquissima Graecorum oratio apud iudices habita nihil fere continuerit praeter testimonia, ius iurandum, calumnias, preces, donec quinto a Chr. saeculo incepere argumenta ex ratiocinatione ducere. Semper autem si quis in iudicium prodierat, ei verendum erat ne vitae examen (ἔλεγχον τοῦ βίου) esset subiturus. Inde specialiter διαβολή vocatur, quidquid ἔξω τοῦ πράγματος profertur." According to Aristotle these technographers do not realize that the focal point of rhetoric as an art is in the *pisteis* (54a 13); and since he says further (14-15) that the *enthymeme* embodies *pistis* one must conclude from his words that the art of rhetoric ultimately resides in the *enthymeme*. He continues his criticism of the technographers, however, and does not return to these *pisteis* until 54b 21-22 where they are now called the *pisteis entechnoi* whose control makes one master of the *enthymeme*. These *pisteis entechnoi* are identified for us for the first time at the beginning of c. 2: 55b 35-56a 4 where we find that they are ἦθος, πάθος and ἐν αὐτῷ τῷ λόγῳ. Unless one has independently decided upon a complete discontinuity between c. 1 and c. 2 there is no reason at all why the passage in c. 2 cannot be used toward an understanding of the phrase in c. 1. This is particularly true since the expression *pisteis entechnoi* is used for the first time after *A* 1, 54b 21-22 at *A* 2, 55b 35, and there is no clear reason from cc. 1 and 2 to think that the phrase is used in a substantially different way. The whole point of this observation is this: since the *pisteis entechnoi* in c. 2 (55b 35-56a 4) include *ethos* and *pathos* one could argue without any difficulty being caused by the text that by the use of this expression at 54b 21-22 Aristotle acknowledges the place of *ethos* and *pathos* in the first chapter. Further the way in which he speaks of *pisteis* and *enthymeme* in c. 1 (54a 13-15 and b 21-22) indicates quite clearly that the *enthymeme* is not identified with any one *pistis*; if anything it has something to do with all three. This is quite critical in any exegesis of these opening chapters, and in c. 2 of this study I will discuss the various meanings of *pistis* in the *Rhetoric* as well as the fact that there is no evidence to identify the *enthymeme* with any one of the three *pisteis*.

Chapter 1 concludes (55b 8-24) with a return to its opening statement on the correlation between rhetoric and dialectic. It also emphasizes further that the art of rhetoric applies to every kind of subject (55b 8, which is picked up again in the definition of rhetoric at the very beginning of c. 2, i.e. 55b 25: περὶ ἕκαστον [see also 55b 31-34, and especially 56a 33]), and that its object is not to persuade but to find those elements in each and every subject which make the subject acceptable: (55b 10-11) τὸ ἰδεῖν τὰ ὑπάρχοντα πιθανὰ περὶ ἕκαστον.

Chapter 2: 1355b 25-1358a 35: The re-statement at the end of c. 1 (55b 16-24) of the correlation between rhetoric and dialectic leads to the definition of rhetoric as a *dynamis*, an ability "to perceive the possibly suasive in any subject" which opens c. 2: (55b 25-26) περὶ ἕκαστον τοῦ θεωρῆσαι τὸ ἐνδεχόμενον πιθανόν. The ἐνδεχόμενον πιθανόν here picks up τὰ ὑπάρχοντα πιθανά of 55b 10-11. We should note that the "suasive" in each text is neutral as far as the subject-matter is concerned. Its "suasive" character is determined by the person as Aristotle says at 56b 28. Therefore the "suasive" can be something absolute or contingent, certain or merely probable. Rhetoric as the art of language for effective discourse is interested in it in so far as it "speaks to" the auditor be it absolute or contingent, certain or generally probable. These *pithana* are, of necessity, related in some way to the subject of discussion whatever it may be. The *techne* of rhetoric, as opposed to other *technai* (55b 27-34), is the ability of the rhetorical art to discern these *pithana* for any subject. Nothing, at the moment, is said directly about what the ἐνδεχόμενον πιθανὸν περὶ ἕκαστον (55b 25-26) is, for it is obviously the task of a treatise on rhetoric to explain it. But when Aristotle takes up the question of rhetorical proof, *pistis* (55b 35-56a 20), he leads into an explanation indirectly. For the material of such proof (*pistis*), when it is ἔντεχνον, must be the *pithana* in any and every subject. (This problem is discussed at greater length in c. 4 of this study on the sources of rhetorical argumentation.)

We now learn (55b 35-56a 20) that there are two kinds of rhetorical *pistis*: artistic (*entechnic*), and non-artistic (*atechnic*: this last is explained in c. 15 of A). The artistic, i.e. *entechnic* because they are the result of method, are ἦθος, πάθος, and ἐν αὐτῷ τῷ λόγῳ which I call πρᾶγμα. (I give my reasons for this word in c. 2; indeed, the terminology is not unknown to students of the *Rhetoric*. BARWICK, for example, speaks without any hesitation of "πραγματικαὶ πίστεις" (see "Die Gliederung. . .", Hermes 57, 1922, pp. 15 ff.). In the course of this explanation Aristotle mentions two things worthy of note to one interested in the coherence of our present text: (a) he refers back again to c.1 and the writers of *technai* and remarks (56a 11-13, 16-17) that they assign no value to *ethos* and give all of their attention to *pathos*; (b) he refers forward (56a 18-19) to his treatment of *pathos* in *B* 1-11. Since the *entechnic pisteis* are such as he has described Aristotle notes (56a 20-35) that one who is to use them must be able to reason, and to handle *ethos* and *pathos* in an intelligent way. This twofold demand of the art makes rhetoric an "offshoot", as it were, of Dialectic and Ethics. He qualifies this, however: i.e. despite misunderstanding on the part of some about rhetoric's relation to Ethics (56a 27-30), rhetoric is, in fact, as was stated at the outset (i.e. c. 1: 54a 1-6), a part of, and like to Dialectic; for rhetoric and dialectic are: (56a 33) δυνάμεις τινὲς τοῦ πορίσαι λόγους.

Aristotle continues this parallel (56a 35-b 26) as he turns to the method of rhetorical demonstration. Rhetoric, like dialectic, uses deduction and induction, i.e. *enthymeme* and example (*paradeigma*). Here (56b 9-10) Aristotle introduces quite explicitly into rhetoric his general system of deductive and inductive reasoning from the *Analytics*. (This passage on the *enthymeme* as syllogism will be studied in c. 3 of this work). Aristotle's promise (56 b 25-26) to compare the nature of *enthymeme* and example is realized in cc. 20-24 of book *B* as most, if not all, commentators note.

Now that he has introduced the method of rhetorical demonstration Aristotle takes up (56b 28-30) the general subject-matter of rhetoric: that which is persuasive (the *pithana* of 55b 10-11, 26) in the subject under discussion. He demonstrates (a) why, in fact, it is the subject of rhetorical discourse: (57a 1-7) "the function *(ergon)* of rhetoric is to attend to those matters about which we are wont to deliberate and for which we have no systems of rules. . .but we only deliberate about matters which appear capable of being one thing or another"; and, (b) 57a 8-21: the place of a reasoned method of argument for such subjects through the use of *enthymeme* and example.

As soon as Aristotle speaks of reasoning by *enthymeme* or example he is involved with sources for these two methods (e.g. 57a 8, 9, 12-13: ἐκ or ἐξ). Consequently at 57a 22-b 25 he takes up the sources for enthymemes, e.g. 57a 30: ἐξ ὧν τὰ ἐνθυμήματα λέγεται. These sources will usually be contingent in character, but can also be necessary, and they are called by the more specific name of *eikota* and *semeia* (57a 30-33). (This passage is discussed in detail in c. 4 of this work.) This particular section on the enthymeme and its source material closes with a few words on the other method of reasoning, example (*paradeigma* 57b 26-36), in which Aristotle indicates what kind of inductive reasoning is implied by *paradeigma*. At 58a 1-2 he draws this section to a conclusion and notes that he has told us now the sources of the *pisteis apodeiktikai*. It should not be necessary to call attention to the fact that these *pisteis apodeiktikai*, even though obviously entechnic in their own right, are not the *pisteis entechnoi* of which Aristotle has been talking (see above pp. 44-46). Indeed, in the light of both the text immediately preceding (57a 22-b 36) and the earlier statement at 56b 6-8 the *pisteis apodeiktikai* can only be *enthymeme* and *paradeigma*.

Aristotle then singles out the *enthymeme* for special consideration (as should be clear the attention he gives to *paradeigma* in the work is minimal). He introduces his remarks with these words: "an extremely important distinction among *enthymemes*, a distinction particularly ignored almost universally, is one which also applies to the dialectic method of syllogisms" (58a 2-4). Substantially the difference, as explained at 58a 4-35 (the end of c. 2), is that some *enthymemes* in their enunciation are general in form and as such can be used without change for disciplines specifically different (58a 12-17); other *enthymemes* are particular and specific in their enunciation and can only be used with a specific discipline (58 a 18-21).

This is the critical passage which, in a treatise centered as it is on the *enthymeme* as the heart of the rhetorical process, states quite clearly that *enthymemes* can be analyzed in particular and in general. The passage also gives the ground for a division which is taken for granted in the treatise. Thus it is possible, as we have already seen, for Aristotle to say in book *B* at 22, 96b 34-5 that he will now take up the general method of *enthymemes*, after telling us at *B* 22, 96b 20 that the first method is the particular method. Both methods are "topical" in character: (58a 11-12) "by rhetorical syllogisms I mean those which have to do with the topics"; both methods have their sources in the *topoi*, either particular or general topics. (This material on the topics is discussed at length in c. 4 of this work.) The important point for us at the moment is that here we are given a clear division of the study of the *enthymeme* as it will be developed in the treatise which is to follow. It is a division which reaches its final achievement in cc. 23-26 of book *B* beginning at 22, 96b 34 and following upon the resumé in cc. 18-22 of the programmatic material of *A* 1-3. Furthermore, this is not a division which should come as a total surprise to one who has read the first two chapters of the work with attention. Aristotle has indicated from the beginning that rhetoric is the art of language which applies to all subjects, *but at the same time* must be able to use the language of somewhat specialized knowledge if it is to use language with any intelligence; to cite a few instances: *A* 1, 54 a 1-3, *A* 1, 55b 8-11, *A* 2, 55b 25-34 read against *A* 1, 54 a 21-55a 3 (where the whole point of the argument is that you must speak to the subject), or again *A* 2, 56a 19-20.

Aristotle concludes c. 2 with a statement (58a 32-35) that his intent is to discuss "first the particular topics; but before doing so let us take up the kinds of rhetoric in order that, after determining the kinds, we may take up separately the substantial characteristics and the propositions for each kind".[50]

Chapter 3: 1358a 36-1359a 29: This brings him in c. 3 (58a 36-59 a 5) to his threefold division of rhetoric and his observation that we must obviously have propositions for these three divisions (59a 6-7), and that these premises (59a 8-10) will be the *eikota* and *semeia* of 57a 22-b 25: "for, universally speaking, a syllogism is formed from premises and the *enthymeme* is a syllogism formed from the premises mentioned" (59a 8-10) (compare 59a 7-10 with *A* 2, 57a 32-33). The word *protaseis* in this passage (59a 6-10) is simply an explanation that the *enthymeme*, as a syllogism, must have *protaseis,* i.e. premises, and that the *eikota* and *semeia* if they are to be used in an *enthymeme* must be in the form of a propositional statement. We see this use at *A* 2, 58a 17-25, 31-32; and *A* 2, 58a 30 suggests that the topics, both particular and general, give *protaseis*. There is no contradiction here. The topics are the ultimate sources to which the rhetorician goes for his *eikota* and *semeia*. (This is discussed in c. 4 of this work.)

Aristotle closes c. 3 with a short, but necessary, statement on the *koina* (59a 11-27) which specify rhetorical discourse and without which such discourse would not begin on any subject. His final statement in c. 3 (59a 27-29) is: Next we must make a separate analysis concerning each of these [the three classes of rhetoric], that is to say, concerning the subject-matter of deliberative, epideictic, and judicial rhetoric". Thus with c. 4 he begins and continues through c. 14 of book *A* an analysis of source material (and thus material for *protaseis*) for the three kinds of rhetoric. Indeed at the end of it he describes the whole process (*B* 1, 77b 16-20) as an "account of the δόξαι (i.e. *eikota* and *semeia* in general) καὶ προτάσεις" for each kind of rhetoric. But he appends at once to this (77b 21-29) that one must not only look to the rational account of the subject-matter (πρὸς τὸν λόγον (b 23)— what I call *pragma*) but also to *ethos* and *pathos*. And certainly a legitimate inference from the text at *B* 1, 77b 16-29 is that if the λόγος gives one δόξαι καὶ προτάσεις so, too, will *ethos* and *pathos*. Thus we are back again at the idea that throughout *A* 4 to *B* 17 we are being told by Aristotle how to seek enthymematic argumentation in a particular way with reference to the subject-matter, the audience, the speaker. Thus *B* cc.1-17 continues the presentation of particular aspects of enthymematic argumentation which are relevant to *ethos* and *pathos*. *Ethos* and *pathos* are not peculiar to any one kind of rhetoric, as *pragma* is, but common to all three, for *ethos* and *pathos* are determined by the audience and the speaker, not the subject-matter. Thus there is no division according to the three kinds of rhetoric.

At chapter 18 of book *B* Aristotle begins the general summation (cc. 18-22) discussed earlier. It serves as a transition to the material which occupies itself with *the general method of reasoning by enthymeme* (see *B* 22, 97a 1-6). And so we have the general topics for inference by *enthymeme*, c. 23; the apparent *enthymeme*, or fallacious reasoning in rhetoric, c. 24; the method to refute rhetorical argumentation, c. 25. The intent of these chapters is more readily discernible when it is understood that rhetorical discourse is discussed here more in terms of the methodology of inference. This is to say that we are given a method which is applicable to all subject-matter to construct, or criticize, discourse in its inferential form. Considered in this way rhetorical discourse is more obviously methodological. In this respect it is like dialectic which was the analogy stressed at the very opening of the treatise.

The final chapter (26) is a brief statement in which Aristotle attempts to clarify two points about the *enthymeme*:

(a) In the first comment he says that "amplification and depreciation" (αὔξειν καὶ μειοῦν) is not a *stoicheion* of *enthymemes*, i. e. not one of the general *topoi* which he took up in c. 23. Since one of these general topics was the "more and less" (*B* 23, 97b 12 ff.) Aristotle may feel that there is need for a clarification. The μᾶλλον καὶ ἧττον is a general *topos*, an axiomatic principle upon which enthymematic argumentation can be built, or as he says here: εἰς ὃ πολλὰ ἐνθυμήματα ἐμπίπτει (03a 19). Such *topoi* are *stoicheia* as he also says here (03a 17) and earlier at *B* 22, 96b 21-22. But the purpose of αὔξειν καὶ μειοῦν is to underline the importance or insignificance of the subject-matter under discussion (and here I read with SPENGEL and ROEMER in excluding ἐνθυμήματα at 03a20, and I believe quite correctly so in the light of *A* 9, 68a 26-27, cf. note 38 *supra*). It fulfils the function of one of the *koina* (cf. pp. 35-39), or as he says at *B* 18, 91b 29-92a 1: "For all men in their discourses must make use of the possible and impossible, and attempt to show, some that a thing will be, others that it has been. Further, the matter of magnitude is common to all discourses, for all men use depreciation and amplification (τῷ μειοῦν καὶ αὔξειν) in deliberation, in praising or blaming, accusing or defending". At *B*19, 93a 15 he calls the procedure τὰς αὐξήσεις.

(b) The second comment notes that refutative *enthymeme* is not a class distinct from constructive *enthymeme*. The only possible reason for insisting on this, as far as l can see, is his fear that his discussion of refutation in c. 25 may have left this unclear (cf. his comment at *Γ*17, 18b 5-6).

With the conclusion of the second book Aristotle has clearly made his magisterial contribution toward a new theory of rhetoric. It is manifest, however, that any study which so intimately involves the *logos* and its artistic (i. e. intelligently ordered) use would be incomplete without a discussion of language and the structuring of language.

It is neither my intention, nor necessary for the purpose of this study, to examine in any detail book *Γ* of the *Rhetoric*. I would like to suggest, however, some general reasons why the book is part of Aristotle's treatise, and some particular points within the book which can be understood best if the work is taken as a part of the whole treatise. Any effort to construct a theory of discourse, no matter how it begins, but most certainly if it begins as Aristotle always began such studies by an analysis of the artistic *synolon*, would be totally impossible without a study of language. From this standpoint there can be no question that such a book should be part of a study of rhetorical theory, nor would the close relation of such a book to books *A* and *B* be surprising. Thus it is that, by and large, neither the presence of this book nor its arrangement is challenged.[51] MARX does deny its unity and argues that it was put together by an editor from two existing works of Aristotle, a περὶ λέξεως (seen now in cc. 1-12) and a μέρη τοῦ λόγου (cc. 13-19), and attached to the first two books.

The study on language which we find in the third book was not only relevant to any theory of rhetoric but was a practice within the whole tradition from the 5th century onward. Furthermore, any person who, like Aristotle, is going to place such emphasis on rhetoric as the art of human discourse, and to locate its core in a mode of inference (the enthymeme) which, precisely by reason of the careful use of language, carries meaning to the whole person (intellect, will, emotions) must obviously give his attention to language and its structure. Primarily because of the strictures of MARX I have reexamined the third book and offer the following brief comments as indicative of its coherence with, and close relation of the first two books.

It can be said of the third book that, while it might possibly stand by itself, it makes sense only in terms of what has preceded it. Chapter 17 (and also 18) with its constant reminiscences would be a mystery without the first two books. Chapters 1-7 with their stress on the persuasive (τὸ πιθανόν) make but small sense without a knowledge from book A of the place of the *pithana* in Aristotle's theory. Statements on *ethos, pathos*, and *reason*, and the interrelation of all three both in *lexis*, and in the structuring of *lexis* (cc. 7, 8, 10, 11, 14-16) bear slight meaning apart from A and B. A study of the thematic development which underlies much of the prescriptive advice in this book confirms this view.

Following the initial statement that we must not only know what we are to say but also how to say it we discover that *lexis* (i. e. language in itself and in composition, cc. 1-12) is ἔντεχνος (Γ1, 04a 16) just as the theory of argumentation in *A-B* was. Further we learn that language is instrumental and important for developing *ethos* (Γ1, 03b 14-18), and that its purpose is simply effective communication with another person *via intellect, ethos, emotions*: Γ1, 04a 1-11. This, of course, is a resumption of the idea of the three proofs of A and B and of the transition at Γ1, 03b 9-10. Throughout cc. 1-12 *lexis* is being analyzed constantly with the expressed purpose of rhetoric in mind: ἰδεῖν τὰ ὑπάρχοντα πιθανά γA 1, 55b 10-11). The dominant factor in this analysis (cc. 2-6) is the audience as it was in his analysis of the nature of rhetoric (A cc. 2-3). Next there follows a more explicit statement (c. 7) that *lexis* must integrate *ethos, pathos, and pragma* (this last, *pragma*, is what I would call the rational analogue, i. e. the statement of the subject as reason apprehends it). Indeed this matter of integration (see c. 7, 08a 10-11) in order to communicate more effectively lies at the heart of the analysis of cc. 1 through 12. In c. 8 the discussion of rhythm is predicated on the need for *lexis* to capture the attention of, and give pleasure to the hearer, to speak to the whole person and not merely to his reason (see c. 8, 08b 27-30, 35-36). Chapters 9-11 stress the rational aspect of *lexis* and emphasize that it must speak to the mind for understanding,[52] and that it should be like *enthymeme* in conferring quick insight and understanding (c. 10, 10b 20-21). This section concludes (c. 12) with an account of the *lexis* proper to each kind of rhetoric as these kinds were analyzed in A and B.

The section on *taxis* (cc. 13-19) is unambiguous and somewhat tedious in its prescriptive character, a section someone might wish to give over to non-Aristotelian authorship.[53] The major thematic concern of these chapters is that the *logos* receive a hearing, since the whole analysis of rhetoric up to this point is meaningless if the *logos* is not received by the audience. Thus in cc. 14-16 Aristotle makes very clear the independent role which *ethos* and *pathos* can have toward this end. It is done almost by way of contrast with logical explanation. Aristotle is fully aware (cc. 14-15) of the part which *ethos* and *pathos* can, and at times must, play by themselves. His comment at c. 14, 15b 5, as well as his stress on logical explanation, however, reveals that he is not happy in saying this. In c. 14 it is possible to see the problem which confronted Aristotle in his effort to make the rational and appetitive side of man the complete object of rhetorical discourse; a problem reflected in the polemic of *A* 1. Here in c. 14 he acknowledges by his statements that *ethos* and *pathos* can come into play independently in rhetorical discourse (surely also one of the reasons behind all of *B* 1-17). But his fear of a return to a purely emotional, non-logical form of rhetoric as a perversion of the art of language is reflected in phrases like those at c. 14, 15a 21-23, 37. The most satisfying use of *ethos* and *pathos* for him is as an integral part of logical demonstration (see c. 16, 16b 23-29, 17a 3-5; c. 17, 18a 38-39). Yet if rhetoric is to exist there must be a hearer and a hearer disposed toward listening. Thus Aristotle admits that this can be achieved by *ethos* and/or *pathos* (see c. 14, 15a 37-b 4, and passim). Logical demonstration is the burden of cc. 17-18 and the work concludes somewhat abruptly with a discussion of the last element in *taxis* the epilogue, which in the tenor of its statements resumes the ideas of c. 13.

In conclusion, then, it must be said that the early chapters of the *Rhetoric* studied in the context of the work itself and Aristotle's philosophy indicate, as does also the analysis of the three books, a unified structure open to no major contradictions. This is not to claim that all problems are fully resolved. It does suggest, however, that our choice of options is limited when we are faced with the kind of problem in the text which has made commentators challenge Aristotelian authorship in part, or Aristotelian organization of the whole work. It does not seem possible that we can readily accept the solution of an "earlier" and "later" rhetorical theory brought into incomplete harmony in our present work. Aside from the fact that the evidence for the content and character of this earlier treatise is neither strong nor convincing the coherence of the *Rhetoric* makes such a solution questionable. The same can be said for those who postulate, as a resolution for the problems they see, a long and short version of the original work which have been brought together inadequately in order to form our present text. The existence of such exemplars is mainly conjectural, and their content is constructed by conjecture in an effort to resolve the problems their authors find in our present text.

Yet, as has been seen, these problems are not intractable and do submit to a reasonable explanation as elements in a coherent development of Aristotle's theory of rhetoric. There are possibly *lacunae* in the text (e. g. book *Γ*), and there are possibly interpolations and editings which have entered the text in the course of time as can be expected in any classical text. The argument, however, that such incursions have affected the substantive parts of Aristotle's rhetorical theory does not stand firm. When we attend to what Aristotle treats as the central principle of his theory, the *enthymeme*, we find a logically consistent development of the theory. In so far as a central principle usually carries with it the ground of unity for all the parts, and confers meaning and significance upon all the elements which form the whole, this could be expected. A study of the *enthymeme* in an effort to discover its meaning as presented by Aristotle oddly enough reveals that not only can we accept the text as received, but also that text statements which appear to militate against the unity and coherence of the text are susceptible to interpretation which makes them both intelligible and acceptable as essential expressions of Aristotle's rhetorical theory.

Notes

[1]See P. DUHAMEL, "The Function of Rhetoric as Effective Expression" The Journal of the History of Ideas 10, 1949, pp. 344-56; E. MADDEN, "The Enthymeme; Crossroads of Logic, Rhetoric, and Metaphysics" The Philosophical Review 61, 1952, pp. 368-76; R. McKEON, "Rhetoric in the Middle Ages" Speculum 17, 1942, pp. 1-32. J. GEFFCKEN, Griechische Literaturgeschichte, vol. 2, Heidelberg 1934, pp. 230, 233 ff.

[2]Cf. *A* 1, 54a 1-55b 24 and *A* 2, 56a 1 ff. (References are to the edition of ROEMER, Teubner, 1923). See D. ALLAN, The Philosophy of Aristotle, Oxford 1952, p. 200; T. GOMPERZ, Griechische Denker, vol. 3-4, Berlin 1931, pp. 367-68; E. HAVET, Etude sur la Rhétorique d'Aristote, Paris 1846, pp. 27-31; W. SÜSS, Ethos, Berlin 1910, p. 126; F. SOLMSEN, Die Entwicklung der aristotelischen Logik und Rhetorik, Berlin 1929, pp. 208-209; E.M. COPE, An Introduction to Aristotle's Rhetoric, London 1867, p. 4, and his commentary, Cambridge 1877, passim under the text numbers cited above; MARX, Aristoteles' Rhetorik, BSG 52, 1900, p. 301. GEFFCKEN, op. cit., p. 231.

[3]J. VATER, Animadversiones ad Aristotelis Librum Primum Rhetoricum, Saxony 1794, p. 10, and L. SPENGEL, Aristotelis Ars Rhetorica I-II, Leipzig 1867, under 1354b 18. J. RUSSO, La Filosofia della Retorica in Aristotele, Naples 1962, p. 82: "E la critica moderna è caduta talora in strane contradizioni proprio su questo punto: dopo aver scoperto che la *Rhetorica* aristotelica è un opera filsofica, e non già un manuale o empirica indagine sullo stile. . ."

[4]For example cf. SOLMSEN, op. cit., pp. 199 f., 202, 226.

[5]See note 2 above and also K. BARWICK, Die Gliederung der rhetorischen TECHNE und die horazische Epistula ad Pisones, Hermes 57, 1922, pp. 16-18.

[6]GEFFCKEN, op. cit., pp. 229-237 with all of his reservations on the work makes this eminently clear. GOMPERZ, op. cit., p. 367: "Hierzu ward A. wohl in erster Linie durch das platonische im 'Phaidros' verfochtene Ideal jener Kunst vermocht. . .die neue Darstellung der Rhetorik so scharf als möglich von ihrer älteren, der bloß empirischen oder routinemäßigen Behandlung zu scheiden."

[7]The deliberately human context within which the rational argument is built in a dialogue represents one conditioning aspect. Another phase of it is the intellectual problem proposed; for example the whole argument of the *Phaedo* on immortality ultimately rests upon that reason which is "the best and the most difficult to refute" (85d). This kind of intellectual problem demands choice, as does also the method of hypothesis in which a series of relevant and plausible hypotheses are considered in order to choose the one which possesses the maximum of truth. In the choice more than intellect is involved. BACON who said that "the duty and science of Rhetoric is, to apply reason to imagination for the better moving of the will" has

clearly analyzed the weakness in Plato's theoretical attitude: "it was great injustice in Plato. . . to esteem of rhetoric but as a voluptuary art. . .And therefore as Plato said elegantly 'That Virtue, if she could be seen, would move great love and affection'; so seeing that she cannot be showed to the senses by corporal shape, the next degree is to show her to the imagination in lively representation: for to show her to reason only in subtilty of argument, was a thing ever derided in Chrysippus and many of the Stoics; who thought to thrust virtue upon men by sharp disputations and conclusions, which have no sympathy with the will of man." (Advancement of Learning, Book II).

[8]Aristotle not only admitted this knowledge, it was an inevitable admission. To say that there is only knowledge of the universal surely has as its corollary that there is only *episteme* of the necessary. Granted that the only true *episteme* for Aristotle is knowledge of the cause, the universal, and the necessary, he could then ask himself just as well as we ask ourselves: what knowledge do we have of the world of things as we apprehend them (*An. Post.* 88b 30-89b 6). His response was direct: that which we find in reality which is constant, but not necessary, can be the object of a kind of knowledge, and it also leads one to seek out the cause, the universal, and the necessary, or truly legitimate *episteme*. *Doxa*, as this knowledge is called, is, in the last analysis, the only valid way to know things which come to be and cease to be, and which, as a consequence, are contingent by the very fact that they are. Indeed it would be otherwise difficult to understand Aristotle's efforts in ethics, poetics, rhetoric (all called *technai* by him) and politics, as well as the object of his inductive methodology. *Doxa* is the manner of knowing in which sensible reality presents itself authentically to man. WEIL'S comment on the *Topics* is to the point (La place de la logique dans la pensée aristotelicienne, Rev. de Metaphysique et Morale 56, 1951, p. 299): "La topique n'est pas une logique du vraisemblable, du plausible, de l'opinion; elle constitue une technique pour extraire du discours le vrai discursif, plus précisément pour en éliminer le faux, à partir de ces connaissances préalables sans lesquelles aucune science ne se conçoit pour Aristote".

[9]*A* 2, 57a 1-5: That about which men deliberate; and men deliberate about all things which are problematic, i.e. appear open to other possibilities (φαινομένων ἐνδέχσθαι ἀμφοτέρως ἔχειν). The phrase: καὶ τέχνας μὴ ἔχομεν means that there is no systematic body of knowledge which would facilitate a resolution of the problem. Yet even in this last instance, as we see at *A* 2, 55b 27-34, rhetoric still has the faculty to discern those elements in any subject of deliberation which are particularly apt to secure a response from the auditor.

[10]*A* 3, 58a 36-59a 5: This analysis is central to the *Rhetoric* and also to the whole domain of human discourse. For it does not simply specify the object of the study of rhetoric and present us with a threefold genus around which the *techne* revolves but it also embraces the major areas of human discourse with which rhetoric as the art of discourse is concerned. Rhetoric, as he tells us at *A*2, 55b 25- 26, is the "*dynamis* (faculty, power) to perceive and grasp the possibly suasive in any given subject, and this is the function of no other *techne*." As such a *dynamis* it clearly finds its completion and fulfilment in its object as presented here. The "possibly suasive" are those elements within any given subject which are likely to bring about a state of mind open to the speaker's thesis. There should be no need to say that for Aristotle in the *Rhetoric* this means an openness to the truth in so far as it can be discerned in a given situation.

[11]A very explicit statement on the ultimate *telos* of rhetoric is found at *B* 18, 91b 8-18.

[12]The whole first chapter is much concerned with this fact. In particular see *A* 1, 55a 14-24; *A* 2, 56a 15 ff., 57a 2-b4; *B* 1, 77b 21; *B* 18, 91b 8 ff.; *B* 25, 02b 31 ff.

[13]From a statement such as *EN* 1139a 3 ff. we are forced to conclude that rhetoric must include that part of the soul which Aristotle calls *to logistikon* as opposed to *to epistemonikon*, that is to say, that it involves *dianoia praktike* rather than *nous theoretikos*; see Ross, Aristotle, op. cit., p. 215, or COPLESTON, A History of Philosophy vol. I, London 1951, p. 328.

[14]See *Metaph.* 993b 21-23. Aristotle states their objects as truth and action. And I would note that he remarks that the practical intellect does not necessarily neglect truth but is concerned with its immediate and relative application to human action.

[15]J. MARITAIN, Creative Intuition in Art and Poetry, New York 1953, p. 47; 44-7 clearly expresses the point Aristotle is making in the introductory chapters.

[16]It would be well to recall the analogy Aristotle draws between medicine and rhetoric; *A* 1, 55b 12 ff.

[17]See *Poet.* 1449b 35 ff. where drama is defined as an imitation of *praxis* and postulates the causes of *praxis*: *ethos* and *dianoia*. There is far more that can be made of this relationship between the *Poetics* and the *Rhetoric* than has been done; in this respect GEFFCKEN, op. cit., p. 230 correctly calls them complementary to each other.

[18]See, for example, J. VAHLEN, Aristoteles' Lehre von der Rangfolge der Theile der Tragödie, Symbola Philologorum Bonnensium, Lipsiae 1867, p. 172, n. 43, and S. BUTCHER, Aristotle's Theory of Fine Art and Poetry[3], London 1902, p. 347. It is true that Aristotle speaks of *ethos* only in the *Poetics*; *ethos* ultimately, however, is nothing more nor less than an established attitude with respect to one's dominant emotional reactions (*EN* 1098a 3 ff.; 1102a 27 ff.; 1105b 19ff.; 1139a 17 ff. are a few places which indicate this), or a firm disposition of the appetitive part of the soul with respect to all the elements which make up this part of the soul. Chief among these elements are the *pathe*. As a matter of fact the very close interrelation between reason and emotion which exists within the soul as it is presented to us by Aristotle can be seen in the study of the *pathe* (*Rhet. B* 1, 78a 20 ff.). These *pathe* are in reality affective dispositions of the mind and as such they are intimately associated with both mental and appetitive activity.

[19]F. MARX, Aristoteles' Rhetorik, BSG 52, 1900, pp. 270 ff.

[20]A. ROEMER, Aristotelis Ars Rhetorica, Leipzig 1923, p. liv.

[21]SOLMSEN who has pursued the work of SPENGEL, VAHLEN, ROEMER and MARX, and who has devised his own theory of our *Rhetoric* as a combination of an earlier and later Aristotelian theory, has this to say: "es war wahrscheinlich nicht einmal Aristoteles' Absicht, die *Rhetorik* mit der Konsequenz und ἀκρίβεια zu einer gedanklichen Einheit zu gestalten, wie sie diesem Stoffgebiet gar nicht gemäß war. . ." Die Entwicklung der aristotelischen Logik und Rhetorik, Berlin 1929, p. 225.

[22]L. SPENGEL, Aristotelis Ars Rhetorica I-II, Leipzig 1867, passim; Über die Rhetorik des Aristoteles, ABA 6, 1851, pp. 455-513. J. VAHLEN, Zur Kritik aristotelischer Schriften (Poetik und Rhetorik), SAWW 38, 1861, 59-148.

[23]C.A. BRANDIS, Über Aristoteles' Rhetorik und die griechischen Ausleger derselben, Philologus 4, 1849, p. 1.

[24]ROEMER, op. cit., p. Lxix; MARX, op. cit., p. 289; P. GOHLKE, Die Entstehung der aristotelischen Ethik, Politik, Rhetorik, Wien 1944, p. 123.

[25]MARX, op. cit., p. 287, and see pp. 301-02.

[26]MARX, op. cit., p. 255. This passage will illustrate the whole endeavor. GOHLKE who accepts it as genuine (op. cit., p. 130 f.) uses it (p. 133) to rearrange part of Book *B*. MARX who finds problems in Book *Γ* demands, as a consequence, a rearrangement of Book *B* at this point. SOLMSEN, (op. cit., p. 32) says of it that it is "extremely unlikely that a later editor manufactured the transition in order to link the first two books to the third".

[27]BARWICK, Die Gliederung. . .,op. cit., p. 16. Of course if one begins with a short and long exemplar of the *Rhetoric*, as ROEMER suggests, there is room to operate. Unfortunately no one alludes to the fact that the content of each such exemplar (if it existed) is unknown; the existence of each depends upon the reconstruction of each interpreter. The general problem has been discussed more recently by V. BUCHHEIT, Untersuchungen zur Theorie des Genos Epideiktikon von Gorgias bis Aristoteles, Munich 1960.

[28]ROEMER, op. cit., pp. xcvii-cii; SOLMSEN, op. cit., pp. 223 ff.; for SPENGEL (Über die Rhetorik. . .) and VAHLEN see note 22 above; MARX, op. cit., pp. 290-300; MARX, pp. 280 ff. also discusses a double enthymeme theory, and see also GOHLKE, op. cit., p. 117 f., 130 ff.

[29]He does not mention *pathos*. A discussion of this and SPENGEL'S reaction can be read in ROEMER, op. cit., pp. xcvii-ci. The omission may be unhappy, but scarcely critical; BAR-WICK, Die Gliederung. . ., op. cit., pp. 19-20 speaking of this passage believes that πάθη are readily thought of in relation to ἤθη, and cites examples thereof.

[30]I would call attention to the way in which Aristotle follows a schema here: after "example" in c. 20 he takes up *gnome* (maxim) in c. 21 which he has already told us (*B* 20, 93a 25) is part of enthymeme. *Gnome* leads him on to c. 22 and to the enthymeme as a syllogism, i.e. a form of inference. It is in speaking of enthymeme as syllogism that he reviews the particular topics and then moves on in c. 23 to its general topics.

[31]SPENGEL, Ars Rhetorica, op. cit., *ad* 1393a 22. In cc. 18-26 κοινόν appears a number of times; it may be of some help toward an understanding of the word to look at all of the instances in which it occurs:

   a) 91b 29 cf. analysis in text
     b32 same as b29, i.e. *megethos* is "common to all speech" like possible, impossible, etc.
     92a 4 same as 91b 29
   b) 92a 2 the adverb: "in a general way" as opposed to: "in particular"
     95a 10-11 "common", "general"
     96b 11-12 "common", "general"
     93a 23-24 the *koinai pisteis* i.e. the general proofs, enthymeme and example, as opposed apparently to what we can call the *idiai pisteis*:
     ἦθος, πάθος, πρᾶγμα which he says he has discussed: ἐπεί περ εἴρηται περὶ τῶν ἰδίων. This is another confirmation of the shift from the particular to the general presentation.
   c) 01a 20 *to koinonikon*
     21 means "common" but the expression is a proverbial one here.

[32]SPENGEL, ibid.; VAHLEN apparently identifies them not merely with the πίστεις but also with the τόποι as well as with δυνατόν, γεγονός, αὔξησις op. cit., pp. 122, 124-25, 128; SOLMSEN, Die Entwicklung, op. cit., p. 225 calls them κοιναὶ προτάσεις; MARX, op. cit. would find *B* 18, 91b 24-92a 7 more appropriately located at the end of *A* 3. ROEMER in a note to *B* 19, 93a 21 in his apparatus locates the problem as Spengel saw it.

[33]See c. 3.

[34]VAHLEN, see note 32 above; COPE, An Introduction, op. cit., pp. 128 ff. where he cites them as four in number; he cites them more correctly as three in the Commentary, op. cit., I, pp. 55-56, and II, p. 175.

[35]"The great and the small" are not "the more and the less" or variations thereof. "The more and the less" is a *koinos topos*: *B* 23, 97b 12 ff. This distinction is often overlooked with consequent confusion.

[36]To avoid misunderstanding, it might be well to remark here that it is clear from the tenor of Aristotle's words that he is writing with both the speaker and the audience in mind.

[37]Aristotle indicates a close relationship between the ἴδια τέλη and one or the other of the κοινά in at least three different places: *A* 2, 57a 1-7, *A* 3, 58b 2-8, and *B* 26, 03a 20-25. In the 57a 1 ff. passage men deliberate about "the possible" not the "impossible".

[38]SÜSS, who appears to have caught the character of these κοινά ("Schließlich gibt es auch gemeinsame Instanzen dieser Art, ohne die kein Genus auskommen kann", op. cit., p. 131) calls them εἴδη on one occasion (133) but also appears to consider them as τέλη (168). The

closest we get is *eidon* describing *auxesis* at A9, 68a 26-27: ὅλως δὲ τῶν κοινῶν εἰδῶν ἄπασι τοῖς λόγοις ἡ μὲν αὔξησις . . .

[39] "Special subjects" within the context of the passage, and in the light of the use of εἶδος in the *Rhetoric* is a strange interpretation of the word. And to translate the term as "special topics" results in the meaningless jumble of the "topic of the topics". No modern commentator to my knowledge has referred the word to the two kinds of enthymeme just mentioned in the text. Such reference would seem to have more point but still does not appear to be correct. SPENGEL does not discuss εἰδῶν in his commentary here, but at 1396b 33 has a comment from which we might conclude that he understands the term to refer the three γένη: "exposuit εἴδη (de quibus vid. I, 2 finem), h.e. τὸ ἀγαθὸν καὶ κακόν, τὸ καλὸν καὶ αἰσχρόν, τὸ δίκαιον καὶ ἄδικον . . ."

[40] See COPE, Commentary II, p. 233, and the more recent translations of RHYS ROBERTS, Oxford 1924; JEBB-SANDYS, Cambridge 1909; FREESE, London 1926; LANE COOPER, New York 1932. Since these interpretations echo fairly consistently the older translations, there is no need to cite the latter. It is possible, however, to find some older works which interpret εἰδῶν as the three kinds of rhetoric. Thus T. GOULSTON in his 1619 edition Aristotelis "De Rhetorica" has: "Ac fere quidem de generibus singulis quae oratori commodata sunt", and his note on the text indicates that he means by "generibus" the three γένη.

[41] See c. 4 on the topics.

[42] In the immediate vicinity of our text: B 20, 93a 28, 94a 17 (on example); B 21, 94b 26, 95b 18 (on maxim); B 22, 96b 24 (on enthymeme). See also B 2, 78b 14, B 4, 81b 33, Γ2, 05a 3, Γ14, 15a 24.

[43] See B 22, 96a 4-b19 which is a summary of his study of the particular topics for each kind of rhetoric, a study that has been the burden of his work from A 4 to B 17. In chapter 4 there is a detailed consideration of these εἴδη, or what Aristotle calls in the passage here ἴδια (96b 15).

[44] On the ἕξεις see Gohlke, op. cit., pp. 133 ff.; SPENGEL'S commentary *ad* 1396 b33.

[45] The significance of the qualifying adjectives τῶν χρησίμων καὶ ἀναγκαίων modifying εἰδῶν is difficult to understand in any of the proposed interpretations of this word. Some take καί as copulative, some as corrective, and both meanings appear possible as is indicated in the interpretation offered in this chapter. As for the qualifying adjectives I do not pretend here to make them any less problematic, but merely to show that for Aristotle they would not be any less probable or possible as attributes of εἰδῶν understood as the three kinds of rhetoric. Aristotle remarks at A 3, 58b 6 f. that the rhetorical *techne* as he understands it is "of necessity" made up of three kinds of rhetorical discourse: ὥστ' ἐξ ἀνάγκης ἂν εἴη τρία γένη τῶν λόγων τῶν ῥητορικῶν. This would appear to mean that if anyone is to make use of this art he must of necessity owing to the nature of rhetoric engage in one or other of the three kinds of rhetoric. In this sense, then, ἀναγκαίων is quite legitimate as an attribute of εἰδῶν. It would also seem quite legitimate to conclude that, since the art of rhetoric realizes itself fully in these three kinds of discourse, what is said of rhetoric may also be said of them; namely that for intelligent action in society they are helpful and useful: cf. A 1, 55a 21 ff.: χρήσιμος δέ ἐστιν ἡ ῥητορική. . ."

[46] These premises are *derived from* particular topics: B 1, 77b 16-20, Γ1, 03b 13-14, A 4, 60b 1-3, A 6, 62b 29-30. They are not topics in themselves.

[47] Aristotle does not use the word γένη in the text, but it is more than clear from a comparison of A 3, 58b 20-28 with the text here, and also from his usual mode of expression in the *Rhetoric*, that he specifically means γένη to be understood here. Thus in our text when he speaks of τόπων περὶ ἀγαθοῦ ἢ κακοῦ he obviously means deliberative rhetoric (cf. A 4, 59a 30-31), while καλοῦ ἢ αἰσχροῦ is epideictic (cf. A 9, 66a 23- 24), and δικαίου ἢ ἀδίκου is judicial

(cf. *A* 10, 68b 1-5). The rest of the sentence is additive and is a summation of the particular topics presented in *B* 1-17.

[48] And one makes enthymemes from propositions (*A* 3, 59a 6 ff.), and these propositions both in content and form are derived from the topics both particular and general.

[49] SPENGEL seems to want to say this (commentary *ad* 1397a 1): "Locos non uni alterive generi, hos enim singulos iam exposuit, sed omnibus tribus communes enumerare vult. . ." The comment of COPE (Comm. II, p. 236) may mean the same.

[50] I.e. the discussion of the substantial characteristics of each kind of rhetoric—στοιχεῖα—, (this word is needlessly confused by some critics, e.g. MARX, op. cit., p. 282), and the selection of propositional statements for each kind which runs through *A* 4-14.

[51] COPE, An Introduction to Aristotle's Rhetoric, London 1867, pp. 277-400 has an analysis and study of this book.

[52] Yet this section with its emphasis on intellectual apprehension contains a continuous undercurrent of the role of *pathos* (*ethos* only indirectly) in such apprehension. It is quite interesting to find the integration of *ethos, pathos, pragma* which is proposed in this study for the enthymeme demanded by Aristotle for *lexis* throughout cc. 1-12.

[53] On the other hand its initial statements on the importance of *apodeixis* (c. 13) are Aristotelian and are a direct return to *A* cc. 1-2. Even MARX, who is most critical of the whole book and who maintains that something new is being introduced here, must say: "Ein neues rhetorisches System, eine neue Theorie ist zudem in der Lehre von der Beweisführung im zweiten Teil des dritten Buches erkenntlich, deren Grundlagen freilich bereits in den beiden ersten Büchern vorhanden sind, deren Bestand aber erst im dritten Buch als bekannt vorausgesetzt wird." op. cit., p. 247.

II

THE CENTRALITY OF THE ENTHYMEME

As soon as it is understood that rhetoric for Aristotle is an activity which engages the whole person in the effort to communicate meaning by way of language a major obstacle toward understanding the *Rhetoric* is removed. We find him where we could, more or less, expect to find him: in the mainstream of Greek rhetorical theory. In any discussion of theory three names are preeminent among the Greeks: Isocrates, Plato, Aristotle. For all of them rhetoric was not a technique but an art, the art of the *logos*. Rhetoric transcended specific intellectual disciplines and was used by man in each discipline in his effort to articulate the world of reality for himself and others by means of language. Although their views have been set in opposition their ultimate observations on the nature of language as the medium whereby man discourses with man are essentially consonant. Each one considered rhetoric as the art of language even though Plato admittedly had his difficulties with it.

Without minimizing their differing attitudes we can say that all three recognized that rhetoric played a central role in the life of man and the polis. When Plato came to write the *Phaedrus* he acknowledged the importance of rhetoric as the art of language, for there can be but small doubt that it is around this subject that the dialogue unfolds. He does insist that the only true rhetoric has its roots in dialectic, and that the only true rhetorician is the philosopher. At the same time his thoughtful reconsideration of the art in the *Phaedrus* would seem to indicate his realization (see the tentative suggestions at 260d, 262c, 269b, d) that rhetoric could indeed serve dialectic which alone has the power to open man on the world of the truly real and knowable. As ROBIN remarks (Platon Oeuvres Complètes IV 3e partie Phèdre, Paris 1947, p. xxxviii): "Enfin dans la dernière section, à cette rhétorique de fait Platon oppose ce qu' on pourrait appeler une rhétorique de droit, rhétorique philosophique qui n'est autre chose qu' une mise en oeuvre pratique de sa dialectique". There can be little question of Isocrates' convictions on the importance of the art. Aristotle made his own position strikingly clear with the opening words of his treatise: "rhetoric is the correlative of dialectic", —as the art of dialectic came into play in the exercise of the intellectual disciplines so did the rhetorical art.

It does not seem to be an exaggeration to say that for all of these men rhetoric, as the art of the *logos*, could bring together the results of the activity of the speculative intellect and those of the practical intellect (the *pragmateia ethike kai politike*) and make them accessible to all for more responsible everyday living in

66

the polis.[1] Rhetoric was certainly not mere speech-making for any one of them; rather it was the heart of the process by which man tried to interpret and make meaningful for himself and others the world of the real. As Aristotle says so well: "Rhetoric is, as it were, a constitutive part of dialectic and is similar to dialectic, as I said at the beginning, insofar as neither rhetoric nor dialectic is a science (*episteme*) concerned with the specific and determinate nature of any subject-matter. They are rather faculties (*dynameis*), so to speak, for providing reasonable explanations" (*A* 2, 56a 30-33).

In other words from what Aristotle says, not formally but certainly explicitly in this passage, rhetoric is general and touches all areas of human knowledge wherein man attempts to convey understanding to another whether it be philosophy, literature, or the physical sciences. This meaning of rhetoric is readily acknowledged in Isocrates, and it is found in the *Phaedrus* when Plato sets down the norms acceptable for an "art" of rhetoric (cf. 277b-c: "whether one is to *expound* or persuade"). Further, it is a meaning clearly at work in all of Plato's dialogues although, strangely enough, never acknowledged there.[2]

A study of the enthymeme in the *Rhetoric* makes it clear that Aristotle's point of departure on the nature of rhetoric begins with the idea that rhetoric is quite simply the art of language. Indeed it does not seem possible to acquire an intelligent grasp of his analysis of rhetoric without an understanding of what he calls the enthymeme and which he considers also in the *Analytics*. In the first place he locates the enthymeme at the very center of the rhetorical process when he says quite explicitly that rhetoric, in the final analysis, directs itself to *pistis* and that the enthymeme incorporates *pistis*: "It is obvious, then, that the *entechnic* method is concerned with the *pisteis*" (*A* 1, 55a 3-4), "enthymeme is the corporeal frame for *pistis*" (*A* 1, 54a 15).

This study is predicated on the fact that once we understand the enthymeme, as Aristotle presents it in the *Rhetoric*, we can come to an informed knowledge of what he means by rhetoric. In actual fact the exegesis of the meaning of ἐνθύμημα in the text not only reveals the specific nature of rhetoric as a *dynamis*, namely something which transcends all particular disciplines, but also the complete relevance and importance of ἦθος and πάθος and the whole complex of *psychagogia* in his theory of rhetoric. With the enthymeme as the foundation block one can discern more readily how rhetoric is the analogue of dialectic and in its own right is a methodology, namely, the artful use of language in the various disciplines, to achieve effective communication, or what Plato has in mind when he writes: καθ᾽ ὅσον πέφυκε μεταχειρισθᾶναι τὸ λόγων γένος...πρὸς τὸ διδάξαι... πρὸς τὸ πεῖσαι (*Phaedr.* 277c).

Few scholars would admit this. A far more typical comment on the *Rhetoric* is that which we find in Ross:[3] "The *Rhetoric* may seem at first sight to be a curious jumble of literary criticism with second rate logic, ethics, politics, and jurisprudence, mixed by the cunning of one who knows well how the weaknesses of the human heart are to be played upon." Most students of the *Rhetoric* would concur with Ross' statement and the attitude finds its way into more general studies. Geffcken, while in general agreement, is still constrained to say more correctly that with the *Rhetoric* we have "eine vollkommen neue Grundlage, einen trotz Aristoteles' Verleugnung der Redekunst als Wissenschaft doch wissenschaftlichen Sinn[4]."

The cause of this general misunderstanding arises in the opening chapters of the *Rhetoric* when Aristotle sets down the theme of his study, and it consists in a misreading of the relationship between πίστις and ἐνθύμημα. The misunderstanding consequent upon this is substantial enough to cause commentators to accuse Aristotle of open contradiction, and even to suspect strongly that the *Rhetoric* is very likely a conflation of two (or more) different treatises.

While it is possible to understand how the mistake arose it is quite difficult to comprehend its long life. There can be no question that for Aristotle the enthymeme was the focal point of his analysis of rhetoric. This inescapable fact is the very thing which has caused dismay among his commentators, and led to the somewhat ambivalent observations already noted. The eminently clear statement of the opening (*A* 1, 54a 1-15) in which we are told that the essence of the whole rhetorical art resides in the *pisteis* and that all *pistis* is incorporated in the enthymeme becomes immediately muddied—or so it would seem to many. These remarks of Aristotle in *A* 1 have caused commentators to believe that the ideal is logical demonstration by enthymeme which is the syllogism of rhetoric. Enthymeme is *pistis* in a preeminent way, but, somehow or other, *ethos* and *pathos* (the emotional aspect which appears to have been rejected: *A* 1, 54a 16-55a 3) are equally *pisteis* as we discover at the beginning of c. 2 (56a 1 ff.).

However, if we restore the enthymeme to the critical center of his analysis where it was placed by Aristotle we discover that there is neither open contradiction in the introduction, nor a lack of unity in the work, and that, least of all, is there cynicism or sophism in Aristotle's theory. It is somewhat surprising that the enthymeme has not been studied with more attention for it was obviously important to Aristotle who made it a subject of study in both the *Analytics* and the *Rhetoric*, and apparently found it of value in philosophy and literature. It is more than clear that it was not understood by those who followed. In the maze of philosophical and rhetorical speculation from the latter quarter of the 4th century onward it came to be catalogued in a rather cavalier fashion as an abbreviated syllogism, an interpretation still common. A reflection of the insignificance to which it was relegated may be found in Roman rhetorical study and Cicero's description of it as a rhetorical device: "*illa ex repugnantibus sententiis communis conclusio, quae . . . a rhetoribus* ἐνθύμημα *nuncupatur.*"[5] The lack of any formal study of the concept in more modern literature is further surprising, and this absence contributes, it seems, to the persistent misunderstanding of the *Rhetoric*.[6] In many ways Aristotle's commentators are in a position similar to that of the scholars of his time: "They say nothing about enthymeme" (*A* 1, 54a 14 f.).

The confusion arises with Aristotle's comments on the *pisteis* and the insistence of his commentators in identifying enthymeme as one of the three *pisteis entechnoi* of *A* 2, 55b 35. By way of introduction it can be said that nowhere in the *Rhetoric*, or indeed elsewhere in his writings, is such an identification made by Aristotle.

The introduction of the *pisteis* at the beginning of his work is quite understandable since Aristotle considers that part of the effort of rhetoric is to elicit in another a correct judgment in instances where the act of judgment is totally free and unconstrained. The *pisteis*, as *A* 1-2, 54a 1-56b 27 demonstrates, are the principal sources which can cause this act of judgment to be made. It is the task of the commentator, as has ordinarily been recognized, to come forward with a rather precise and determinate meaning of this term πίστις if at all possible. Traditional exegesis has identified the term with the three artistic proofs, the *pisteis entechnoi*. It then makes the further move of identifying the three *pisteis entechnoi* as *ethos, pathos* (thus the contradiction often talked about), and *enthymeme*.[7] These three, then, become the means, or modes of proving or demonstrating.

The identification is partially, but not fully, justified by the text of Aristotle. Nowhere does Aristotle explicitly identify enthymeme with the *pisteis entechnoi*, as he does identify *ethos* and *pathos* with them. This point should be kept in mind. Without difficulty one can show Aristotle's clear reference of *ethos* and *pathos* to these *pisteis* (*A* 2, 56a 1-19). There is no such clear conjunction of *enthymeme* with *pistis* where *pistis* means one of the three *pisteis entechnoi*, and there is no clear evidence that the third of the three *pisteis entechnoi* is the *enthymeme*.

In actual fact the word πίστις in Aristotle's text will not sustain the univocal interpretation (i. e. proof, way of proving) which has been imposed upon it. The assumption of such a univocal meaning has generated some of the difficulties about the coherence and unity of the text. In reality the word *pistis* has a number of meanings in the text, and it is necessary to discriminate among them for an understanding of the text and the meaning of enthymeme.

A few comments by way of preface are necessary. First of all the word *pistis* occurs within the text 41 times (22 times in *A*, 7 in *B*, 12 in *Γ*) and offers sufficient evidence within the text for its exegesis. Secondly, it is essential to recognize that the interpretation of *pistis* presented here is the direct consequent of an effort to determine the meaning of enthymeme which Aristotle makes the key concept of his rhetorical analysis. This problem of the meaning of enthymeme arises in the text and its solution is sought there. In this attempt no pre-conceptions about any theories of language were brought to the text. The only question put to the text was: what is meant by enthymeme? In the absence of any formal studies of the enthymeme the interpretations offered either raised problems with the text, or reduced the enthymeme to a truncated syllogism. Both were possibilities. However, the more Aristotle's text, together with its many interpretations, was studied, the more it began to emerge that the text became tractable and understandable with the explanation offered here, even though this explanation with its strongly organic theory of language may sound to some more modern than ancient. Aristotle's text conveys the strong impression of a theory of discourse which asserts that discourse in all areas, but particularly in the area of the probable and contingent, is never purely logical and notional. It must attend also to the audience and to the confrontation of speaker and audience (*ethos* and *pathos*). The notional exposition of the subject is insufficient in the sense that "demonstrations have no power of persuasion". In the text one is continually aware of the fact that persuasive discourse must be alert to the attitudes, convictions, beliefs of the auditor and speaker. This theory of the integral character of persuasive discourse is contained in Aristotle's statements on the *pisteis* where he directs our attention to those qualities which must be considered in the presentation of a subject, namely, the logical and emotive aspects. The causes of persuasion and conviction reside not only in the rational explanation of the subject (the *pisteis pragmatikai*), but also in the character of the audience and speaker and in their emotional resonance with the subject (the *pisteis ethikai* and *pathetikai*). While the *rational explanation*, or *ethos*, or *pathos*, may be used independently to win assent or conviction (cf. pp. 51-52), Aristotle appears to affirm clearly that their effective and proper use is by being brought together in deductive and inductive argumentation.

When we discriminate among Aristotle's various uses of *pistis* his understanding of the nature of language in discourse reveals itself. Basically there are five meanings of the word in the work. Two of them can be put aside fairly quickly. Both are technical expressions. One occurs at *A* 14, 75a 10 and means "pledge" or "word of honor". The other appears in the third book where he discusses t he various "parts" of speech. Aristotle uses *pistis* as the technical term for that part of a speech wherein one formally demonstrates one's thesis or proposition. The clear instances of this all appear in the singular, e.g. *Γ* 13, 14a 35, b 8, 9; *Γ* 17, 18a 18. There are a few instances which are not as clear and can be questioned as will be seen later.

This leaves us with the three critical meanings of *pistis* which are first met in the opening chapters of the work. These meanings are: (1) *pistis* as a state of mind, i. e. belief or conviction, which results when a person accepts a proof or demonstration; (2) *pistis* as the logical instrument of the reasoning process in deduction or induction; (3) *pistis* as source material, material which comes from the *logical analysis* of the subject, from the study of the *character* of the speaker or audience, and from the study of the *emotional context* potentially present for this audience in this subject and situation. As the source of conviction *pistis* in each meaning—which is *ethos, pathos*, and not enthymeme but what I call *pragma*, the logical aspect of the subject—carries probative force either in itself, or most effectively when it is organized in a form of deductive or inductive inference.

1) *Pistis* is used to represent the state of mind, namely, conviction or belief, at which the auditor arrives when the correctly chosen aspects of the subject-matter are placed before him in an effective manner. In the opening chapters this meaning usually appears in a verb form, *A* 1, 55a 5; 2,56a 6,19 (or later on 8,66a 11). The noun is found in this sense at *A* 9,67b 29; *B* 1,77b 25. The use at *B* 20, 94a 10 is to my mind questionable, see p. 60 below.

2) In its second meaning *pistis* is the word used for a methodological technique, illustrated best perhaps by Aristotle's comment at *A* 2, 56b 6-8: "all men make their proofs (τὰς πίστεις ποιοῦται) in a demonstrative way either with examples or enthymemes; aside from these two there is nothing else". In this sense *pistis* means the logical instrument used by the mind to marshal the material into a reasoning process. It is a method which gives the matter a logical form, so to speak, and thus produces that state of mind in the auditor which is called belief, *pistis*. For, as Aristotle remarks (*A* 1,55a 5-6), belief or conviction is the result of some kind of a demonstrative process. It is this meaning of *pistis* which is applicable primarily to *enthymeme*, but also to *paradeigma* (example). For in rhetoric *enthymeme* (the process of deduction) and *paradeigma* (the inductive process) are the logical instruments which one is to use in constructing argumentation directed toward *krisis*, or judgment, on the part of another (*A* 2, 56a 34-b 27).

At *A* 1, 55a 4 Aristotle speaks of *pisteis* which very probably are the *entechnic pisteis* (see p. 64), and then explains that *pistis* is a kind of proof or demonstration: "For it is clear that the entechnic methodology is concerned with the *pisteis* and that *pistis* is a kind of demonstration". This specification of *pistis* as a kind of proof, demonstration, is compatible with the idea of *pistis* as deduction or induction (the second meaning) and also as the source of conviction (the third meaning, see p. 60). However, it exemplifies the somewhat casual way in which Aristotle uses *pistis*. For he continues (55a 5-6) with an explanation of "kind of proof, demonstration" which says that the ἀπόδειξις ῥητορική is the enthymeme and that the enthymeme is a συλλογισμός τις (8). In effect he is saying that *pistis* as rhetorical *apodeixis* is enthymeme, the syllogism of rhetoric. He uses *pistis* in this same way as a technique for inference at *A* 2, 56b 6-7 where he joins enthymeme (deduction) and *paradeigma* (induction) as the only two ways to demonstrate. At *A* 2, 58a 1 enthymeme and *paradeigma* are quite clearly contained in the phrase *pisteis apodeiktikai*, just as they are called the *koinai pisteis* at *B* 20, 93a 23-24 (I believe that πίστεων at *A* 1, 55a 7 also refers to enthymeme and *paradeigma*, but it could be a more generic use of the word.) *Pistis* at *B* 20, 94a 10 with the explicit reference to enthymeme and *paradeigma* as the forms of *apodeixis* is probably used in this meaning of logical instrument: "for the ways of proving are by means of these [i.e. enthymeme and paradeigma]". In the same way *pisteis* at *B* 1, 77b 19 with its close correlation to, and explanation by *enthymemata* can be taken in this sense.

In the third book there are a number of instances of the use of the plural form, *pisteis*, which, while they occur in the section on the parts of a speech, do not appear to be the technical use of *pistis* to denote a part of the speech. These appear at *Γ* 13, 14b 10-11; *Γ* 17, 17b 21, 18b 6, 8, 23. A comparison of 14b 10-11 and 18b 6, 8 with the text at *B* 22, 96b 23-28, *B* 25, 02a 31-35 and *B* 26, 03a 16-31 makes it clear from the similarity of language that Aristotle is talking about refutative or demonstrative enthymemes. Furthermore the whole context of c. 17 is concerned with the use of *paradeigmata* and *enthymemes* so that it would seem reasonable to conclude that *pistis* at 17b 21 and 18b 23 also refer to these two logical instruments. (c. 17 is discussed in the final chapter of this study.)

This leaves six instances of *pistis* in this second meaning of logical instrument which could be argued, i.e. *A* 6, 63b 4; *A* 7, 65b 20; *A* 8, 66a 18; *B* 12, 88b 30; *B* 18, 91b 26; *Γ* 16, 16b 34. In each of the first five instances which occur at the conclusion of a list of particular topics we are told that it is from these topics (̓ξ ὦν) that one is to take his πίστεις. But we also know that the sources of argumentation by enthymeme are the topics (cf. *A* 2, 58a 10 ff.). If this is so, *pisteis* in these instances can refer to enthymeme and by extension to *paradeigma* which is the second form of proof, namely, that by induction. It is possible, however, that πίστεις in these instances and also at *Γ* 16, 16b 34 refer to the third meaning, the sources which induce a state of belief or conviction.

3) In its third meaning *pistis* signifies source material, that which can induce in the auditor, if properly used, a state of mind which is called belief, or conviction. In this meaning Aristotle is not saying the same thing as he does in his use of *pistis* in meaning (2). These sources of belief, however, are called *pistis* by the same kind of intrinsic denomination by which he has used this word to indicate belief itself (meaning (1)), and the inferential method to establish belief (meaning (2)). That which can induce conviction in an other, the *endechomenon pithanon* (*A* 2, 55b 26) which is possibly suasive to an other (*A* 2, 56b 28), he calls *pistis* also, and he uses the word of both the *entechnic pisteis* (*A* 1, 54b 21; *A* 2, 55b 35) and the *atechnic pisteis* (55b 35). In the art of rhetoric as subject to reason Aristotle locates the sources of belief or conviction in three general areas *ethos, pathos, logos*. These he calls the *entechnic pisteis* and *pistis* in this sense of source material is to be found *in* each of these categories: ἐν τῷ ἤθει κτλ. (*A* 2, 56a 2-3). They are the sources. Insofar as any *ethos, pathos, logos* results in each instance from a whole set of constituent elements which make the particular *ethos, pathos, logos*, each of the three cannot be conceived independently of its parts. A particular *ethos*, for example, consists of the elements which constitute it. Further, insofar as these elements (which Aristotle investigates between *A* 4 and *B* 17) are simply the material to be used to construct the particular *ethos, pathos, logos* and thus help to establish credibility and eventually win belief or conviction from an other, when Aristotle calls *ethos, pathos, logos* the *pisteis entechnoi* he is obviously using *pistis* in a meaning different from the other two uses. *Pistis* is now used to specify the sources of conviction or belief in three general categories. As he says at *A* 2, 56a 5: *ethos* makes the speaker ἀξιόπιστον, is the source of his credibility. At *A* 9, 66a

23-28 Aristotle repeats the idea: "We must next speak about virtue and vice and of the honorable and dishonorable insofar as these are the *telos* of one who praises or blames. For at the same time that we speak on these subjects we also happen to reveal those qualities *from which* we will be accepted as of a certain nature with respect to *ethos* which was the second *pistis*. As a matter of fact *from the same sources* we will be able to make ourselves and another worthy of belief in relation to *arete*."

What may cause confusion in this use of *pistis* is contained in the very nature of anything which is a source of credibility or conviction. In a passive sense it is that which makes a person credible (ἀξιόπιστος), the source of the credibility. But once acquired such a source can, in an active sense, operate as that which causes belief in the other. In any particular subject-matter of discourse these sources are varied and frequently indifferent. The art of rhetoric is, in part, the intelligent selection of these sources in each area (*ethos, pathos, logos*) for a particular subject, and this is precisely what Aristotle attempts to illustrate through *A*4-*B*17. If they are chosen with reason and care there is no question that by themselves they can lose their passive character and can, in an active sense, effectively contribute to belief or conviction in the auditor without further organization into deductive or inductive argument. Indeed, Aristotle is not precise in the way he uses *pistis* in this meaning and frequently it seems to carry this active sense (cf. the uses of *pistis* through pages 58-66). However, Aristotle definitely expresses the view that in every subject of discourse there is material which can lead an other to belief, and it is to be sought in the way in which the subject is presented by the speaker, his *ethos* (attention is also given to the *ethos* of the auditor); in the tonal resonance within the subject, its emotional ambience for the auditor, *pathos*; and in the factual evidence of its own truth which the subject offers, its *logos*. These are called the three *entechnic pisteis*.

Before proceeding it is necessary to determine these *entechnic pisteis* because much of the confusion in interpreting the *Rhetoric* arises here. In Aristotle's words the *entechnic*, or artistic *pisteis* are (*A* 2, 56a 1-4): ἐν τῷ ἤθει τοῦ λέγοντος ... ἐν τῷ τὸν ἀκροατὴν διαθεῖναί πως ... ἐν αὐτῷ τῷ λόγῳ διὰ τοῦ δεικνύναι Γ φαίνεσθαι δεικνύναι. The accepted way of interpreting this is to call the *entechnic pisteis* ἦθος, πάθος, ἐνθύμημα. The identification of the last is the problem. There does not seem to be any way in which this phrase can be specified as "*enthymema*". Any effort to argue that interpretation from the phrase itself would have to work from *logos* and *deiknunai*. If we take *deiknunai* and argue from the parallel use of the word at *A* 2, 56a 35-b 8 we would then have to interpret the expression in our passage not only by *enthymema* but also by *paradeigma*. There is no reason why the word at 56a 4 and 20 should be interpreted to mean exclusively inference by syllogism, and so enthymeme the syllogism of rhetoric. (*deiknunai*, for example, at *A* 13, 74a 9; *B* 5, 83a 10, 7, 85a 31 which are the only three times it occurs between *A* 4 and *B* 17 means mostly "show, show forth, prove," or in BONITZ' explanation "universe demonstrandi, exponendi, explicandi vim habet".)

There may be some point in arguing from *logos* at 56a 4 since the Greek text makes it coequal with τῷ ἤθει and τῷ . . . διαθεῖναί πως. Owing to this correlation of *logos* with the other two *pisteis* it appears to be something independent and it does seem that *logos* here (and quite likely at 56a 19) has not quite the same meaning as it has in the immediate text when used with *ethos* 56a 5, 9 (διὰ τοῦ λόγου), and *pathos* al4 (ὑπὸ τοῦ λόγου) where it apparently signifies "speech, spoken word, discourse"[8]. However, in contradistinction to the *ethos* of the speaker which is revealed by his speech, and to affecting the auditor in a certain manner which is done by the use of speech, *logos* at a4 seems to mean something like "the explanation, the factual evidence of the subject," the subject viewed in its logical aspect, its internal, rational coherence and significance. At *B* 22, 96b 3 which in its expression is similar to our statement at 56a 4 *logos* appears to have this meaning. We are told that we cannot set forth a subject by *logos* without the *hyparchonta* of the subject (96b 8) which are highly defined (8) and most particular to the subject (9), indeed, in the example Aristotle offers here the *hyparchonta* must be ἴδια (15), all of which mean specific facts which explain the subject.

Thus it is that the phrase ἐν αὐτῷ τῷ λόγῳ should be called something like τὸ πρᾶγμα, and signify the subject of discourse in its purely logical character which speaks to the intellect of the auditor, just as *ethos* and *pathos* are aspects connected with the subject which transmit significance to his emotions, feelings, and will.[9] There is no textual evidence for calling this third *pistis* (ἐν αὐτῷ τῷ λόγῳ) ἐνθύμημα as commentators do. I call it πρᾶγμα because Aristotle explains it in such a way (*A* 2, 56a 19-20) as to justify some such term, and because I discovered that in the *Rhetores Graeci*[10] Minucianus calls the three *pisteis* (πίστεων τρία εἴδη *A* 2, 56a 1): ἠθικαί, παθητικαί, λογικαὶ αἱ αὐταὶ καὶ πραγματικαί, and that Dionysius of Halicarnassus,[11] who appears to have discerned something of the character of the Aristotelian enthymeme, speaks of the three *pisteis* as πρᾶγμα, πάθος, ἦθος. The third *pistis*, then, derives from those aspects of the subject which are the logical, rational, elements in the subject which can be apprehended by reason.

The three *pisteis entechnoi, ethos, pathos, pragma*, can be used independently as a way of winning belief or conviction as far as the evidence of the text is concerned. This is done simply by presenting a series of ethical, emotional, or purely logical reasons for the acceptance of one's proposition. And in passages such as those at *A* 6, 63b 4; *A* 7, 65b 20; *A* 8, 66a 18; *B* 12, 88b 30; *B* 18, 91b 26 the word *pisteis* can be so interpreted. Such a presentation would still not constitute a formal way of proving or demonstrating as far as Aristotle is concerned in the *Rhetoric*. At the very most one would have an enumeration of ethical, emotional, or logical appeals to the audience. And while this independent use of the three *entechnic pisteis* can be accepted the argument for it within the context of the first two books is not strong.

For what we possess in *A* 4-*B* 17 where Aristotle considers these three *pisteis* is an account of particular topics in the area of *pragma* (*A* 4-14), *pathos* (*B* 2-11), *ethos* (*B* 12-17). These topics are meant to provide the means primarily for deductive argumentation by *enthymeme*, but also for inductive argumentation by *paradeigma* which are the only ways in which to demonstrate anything as we have seen. If Aristotle calls these particular sources for argumentation the *pisteis entechnoi* he tells us at the same time that as particular topics they are sources for the enthymeme which is one of the two *koinai pisteis*. As a final confirmation that these *pisteis entechnoi*, considered as particular topics, are viewed by Aristotle as sources for argumentation we have his statement at *Γ* 1, 03b 6-9: "There are three things in discourse which demand systematic treatment, first the sources of proofs . . . we have spoken of the *pisteis* and from how many sources they come, namely, that they come from three sources, what kind they are, and why they are only three".

The first three instances of the use of *pistis* in the *Rhetoric* are at *A* 1, 54a 13-15, b 21; 55a 4. Aristotle here speaks of these *pisteis* as the substantial element in rhetoric as an art. At *A* 1, 54 b 21 they are called the *entechnic pisteis*. In each of the three instances these *pisteis* are connected in the text with enthymeme in such a way that one understands that control of these *entechnic pisteis* makes one master of the enthymeme, e. g. *A* 1, 54b 22: ὅθεν ἄν τις γένοιτο ἐνθυμηματικός "whereby one becomes master of the enthymeme". Further, enthymeme incorporates *pistis* (*A* 1, 54a 15). In each instance the word ἔντεχνος is used. In Aristotle the word is only used here and at *A* 2, 55b 35-37 and *SE* 172a 34-36. In each citation the word appears in a context which implies a *technique for reasoned statement*, a method for logical presentation. Thus we are told at *A* 1, 55a 4 that the *entechnic methodos* is one that involves these *pisteis* (περὶ τᾶς πίστεις; and the *pisteis* here are apparently those of *A* 1, 54b 21: the *entechnic*. This passage together with *A* 1, 54a 13-15, b 21 and the entire development of *A* 4-*B* 17 suggests that these *pisteis entechnoi* are distinct from but related to enthymeme, that they are used by enthymeme.

Other instances of *pistis* in the sense of the source material suitable to effect conviction or belief are: *A* 2, 56a 1 (and *pisteis* is understood at 2-3), 13, 21; *A* 15, 75a 22, 77b 12; *Γ* 1, 03b 7, 9. I find questionable the use at *A* 6, 63b 4; *A* 7, 65b 20; *A* 8, 66a 18; *B* 12, 88b 30; *B* 18, 91b 26; *Γ 16, 16b 34* (cf. above p. 60).

There is an obvious necessity to recognize difference in Aristotle's use of *pistis* throughout the *Rhetoric*. VATER, for example, realized this when he distinguished the *entechnic pisteis* between those used in a *sensus latior* as *pisteis* ("quae arte comparantur rationes faciendae fidei", e.g. *A* 2, 55b 35 ff.) and a *sensus angustior* ("quae solius oratoriae sunt propriae", e. g. *A* 1, 54b 21).[12] But VATER did not see, nor for that matter did anyone else, that there is still difficulty unless we clearly differentiate between *pistis* as source material (ἦθος, πάθος, πρᾶγμα) and *pistis* as a methodological technique, or a means for organizing demonstrative argument. The ostensible result of such a discrimination is that we are faced with a distinct break with the traditional exegesis of the text. While this does cause one to proceed with caution, still the discovery of a more meaningful and intelligent coherence in Aristotle's exposition strengthens one's confidence.

In the accepted interpretation Aristotle is attacking earlier technographers for their neglect of logical proof (A 1, 54a 13, 15; b 21), namely, the use of the enthymeme. Consequently when Aristotle identifies the three kinds of *pisteis* at A 2, 55b 35 ff. his remarks on the logical character of the third *pistis* (A 2, 56a 3-4) are immediately taken to refer to the enthymeme. Thus we find that the *pisteis* are interpreted as three independent modes of rhetorical demonstration: non-logical (or quasi-logical) demonstration by the use of *ethos* and *pathos*, and logical demonstration by means of the *enthymeme*, the syllogism of rhetoric. The consequence, however, of this exegesis is a series of insoluble difficulties in Aristotle's opening chapters—a place where one would not ordinarily expect an author to falter. The exegesis labors under the following problems:

1. It assumes a univocal and very limited meaning for *pistis* which is certainly not possible as we have already seen.
2. It ignores the fact that *paradeigma* is the correlative of enthymeme as a method for demonstration.[13] The fact of such an obvious correlation made by Aristotle forces one to ask the meaning of the statement found at A 2, 56a 1 ff.: πίστεων τρία εἴδη. Obviously if we argue that the third *pistis* is enthymeme then we must acknowledge that there are not three *pisteis* but four: ἦθos, πάθos, ἐνθύμημα, παράδειγμα. It is difficult to believe that Aristotle did not see this.
3. It is equally difficult, and no one fails to see this difficulty, to understand how Aristotle could slip into such open contradiction in his introductory chapters, and that, too, without the slightest perturbation on his part. Obviously, if rhetoric concentrates its effort on logical demonstration, or demonstration by the enthymeme which is *pistis par excellence*, Aristotle's extensive treatment in the *Rhetoric* of *ethos* and *pathos* is meaningless. Not only have we no grounds whatsoever for accepting his critique as in any way different from that of his predecessors, but there is no reason why it can't be as readily dismissed as Aristotle's own dismissal of his predecessors' work on the psychology of the person as an improper extension of the rhetorical endeavor: ἔξω τοῦ πράγματos (A 1, 54a 15 ff.).
4. There is another rather substantial difficulty which arises as Aristotle develops the theory of the enthymeme and discusses the sources from which statement by way of the rhetorical syllogism can be derived. He calls these sources the εἰκότα, σημεῖα, and τεκμήρια. He will also speak of special topics as sources for enthymeme. And yet all of these sources for the premises of an enthymeme are in turn derived from *ethos, pathos* and what I have called *pragma*. Obviously in this kind of analysis on the part of Aristotle the

enthymeme, as a logical instrument, is set apart from its sources: *ethos, pathos, pragma*. If no distinction is made between *pistis* as source material and *pistis* as a means of reasoning, Aristotle is forced into a rather strongly illogical and confused statement when he enlarges his initial comments on enthymeme.

If we follow with more care the text which Aristotle has given us we do arrive at a far more intelligent statement on the nature of rhetoric which is not only more consonant with the rest of the work but makes it perfectly easy to understand why Aristotle insists upon the centrality of the enthymeme for a valid understanding of the art of rhetoric. For we begin to realize that, in the last analysis, the enthymeme is the capstone whereby the *logos* is artistically structured in discourse.

In justice to Aristotle's endeavor, and in the light of the work of Isocrates, as well as a statement like that of the *Phaedrus*, we must locate the task which a theorist on the art of rhetoric faced. To begin with, in any confrontation of two minds on the truth or falsehood of an open subject, which is to say a subject which is contingent and subject to change, a common ground for intelligent discourse must be found. Meaningful discourse on any subject open to further deliberation or consideration must begin on ground acceptable to the persons engaged in discourse. This personalistic process is present and can easily be discerned in any Platonic dialogue. And as soon as we say "persons" we must accept the fact that the person as an integral entity enters into reasoned discussion. As a totality of intellect, will, and emotions, he approaches and attempts to resolve the problematic thesis placed before him. As Aristotle says at *A* 2, 56a 21 ff.: "Since the sources of conviction come through these three it is clear that mastery of these sources must be acquired by the person who can reason, has the ability to discern character, the virtues, and thirdly the emotions, that is to say the nature, the quality, and source of each emotion and how it is produced . . ."

There would seem to be no question that it is this which Aristotle has in mind when he speaks of the ὑπάρχοντα πιθανά which are to be found in any subject (*A* 1, 55b 10-11). The *endechomena pithana* (*A* 2, 55b 25-26), those potentially acceptable and convincing aspects of the subject, are the elements in the subject which are meaningful to this person or group of persons. They are different for a different person or group as any number of comments of Aristotle indicate. These constitutive elements of the subject of reasoned and persuasive discourse are Aristotle's *entechnic pisteis*: *ethos, pathos, pragma*. As *pisteis* they are understood as source material and are a part of the entechnic method, *A* 1, 55a 4: ἡ μὲν ἔντεχνος μέθοδος περὶ τᾶς πίστεις ἐστίν; this is the method proper to rhetoric, by which word Aristotle means: human discourse subject to both art and reason. For both ideas lie behind his use of τεχνος and μέθοδος. From *A* 1, 54a 1-11 we should expect that a τέχνη is a guide for action that is reasoned, reasonable, and capable of explanation. *Techne* enables one to examine the causes of correct action (*A* 1, 54a 10-11); and as he says at *A* 2, 55b 37 ff. the *entechnic pisteis* are those which are derived as the result of a systematic method. Aristotle elaborates the meaning further by insisting that as reasoned activity the *dynamis* of rhetoric is the developed ability, or insight, which scans the whole subject-matter and selects with care the *endechomena pithana* which will carry meaning to the auditor (*A* 2, 55b 25 ff. and *A* 2, 56b 28 ff.). This methodology can be taught, and so eventually he himself will discuss in the *Rhetoric* the various *entechnic pisteis*. Furthermore, once the *entechnic pisteis* for the particular subject-matter have been chosen, they should be given form and organized effectively in a demonstrative process which will either be deductive or inductive: enthymematic or paradeigmatic. Thus the three *entechnic pisteis* which possess a potential probative force are integrated by means of the two *pisteis* which are the logical instruments: enthymeme and *paradeigma*.

Thus the various ways in which Aristotle has employed *pistis* come together in the final act of rhetorical demonstration or *apodeixis*. The substance for the demonstrative presentation is the source material drawn from *pragma, ethos, pathos* (*pistis* as source material); this is put into a form of deductive or inductive reasoning (*pistis* as a methodological instrument) which creates conviction, or acceptance in the mind of the auditor (*pistis* as a state of mind). The first two steps represent Aristotle's *entechnos methodos* (*A* 1, 55a 4), the last is the object and goal of the methodology.

In introducing the inferential process of deduction and induction, namely, the *enthymeme* and *paradeigma*, Aristotle has brought into rhetoric his logical system of deductive and inductive reasoning which for him is absolutely necessary for all *apodeixis*.[14] As a logical instrument the enthymeme is the syllogism of rhetoric (*A* 2, 56b 5) which uses the material offered by the *entechnic pisteis* and marshals it into an effective form of demonstration. It is, in fact, Aristotle's introduction of the inferential methodology of his philosophical system into the field of rhetoric.

In the light of the preeminent role Aristotle assigns to the syllogism—and in the *Rhetoric* to the *enthymeme* in comparison with *paradeigma*—as the mode of demonstration it is not difficult to understand what he means when he speaks of the enthymeme as κυριώτατον τῶν πίστεων (*A* 1, 55a 7). His remark, however, that it is the σῶμα τῆς πίστεως (*A* 1, 54a 15) appears most natural and quite intelligible, since, as syllogism, it is quite manifestly the container, that which incorporates, or embodies, the *pisteis entechnoi* imposing form upon them so that they may be used most efficaciously in rhetorical demonstration. It does not appear incorrect to say that in the field of demonstrating the probable, which is, by and large, the demonstration of rhetoric, the enthymeme parallels the role of *apodeixis* in the area of metaphysics, just as the practical syllogism plays a similar role in his ethics.

By way of conclusion if we compare Aristotle's analysis with the little we know of the heterogeneous and mechanical contemporary analyses of the art[15] we find a remarkable synthesis of the method of rhetorical discourse in Aristotle. In his treatise we find that fundamentally:

1) there are two methods of demonstrating or proving:
   enthymeme (deduction), *paradeigma* (induction).
2) there are two major sources for the two methods:
   a) particular topics—these will provide the individual *eikota, semeia, tekmeria* in each of the three major areas which primarily give rise to belief: *pragma, ethos, pathos*. These last can be used independently but they are meant to be used by the *enthymeme* from Aristotle's statements—and presumably by *paradeigma*.
   b) general topics—inferential forms to be used by enthymeme from what Aristotle says in the *Rhetoric*. But it is clear that the inductive process can use them by citing examples that prove the general principle each general *topos* asserts.

Independently of all that has been said thus far a careful reading of the *Rhetoric* would confirm the view that the enthymeme is central to Aristotle's exposition of the nature of rhetoric. Unfortunately the development of rhetorical study after Aristotle in the direction of petty detail and technique turned the study back toward the character of some of the pre-Platonic discussion such as is suggested in collections like SPENGEL'S Technon Synagoge or RADERMACHER'S Artium Scriptores. The consequence of this development was that rhetorical treatises became handbooks of "good" speaking and writing whose character is rather well described by Cicero: "*scripsit artem rhetoricam Cleanthes, Chrysippus etiam, sed sic ut siquis obmutescere cupierit nihil aliud legere debeat*" (*de Fin.* 4.7). A reading of SPENGEL'S commentary on the *Rhetoric* reveals a fairly constant failure on the part of later technographers to understand Aristotle's work. As a consequence whatever assistance which might have been expected from post-Aristotelian rhetorical study toward an understanding of the enthymeme is non-existent. Any attempt to determine its meaning must be made primarily from Aristotle's statements, and of these Ross represents a not uncommon viewpoint: "The enthymeme is discussed in many passages of the *Rhetoric*, and it is impossible to extract from them a completely consistent theory of its nature". (Aristotle's Prior and Posterior Analytics, Oxford 1949, p. 499). Oddly enough there has not been any formal study of the Aristotelian enthymeme aside from the related studies of J. McBURNEY, The Place of the Enthymeme in Rhetorical Theory (diss. U. of Michigan, no date), and FR. SOLMSEN, Die Entwicklung der aristotelischen Logik und Rhetorik, Berlin 1929. Each of them is helpful but limited in its contribution to a full understanding of the role of the Aristotelian enthymeme in rhetoric.

The very first observation which could be made with respect to Ross' comment is that both the word ἐνθύμημα and the meaning which it carries in the *Rhetoric* is novel. And if we are to discover what Aristotle intended by the word we must do so primarily in his own writings. It is still true, however, that the antecedent history of the word and its denotation, insofar as they can be traced, gives some slight evidence for a meaning which makes Aristotle's specification of the word and the concept as we find it in the *Rhetoric* more understandable. This is what could be expected insofar as Aristotle usually worked within the historical context of ideas and was quite conscious of their development. At the same time there can be no doubt that the enthymeme for Aristotle clearly represents the introduction of his newly discovered theory of inference by means of the syllogism into the field of rhetorical study. As a matter of fact this new and formal mode of reasoning seems to have been instantly successful and rather quickly adopted by his contemporaries. At least this would seem to be a safe deduction from a comment on Eubulides, a contemporary of Aristotle and the reputed instructor of Demosthenes. We are told by Diogenes Laertius (II. 108, Oxford 1964, ed. H. LONG) that Eubulides quarreled with and criticized Aristotle. Yet we read in Philodemus (ed. SUDHAUS, Teubner 1892) (I. 84. 31 ff.), that Eubulides was contemptuous of speeches that did not possess syllogisms.

The provocative question still remains, however, as to why Aristotle chose the word ἐνθύμημα for the syllogism of rhetoric. In the light of *Topics* 162a 15 ff.: "a philosopheme is an apodeictic syllogism, an epicheireme a dialectical syllogism, a sophisma an eristic syllogism, an aporeme a dialectical syllogism which concludes to a contradiction" one would expect that the word is more than a mere name for rhetorical syllogism. Indeed, if an epicheireme is an inference "from probabilities" (*Topics* 100a 30), one might rightly expect that when Aristotle calls rhetorical inference which argues "from probabilities" an enthymeme he has some further purpose in mind. Insofar as the usual quality of words ending in ἄμα is to designate the result of the action involved this would seem to imply that something more than simple logical inference is at issue in the use of ἐνθύμημα, as it is also in φιλοσόφημα, ἐπιχείρημα, etc.

In view of the fact, as has been said, that Aristotle worked within the tradition of his predecessors[16] one could expect the pre-Aristotelian literature to throw some light on the meaning of the word. Yet the common interpretation of ἐνθύμημα in pre-Aristotelian literature is "thought", an act of the mind, as VOLKMANN (Die Rhetorik der Griechen und Römer, Leipzig 1885, p. 192) observes, interpreting it by ἐννόημα. This, of course, reveals no quality peculiar to rhetorical syllogism which could not be found in any other kind of syllogism. Furthermore such a correlation between enthymeme and "thought" would on the face of it be rather strange. In a language which has recognized from its earliest literary remains a distinction between θυμός and νοῦς an identity between ἐνθύμημα and ἐννόημα might be justifiably suspect. It is a common axiom on the part of students of the language to attribute a certain precision and care to the Greeks in their use of words. And the evidence for such care is present in the distinction between ἐνθυμέομαι—

ἐννοέομαι; ἐνθύμημα—ἐννόημα; ἐνθυμηματικός—ἐννοηματικός. To have something ἐν θυμῷ is not simply to "have a thought". The use of the word θυμός in the literature as the principle of feeling and thought does not permit such a precisive identity with "thought" as has been made. ἐνθύμιος for example = taken to heart, and ἐνθύμιον ποιεῖσθαι τι= ἐνθυμεῖσθαι: to take to heart, have a scruple about (*Thuc.* 7. 50). WILAMOWITZ has recognized this in two different places,[17] yet he is not too certain of the meaning of ἐνθύμημα. In the *Menander* (81) he tells us that originally the idea of *enthymios* was in *enthymema* but leaves it unclear as to whether this meaning is applicable to the use of the word in rhetoric. In the *Herakles* (186) he would derive the rhetorical term from the verb form and limit it to the meaning: ὅτι ἐν θυμῷ ἐστιν. Still a few lines later he must admit that the verb can be used in the broader sense such as is found in the Thucydides citation above, a meaning which he himself accepts for *enthymios*.

Since it is quite clear by now that in Aristotle ἐνθύμημα is not simply logical demonstration by syllogism the effort to discover whether something more than "thought" or "reason" resides in the pre-Aristotelian usage merits consideration. For it may point both to the reason why Aristotle used this term for the syllogism of rhetoric and what he may have had in mind by the rhetorical syllogism.

A survey of the general literature yields relatively little on the use of the noun, ἐνθύμημα, as well as the adjective and verb form.[18] There are two authors who use ἐνθύμημα more frequently: Xenophon and Isocrates. Of the latter WILAMOWITZ remarks somewhat assuredly: "Der rhetorische terminus ist von Isokrates geprägt; von Aristoteles aufgenommen" (Menander, 81). Xenophon employs the word in several works: *Cynegeticus* 13.9.3; *Hellenica* 4.5.4; 5.4.51; *Oeconomicus* 20.24; *Anabasis* 3.5.12; 6.1.21. In all of these instances the denotation "thought" certainly seems acceptable to the text, and it is so interpreted. But it would certainly be an over-simplification of the text to say that this is always the exclusive denotation of the word.[19] In Isocrates' use of the noun the same conclusion would have to be drawn. ἐνθύμημα is used in *Panathenaicus* 233a; *Evagoras* 190e, 191a; *Against the Sophists* 294d; *Antidosis* 319d. All of these passages are usually translated by some form of "thought", e.g. E. S. FORSTER on *Evagoras* 190e (Isocrates Cyprian Orations, Oxford 1912) "'those ideas which concern the actual facts'. ἐνθύμημα is here used in its literal sense; later in Aristotelian logic it has the meaning of 'a syllogism drawn from probable premises'".[20] It is, of course, the literal sense which is at issue. For example one might ask what kind of "thoughts" a phrase like ἐνθυμήμασιν ὀγκωδεστέροις could possibly be (*Antid.* 319d)? Again how is it possible to interpret, as is done, *Ag. Soph.* 294d as "thoughts" e. g. "to adorn with striking thoughts"? It is difficult to understand the use of the verb καταποικίλλω in this manner; unfortunately Isocrates uses the word only here. He does, however, use ποικιλία and in each instance it refers to the use of rhetorical devices and varieties of style, and this is a meaning far more in keeping with the image imbedded in the root word.[21] Furthermore a study of each of the passages cited above for his use of enthymeme reveals clearly that Isocrates is talking about style and the techniques and variety of style. Consequently we would have to conclude that when he uses enthymeme he may well be speaking not about "thought," but a figure of thought, that is, thought developed and expressed in a certain way. There is no evidence to demonstrate that he is talking simply of "thought". As a matter of fact when he wants to say "thought" he uses the more likely word διάνοια in the very passage of the *Evagoras* (191a) where he has just used ἐνθύμημα.

Turning from the general works of literature to the pre-Socratics and the technographers, the evidence for ἐνθύμημα is restricted. Among the pre-Socratics the only mention of the word occurs in a fragment about Nausiphanes the probable preceptor of Epicurus.[22] The importance of the Nausiphanes citation is that it makes a distinctly Aristotelian statement by correlating *enthymeme* with *syllogism*, and *paradeigma* (example) with induction: The text itself (DIELS-KRANZ, Die Fragmente der Vors. II, p. 249, 38 f.) indicates that syllogism is apparently understood in the technical sense given to it by Aristotle. This is inescapable from the parallelism of the four terms. Nausiphanes (b. ca. 360) was certainly a contemporary of Aristotle, and if the citation antedates Aristotle it would obviously be significantly important. While VON ARNIM believes that Aristotle is dependent upon Nausiphanes the point is disputed by SUSEMIHL and VON FRITZ.[23] In actual fact until evidence is on hand that Aristotle is not the author of the technical meaning of συλλογισμός as the instrument for deductive reasoning the presumption must be that Nausiphanes depends on Aristotle for this correlation of syllogism-enthymeme. Most assuredly there is no assistance from the fragments of Nausiphanes which we possess in securing even the possibility of such an authorship for him; and there is absolutely no evidence in any other author prior to Aristotle which makes such a correlation of *enthymeme* with syllogism, and *paradeigma* with induction.

When we turn to the remains of the pre-Aristotelian technical writing on rhetoric we find the word ἐνθύμημα used by only two of the technographers. From the evidence there is no question that the first of the two, Alcidamas, whose writing is known to Aristotle[24] did not think of ἐνθύμημα as συλλογισμός. If we couple this with the fact that the other technographer, Anaximenes, does not understand enthymeme as a syllogism the likelihood that Nausiphanes pre-dates Aristotle in this matter becomes weaker still. While it is questioned that Alcidamas wrote a *techne*, the work which concerns us is his περὶ σοφιστῶν.[25] The work is not technographical in character, and there is consequently nothing like a definition of the word ἐνθύμημα which actually appears thirteen times in the speech (nos. 3, 4, 18 (bis), 19 (bis), 20 (bis), 24 (bis), 25 (bis), 33). It is used as a term which is accepted and understood; it is never explained. As a student of Gorgias and, in turn, the putative teacher of Aeschines, Alcidamas was a contemporary of Isocrates (Tzetzes, *Chiliades* 11. 670; 746), and like Isocrates he called his art: rhetoric-philosophy (*Peri. Soph.* no. 2). A reading of this work on the Sophists does encourage the view that Alcidamas belongs to the tradition which is usually accepted for the Sophists, namely, that of an eminently practical and somewhat mechanical, rather than theoretical, understanding of the art of rhetoric. The justification of this ascription to all the Sophists without discrimination can be questioned (cf. Introduction). In all probability, however, it does represent one phase of rhetorical study, and it can be seen at greater length and in more detail in the *Rhetoric to Alexander*. The burden of Alcidamas' essay is an attack on written speeches and logography in general, and in reading it one receives the impression that it is an attack upon Isocrates and his theory of carefully prepared discourse.[26] Cicero sums up rather well Alcidamas' concern for facility in speaking even at times to the neglect of what is said (e. g. *Peri Soph.* no. 20): *"rhetor antiquus in primis nobilis . . . cui rationes . . .defuerunt, ubertas orationis non defuit"* (*Tusc. disp.* 1. 48. 116; in its own way this is reminiscent of a comment made about Anaximenes: "a spate of words, a trickle of sense" (Stobaeus, *Florilegium* 3.36.20). From his own apologia (nos. 29-34), however, as well as his insight into what can be called the primary structural elements of rhetorical discourse (subject-matter, *taxis*, and *lexis*, v. no. 33) it would be wrong to dismiss Alcidamas as a careless or haphazard rhetorician. His obvious concern with discourse and the definition of rhetoric attributed to him which is rather Aristotelian[27] in tone indicates his concern with rhetoric as a discipline. We read in the *Rhetores Graeci* (ed. WALZ, Stuttgart, 1833), 7.1.8.18-24 that "the followers of Alcidamas" define rhetoric in this way: "rhetoric . . . is *dialogike*, and *dialogike* is thus defined: δύναμις τοῦ ὄντος πιθανοῦ". Obviously if Alcidamas wrote a *techne* and discussed enthymeme Aristotle might very well have incorporated his ideas.

We can only work, however, with the text of the *Peri Sophiston*, and the effort to interpret ἐνθύμημα here faces precisely the same problem found in the other pre-Aristotelian literature. Enthymeme, as it occurs in the work, does not mean syllogism.[28] Further it cannot mean "thought" without any qualification, a simple act of the mind, although BLASS who is the only one to consider the word inclines to this meaning which he interprets as "Auffindung der Gedanken". Alcidamas has a variety of word forms for the act of thought: φρονέω (nos. 1, 2, 6, 10, etc.), οἴομαι (nos. 2, 14, 20), νομίζω (nos. 2, 5), διανοέω (no. 24) to mention a few. He also recognizes noun forms of διάνοια (nos. 16, 24, 28, 32) and cognates such as ἀγχίνοια (no. 16), πρόνοια (nos. 23, 33). In itself this recognition on the part of Alcidamas of terms for the act of thinking does not exclude ἐνθύμημα from denoting simply and exclusively "thought". Yet doubt does begin to arise when we find him (no. 16) calling the activity of the mind in written composition διάνοια and making a clear distinction (no. 24) between ἐνθύμημα and διάνοια. The latter is used together with its verb form to express the action of the mind. Finally he describes the activity of the mind in extemporaneous discourse by διάνοια. The evidence from each instance of his use of the word ἐνθύμημα suggests that

Alcidamas is using it, as Isocrates does, to denote something like a figure of thought—but not simply for thought itself. There is no indication that this figure of thought is antithesis, or opposition, or contrast. While it is something more than a mere act of the mind, there is no clear evidence that it means "thought" as the act of the whole person: mind, will, emotions, feelings. ἐνθύμημα is something more than notional apprehension (an act of the intellect only), but we have no certain indication that it is real apprehension: an act whereby the mind grasps something as a reality known to the whole man, an object of experience, the process which he describes so well when speaking of discourse as ἔμψυχος, discourse which is living and real (no. 28).

There is little or no point in introducing Theodectes in an effort to discover the meaning of enthymeme prior to Aristotle.[29] While we have evidence for a treatise (or treatises) from his hand the only access we would have to its content would be by way of reconstruction almost exclusively from Aristotle's *Rhetoric*. Aside from the usually tenuous character of such undertakings its futility in the present instance is more than evident. Indeed the other pre-Aristotelian technographer, Anaximenes, presents many problems of his own.[30] But we do possess a *techne* with which to work, the so-called *Rhetoric to Alexander*, a title acquired from the prefatory epistle which is considered a late forgery. Until the time of Victorius this work was attributed to Aristotle but it is now accepted as very probably the *techne* of Anaximenes a pupil of Diogenes the Cynic and Zoilus the rhetor.[31] Since we have this treatise on rhetoric and the word enthymeme appears in it there is need to locate this work with reference to Aristotle. The evidence points rather sharply toward a period prior to Aristotle's *Rhetoric*. This is so independently of whether or not we accept the author as Anaximenes whose *floruit* on the evidence of Diodorus (15. 76. 4) is 366 B.C. making him a contemporary of Plato, Isocrates and Aristotle. Insofar as the reasons for dismissing Anaximenes as author are not compelling there seems to be no reason not to speak of him as the author. The last datable event in the treatise is the Corinthian expedition to assist Syracuse under Timoleon ca. 343/2 (c. 8, 1429b 18 ff.). Taken together with Diodorus this would give us an approximate date for Anaximenes of 380-320 and place the treatise possibly about 340. This coincides fairly closely with the date generally accepted.[32]

The substantial material of the treatise would certainly favor a period of time prior to Aristotle's work in the *Rhetoric*, for in matters of critical importance there is no indication of any awareness of Aristotle's work. This is difficult to accept,[33] for certain things, whether Anaximenes wished to acknowledge them or not, such as a bow toward a definition of rhetoric, or a discussion of ἦθος would seem inevitable in a post-Aristotelian work. Yet neither appears, and their absence is incomprehensible. On the other hand there are a striking number of similarities between the two treatises.[34] There has been an effort to explain these by Aristotle's and Anaximenes' use of a common source: our unknown Theodectes. A more likely explanation would be Aristotle's use and development of the work of Anaximenes.

This last point might very well be confirmed by the statements of each man on enthymeme. For it is certainly possible to understand Aristotle on enthymeme with Anaximenes as a reference work. Anaximenes' statements on the enthymeme, after Aristotle's work in the *Rhetoric*, are quite beyond comprehension.

In Anaximenes we first meet ἐνθύμημα (c. 7, 1428a, 16 ff.) as a species of what is called by the general name πίστις. As such it is one of seven types of *pistis* among which are *eikota, paradeigmata, gnomai, semeia* and *elenchoi*. About the only parallel one could devise between this statement and Aristotle is that Anaximenes' *pistis* is in concept similar to what Aristotle calls *pistis entechnos*. This statement is followed by a definition of each of these species and finally at c. 10, 1430a 23 ff. we reach a definition of enthymeme: "Enthymemes are oppositions not merely in language and action but in all other things as well. You will acquire many of them by inquiry, as was noted under the investigatory branch of rhetoric, and by examining whether the speech is anywhere in opposition to itself or the actions in opposition to justice, the law, the expedient, the honorable, the possible, the facile, the probable, the character of the speaker, or the character of the circumstances."

Perhaps the most pointed comment on this definition, in respect to what is being said in this chapter, is the most recent observation of GRUBE (A Greek Critic: Demetrius on Style, Toronto 1961, p. 160): "at 1430a 24 the word is defined as contradiction . . . The meaning contradiction is quite unique". Grube is of the opinion that the word as found elsewhere in the treatise, e.g. cc. 22, 32, 1434a 36, 1438b 35 "seems to have the Aristotelian meaning", by which GRUBE understands "a rhetorical syllogism". It does not seem possible to derive "rhetorical syllogism" from either of these passages. Indeed in all that Anaximenes has to say about enthymeme[35] in the rest of the work there is nothing which would substantially change the definition given above, and it is certainly not the Aristotelian understanding of the enthymeme.[36] We can, as has been done above, interpret the definition of Anaximenes in a less restrictive way than GRUBE, and in a way to which the Greek word readily submits, namely as opposition, not contradiction. This still leaves enthymeme in Anaximenes as a species of opposition which is found in language or reality either naturally or, as we see at 14, 1431a 34-5, artificially, that is to say, subject to the speaker's ingenuity in devising it. If we were to seek an exact parallel to this in Aristotle we find it in the enthymeme which he derives from the general topic of opposites (*B* 23, 97a 7 ff.). Interestingly enough this is the first general topic for enthymemes given by Aristotle which might indicate that he finds this quality of opposition of some importance for the enthymeme. It should also be noted that in this same passage Aristotle remarks that Alcidamas uses this formal topic from opposites in his *Messiancus*. This might also indicate that Anaximenes' usage is not particularly unique for the rhetoricians. The fact remains, however, that the technical meaning given to enthymeme by Anaximenes is substantially different from Aristotle's.[37] Obviously this creates a rather intolerable difficulty if Anaximenes is writing after the time of Aristotle's *Rhetoric*. On the other hand a number of intriguing parallelisms become understandable if we accept the possibility that Aristotle introduced his new methodology of reasoned inference by syllogism into the rhetorical *pragmateia* with the work of Anaximenes in mind. Many of the statements which the two authors make yield to this possibility. The reverse process permits of no other reasonable explanation save the questionable common source already mentioned.

One of the very first qualities we find in the enthymeme of Anaximenes is that it should be expressed with brevity (c. 10, 1430a 36-8): "compactly and in as few words as possible". In Aristotle's whole discussion of enthymeme brevity is such a significant matter that his comments have been traditionally interpreted to mean that the enthymeme was an abbreviated syllogism.[38] Related to this idea of brevity in the enthymeme are Anaximenes' comments on *asteion legein* and the enthymeme. Aristotle also joins the two (*Γ* 10,10b 20 ff.), and for both Aristotle and Anaximenes the dominant idea in *asteion legein* is brevity.[39] This matter of brevity and antithesis (ἐναντίωσις) in the enthymeme of Anaximenes is important and we shall return to it presently. For it appears possible that Aristotle is not simply using Anaximenes but with the introduction of his theory of reasoned argumentation into the field of rhetoric is developing ideas of Anaximenes into a more ordered presentation of his own centered around his inferential methodology. There are a number of things which encourage this line of thought. At c. 7, 1428a 16 ff. Anaximenes speaks of two kinds of *pistis*. Although he does not specify them as *entechnic* and *atechnic*, as Aristotle does at *A* 2, 55b 35 f., his explanation makes it eminently clear that the same distinction is at work. Anaximenes places among the *pisteis entechnoi*: *eikota, tekmeria, semeia, enthymemata, paradeigmata*, and says that these *pisteis* are derived from words, persons, and circumstances, or the reality itself (c. 7, 1428a 16-23). Aristotle, as we know, also speaks of the *entechnic* proofs, by which he means those which the speaker devises, and he derives them from persons and the circumstances or the reality itself (*A* 2, 56a 1-20; and see above pp. 60 ff.). Very early in his treatise, however, Aristotle declares that the only way in which we can reasonably demonstrate anything is by deduction (*enthymeme* in rhetoric) and induction (*paradeigma* in rhetoric) and these become for him the *pisteis par excellence* of rhetoric: the *koinai pisteis*. This he calls the entechnic methodology of rhetorical demonstration (*A* 1, 55a 4). Aristotle then proceeds further. For him *eikota* and *semeia* are not correlates of enthymeme as a form of *pistis* but rather are sources for reasoning by enthymeme, the rhetorical syllogism (*An. Pr.* 70a 10). Aristotle would also agree in general with Anaximenes (c. 14, 1431a 39-42)[40] that the enthymeme is the source of probable knowledge. He is not, however, satisfied with this. Rather we find in Aristotle a radical reorganization of the ideas. All of Anaximenes' *pisteis* produce only opinion with one exception: certain kinds of *semeia* which effect certain knowledge (c.14, 1431a 42: καὶ σαφῶς εἰδέναι). In Aristotle, on the other hand, we find a very clear division of *semeion* (*A* 2, 57b 1 ff.) into *tekmerion* the source of certain knowledge, and *semeion anonymon* the source of probable knowledge. Insofar as *semeia* in Aristotle are not correlates of enthymeme as a type of proof, but rather are sources for reasoning by the rhetorical syllogism, Aristotle has simplified the process and made possible inference by enthymeme which will give both probable and certain knowledge.

Another area in which this radical re-formation can be seen is the relationship between enthymeme and maxim (*gnome*). Anaximenes stresses the close connection between the two. Aristotle also emphasizes it[41] particularly in *B* 20, 93a 25-26 where he calls maxim a part of enthymeme. Once again we find in Aristotle an advanced and more developed analysis of matter seminally present in Anaximenes. With Anaximenes Aristotle distinguishes enthymeme from maxim but like Anaximenes he perceives a close relation between the two and brings them together stating that: enthymemes are to all extents and purposes syllogisms concerned with human actions as maxims are concerned with human actions, consequently the conclusions or the premises of enthymemes are *gnomai* with the syllogistic form omitted (*B* 21, 94a 25-9). Where Anaximenes speaks of enthymeme (c. 32, 1438b 30 ff.; c. 36, 1442b 33 ff.) as a means of confirming (βεβαίωσις) your proof Aristotle places the full weight of rhetorical demonstration in the enthymeme itself at the very beginning of his treatise. For Anaximenes the enthymeme is a kind of mechanical device external to and shoring up demonstration, as can readily be seen in comments on its use in cc. 32, 36 above, or again in c. 35 on encomiastic oratory. Aristotle has made the enthymeme the integrative force in rhetorical demonstration, but in doing this he stresses in the enthymeme the very qualities which underlie all of Anaximenes' statements about it. The characteristic prominent in the enthymeme of Anaximenes is its ability to express the substance of an argument in a concise and emphatic manner precisely because it brings the issue into sharp focus by contrast. The enthymeme, as Anaximenes understands it in the treatise, is grounded in the idea of contrast and opposition. USENER (Quaestiones Anaximeneae, op. cit., p. 37f.) underlines this fact rather emphatically, for he finds the enthymeme of Anaximenes totally foreign to both the theoretical and practical ideas of Greek rhetoric. Usener would locate it, if anywhere, in Greek eristic. Yet it is precisely in this idea of contrast that there is a likely relation between the more developed enthymeme theory of Aristotle and the enthymeme of Anaximenes. The theory of learning, if we can call it such, continually at work in the Aristotelian enthymeme is a form of contrast and relation between two things: known-unknown; more known-less known.[42] He expresses this rather pointedly at *B* 24, 01a 4-6. Convinced as he was that "opposites become better known when set side by side" (*Γ* 17, 18b 4) he tells us at *B* 24, 01a 4-6 that a condensed and antithetic form of expression belongs to the enthymeme: χώρα ἐστὶν ἐνθυμήματος. This aspect of contrast and opposition in the enthymeme is discussed in more detail in c. 3 of this study. The point of interest at the moment is that once again Aristotle could easily be thought of as developing in his enthymeme theory the material he found in the *Rhetoric to Alexander*—if not doing so in actual fact.

Consequently, despite certain inadequacies, the evidence on hand as to the meaning and the use of ἐνθύμημα both in Greek literature and in the rhetorical writing prior to Aristotle encourages one to think that Aristotle worked in rhetoric as he always did, namely, within the historical tradition. While it is quite easy to say that he simply adopted a term of no particular significance there are no reasonable grounds on which to do so. Why, or how, he came to select the word ἐνθύμημα is not known; but we do know that his general approach to a problem was to work from out of the tradition, and, as we have seen, we find the word in the tradition. We find further that in the general literature and the technographers it is used in ways which suggest similarities to Aristotle's enthymeme. We discover that it signifies something that is more than a simple act of the mind, an act grounded only in reason. Its usage appears to implicate an act of the whole person, his emotions and feelings as well as his intellect. When it becomes a technical term of rhetoric, such as it appears in Anaximenes, we find it described as a form of brief, pointed opposition, echoes of which we again come upon in Aristotle's comments on his own enthymeme. A study of Aristotle's enthymeme as used in the *Rhetoric* reveals that it cannot be equated completely with syllogism interpreted as the rational demonstration of the subject. Aside from other difficulties with such an interpretation it does seem that if Aristotle wanted to understand the syllogism of rhetoric in this way he could easily have called it a syllogism without further qualification. There was no need to say that the syllogism of rhetoric has a particular name: the enthymeme (*A* 1, 55a 6), that it is a kind of syllogism (συλλογισμός τις, a8), observations which imply in themselves the differences he himself suggests at *A* 1, 55a 8-14. The evidence from the text suggests that the enthymeme is not a demonstration by reason alone. Aristotle makes it clear in the *Rhetoric* that in the effort to effect judgment and decision whose consequences involve the one judging, and further to do this in the area of the probable and contingent, one must seek out as sources to convince not only the rational explanation of the subject (*pragma*) but also the emotive elements in the subject (*ethos* and *pathos*). If this is so, then his significant contribution to the art of rhetoric, a contribution which truly made it the art of discourse grounded in reason, namely, the introduction of the theory of deductive and inductive argumentation, should reflect the sources of conviction and belief. The deductive process cannot be the simple scientific syllogism, the syllogism of pure reason. Not only does the modality of the subject-matter in rhetoric prevent this, but the very object intended by rhetorical argumentation, i. e. personal conviction which will motivate personal action, does not permit it. Such a goal calls for assent on the part of the whole person: intellect, will, emotions; and, ideally, these should find their way into any demonstrative process be it by deduction or induction. And so it is proposed here that, since the word ἐνθύμημα carried with it in the tradition a sense of form and denoted something more than an act of mere reason, Aristotle used the word which best suggested what he had in mind by the rhetorical syllogism.

Notes

[1]We have the evidence of Socrates' extended concern in the *Apology* with the substantial problem of ἡ ἐπιμέλεια τῆς ψυχῆς clothed in the concrete terms of his own life; or Demosthenes' analysis of the implications of the idea of freedom (*eleutheria*) for the city-state in his *Crown Speech* 53ff.; or Pericles' discussion of the responsibilities of citizenship (*politeia*) in his funeral oration: "for the Athens I have celebrated is only what the heroism of these and their like have made her" (Thucydides 2.42). In the *Politicus* 304d f. Plato assigns to the true statesman just such a control of the art of rhetoric; and in the *Phaedo* 89d-90d he speaks of the unfortunate and harmful consequences of misology as a result of which men blame discourse rather than their own inabilities and their lack of trained skill with language. The consequence is that such men "continue to spend their lives hating and reviling discourse and deprive themselves of truth and knowledge concerning reality".

[2]This question deserves more attention than it has apparently received. It would not be difficult to sustain the thesis that Plato's work demonstrates in detail the philosophical analysis of the *logos* which we have in the *Rhetoric*. There is a limited admission of this, for example, in G. E. MORROW, Plato's Conception of Persuasion, The Philosophical Review 62, 1953, pp. 234-250. MORROW argues that Plato intended to use the 'philosophical rhetoric' which he outlined in the *Phaedrus*, and did in fact make use of it, particularly in the educational theory of the *Republic* and the *Laws*.

[3]W.D. ROSS, Aristotle, London 1953, p. 275.

[4]J. GEFFCKEN, Griechische Literaturgeschichte, Heidelberg 1934, vol. 2, pp. 232, 234.

[5]Cicero, *Topica*, 14.56 (ed. BORNECQUE, Paris, "Les belles lettres" 1960); see also Demetrius περὶ ἑρμηνείας, no. 30 (Rhetores Graeci, ed. SPENGEL, Teubner 1856, vol. III).

[6]In the most recent study of Aristotle by G.E.R. LLOYD, Aristotle: The Growth and Structure of His Thought, Cambridge 1968, p. 273, the *Rhetoric* is dismissed with a series of inconsequential observations of which the following is typical: "Just as in the *Sophistici Elenchi*, for example, he considers how to deceive your opponent in argument. . .so too in the *Rhetoric* he discusses the tricks of the trade, the various devices the public speaker may use to win his case."

[7]These proofs are called the "non-logical" (*ethos* and *pathos*) and the "logical" (*enthymeme*) methods of proving. The inconsistency of Aristotle damning "non-logical" *pistis* in the opening pages A 1, 54a-b, and shortly later incorporating it with "logical" (A 2, 56a 1 ff.), is so obvious that one does not have to subscribe to the inerrancy of Aristotle in refusing to believe that he was incapable of recognizing what many commentators over the centuries have perceived. See COPE, An Introduction to Aristotle's Rhetoric, London 1867, pp. 90 ff., 140 ff., and his Commentary, Cambridge 1877; E. HAVET, Étude sur la Rhétorique d'Aristote, Paris 1846, pp. 27-31; J.S. VATER, Animadversiones ad Aristotelis Librum Primum Rhetoricum, Saxony 1794, pp. 10-13 is more circumspect but does not remove the problem, nor does Spengel in his commentary (Lipsiae 1867): see *sub* 1354b 18.

[8]At A 8, 66a 9-10 I would take *logos* in δι ἀποδεικτικοῦ λόγου as rational explanation (i.e. *logos* at 56a 4, 19) since *apodeiktikos* can be a synonym of *didaskalikos*, cf. *Met.* 1073a 2, *SE* 165a 39.

[9]One has but to consider the explanation of *ethos* and *pathos* in A 2, 56a 5 ff., and the statement made about ἐν αὐτῷ τῷ λόγῳ in 56a 19-20. In this first book from A 4, 59a 30 onward when Aristotle discusses the material topics for the premises of enthymemes in the three genera

of rhetoric we find that he is deriving them from the subject-matter under discussion, i.e. what is here called "pragma".

[10]*Rhetores Graeci*, vol. IX, p. 601 (ed. WALZ, Stuttgart 1832); see also vol. V, p. 506.

[11]*Lysias*, nos. 16 ff. (edd. USENER-RADERMACHER, Teubner 1965). In view of the general misunderstanding of the Aristotelian enthymeme among the subsequent technographers, possibly caused by the withdrawal of Aristotle's works, it is very instructive to see this understanding in Dionysius who was writing at a time shortly after Aristotle's works were quite probably accessible once again for study. Demetrius (*Peri Hermeneias*) frequently uses *pragma* as "subject-matter" (cf. 22.11.75). VOLKMANN, Die Rhetorik der Griechen und Römer, Leipzig 1885, p. 177 says that this use of πίστεις πρᾱγματικαί goes back to Aristotle A 2, 56a 1-4; see also SÜSS, Ethos, Berlin 1910, pp. 126, 147 who speaks of this third *pistis* as πρᾱγμα, and has this comment (p. 147): "...was die Isokrateer πρᾱγμα nennen, Aristoteles aber die πίστις ἐν αὐτῷ τῷ λόγῳ. . ." SPENGEL in his commentary (*sub* 1356a 21) apparently identifies this third *pistis* with enthymeme, but his remarks on 1354b 18 would appear more to the point when he speaks of this *pistis* as "ex re ipsa".

[12]VATER, Animadversiones, op. cit., p. 13. The multiplicity of meaning present in πίστις, inescapable as it is, has never been discussed by students of the work and it was challenged by G. WIKRAMANAYAKE, AJP 82, 1961, pp. 193-6; his objections were competently answered by J. LIENHARD, AJP 87, 1966, pp. 446-454.

[13]This is stated a number of times in the *Rhetoric*; see especially *B* 20, 93a 23; also *A* 2, 56b 6 ff.; *A* 9, 68a 29 ff., *B* 18, 92a 1 ff.; *B* 20, 94a 9 ff.; *Γ* 17, 18a 1 ff.; it also appears in *An. Post.* 71a 9-11.

[14]In the *Posterior Analytics* 71a 1-11 Aristotle begins an attempt to show that all learning and teaching arises from pre-existing knowledge as can be seen in a study of the theoretical sciences, or from a study of the argumentation used in all reasoning: syllogism and induction, both of which teach through that which is previously known. He continues by stating the parallel in rhetoric of enthymeme and example to syllogism and example: in the same way rhetoricians persuade, either through examples which is induction, or through enthymemes which is syllogism.

[15]*Phaedrus* 266 d-3 speaks of *prooimion, diegesis, martyriai, eikota, pistosis, epipistosis,* and Aristotle *Γ* 13, 14b 14ff. of *diegesis, epidiegesis, prodiegesis, elenchos, epexelenchos;* cf. also RADERMACHER, Artium Scriptores, Wien 1951, pp. 34-35 (B.II.23), p. 133 (B.XXII.9), pp. 209, 213, 214-215 (C. 21, 32, 36).

[16]For the *Rhetoric* a casual reading of either Spengel's *Synagoge Technon*, Stuttgart 1828, RADERMACHER'S Artium Scriptores, Wien 1951, or SPENGEL'S commentary on the *Rhetoric* (Lipsiae 1867) will give clear confirmation of this. As SPENGEL notes in the *Synagoge*, p. 173: "philosophus ille suas sententias saepe non minus quam Plato priorum. . . rationibus apfacit."

[17]WILAMOWITZ, Herakles II, Berlin 1895, p. 162; Menander: Das Schiedsgericht, Berlin 1925, p. 81; as he suggests *enthymios* had a specific meaning for fifth century Athenians: "was religionem habet, was gewissensscrupel macht".

[18]The source for the following is always the *index verborum*, if it exists, combined with whatever other resources that offered themselves. *Homer*: no noun; *enthymios* is used. *Hesiod*: no form. *Herodotus: enthymios* once, and with meaning "scruple". *Thucydides: enthymios, enthymia* in sense of "religio"; verb; and *enthymesis* once. *Aristophanes*: verb appears four times; scholiast on *Nubes* 317 interprets γνώμην by ἐνθυμήματα even though νοῦν occurs in the same line. *Aeschylus*: verb appears once and Italie interprets as "curare, aegre ferre". *Sophocles: enthymios* twice; noun twice: *OC* 292, 1199 both obviously not susceptible to the simple translation "thought" as Wilamowitz recognizes for 1199 (Menander, op. cit., p. 186).

Euripides: *enthymios* twice; *enthymesis* in *frg.* 246. *Pindar:* no form of verb, adjective, noun. *Plato:* verb appears. *Lysias:* verb form frequently.

[19]I will cite only the *Anabasis* as an example. The first citation will tolerate "thought", "idea", "notion". The second will not do so at all. Within the immediate context there are four verbs for thinking, including διανοέομαι; the ἐνθυμήματα in the text are the result of his hopes, thoughts, and desires which is clearly shown by the adjective τοιαῦτα which in turn makes ἐνθυμήματα the sum of the preceding actions. This passage is followed by the verb ἐνθυμέομαι, which, in the context, means an act that results from reason, feelings, the whole person, as the sentence shows.

[20]More recently R. FLACELIÈRE has given slight leeway (Isocrate: Cinq Discours, Paris 1961, p. 89, interpreting enthymeme as: "(de θυμός): réflexion, pensée, idée".

[21]For example cf. M.L.W. LAISTNER on Philip, 27 in Isocrates: De Pace and Philippus, New York 1927.

[22]Unfortunately most of the information on the teaching of Nausiphanes comes through Philodemus from a polemic written against the rhetorical doctrine of Nausiphanes by the Epicurean Metrodorus of Lampsacus.

[23]H. VON ARNIM, Dio von Prusa, Berlin 1898, p. 59; F. SUSEMIHL, Aphorismen zu Demokritos, Philologus 60, 1901, pp. 190-1; K. VON FRITZ, RE XVI, 1935 p. 2026 argues against VON ARNIM that the dependance of Nausiphanes on Aristotle is possible.

[24]Aristotle refers to his works on four occasions in the *Rhetoric*: *A* 13, 73b 18, *B* 23, 97a 12 (*Messeniacus*); *B* 23, 98b 10-19; *Γ* 3, 06a 1-b19. The citations indicate an intimate knowledge of the speeches of Alcidamas; on which see BRZOSKA on Alcidamas in RE I, 1894, p. 1534; BLASS, Die attische Beredsamkeit II², Leipzig 1872, p. 351 correctly observes that Aristotle preferred Isocrates to Alcidamas. After Aristotle the first notice of Alcidamas is in Demetrius περὶ ἑρμηνείας 12, and Dionysius of Halicarnassus *de Isae.* 19, neither of which contributes in any way to the problem here.

[25]The text used here is that of RADERMACHER, Artium Scriptores, Wien 1951, pp. 135-141. This work of Alcidamas is generally accepted as genuine; his *Palamedes* is questioned. VAHLEN, Der Rhetor Alkidamas (Sb. d. Wiener Ak. 1863); BRZOSKA, RE I, 1894, pp. 1533-9; BLASS, op. cit. pp. 345-64; BAITER-SAUPPE, Oratores Attici, Turici 1839-43, pp. 154-69; SPENGEL, Synagoge, Stuttgart 1828, pp. 172-180; H. RAEDER, Alkidamas und Platon als Gegner des Isokrates, RhM 63, 1908, pp. 495-511; K. HUBÍK, Alkidamas oder Isokrates, WS 22, 1901, pp. 234-251; L. ROBIN, Phèdre, Paris 1947, p. clxv. Dionysius of Halicarnassus in *Ep. ad Amm.* I. no. 722 attributes to Alcidamas a *techne* antedating Aristotle. The only strong evidence for this *techne* is a definition of rhetoric attributed to him in *Rhetores Graeci* (ed. C. WALZ, Stuttgart 1833), VII. 1.8.18-24. This same citation would indicate that Alcidamas did have a school of followers (οἱ περὶ τὸν᾿ Ἀλκιδάμαντα) which BLASS (op. cit., p. 351) denies.

[26]RAEDER, op. cit., p. 498, HUBÍK, op. cit., p. 240, SPENGEL, Synagoge, p. 174. For what it is worth HUBÍK, RAEDER, BRZOSKA assume that this work of Alcidamas is a reply to Isocrates' *Against the Sophists*. Such an exchange might have occurred for there does appear to be a reference to our work in the *Panegyricus* 11; and *Philippus* 25-27, *Epist.* I.2-3 could well be rejoinders to statements in this work.

[27]Cf. *Rhetoric*, *A* 2, 55b 25-6; see also SPENGEL, Synagoge, p. 173, BLASS, op. cit., p. 348 n.1.

[28]Aristotle does say (*B* 23, 97a 7-12, *B* 23, 98b 10-19) that he finds certain general topics which he himself uses as a source for inference by enthymeme in the *Messeniacus* of Alcidamas. But there is nothing more unusual in this than in BLASS (op. cit., p. 355) finding deduction and induction in the *Peri Sophiston*. All are very natural modes of reasoning and one would and could expect to find them prior to their formalization by Aristotle in the *Organon*.

[29]SOLMSEN, Drei Rekonstruktionen zur antiken Rhetorik und Poetik, Hermes 67, 1932, pp. 133-54 and RE X, 1934, pp. 1722-34 discusses the problem of Theodectes; as P. GOHLKE observes, we know nothing of his so-called treatise and the one reference to it in the *Rhetoric* Γ9, 10b 3 fits cc. 27-29 of the *Rhetoric to Alexander* perfectly: Die Entstehung der aristotelischen Ethik, Politik, Rhetorik, Wien 1944, p. 114.

[30]P. WENDLAND, Anaximenes von Lampsakos, Berlin 1905; H. USENER, Quaestiones Anaximeneae, Göttingen no date; A. IPFELKOFER, Die Rhetorik des Anaximenes, Würzburg 1889; E.M. COPE, An Introduction to Aristotle's Rhetoric, London 1867; C. ROBERT, Anaximenes, RE I, 1894, pp. 2086 ff.; M. FUHRMANN, Anaximenis Ars Rhetorica, Lipsiae 1966, whose text I follow in the citations.

[31]Dionysius of Halicarnassus, *ad. Amm.* 2, *de Isae.* 19 mentions a *techne*, and from Philodemus *Rhetorica II,* ed. SUDHAUS, p. 254, 21 ff. and Quintilian 3.4.9, we learn that he was apparently concerned with rhetorical education in order to turn out orators in the field of judicial and deliberative oratory. IPFELKOFER, op. cit., p. 8 ff. gives a history of the scholarship on this problem, as does USENER, op. cit., p. 1 ff. Among the many who would agree with Victorius the following can be mentioned: IPFELKOFER, USENER, SPENGEL, WENDLAND, ROBERT, WESTERMANN, BLASS. Recently V. BUCHHEIT, Untersuchungen zur Theorie des Genos epideiktikon von Gorgias bis Aristoteles, Munich 1960, challenged this ascription, and G. GRUBE, A Greek Critic: Demetrius on Style, Toronto 1961, pp. 156-63 questions the attribution to Anaximenes arguing exclusively from Quintilian; but he does accept the fourth century date. Fuhrmann comments (p. xl) on recent challenges of Quintilian: "equidem hanc nimiam diligentiam non probo; nam si Rhetoricam ad Alexandrum paulo post annum 340 a. Chr. n. a sophista quodam scriptam esse constat, utrum Anaximeni an aequali alicui attribuamus quid refert?"

[32]BLASS, op. cit., p. 391 and notes 2,3; ROBERT, op. cit., p. 2090; USENER, op. cit., p. 23.

[33]A reading of the treatise without recourse to the discussion of the problem in the secondary sources definitely impresses one with the affinity of the material in general to the pre-Aristotelian technical writing. The work does reveal unity of concept and composition which argues to a single author. And yet the general division of rhetoric into three kinds with seven species is a cumbersome systematization which one could call post-Aristotelian with only great lenience. It is clear that in the treatment of *eikos* and all matters connected with logic, as COPE remarks (Introd., p. 421), the author demonstrates an ignorance of what Aristotle has said; and this can also be stated for his discussion of *tekmerion*. All of the technographers after Aristotle took up Aristotle's theory on *tekmerion* (v. SPENGEL'S commentary at 1357b 6 and RADERMACHER, Artium Scriptores, p. 215); our author ignores it. It is again quite difficult to explain how this *techne*, emphasizing as it does the elementary idea of persuasion at any cost, could come after Aristotle's *Rhetoric* without even the slightest discussion of the firm Aristotelian position on this point. The more one involves oneself with the problem the more inclined one is to agree with IPFELKOFER, op. cit., p. 13 that the only way one can explain the *Rhetoric to Alexander* is that it is written "ohne alle Kenntnis der aristotelischen Rhetorik" and indeed prior to it; see also WENDLAND, op. cit., p. 27: "In dem Texte des Lehrbuches ... ist ... unsere aristotelische *Rhetorik* nirgends benutzt"; ROBERT, op. cit., p. 2093; SPENGEL, Die Rhetorica (des Anaximenes) ad Alexandrum kein Machwerk der spätesten Zeit, Philologus 18, 1862, pp. 604-646. Isocrates has been proposed, and also rejected, as the influence on this work. Whether he is or not is immaterial to this discussion save in the matter of the four-fold division of a speech which is Isocratean in character. For here again it is difficult to understand how anyone writing after Aristotle could disregard Aristotle's ridicule of such divisions in Γ 13, 14a 31 ff. FUHRMANN (pp. xl-xli) speaks of the relationship to Aristotle.

[34]Even though it is difficult after reading the *Rhetoric to Alexander* to accept it as post-Aristotelian one can discern reasons for the arguments about its relation to Aristotle's work. Despite rather

firm convictions on the matter I must admit that to find in the work the presence, on occasion, of divisions, definitions, and specifications of terms such as one is accustomed to meet them in Aristotle is a cause for wonder, e.g. c. 1, 1421b 7-1423a 12. I do not know that this fact can be explained with WENDLAND (who rejects later interpolation of the text with Aristotelian material) by saying that Aristotle in re-working an earlier *Rhetoric* of his own used the *techne* of Theodectes which had also been used by Anaximenes. Aside from the fact that such an explanation raises a further problem of an earlier form of the present *Rhetoric*, and so an enterprise of higher criticism still unsatisfying in its results, it is quite possible to explain the similarities by Aristotle's use of Anaximenes in which he took what was acceptable and rejected that with which he could not agree. Certainly the matters common to each are striking. Anaximenes (c. 2, 1423a 13 ff.), like Aristotle, considers the object of deliberative oratory: at c. 1, 1421b 15 ff. he discusses the various τέλη of rhetorical discourse but without the much more sophisticated analysis of Aristotle. Anaximenes' two kinds of *pisteis* (c. 7, 1428a 16 ff.) roughly parallel Aristotle's *pisteis entechnoi* and *pisteis atechnoi*, and his discussion of *semeion* (c. 12, 1430b 30 ff.) is quite similar to Aristotle's definition. It is also of interest to note that, while Anaximenes (c. 15, 1431b 23-6) speaks of using enthymemes as ἐπίλογοι to witnesses, Aristotle uses the same word when he recommends that *paradeigmata* be so used with enthymemes (*B* 20, 94a 11). The discussion of *gnome* (c. 14, 1431a 35 ff.) in Anaximenes and in Aristotle also bears comparison. These are some of the more obvious instances of a relationship between the two. Insofar as these relations represent technical matters of rhetoric present for the most part in precisely this way in none of the earlier writing it seems quite probable that if there is a relationship between the two it is Aristotle re-working Anaximenes.

[35] ἐνθύμημα is found in Anaximenes in the following places: cc. 7, 1428a 21; 10, 1430a 23-39; 14, 1431a 28-39; 15, 1431b 26; 18, 1432b 27, 1433a 26; 20, 1434a 4 (verb form); 22, 1434a 35; 32, 1438b 34 (or, ἐπενθυμήματα), 1439a 6 (ἐνθυμηματώδεις), 20, 34, 1440a 23; 35, 1441a 20, 40, b11; 36, 1442b 39, 1443a 3, b42.

[36] SPENGEL, *Anaximenes Ars Rhetorica*, Leipzig 1847, p. 162: "Aristoteli ἐνθύμημα genus probationis est ῥητορικὸς συλλογισμός quaevis sententia cui ratio addita est, *Rhet.* I.2; II.21-2, Anaximeni, ut Isocrati aliisque oratoribus, species, sententia cui qualiscumque ἐναντίωσις inest". In actual fact there is little in Anaximenes' definition of enthymeme to distinguish it from his definition of *tekmerion* (c. 9), aside from the greater extension of enthymeme, a fact which he recognizes himself in c. 14.

[37] And yet in the one place where Anaximenes uses the verb form (c. 20, 1434a 4) he does so with a meaning found throughout the literature.

[38] Aristotle's phrase at *Γ* 18, 19a 19: τὰ ἐνθυμήματα ὅτι μάλιστα συστρέφειν δεῖ can be compared with Anaximenes on enthymeme 10, 1430a 36-8: δεῖ δὲ τούτων ἕκαστα συνάγειν ὡς εἰς βραχύτατα καὶ φράζειν ὅτι μάλιστα ν ὀλίγοις τοῖς ὀνόμασι; see also 18, 1432b 25-7, 1433a 25-26.

[39] For Aristotle see either COPE, Commentary III, p. 107 n. 1, or SÜSS, Ethos, Berlin 1910, p. 176, and of course the text. For Anaximenes see 15, 1431b 25-6: "unless you wish to express an enthymeme briefly for the sake of *asteion*" and 22, 1434a 34-7. This last is quite interesting. Not only does it offer by implication a suggestion similar to Aristotle, namely, that a good enthymeme is such that, when enunciated in part, the hearers grasp the rest of the meaning (*B* 23, 00b 30-4; *Γ* 10, 10b 20-8), but it urges explicitly that only half the enthymeme can be spoken so that the hearers may complete it (with which cf. *A* 2, 57a 16-21). The passage also implies (1434a 38-40) that one should not use enthymemes one after the other; on this point see Aristotle *Γ* 17, 18a 6. Rather than the use of a common source (WENDLAND) these passages suggest that Aristotle in developing his own theory is modifying and incorporating Anaximenes.

[40]From the text enthymeme is clearly included in the phrase τῶν προειρημένων ἁπάντων and so it, like the others, only effects opinion.

[41]Anaximenes first distinguishes between enthymeme and *gnome* (c. 14, 1431a 35-8), and in every subsequent mention of enthymeme in his text (cf. note 35) he joins it with *gnome*. This could well be compared with Aristotle *B* 21, 94a 22-b 12; in particular the definition of *gnome* in c. 11, 1430b 1-b 29 should be compared with Aristotle *B* 21, 94b 7-12 where one can discern the kind of analysis which is going on in Aristotle with respect to the matter found in Anaximenes.

[42]J.M. LeBLOND, Logique et Méthode chez Aristote, Paris 1939, pp. 21-4, in his analysis of the methodology of the *Topics* finds it radicated in opposing viewpoints of a problem.

III

THE ENTHYMEME AS THE METHOD
OF RHETORICAL ARGUMENTATION

Aristotle, then, gives us two logical modes of demonstration which organize the material of discourse, enthymeme and example. They are the correlatives of syllogism and induction which in his philosophical treatises is the methodology whereby we move toward further knowledge of the world of reality. In the *Rhetoric* he calls them (*B* 20, 93a 23) the κοιναὶ πίστεις for all rhetorical discourse and they so dominate his analysis that both discourse and speakers may be qualified as either παραδειγματώδεις or ἐνθυμηματικοί (*A* 2, 56b 1-27) and some kinds of discourse are more suited to one type of reasoning, some to another.[1] The grounds for this distinction reside in the nature of deductive and inductive inference as Aristotle says at *A* 2, 56b 11-18, a passage unnecessarily confused by the commentators.[2]

To reason deductively is to reason from the general rather than from the particular which is induction. Obviously deduction requires from the auditor a larger intellectual grasp of a problem, more sophisticated skill, attention and critical discernment. This point is made quite well in *Problemata* 18.3 (a work not by Aristotle but clearly representative of the Aristotelian tradition): 'men learn with less effort from examples for they learn individual facts; enthymemes on the other hand are a demonstration from universals which we know less well than particulars'. The statement is an accurate echo of Aristotle for he says fairly much the same at *A* 2, 57b 27-30 and *A* 2, 56b 14-18. It is also the reason why he observes at *Topics* 105a 16-19 that induction ("example" in the *Rhetoric*) is more persuasive, and clear, and experientially more known, although syllogistic reasoning is more forcible and effective.[3] Again he remarks at *Topics* 157a 18-20 that induction should be used for those less skilled in reasoning but syllogism for the more dialectically skilled mind.[4] Induction is clearly more appropriate for the ordinary person since it permits more ready comprehension and understanding.

In spite of these difficulties found in deductive inference it occupies a prominent position for Aristotle in rhetorical discourse. This is clear from the fact that the enthymeme is the center of his analysis of rhetoric. He insists that the enthymeme is a syllogism and frequently makes this identification in the *Rhetoric*: *A* 2, 56a 22,b 5; *A* 2, 57a 23; *B* 21, 94a 26; *B* 22, 95b 22; *B* 23, 00b 27 ff.; *B* 25, 02a 29 ff. He underlines the identification further when, in explaining what the enthymeme is, he repeats the formula used to define syllogism in the *Prior Analytics* (24b 18-26) and the *Topics* (100a 25 ff.; 165a 1 f.).[5] In the light of his statements on the syllogism in the *Prior Analytics* there is no problem here. At 25b 26-31[6] he observed that the syllogism has a wider extension and includes more than strict scientific demonstration. It is, so to speak, a genus for other species of deductive reasoning and as far as the structure is concerned in his definition at 24b 18-26 a syllogism is the same whether it occurs in formally scientific, in dialectical or rhetorical argumentation. This is the whole point of his comment in the *Topics* 162a 15 ff.: "a philosophema is an apodeictic syllogism, an epicheirema a dialectical syllogism, a sophisma an eristic syllogism, an aporema a dialectical syllogism which concludes to a contradiction". Had he continued with an addition which we can make from *Rhetoric A* 2, 56b 4-5 in precisely the same language "the *enthymema* is a rhetorical syllogism" (ἐνθύμημα μὲν ῥητορικὸν συλλογισμόν) we would have here a fairly complete statement of his use of syllogism. It is, of course, quite possible that the enthymeme is not mentioned because he had not yet brought his theory of the syllogism into the field of rhetoric. In any event his analysis of the enthymeme as a form of syllogistic inference clearly locates it with the other kinds of syllogism mentioned in the *Topics* passage.

Before considering more closely the structure, or form, of the enthymeme and the modality of the kind of statement it makes let us glance briefly at some of the implications for Aristotle's theory of rhetorical discourse which follow upon the fact that the enthymeme is the syllogism of rhetoric. In building his theory of rhetoric around the syllogism despite the problems involved in deductive inference Aristotle stresses the fact that rhetorical discourse is discourse directed toward knowing, toward truth not trickery. To one acquainted with Aristotle it should be evident that syllogism and induction are inextricably connected with the demonstration of truth. From the analogy drawn between "enthymeme-example" as the rhetorical forms of "deduction-induction," Aristotle directs rhetoric toward the demonstration of the true. Indeed the view of the *Rhetoric* as a collection of sharp techniques, a sophist's *vademecum*, is not only false but irreconcilable with the whole tenor of the work and such explicit statements as *A* 1, 54b 10; *A* 1, 55a 17-8, 21-3, 31-3, 37-b 7; *B* 24, 02a 23-8 and the entire discussion of apparent enthymemes *B* 24, 00b 35-01a 28. In so emphasizing the role of discursive reasoning Aristotle rejects decisively the Platonic criticism of rhetoric in the *Gorgias* 465d-466a, a rejection made more specific by his repetition of certain key words of Plato. Rhetoric is no longer a "part of flattery" (μόριον κολακείας 466a) but a "part of dialectic" (μόριόν τι τῆς διαλεκτικῆς *A* 2, 56a 31); it is the "counterpart of dialectic" (ἀντίστροφος τῇ διαλεκτικῇ *A* 1, 54a) not the "counterpart of cookery" (ἀντίστροφος ὀψοποιίας 465d).[7] If rhetoric is so clearly related to dialectic, a discipline whereby we are enabled to examine inferentially generally accepted opinions on any problem whatsoever (*Topics* 100a 18-20),[8] then it is the rhetorical syllogism which moves the rhetorical process into the domain of reasoned activity, or the kind of rhetoric Plato accepted later in the *Phaedrus*. It is also the rhetorical syllogism which relates *Rhetoric, Topics,* and *Analytics.* For example at *A* 1, 55a 8-14 Aristotle notes that the individual who knows the sources and the methodology of the syllogism would be naturally equipped to develop enthymemes. He makes one restriction however: this individual must know the subject-matter of the enthymemes and the specific difference between an enthymeme and the scientific syllogism.[9] From this we might conclude that in its structural form the enthymeme is like all syllogism but that in the character of the statement made it will be different from the scientific syllogism. Insofar as the primary concern of rhetoric is discourse in the area of the probable it would appear that the modality of all of its statements would be probable and that it would be like the dialectical syllogism in this respect. There is, however, reason to believe that Aristotle has not so restricted the enthymeme but has given it the right to use certain as well as probable statement (cf. *infra*, pp. 91-92). This means that discourse in rhetoric can reach beyond probable knowledge. From Aristotle's statements one can conclude that in the modality of its premises the rhetorical syllogism is usually like the dialectical syllogism but sometimes like the scientific syllogism (*apodeixis* in its strict meaning). The enthymeme appears to be a form of inference which may partake of both the nature of the dialectical and the scientific syllogism.

Let us turn now to what Aristotle has to say about the form of the enthymeme. From his statements there is nothing to indicate that he did not consider the enthymeme to be an ordinary syllogism of three statements. Thus in structure its power like that of any syllogism resides in its ability to sum up the implications and scope of an argument in a fairly precise, condensed, and reasoned inference of two premises and a conclusion. While this position of Aristotle on the form seems clear enough the enthymeme from the earliest times has been defined as a truncated syllogism in form, a syllogism with a suppressed premise or an omitted conclusion.[10] The debate on specifying enthymeme by its structural form as an abbreviated syllogism has been continuous and is still common. Yet in 1729 FACCIOLATI (following PACIUS) wrote: "Nego enthymema esse syllogismum mutilum . . . Nego, inquam, et pernego enthymema enunciatione una et conclusione constare, quamvis ita in scholis omnibus finiatur et a nobis ipsis finitum sit aliquando. . ." In support of Facciolati the very most that can be said is that the statements of Aristotle would favor an abbreviated form but do not make such a form an essential part of the enthymeme in contradistinction to the ordinary form of the syllogism.[11]

The two passages where Aristotle seems to justify those who define the enthymeme as an abbreviated syllogism do not permit one to draw such an absolute conclusion. The first is at *A* 2, 57a 16-17 and it is followed by an example which is meant presumably to be a syllogism without a major premise. The text and context are more than clear and all that can be drawn from them is that the enthymeme should not be a long inferential process and often may permit the ellipsis of a premise. The second passage *B* 22, 95b 24-26, although it is interpreted by COPE to mean an abbreviated form, is not at all that explicit in its statement. The key word is πάντα, but this is explained by Aristotle at lines 26,30-32 and it means quite simply (a possibility even COPE must admit) that one should not introduce all kinds of unnecessary argumentation.

We cannot say, then, that the enthymeme is by definition an abbreviated syllogism and yet all of Aristotle's remarks on it are rather well summarized at Γ 18, 19a 18-19: "enthymemes should be condensed as much as possible. There is a definite predilection for enthymeme as a brief, direct and compact inference, and possibly in an abbreviated form. The reason for this attitude of Aristotle is determined by the factor which always plays a key role in his analysis of rhetoric: the audience. Here specifically it is his concern about the ability of the auditors to acquire the knowledge and understanding introduced by the deductive process. Aristotle states this fairly early at A 2 57a 3-4, 11. At B 23, 00b 30-34 we learn that the best enthymemes are those which, while substantial in content, are nevertheless apparent to the audience when first enunciated, or shortly thereafter. Aristotle is concerned that the audience acquire knowledge, but knowledge which he qualifies as μάθησις ταχεῖα: a quick, comprehensive grasp of the problem (Γ 10, 10b 10-12, 20-21, 25-26; B 23, 00b 31-34; A 2, 57a 21). It is essential that understanding come across to those engaged in discourse quickly and effectively; as he says at 10b 20-21: "of necessity a style and enthymemes which possess elegance (ἀστεῖα) are those that give us μάθησις ταχεῖα". He makes this point more explicit at 10b 27-36 where he says that such a rapid insight is achieved in three ways: 1) by enthymeme with respect to thought, 2) by antithesis with respect to style, and, 3) in language by metaphor. The point at issue here for Aristotle is the most effective way to convey to an other this quick, comprehensive insight, and he centers his attention on the three components which mediate it, namely, thought, language, style. From what he says we may suppose that enthymeme does it by the way in which it organizes the thought, since clearly style does it by the way in which the idea is emphasized by sentence structure, and in language it is the structure of analogy, in metaphor which obtains the same result.

Each contributes to μάθησις ταχεῖα, and one cannot help but note that their underlying logic is a movement from idea to idea, or statement to statement, e. g. "this" and so "that", or, "if this is so" then "that is so". Indeed somewhat earlier Aristotle joined the enthymeme quite closely with the antithetic style saying quite simply that this style is the *locus* for enthymematic statement (χώρα ἐστὶν ἐνθυμήματος B 24, 01a 4-6). The particular logic of the antithetic style for effective communication of thought is revealed at B 23,00b 28-29: "when two things are set beside one another they are more clear to the hearer". Antithesis is based on a relationship between two concepts or propositions whereby we move directly, concisely, and with new knowledge from the known concept or proposition to the less known. The movement is quite similar to that which takes place when a syllogism is shortened.

These statements of Aristotle which favor a shortened syllogistic structure for the sake of the auditors indicate his desire that the language of discourse speak to the hearers in an immediate and direct way even when the syllogism is used. The introduction of his major mode of demonstration into rhetorical theory could work against such immediacy. For deduction develops usually from the area of more general principles, of concepts in themselves, or of the more universal ideas entailed by the subject itself. Such discourse can easily lose itself in theoretical analysis and lose rapport with those not sufficiently skilled to follow a line of deductive reasoning, or to perceive its relevance. In suggesting a modification of the form Aristotle apparently wishes to retain the strength which deductive demonstration contributes to discourse as a reasoned activity, and at the same time to make this power more accessible to a general audience. We have an example of how effective this can be in the *First Olynthiac*. Demosthenes works from the major premise that "freedom involves self-sacrifice and personal responsibility" (2-6)—a secure general principle which would command assent, but whose development would carry little weight in the situation. Thus this major premise is never formally articulated. Demosthenes develops the minor which is more immediate and obvious: "our freedom is here and now at issue" (2), and the conclusion: "we must make sacrifices and assume our responsibilities". The power of the argument is patent: the immediate concern about the danger and how to cope with it is raised to a level which grounds the whole motive for action in a principle acceptable to most, if not all, men.

In many ways this permissible modification of the syllogistic form on Aristotle's part appears to be caused by a desire to make the constraining force inherent in deductive inference as immediate for an ordinary audience as the appeal of induction.[12] This would appear to be the point of his comment at *B* 22, 95b 22-25 where he remarks that he has previously discussed three facts about the enthymeme: that it is a syllogism; how it is a syllogism; and in what way it differs from a dialectical syllogism.[13] He explains this last point immediately with the comment that those who use the enthymeme "must not draw the conclusion from an extended series of inferences (πόρρωθεν) nor include all relevant material". If we ask where he has engaged in such a discussion the only likely passage is *A* 2, 56a 35-57a 21. In this section he notes, among other things, that the enthymeme is used with an audience "which is not able to comprehend in all its detail an argument built of many stages nor able to reason through an extended series of inferences" (*A* 2, 57a 3-4). There is an obvious relation between these two passages in the demand for conciseness in the rhetorical syllogism. As a further point Aristotle seems to contrast the syllogistic process in rhetoric and dialectic. The point of the contrast is that dialectic employs a series of interrelated syllogisms which develop an argument to a conclusion. The rhetorical syllogism must capture the evidence forcefully enough to stand alone. When Aristotle writes as he does at *A* 2, 57a 7-10 he can only be describing the dialectical syllogism: "it is possible to construct syllogisms and draw conclusions from evidence that is itself the result of syllogisms or from evidence not demonstrated by syllogism but in need of syllogistic proof since it is not probable." The dialectical syllogism as seen in the *Rhetoric* permits an extended inferential process leading to a conclusion. A moment's reflection on the nature of dialectical argument would recall that it is a detailed and analytic inquiry which advances gradually from a set of initial hypotheses or statements through detailed reasoning to a tentative conclusion. In contrast to this the enthymeme confines its demonstrative or probative statement to a concise and direct form, and one which may be shortened. Indeed this difference would seem to be more properly the point of the well-known distinction of Zeno between dialectic (the closed fist) and rhetoric (the open hand): "*Zeno . . . manu demonstrare solebat quid inter has artes interesset, nam cum compresserat digitos pugnumque fecerat, dialecticam aiebat eiusmodi esse; cum autem diduxerat et manum dilataverat, palmae illius similem eloquentiam esse dicebat.*" (Cicero, *Orat.* 32.113).

Let us now consider the kind of statement permitted by the rhetorical syllogism. The syllogism as inference will differ with the character of its propositions or premises. If their modality is apodeictic they assert necessary relations, if problematic they affirm contingent or possible relationship. Obviously the character of knowledge achieved in the conclusion will differ. As has been said rhetoric for Aristotle concerns itself mostly with problematic statements and probable knowledge. Its object is to secure a position as far as that can be done which will enable one to engage in intelligent, reasonable, and human action, or to confirm a position taken as rational and acceptable or simply to speculate on the acceptability or non-acceptability of a proposal. These are all legitimate objects for discussion in the area of conditioned and consequently probable human situations. In view of this contingency of subject-matter of rhetorical discourse (*A* 2, 57a 14-15) we might accept that the enthymeme would be confined to problematic modal propositions and would reason to probable conclusions.

There are, however, some observations of Aristotle which demand attention insofar as they extend the character of inference by enthymeme and consequently the nature of rhetorical discourse. Neither the observations nor their consequences are formally developed by Aristotle. He assumes that they are known from his other works (e. g. his comment at *A* 2, 57a 29 ff.). At the same time they widen the horizon of rhetorical discourse and locate his study of rhetoric in the context of the *Phaedrus*. They extend the *vis loquendi* of rhetoric to forms of discourse which could certainly include philosophical discourse and they indicate that for Aristotle rhetoric is the art of the *logos* in all avenues of discourse (a more detailed discussion of the reason for this is taken up in c. 4 following). They imply that for Aristotle, as for Plato, "the art of rhetoric, viewed in its totality, would be a kind of *psychagogia* (i.e. influencing the whole person) by the use of language" (*Phaedrus* 261a 7-b2) in every area of concern to men, even that of philosophical discussion. This interpretation is dictated by Aristotle's introduction of apodeictic modal propositions into rhetorical discourse. With this material which Aristotle calls *anagkaia* and *tekmerion* (*A* 2, 57a 22-b 25) rhetoric is moved from the realm of probable statement and knowledge to knowledge which Aristotle specifically designates more strictly as philosophical knowledge: the knowledge that a thing cannot be other than it is (*An. Post.* 88b 30-32; 71b 10-12). Of course for Aristotle philosophic knowledge in its full sense is not simply knowledge (as we have it here) of the unconditioned. It is knowledge both of the fact and of its cause as well. The kind of necessity we have in the *anagkaia* of rhetoric will permit one to conclude only to knowledge of the fact in the conclusion, not to the reasoned fact. To this extent the rhetorical syllogism which infers from *anagkaia* differs from the scientific syllogism or strict *apodeixis* as seen, for example, in the *Posterior Analytics* 71b 9-24. Rhetorical inference while called *apodeixis* (e. g. *A* 1, 55a 5-7; *B* 25, 03a 10-15) does not carry with it the same demonstrative force of scientific *apodeixis*. And yet one cannot overlook the fact that by this necessary subject-matter Aristotle has drawn rhetoric within the orbit of what is more properly philosophic discourse. This fact was recognized by Stephanus in his commentary on *A* 2, 57a 22 ff. where he speaks of this as another instance of what he calls "the communion of philosophy and rhetoric" (*Commentaria Graeca* vol. 21, p. 263. 5-10). Aristotle gives rhetoric the right to certain as well as probable knowledge, a right claimed at least by Isocrates in his theory of rhetoric and often exercised by Plato in his dialogues. This extension of rhetoric beyond the area of the contingent and the probable with which it is generally identified should not be surprising. Aside from the fact that there is the initial correlation between rhetoric and dialectic (the methodology of inquiry) there are throughout the *Rhetoric* a number of cross-references to what Aristotle calls his work on dialectic, analytics, ethics. He gives the justification for such reference fairly early at *A* 1, 55a 14-18 where he remarks that the reality (τὸ ἀληθές) which is ordinarily the concern of philosophical speculation is the legitimate object of rhetorical discourse just as the faculty (the intellect) which directs itself upon this object is the same in each discipline. Later at *A* 4, 59b 8-12 he states: "Indeed what we have had occasion to declare previously is true: that rhetoric is composed of the science (*episteme*) of analytics, of the science of politics relative to ethics, and is partly like to dialectic and sophistic".[14]

The instrumentality of the enthymeme as the major form of rhetorical inference in Aristotle's theory of rhetoric underscores the transcendence of rhetoric as a *techne*. Aristotle speaks of this transcendence early in the treatise (*A* 1, 55b 8-9; *A* 2, 55b 31-34, 56a 30-33) in calling rhetoric a *dynamis* which stands apart from the *dynamis* of the specific disciplines. When this power is located we discover that it resides ultimately in the artistically effective control of language as it is used to speak to the other. This is intrinsic to rhetoric. As the instrument of rhetorical argumentation the enthymeme possesses a similar universality by reason of its form. By reason of the matter which it may legitimately organize into inference it is free to use the varied sources of knowledge wherein man speaks to man. This is simply to say that while we must acknowledge that the formal and primary denotation of rhetoric and rhetorical argumentation is discourse directed toward effecting judgment on open questions we cannot think that this primary objective confines its effort exclusively to the area of practical reasoning as opposed to speculative reasoning, or to the area of the problematic as opposed to the certain—at least this appears to be the firm implication of statements such as those at *A* 1,55b 8-9; *A* 2, 55b 25-26; 31-33.[15] Where judgment is the final objective, even judgment directed toward action, every facet of human knowledge which makes judgment possible is legitimate material for discourse. This can, and frequently will, mean certain as well as probable knowledge. When Aristotle in his analysis of rhetoric brought syllogistic reasoning into the realm of ordinary human discourse he utilized a vehicle which by its general character in his work assumes an effort at reasoning, and consequently assumes an effort at rational discourse as opposed to sophistry. Furthermore in the manner in which he developed the methodology of the enthymeme in the *Rhetoric* he presented us with a more substantial answer to the problems raised by those who had discussed rhetoric. For the methodology of the enthymeme involves the range of human knowledge at man's disposal for intelligent discussion as well as the whole complex of human psychology.

It is interesting to note that in the study of the *Rhetoric* there is rarely any discussion of what Aristotle calls the apparent enthymeme (*B* 24) and the refutative enthymeme (*B* 25). The reticence is surprising since they represent another aspect of the enthymeme and an understanding of them would seem necessary to a full comprehension of enthymeme and enthymematic reasoning. In the present context they are particularly relevant and instructive for they confirm the three points just mentioned in the discussion of the enthymeme as the instrument of deductive reasoning: 1) the fact that rhetoric is concerned with truth, 2) the structural form of the enthymeme, and, 3) the character of its subject-matter. For Aristotle's critique in these chapters of the apparent and refutative enthymeme assumes that it is an ordinary syllogism of three propositions in which the premises correctly enunciate reality as it can be known in what is generally a conditioned human situation. Aristotle gives the larger part of his attention to the apparent enthymeme, and it is well to understand the intent of his discussion.

We can locate this fairly well if we recall his comment (*A* 1, 55a 29-33) that rhetoric must be able to contend with false argumentation, or his words in the *Sophistici Elenchi* (165a 24-27): "To employ a single point of comparison: it is the task of the one who has knowledge to speak the truth with respect to each subject in which he is learned and to be able to expose the individual who uses false reasoning."

Assuredly Aristotle's concern with false reasoning is not with deception as a constructive element in the art of rhetoric. On the contrary its purpose is to defend the *logos* against misleading and incorrect argument. His discussion of the apparent enthymeme allows no doubt that Aristotle viewed the rhetorical syllogism as inference that is valid and genuine both in its formal structure and material content.

For the ground on which his critique of the apparent enthymeme rests is that it is false inference either in form or content. Thus it is clear that rhetorical discourse directs itself, within the limits usually imposed upon it, to the exposition of the true. What is wrong with the apparent enthymeme is that somewhere it is involved with a misrepresentation of reality as it is, and as it can be known. Aristotle's sense of the inadequacy of the fact that there is no name for the false *rhetor* and false rhetoric (*A* 1, 55b 17-21) is sharply pointed here. His argument in his presentation of the apparent enthymeme implies that there is a false rhetoric and that it is grounded in fallacious argumentation, in the failure or the refusal to present the truth as it can be known in a given situation.[16]

From all that Aristotle has said of inference by syllogism in the *Analytics* apparent enthymeme which leads to error will be false inference either formally or materially or both. This is to say that an apparent enthymeme will be deficient either in its form as a syllogism in one of the three figures of syllogism, or in the content of the statements it makes in its premises. One cannot argue that what makes an enthymeme "apparent" is that it only yields probable knowledge. The major burden of rhetorical argumentation, as Aristotle recognizes, consists in reasoning to probable conclusions from sources which give probable statements. The very same situation exists in the *Sophistici Elenchi* whose relation to the rest of the *Topics* is often considered parallel to the relation of our chapter 24 on apparent enthymeme to the rest of the *Rhetoric*.[17] No one obviously would deny that the basis of the dialectical syllogism is to reason from probabilities to probable conclusions. Consequently when Aristotle discourses on apparent dialectical syllogisms in the *Sophistici Elenchi* he certainly does not find their falsity in the fact that they infer the probable. The only foundation for their "apparent" syllogistic character would be that either they are not proper syllogisms, or do not reason from the truly probable. In the light of everything he has said in the *Rhetoric* up to chapter 24 the same should be true for the apparent enthymeme. If chapter 24 makes any contribution to our understanding it should reveal that apparent enthymemes fail either in correct syllogistic form, or in reasoning from the apparently (but not truly) probable, or in both. In each instance the apparent enthymeme does not validly demonstrate even probable knowledge but merely gives the appearance of demonstrating: φαίνεσθαι δεικνύναι (*A* 2, 56a 36).

It has been said that Aristotle would not consider formal fallacy since it would be so transparent. Yet when we turn to the *Topics* (100b 23-101a 4) we find him distinguishing inference which is false in two ways: (a) inference which is formally false: an *apparent syllogism* from probable or apparently probable premises (from 101a 3-4 an "apparent syllogism" is not a syllogism since it appears to reason but does not reason), and, (b) the syllogism which is materially false: a syllogism from apparent but not true probabilities. This distinction is just as clearly made at 165b 7-8.

In terms of this distinction, then, an apparent enthymeme is not an enthymeme which concludes to probable knowledge, but rather an enthymeme which is defective to the extent that it will not conclude to a statement of any kind, not even probable, save one which is false. When we turn to the *Rhetoric* (*B* 24) and study the sources from which the apparent enthymeme is derived we find that the nine topics given as the sources confirm this distinction insofar as they are sources which occasion either formal or material fallacy.[18] These topics present sources which cause either invalid form or fallacy in the statement of the premises.[19] In the *Sophistici Elenchi* (165b 23 ff.) these two general classes of false reasoning are called *in dictione* and *extra dictionem*.[20] While Aristotle explicitly mentions only one of them (*in dictione*) in the *Rhetoric* a comparison of our passage in the *Rhetoric* with that of the *Sophistici Elenchi* indicates that he is speaking about both. A glance at the topics in the *Rhetoric* shows that topics V, VI, VII effect a false statement in one of the premises and therefore an inference which is materially false. The other topics are connected with form: topics Ib, II, VIII, IX give an inference which is formally invalid while topics Ia and III yield no inference at all.

One of the sources for apparent enthymeme, topic IV fallacy of *semeion*, has been omitted and the reason for this should be obvious. The whole burden of the *Rhetoric* to this point is that one of the sources for valid enthymeme is *semeion*. A ready but somewhat superficial solution to this apparent contradiction would be to suggest that Aristotle is speaking here at *B* 24, 01b 9 ff. of those *semeia* which are the *semeia anonyma*: non-necessary signs. The use of the word ἀσυλλόγιστον at b10, 13 might seem to strengthen this suggestion when we recall the use of the same word at *A* 2, 57b 14 and 24 in reference to these same *semeia anonyma*. Since Aristotle never challenges the *tekmerion*, or necessary sign, we could then argue that these *semeia anonyma* which are contingent and non-necessary will never give certain knowledge and can only be used as the source of probable knowledge. In this respect one might consider them false and misleading. The only difficulty with this interpretation should be fairly obvious from what has been said: the task of rhetoric by and large is grounded for Aristotle in reasoning to probable conclusions. He has no problem about the validity of the probable as one of the sources of knowledge. Therefore he cannot be discarding non-necessary signs here as sources of valid enthymemes because of their reasoning to probable knowledge.[21] If he is calling enthymemes derived from *semeia anonyma* apparent enthymemes (and as he says at *B* 24, 00b 37 "apparent" means not an enthymeme but only with the appearance of being an enthymeme) we have the same kind of nonsensical statement which is wrongly urged against his presumably contradictory statements in the first chapter of Book *A* on *pathos* and *ethos*. The problem is further complicated by the fact that these comments at *B* 24, 01b 9 ff. are not passing observations. He makes similar statements on *semeia anonyma* in the *Prior Analytics* 70a 3 ff. and the *Sophistici Elenchi* 167b 8 f.

What, then, can Aristotle mean by these comments on sign at *A* 2, 57b 10-25; *B* 24, 01b 9-15; *B* 25, 03a 3-6; *An. Pr.* 70a 3-38; *SE* 167b 8-11? While a number of these passages speak of *semeia* without specification there is no need, as has been said, to complicate the problem since Aristotle accepts the validity of inference by necessary sign which he calls *tekmerion*. The passages question the validity of inference by non-necessary sign, the *semeion anonymon*. Aristotle gives the inescapable impression that any inferences from *semeia anonyma* are invalid and so false. He bases their falseness on the fact that the *semeia anonyma* can only be used in the second or third figure syllogism and used only in a way which gives a formally invalid inference.[22] His examples make this clear, e.g. *A* 2, 57b 19 ff. for the second figure (Everyone with fever breathes rapidly, This man breathes rapidly, This man is with fever); *A* 2, 57b 11 ff. for the third figure (Socrates is wise, Socrates is just, The wise are just). Obviously sign enthymemes developed in this way will be formally invalid. In his second figure example Aristotle violates a basic law of his syllogism (a distributed middle term), and in his third figure example he concludes to a statement not warranted by the premises. Indeed if Aristotle had drawn the correct conclusion in the third figure: Some wise men are just, the *semeion* argument is not only valid but helpful for it does enable us to establish a proposition that can be of assistance in developing a thesis.

Here, then, is the difficulty. Aristotle in his statements on *semeia anonyma* appears to say that enthymemes drawn from them will be necessarily invalid formally. If this is so then enthymemes from *semeia anonyma* would be "apparent enthymemes" and we do have a substantial contradiction.

In opposition to this we must acknowledge the following. Aristotle tells us in the *Rhetoric* that sign—without any qualifications—is a source for enthymematic reasoning (*A* 2, 57a 30-33); and we have no reason to think that the reasoning is any less valid than that from *eikos* also mentioned here as a source. Almost by way of confirming this he uses a *semeion anonymon* in a valid inference in the *Prior Analytics*, 70a 25 ff. This sign has the same intrinsic value as that used invalidly at 70a 20 ff. The difference is simply that at 70a 25 ff. he uses *semeion* in the first figure syllogism and makes a formally valid inference. If this is so *semeia anonyma* enthymemes do not of themselves necessarily implicate formally invalid inference. Stephanus in his discussion of sign argument (*Commentaria Graeca* vol. 21, pp. 264 ff.) would agree. Writing on Aristotle's statements on sign at *A* 1, 57b 1 ff. he maintains that the *semeia* will yield a valid inference if they are formally and materially valid. By way of confirmation he notes that commentators take the *semeion anonymon* enthymeme on quick-breathing (which Aristotle has placed in the second figure and in a formally invalid inference) and give it valid form by placing it in the first figure. When we turn to Aristotle's remarks on fallacy in sign arguments at our passage in the *Rhetoric B* 24, 01b 12-15 there is further difficulty. His example does not illustrate formal fallacy which is apparently the point of all his strictures against *semeia anonyma* enthymemes. The example he gives on

Dionysius is in fact involved in a material not a formal fallacy. The major is a false statement. It is only "apparently" probable, not truly probable, that "every bad man is a thief". There is no ground for thinking that "badness" is in any way a sign which leads to the predicate "thief". This sign argument is materially false and this was recognized by the commentator Anonymus (*Commentaria Graeca* vol. 21, p. 151) who says quite correctly that there is no syllogism here "because the major premise is false", even though the inference is in valid form. This evidence that *semeion* does not of itself involve invalid inference is strengthened by two other statements of Aristotle in the *Prior Analytics*. At 70a 6-7 he explains *semeion* as "that which by its nature tends to be a demonstrative premise that is either necessary or generally accepted". Now a πρότασις ἀποδικτική as ordinarily used by Aristotle even with the qualification here of ἔνδοξος means one that establishes a solidly firm relation between subject and predicate. And as BONITZ says of the phrase βούλεται εἶναι (which accordingly I have translated: "by its nature tends to be") "significatur quo quid per naturam suam tendit". Shortly later at 70a 37-38 Aristotle remarks "in all *semeia* truth is present". Both the text and context of the chapter make it clear that the kind of truth he has in mind here is truth which results from inference by syllogism. To interpret the phrase in a restrictive sense, e. g. "there is truth in *semeia*" is gratuitous, if indeed meaningful.

It certainly does not appear, then, that enthymemes from *semeia anonyma* are of themselves invalid. The most extreme judgment which Aristotle's statements would warrant would be that *semeia anonyma* enthymemes may not be, by the very fact that they are *semeia anonyma*, intrinsically valid for probable argumentation. But we certainly cannot say what his comments here (*B* 24, 01b 9-15) and in the other passages seem to imply, namely, that such enthymemes are *intrinsically invalid* for probable argumentation. Aristotle's analysis of sign inference in the *Rhetoric, Analytics* and *Sophistici Elenchi* appears to labor under the same kind of incompleteness of statement which Ross notes in some detail (pp. 491-495 of his commentary on the *Analytics*) for the analysis of counter-argumentation in chapter 26 of the *Analytics* which immediately precedes our c. 27 on sign-inference. As a further indication of this possible incompleteness and uncertainty we may point to the somewhat confusing comments in the *Sophistici Elenchi* and our passage in the *Rhetoric* specifically *B* 24, 01b 9-15 and 20-30. The *Rhetoric* mentions the fallacy from sign and the fallacy from consequents as two distinct and separate fallacies with their own examples. In the *Sophistici Elenchi* there is no mention of fallacy from sign; fallacy from consequents is discussed. We are told further that fallacy from sign is the same as the fallacy from consequents, e.g. "in the *Rhetoric* demonstrations from sign are from consequents" (167b 8-11). Then to make the problem more confusing the example used to illustrate sign fallacy (167b 10-11) is the example used in the *Rhetoric* to illustrate the fallacy from consequents.

We would have to admit, however, when we turn to the statement on the apparent enthymeme in the *Rhetoric* that the results for the nature of the enthymeme far outweigh the inadequacies of the explanation of fallacy from sign. In the criticism of the enthymeme which is only apparent and not a true enthymeme we acquire a firm and clear illustration of the form and character of enthymematic reasoning. Many aspects of the enthymeme, which up to this point in his treatise has been presented positively, are confirmed by his critique of the apparent enthymeme. We are also put in possession once again of Aristotle's conviction that the object of rhetorical discourse is truth, a theme he sounded in the opening chapter, *A* 1, 55a 19-b 24.

His brief study of refutation (*B* 25, 02a 29-b 13) restates both of these ideas. It concentrates almost exclusively upon the enthymeme and deductive reasoning (in which he assumes at all times a syllogism of two premises and a conclusion). The study, however, also incorporates the other mode of demonstration, induction. The statement on refutation is fairly simple and explicit. When of necessity we go behind some of the comments in an effort to understand them more fully we must turn to the *Prior Analytics* and the *Sophistici Elenchi*. Once again we discover an unclearness which characterized his words on the apparent enthymeme from *semeion*.

Refutation is called λύσις in the *Rhetoric* and it is described in the *Sophistici Elenchi* 176b 29-30 as "the exposure of false reasoning" (see also *Topics* 160b 33-35). We are told in the *Rhetoric* that it works either by counter-syllogism or by a specific objection against one of the premises or the conclusion. At once it is clear that the methodology of demonstration (deduction-induction) comes into play in refutation. For we refute either by counter-inference or by instancing one or more facts contrary to a statement made. The first method is the refutative enthymeme. It is clearly not some special "kind" of enthymeme. Aristotle tells us (*B* 25, 02a 32-33) that it argues from the same *topoi* as the demonstrative enthymeme, and at *B* 22, 96b, 23-28 we learn that it bears the same relation to the demonstrative enthymeme as *elenchos* does to the dialectical syllogism.[23] Indeed he calls the refutative enthymeme the elenchic enthymeme (*B* 22, 96b 25) and it is more than clear from his comments (*B* 22, 96b 26-28) that what he said of *elenchos* and syllogism in the *Sophistici Elenchi* (164b 27-165a 3) is strictly referable to the deictic and elenchic enthymeme. As *elenchos* and the dialectical syllogism are both syllogisms, one destructive, the other constructive, so are the elenchic and deictic enthymemes both enthymemes. Any difference between them resides solely in the fact that the elenchic enthymeme (just as *elenchos* itself) is inference directed to disprove the conclusion reached by the deictic enthymeme it is refuting. Indeed this explanation is precisely that which Aristotle himself gives in a more explicit manner at *B* 26, 03a 25-31. At *Γ*17, 18b 2-6 ff., the one other place in which he speaks of the refutative enthymeme, he repeats once again that the refutative enthymeme does not differ essentially from the demonstrative enthymeme. In calling our attention to the fact that refutative and demonstrative enthymemes use the same topics and that these topical sources are usually probabilities Aristotle throws light on an earlier passage often criticized, e.g. *A* 1, 55a 29-36. He readily acknowledges (*B* 25, 02a 33-35) that, since the sources for enthymeme are probabilities, opposing probabilities are often possible. Thus there is ample opportunity for anyone to make use of a refutative enthymeme which can infer a conclusion negating the conclusion of a demonstrative enthymeme. Of more significance, however, is the fact that *A* 1, 55a 29-36 now becomes rather obvious, although most opponents of his *Rhetoric* still succeed in misreading it. There, in what has been taken as an admission of the sophistry intrinsic to the rhetorical *techne* Aristotle said that rhetoric by its very nature can demonstrate opposites—not that it should as he attempts to make clear shortly later at *A* 1, 55b 10-24 since this is not its purpose. As can now be seen the general character of its subject-matter, the contingent and probable, rather readily lends itself to such action. To determine the character of rhetoric or anything else, however, from the misuse to which it is open is its own kind of sophistry as Socrates once remarked.

Refutative enthymeme is one kind of λύσις. The second type Aristotle calls *enstasis*. While a relatively coherent explanation of *enstasis* can be obtained from the *Rhetoric* it is not very satisfying and if we move out of the *Rhetoric* into the *Analytics*, the *Topics* and the *Sophistici Elenchi* where he also discusses the subject the picture becomes more confused. The cause of the problem is fairly simple: Aristotle has apparently given a perfectly valid double method of refutation: 1) a form of deduction in counter-syllogism (counter-enthymeme in rhetoric), and, 2) what can be called a form of induction in *enstasis*. When, however, we examine his statements on *enstasis* more closely the distinction disappears. Some refutation by *enstasis* appears to be syllogistic in character. In the *Rhetoric enstasis*, or objection as it may be called, is clearly denied a deductive character (*B* 25, 02a 31-32; *B* 26, 03a 31-32), and it appears to be what Aristotle had in mind by using the word itself: i.e. to block an opponent's way by denying one of his premises. We are told that it is not an enthymeme but rather a probable proposition which makes clear either that the opponent has made a false statement in one of the premises (ψεῦδός τι εἴληφεν), or that his reasoning is invalid (οὐ συλλελόγισται) (*B* 26, 03a 32-33). This explanation corresponds remarkably well with the definition of *enstasis* given in the *Analytics* at 69a 37: "an *enstasis* is a premise opposite to another premise". It also fits quite well the distinction between counter-enthymeme and objection that is assumed at *Γ* 17, 18b 5-22 and in the *Topics* 160a 39-b 13.

Turning from this to the four topics for *enstasis* which Aristotle names and illustrates (*B* 25, 02a 35-b13) one could still accept the propositional character of *enstasis* as an inductive instance against the statement in one of the premises or the conclusion of the demonstrative enthymeme—a process shown rather well at *Topics* 157a 34-157b 33. A more careful study, however, does cause problems. Despite the clear statement on *enstasis* in the *Analytics* passage just cited there is no question that Aristotle's explanation in what follows upon it is made in terms of his figures of the syllogism and clearly assumes that *enstasis* is syllogistic in character. "The kind of ἔνστασις dealt with in the present chapter [our passage, 69a 37 ff.] turns out to be a perfectly normal syllogism."[24] The propositional character of *enstasis* disappears and its distinctness from counter-syllogism is certainly clouded. This confusion is not removed by the passage in the *Topics* 160a 35-161a 15, in the *Sophistici Elenchi* 176b 29-177a 8, nor, in actual fact, in the *Rhetoric*. Superficially, as was said above, one could accept the *Rhetoric* passage as keeping the distinction between counter-syllogism and *enstasis* and COPE (Commentary, and Introduction) as well as SPENGEL (Commentary) so accept it. The fact is, however, that if we understand the first topical source (as it is usually interpreted) to mean "from the enthymematic statement itself", then one of the two examples which Aristotle gives of this kind of *enstasis* is in reality counter-enthymeme. Its value as refutation is otherwise not discernible. Aristotle says (*B* 25, 02a 37-b 4): "By the phrase 'from itself' I mean, for example, if the enthymeme should intend to demonstrate that love is good, *enstasis* can assume two forms: for one may assert as a general proposition that all privation (want) is evil, or, as a particular statement that Caunian love would not be used as a commonplace if there were not indeed evil loves". It is quite easy to understand how the specific instance of incestuous love seriously challenges the unqualified statement that "love is good". It does not appear, however, that there is any effective refutation to this statement in the counter-proposition "all privation is evil" unless this is developed as an enthymeme directed specifically against the enthymeme developed from "love is good". This kind of statement "all privation is evil", while it may convey meaning to members of the Academy and need no proof, is used as an example here of a kind of refutation, and it makes no sense as an isolated proposition in the example given. It does take on meaning as a stage in a counter-inference. In other words this kind of *enstasis* appears to be the kind of *enstasis* described in the *Analytics* (69a 37-b 37; Ross, Commentary, says that it "agrees exactly") which is in fact counter-syllogism.

Thus the distinction established between *enstasis* and counter-inference is undermined in this first topic for refutation by *enstasis*, just as it is in *Analytics* 69a 37-b 37. On the other hand it is interesting to note that the distinction is preserved in the other three topics. These three topics for *enstasis* refutation correlate exactly in name and order of presentation with the other types of *enstasis* at the end of the *Analytics* passage. There Aristotle only mentions the types in order to say that they should be given further consideration (69b 38-70a 2). He does not enter upon such a consideration but it is found in the *Rhetoric* for each of the topics. Topic I, on the other hand, is the kind of refutation which is discussed in the *Analytics* where we find that it is not only called *enstasis*, but in reality is a form of counter-syllogism.

There is, then, in Aristotle's account of refutation (λύσις), as in his account of fallacy from *semeion anonymon*, a degree of ambiguity and uncertainty. However, that which does emerge from his discussion of refutation is of more importance. This is the clear evidence that for Aristotle the methodology of deductive and inductive inference is the root of all rhetorical argumentation, even refutation. At the very beginning of his study Aristotle indicated that his study of rhetoric was grounded in the idea that the *logos* was a peculiar property of man and consequently something which merited study and structure (*A* 1, 55a 38-b 2). His structure was announced quite early when he stated that rhetoric could be submitted to method (*A* 1, 54a 4-8) and that the methodology would revolve about the *pisteis* (*A* 1, 54a 13). Eventually this methodology assumed its dominant form in the process of deduction and induction, with the deductive process of the enthymeme receiving the larger part of his attention. His analysis of rhetoric developed around this central core: enthymeme and example incorporate the *entechnic* method and enable one to give form to the sources in the effort to communicate knowledge and conviction. Everything proper to the art in the first two books pivots on this axis and when we arrive at the conclusion of the second book and the defense of the *logos* we discover that the deductive and inductive process is still at work.

Notes

[1]At *A* 9, 68a 29 ff. we learn that examples are best for deliberative rhetoric (restated at *B* 20, 94a 6 f. with the reason given: the future is like the past), enthymemes for judicial, since the past lends itself to demonstrative proof and to the examination of causes. This statement at *A* 9, 68a is repeated in substance at *Γ* 17, 18a 1-5. Aristotle does not stress this point and if one is tempted to push the distinction too far his comment at *Metaphysics* 995a 6-12 should be considered. SPENGEL observes (Commentary s. 1356b 21-2) that Demosthenes is enthymematic, Cicero paradeigmatic in character.

[2]See SPENGEL, Commentary at 1356b 10.

[3]See *An. Pr.* 68b 32-37, Alexander on *Top.* 105a 10 who has an intelligent observation on induction and syllogism in which he notes that the quality of induction is suasiveness (*pithanon*) but that of syllogism coercive in its demand for assent (*anagkaion*).

[4]See also *Top.* 164a 12-14; *Prob.* 18.3 and the commentary of SEPTALIUS to this last (In Aristotelis Problemata Commentaria, Lyons 1632): "et sicut inductio maiorem in se verisimilitudinem continet, et planior, faciliorque est. . .ita syllogismus maiorem probandi vim in se habet et ad contradicendum est efficacior". He then adds the comment that in the first book of the *Rhetoric* examples are to be used with the ordinary person but enthymemes with the learned. This is a distinction which Aristotle could not have made in the *Rhetoric* but it does underlie some of his thinking on the enthymeme and is one of the reasons why the shortened form of the enthymeme, while not of its essence, is still of primary importance. Aristotle was conscious of the greater demonstrative and suasive power of the enthymeme when compared with example.

[5]As is generally known there has been question of the meaning of "syllogism" in the *Topics*. It is used in a technical sense as understood above and also in a broad sense of "reasoning". The difference in usage has since MAIER's time (Syllogistik des Aristoteles II.2, p. 78) been one of the grounds for distinguishing between an earlier *Topics* (usually books 2-7.2) and a later *Topics* (1.7, 3-5, 8, 9). It is also acknowledged that the earlier *Topics* has small additions from the later *Topics*. There is some added testimony for this early-later format from other evidence gathered by GOHLKE and HUBY (see P. HUBY, 'The Date of Aristotle's *Topics* and its Treatment of the Theory Ideas', *CQ* N.S. 11-12, 1961-62, pp. 72-80 for further reference). BRUNSCHWIG in his recent edition of the *Topics* (Aristote Topiques I-IV, Paris, 1967) while

he does say that there is no relation between "syllogism" in the *Topics* and the *Prior Analytics* (p. xxx: "on en chercherait en vain, dans les Topiques, la structure charactéristique . . .") does admit (p. xxxi) its presence as understood here in the text. Yet he cannot accept (p. xxxi, note 1) any correlation between the two passages in the *Analytics* (24b) and *Topics* (100a). On the other hand A. MANSION (Symposium Aristotelicum, Paris 1961, pp. 66-67) has argued effectively that at 100a 25 ff., 164b 27-165a 2 syllogism is to be understood in its technical sense (". . .il est difficile de croire que le même raisonnement appelé *syllogismos* dans les *Topiques* y ait été conçu comme un raisonnement dont la forme spécifique n'avait pas encore aux yeux de son auteur celle d'un syllogisme véritable, du fait que, à ce moment, Aristote n'avait pas encore élaboré dans son esprit cette forme fondamentale du raisonnement désignée finalement par le terme: συλλογισμός). LE BLOND (Logique et méthode chez Aristote, Paris 1939) would also argue (p. 30) that in the later section of the *Topics* such as 100a 27 the word is used in its technical sense. Consequently owing to the lack of evidence for the date of the final revision of the *Topics* there is no problem in assuming that the constant cross-references to the *Topics* in our *Rhetoric* are to the revised edition particularly in view of the fact that throughout the *Rhetoric* "syllogism" is only understood in a technical sense.

[6]Thus a statement like COPE's on A 2, 56a 22 (Commentary I, p. 33) should be read with care: "συλλογίσασθαι improperly applied here, as ἀπόδειξις above, I 11.p. 19 to *rhetorical reasoning*". *An. Post.* 71b 23-5 again admits the possibility of syllogism without *apodeixis*.

[7]At A 2, 56a 27f. Aristotle's use of ὑποδύεται is another echo of Plato. At 464 c-d speaking of the way spurious arts insinuate themselves into the genuine arts which minister to the mind and body Plato charges rhetoric, a mere *eidolon* of *dikaiosyne*, with the attempt to usurp the place of *dikaiosyne* which (with *nomothetike*) constitutes the genuine art of πολιτική. Aristotle takes up the word and remarks that rhetoric "slips into the guise of πολιτική", as do those who lay claim to it, for two reasons: a) the close relation of rhetoric to "the science of ethics which may be rightly called politics", and, b) the misunderstanding [of this relationship] by the practitioners of the art, or their pretentiousness, or other human failings. Without pressing the matter further Aristotle's assertion in his opening lines (A 1, 54a 9-11) that rhetoric is an art since it submits to reason is in direct opposition to Plato's claim that rhetoric is no art since it does not submit to reason (465a).

[8]W. D. ROSS, Aristotle's Prior and Posterior Analytics, Oxford 1949, p. 484 speaks somewhat to the point: "The object of dialectic and rhetoric alike is to produce *conviction* . . . Many of their arguments are quite regular syllogistic ones, formally just like those used in demonstration. But many others are in forms that are likely to produce conviction, but can be logically justified only if they can be reduced to syllogistic form; . . . The distinction between dialectical and rhetorical arguments is logically unimportant. They are of the same logical type . . ."

[9]WAITZ, Aristotelis Organon, Leipzig 1844, commenting on *Posterior Analytics* 82b 35: "Unde fit ut λογικόν idem fere sit quod διαλεκτικόν . . . id quod non ad ipsam veritatem pertinet, sed ad disserendi artem qua sententiam sive veram sive falsam defendimus". When he comes to our passage in the *Rhetoric* he continues: "quamquam 1355a 13. . .quum λογικὸς συλλογισμός et hic et in iis quae proxime sequuntur opponatur rhetorico syllogismo (ἐνθυμήματι), veram demonstrationem significare videatur".

[10]Planudes, for example, *Rhetores Graeci*, ed. WALZ, Stuttgart 1832, vol. 5, pp. 403.10-404.2, makes a distinction between dialectical syllogism and enthymeme which he claims is that of Alexander. The gist of it is that the dialectical syllogism uses all three propositions while the enthymeme need not state all the premises or may omit the conclusion. Anonymus (*Commentaria in Aristotelem Graeca*, Berlin 1882-1909, vol. 21, p. 2.26-27; p. 130.22 ff.) understands the enthymeme to omit a premise. Alexander in his commentary on the *Topics* 100a25 (*Commentaria*, vol. 2 part 2, p. 9.13-21) speaks of the enthymeme as a shortened syllogism, as does Philoponus on *An. Post.* 71a 1 (*Commentaria*, vol. 13, p. 6.2-3). The same is true of

Minucianus (*Rhetores Graeci*, ed. SPENGEL, Teubner 1894, vol. 1, p. 343.4-11) who gives a definition accepted by VOLKMANN (Die Rhetorik², p. 192). See also W. KROLL in Das Epicheirema, Sb.d.Ak.d. Wissenschaften in Wien, 216 (1936-37), p. 2; H. MAIER, Die Syllogistik II.1, p. 476, COPE in his Commentary and An Introduction to Aristotle's Rhetoric (with the exception of his passing comment on p. 103 of An Introduction).

¹¹Thus the distinction of form is hardly as insignificant as Ross would make it: "purely superficial characteristic" (Aristotle's Prior and Posterior Analytics, p. 500) or MADDEN in "The Enthymeme", The Philosophical Review 51, 1952, pp. 375-376. Nor again is it as essential as MAIER (Die Syllogistik, p. 476), COPE (Commentary II, pp. 209-221-222) and others would consider it. As shall be seen later a study of the sources of the enthymeme (*eikota* and *semeia*), of its inferential forms (*koinoi topoi*) favors an abbreviated form. For example, *eikota* are general probabilities in which frequently the minor premise may be assumed; *semeia* permit either a major or minor premise to be omitted, e.g. *A* 2, 57a 19-21; and the *koinoi topoi* offer a form of inference which is usually a relation; if x then y, a form in which either a premise or a conclusion may be assumed depending upon the evidential immediacy of the topic used.

¹²In actual fact a study of the character of induction, or example, as it is presented in the *Rhetoric*, reveals a structure of inference analogous to that of the abbreviated syllogism. Even when we admit that inductive example is not quite the same as ordinary induction (*A* 2, 57b 26-30; *B* 20, 93a 26-27), yet if both kinds of induction are to work successfully a mental process similar to that met in the enthymeme in its abbreviated form is called for. Example makes its induction from particular to particular, or inference by resemblance. However in such inference the mind always assumes as its ground the general proposition which is being inferred about one particular by means of another particular. On "example" cf. *An. Pr.* 69a 13-16; Alexander on the *Topics* (*Commentaria*, vol. 2 pt. 2, pp. 85.28-87.14); Zeno in *Stoicorum Veterum Fragmenta* (ed. VON ARNIM) vol. I.83.

¹³The kind of reasoning called for in the *Topics* is concerned with detailed investigation. As E. WEIL says quite well (La place de la logique dans la pensée aristotélicienne, Rev. de Met. et Morale 56, 1951, p. 295); investigation by the method of the topics is to subject the terms of a proposition, of philosophical theses, or of a particular *scientia* to the demanding investigation of substance, genus, species, accident etc. Or as BRUNSCHWIG (Aristote, Topiques p. xxix) indicates: method in the *Topics* is "d'élaborer une argumentation tendant à établir la proposition contradictoire de celle que soutient le répondant". Without question this is usually closely articulated argumentation developed through a series of steps. We may correctly assume that when Aristotle revised the *Topics* and introduced to it the methodology of syllogistic reasoning he intended topical inquiry to use the syllogism where possible. Owing to the nature of topical inquiry this would necessitate a series of inferences developed one from another. This is an assumption but the grounds for it are strong: a) in the *Rhetoric* syllogism is used only in its technical sense, b) consequently when Aristotle speaks of a difference between rhetorical and dialectical syllogism there is certainly no reason to conclude that the difference resides in the meaning of "syllogism", c) particularly is this so when his statements suggest quite strongly that the difference lies in the length of the inferential process. In a well reasoned statement WEIL (La place de la logique. . .p. 286 note) argues that the *Analytics* never replaced the *Topics* as a methodology for Aristotle as the very fact of the revision of the *Topics* with the introduction of the syllogism would confirm. He further comments (p. 302) that the true dialectician proceeds to his examination of a problem according to the rules of the syllogistic methodology ("le vrai dialecticien est celui qui procède à l'examen selon les règles de la technique syllogistique").

¹⁴The word "analytics" causes concern to the commentators here. Yet the manuscript tradition is for the word and there is no conceivable reason at this particular place in the text for any copier or editor to insert such a word. In most cases where the word is cited the references are to

forms of reasoning or the formal logic of the *Prior Analytics*. When there is discussion, however, of the apodeictic modality of propositions the reference would be to the material logic of the *Posterior Analytics*. The discussion of *anagkaia* and *tekmeria* involves sources for propositions which are properly the subject of the *Posterior Analytics*. While commentators refer citations such as *A* 2, 57a 29 and *B* 25, 03a 12 to the *Prior Analytics* the matter is open to question. For there is no absolute way, when "analytics" is used, to know whether Aristotle meant the *Prior* or the *Posterior Analytics*. Usually when Aristotle wanted to make such a distinction he spoke of the *Prior* as "on the syllogism", "in the first" (cf. WAITZ, Organon, p. 336, Ross, Aristotle's Prior and Posterior Analytics, p. 1). Without entering into the question there is the same problem with citations of the word "dialectics". It is not possible to assert that these are references only to the *Topics*. There are clear cases where the *Prior Analytics* must be understood, e.g. *A* 1, 55a 9 (certainly the *Topics* does not study the syllogism and it has nothing to do with strictly demonstrative syllogisms at *A* 1, 55a 13); *A* 2, 56a 36 (where Dionysius Halicarnassus (*Ep. ad Amm. I.* 730 ff.) citing this passage of the *Rhetoric* almost verbatim reads "analytics" for the text reading "dialectics"; for the text and context "analytics" makes much more sense); *B* 22, 96b 25-26 (where the reference can be both to the *Prior Analytics* 66b 4 ff. and the *Sophistici Elenchi* 168b 27 ff.). In general it could be said that Aristotle's correlation of rhetoric with dialectic, analytics, and ethics is not at all discordant with the statement made by "good *logos*" in the *Phaedrus* at 260d: "and I will make a boast: without me the man who knows truth will not master the art of persuading".

[15]Isocrates in the *Antidosis* 256 speaks of rhetoric as the faculty "whereby we struggle with subjects open to dispute and examine matters which are unknown to us". Intelligent decision requires understanding first and the Aristotelian approach to rhetoric is that of a methodology to reach understanding. The challenge implicit in Aristotle's analysis of rhetoric is to the person, for the person must resolve through decision the inner tension generated by the problematic. Rhetorical discourse is simply the method to place before him the means for making the decision as intelligently as possible.

[16]Aristotle faced the same problem in the *Topics*. The technique of the sophist and the dialectician can no more be separated than that of the sophist (false rhetor) and the rhetorician: the technique in each instance is the same. Because of the introduction of eristic into legitimate dialectics in the *Topics* scholars have drawn the same conclusion that they have made with regard to the *Rhetoric*, i.e. that both methodologies are studies in sophistical argumentation. This reveals a failure to comprehend the character of both disciplines as *technai* and to understand that both the true dialectician and rhetorician, from Aristotle's statements, want (a) as their starting point, propositions truly held by men, and, (b) as their goal, the acquisition of truth in a given problem. Neither methodology is a game. The *Topics* offer a method to move discursively toward the true, *Rhetoric* a method for the effective communication of the true as it can be apprehended.

[17]In the light of *A* 2, 56a 34-b 2 the parallelism spoken of would seem well founded.

[18]The numbering is that of ROEMER's text. In view of all that has been said it is difficult to understand how MAIER's statement (Die Syllogistik II.2, p. 493, also note 1) that the *rhetor* may legitimately use the apparent enthymeme can be right.

[19]In this respect the topics for the apparent enthymeme are quite similar to the particular and general topics for the valid enthymeme; we discover that they offer sources for the content of the premises or for the form of syllogistic inference.

[20]WAITZ (Organon), sees the distinction and expresses it this way: "Vitia quae in redarguendo admittuntur aut in dictione sunt. . .aut non in dictione . . . Alterum vitium positum est in prava verborum interpretatione (Wortverdrehung), alterum in falsa argumentatione (Schlußfehler)." The difficulty with this interpretation, however, is that it seems rather clear that what he calls *in dictione* fallacy is really the fallacy that attacks valid form (Schlußfehler), while his *non in dictione* fallacy is one that attacks the character of the statement in the premises.

[21]In a passage at *Sophistici Elenchi* 167b 8-11 Aristotle states that in rhetoric signs involve the fallacy of consequent. WAITZ (Organon), in a note s. 167b 8, appears to accept this and to see the opposition in b 8-13 between rhetoric (which seeks verisimilitude) and analytics (which seeks truth). One cannot conclude from Aristotle's statement here that reasoning from sign is *in se* fallacious. To conclude correctly to the probable (even to verisimilitude), as rhetoric frequently does, is not the same as concluding to what is false.

[22]In this respect it is noted again that Aristotle's critique in all passages assumes that the enthymeme is like the syllogism in structure, i.e. two premises and a conclusion. W. HAMIL-TON (Lectures on Metaphysics and Logic, Boston 1867) is still to the point (p. 276): "I shall therefore. . .show that. . .the restriction of the enthymeme to a syllogism of one suppressed premise cannot be competently maintained". He goes on to argue (pp. 276-281) correctly that neither the *Organon* nor the *Rhetoric* gives any textual support for this common understanding of the enthymeme.

[23]COPE (Commentary II p. 332) experiences some difficulty in reconciling *B* 22, 96b 23-28 with our passage at *B* 25, 02a 31 ff. However, εἴδη δύο at *B* 22, 96b 24 means no more than "kind" in a very broad use of the word such as we find it at *B* 20, 93a 28, *B* 20, 94a 18 when used of example and *B* 21 94b 26 of maxim. Indeed our statement here at *B* 25, 02a 32-33 is most probably repeated at *B* 26, 03a 30 where αὐτοῖς contrary to the common interpretation of "arguments", "instruments" more likely stands for "the same topics". For in actual fact *topoi* is the subject around which the various problems posed in this c. 26 are resolved. The clause (*B* 26, 03a 30) should probably be translated: "for both (deictic and elenchic) enthymemes use the same topics".

[24]Ross, Aristotle's Prior and Posterior Analytics, p. 495; on pp. 491-494 he explains the difficulty well. E. POSTE, Aristotle on Fallacies, London 1866, pp. 144-147, 192-202 is also to the point.

IV

THE SOURCES OF RHETORICAL ARGUMENTATION
BY ENTHYMEME

Once the general form of the enthymeme as the syllogism of rhetoric is determined the next question which arises is the kind of subject-matter which is used by the rhetorical syllogisms in the development of an argument. For the quality, or the modality, of the subject-matter used in the premises will control the kind of knowledge attained in the conclusion. Aristotle states that the sources for argument by enthymeme are the *eikota* (probabilities) and *semeia (A* 2, 57a 32-3) and then proceeds to specify *semeia* into non-necessary signs (*semeia anonyma*) and necessary signs (*tekmeria*) (*A* 2, 57b 3-5). Somewhat later (*B* 25, 02b 13-25) he appears to introduce another source: example. In as far as this appears to be in direct opposition to his statement that the two instruments of rhetorical demonstration are enthymeme for deduction and example for induction this remark at *B* 25 should be clarified before we move on to a discussion of the *eikota* and *semeia*. A substantial question is raised by this statement of Aristotle at *B* 25, 02b 13-14: does *paradeigma* disappear as an independent and coordinate method of rhetorical demonstration; if not, what is the possible meaning of Aristotle's statement? Ross in his commentary on the *Prior and Posterior Analytics* (pp. 499-500) offers a solution which is not adequate to the statements in the *Rhetoric*.[1]

In reply, then, to the question posed: *paradeigma* does not cease to be a coordinate instrument with enthymeme for rhetorical demonstration; it remains one of the two *koinai pisteis*. The point whtch Aristotle is making is a rather simple one.[2] Example may be a source of enthymeme insofar as example (or examples, *B* 25, 02b 17) can give you a probable universal principle or truth from which you may then reason by the use of enthymeme to a particular conclusion. Example gives the universal by that "flash of insight by which we pass from knowledge of a particular fact to direct knowledge of the corresponding principle.[3]" It is an operation of the mind in which the mind transcends sense experience, even one instance of it, and perceives the universal inherent in the terms and their necessary connection. In actual fact a moment's reflection will show that in using an example some transition to the universal has already been made by the mind if the mind is to discern any likeness or relevance of the example in the first place. Thus in our passage example is nothing but the ground for educing a general proposition or principle. This proposition is then employed independently as a premise in the enthymeme. As a source of enthymeme example is no more a "part of" enthymeme than induction is a "part of" syllogism in such a statement as *An. Post.* 81a 40-b9:[4] "demonstration is from universals, induction from particulars; but it is impossible to perceive universals without induction."

Returning, then, to the sources originally given by Aristotle, the *eikota* and *semeia*, the first task is to discover what difference, if any, exists between them. From the *Rhetoric* there is no doubt that in Aristotle's mind there is a difference in both concepts. And he expresses this with a brief and pointed comment in *An. Pr.* 70a 2-3: "*eikos* and *semeion* are not the same thing." The precise nature of the difference is not perhaps as sharp as one could wish, yet it is not as elusive as HAVET makes it: "Tout le second chapitre du premier livre est très-pénible à déchiffrer. Le distinction de l'εἴκος, du σημεῖον, du τεκμήριον, n' est pas plus nette que celle du syllogisme et de l' enthymème. Je ne pourrais le faire bien voir qu' en le traduisant; mais à quoi bon traduire des choses aussi peu satisfaisantes.[5]" Those who attempt a distinction between the two sources develop their distinction on the kind of knowledge obtained when these sources are used in the rhetorical syllogism. Thus for some[6] an enthymeme built upon *eikota* will give what is called the "ratio essendi" of the fact stated in the conclusion, that is to say the explanation why this conclusion actually is. The premises, in other words contain the reasons for the fact stated in the conclusion. A *semeion*-enthymeme, on the other hand, presents the "ratio cognoscendi" of the fact stated in the conclusion, namely, the grounds on which one can acknowledge that the conclusion exists without, however, being able to explain the reason why the conclusion as stated is valid. One could question the distinction on the ground that an *eikos*-enthymeme might very well give the "ratio cognoscendi" of the fact for there does not appear to be anything intrinsic to the logic of the *eikos*-enthymeme which would justify the absoluteness of the distinction. But the most immediate difficulty with this explanation is that one would wish to know what difference exists between non-necessary *semeion*-enthymemes and necessary *semeion*-enthymemes. Ross in his commentary on the *Prior Analytics*[7] gives his attention to all three sources and distinguishes them in this way: 1) enthymemes from non-necessary signs are syllogistically invalid, 2) those from *eikota* argue merely from probability, 3) enthymemes from necessary *semeia* are syllogistically valid but may not give "the reason for the fact stated in the conclusion but only a symptom from which it can be inferred." There are difficulties with this proposal. The statement about non-necessary sign enthymemes is open to question as we have already seen in the discussion of the apparent enthymeme. Moreover from the nature of non-necessary signs valid syllogistic inference from them is clearly as much an inference from probability as inference from *eikota*. As far as necessary signs are concerned one cannot dispute the statement that they will only permit an inference that is absolutely secure on the fact reached in the conclusion, but not the reasoned fact. If Aristotle, however, does differentiate between these three sources for rhetorical reasoning he must see some distinction in the kind of argumentation they allow. Further study of *eikos, semeion anonymon* and *tekmerion* leads one to conclude that the difference resides in the certitude with which one can affirm one's conclusions from each source. As a general guide it can be said that enthymemes developed from *eikota* and *semeia anonyma* represent the kind of reasoning which can be found in Aristotelian dialectics, while those from *tekmeria* present more the character of scientific reasoning as found in his *Analytics*. Once again we have the rhetorical *pragmateia* bringing together the field of probable and certain knowledge. From all that has been said thus far this should not be unexpected.[8]

In the *Rhetoric* (A 2, 57a 34-b 1) Aristotle defines *eikos* in this way: "that which generally happens, not 'generally' in any unlimited sense of the word; rather its extension includes all reality which can be other than it is, and in this area its relationship to that reality to which it is an *eikos* is like that of any universal to a particular." Expressed more directly we have this: with reference to any reality that has a number of possibilities an *eikos* is that possibility which usually happens. An example of such an *eikos* would be the statement that "parents love their children".

There are one or two things to be noted here. *Eikos* is not that which simply happens. In this sense it would apply without any qualification to sheer chance among other things, or to anything possible, for example to that aspect of the possible spoken of in *An. Pr.* 32b 10-11: the indeterminate.[9] Such an understanding of *eikos* leads to the absurdity criticized in *B* 24, 02a 8-16: the improbable is probable, because many improbable things happen. If the enthymeme as a syllogism is reasoned inference then its sources must be reasonable and rational. *Eikos* in the sense of the "indeterminate" is neither; and, if anything, it would be a source for sophistic reasoning as is indicated at *B* 24, 02a 16 ff. In the *Rhetoric eikos*, or the probable, possesses a note of stability and permanence. This stability is described well when Aristotle makes *eikos* a kind of universal with respect to individual probabilities (*A* 2, 57b 1). While this stability is not inherently necessary yet it is not subjective and extrinsic. It is intrinsic and objective since it is grounded in reality. This relative intrinsic necessity is aptly described in the *Nicomachean Ethics* 1112a 18-b 11. There Aristotle speaking of deliberation (which is, of course, the occasion of rhetorical discourse, e. g. *A* 2, 56b 37 ff.) tells us that deliberation involves things which follow certain general rules, things calculable with probability. Further at *Metaphysics* 1027a 20-21 he states that with respect to such a stabilized contingent (τὸ ὡς ἐπί τὸ πολύ) there can be knowledge: e.g. all *episteme* is of that which is always (τοῦ ἀεί) or of that which is for the most part (τοῦ ὡς ἐπὶ τὸ πολύ). In the *Prior Analytics* (32b 20 ff.) this is carried further and we learn that this kind of stable contingent can be used in a demonstrative syllogism.

In the *Rhetoric*, then, there is a clear emphasis placed upon *eikos* as something which is permanent and stable. The reason for the emphasis becomes manifest when one considers other Aristotelian statements such as those mentioned above: namely, that *eikos* offers ground for reasonable inference and can be known (cf. *EN* and *Met.* passages above). As such it can lead to further knowledge, and thus the rhetorical enthymeme which uses *eikos* as a source is a way to a knowledge which is both reasonable and wholly acceptable to the mind. In Aristotle that which is ὡς ἐπὶ τὸ πολύ leads one to seek both the universal and the cause which are the ultimate foundation of *episteme*. *Eikos* represents the kind of reality mentioned by Aristotle when speaking of the different kinds of knowledge in the *Posterior Analytics*. There are, we are told, things in the order of reality which "are true, and yet capable of being other than they are" (88b 32-33). These are the object of *doxa*, one of the states of mind which can know the true. *Doxa* can know the real and the true, not with scientific knowledge since it originates with that which is contingent, but nonetheless with knowledge since it is concerned with that which is and which possesses a certain stability.[10] The possibility of such knowledge is readily accepted in the *Prior Analytics* (70a 4 ff.): "that which men *know* (ἴσασιν) happens or does not happen, is, or is not, for the most part in this way,—that is an *eikos*." Aristotle illustrates this with an example of such an *eikos*: our knowledge that those who are resentful hate.

Since knowledge is possible with regard to this *eikos* we obtain through it the means whereby we may move to other knowledge in the same order. That is to say that we can have in *eikos* the basis of suasive and probable demonstration. As he says (*An. Post.* 87b 22 ff.): "every syllogism works through propositions which are either necessary, or, for the most part true; if necessary, the conclusion is necessary; if for the most part true, such, then, is the conclusion." The enthymeme represents the latter kind of syllogism. As a matter of fact it is precisely in its use in such a demonstrative process that the analysis of *eikos* is carried further in the *Rhetoric*. In *B* 25, 02b 21 ff. we are told that because of the non-necessity of *eikos*-enthymemes they are always open to objection, since the very nature of *eikos* occasions this. However, the only kind of objection which invalidates such argumentation is not an objection which shows the conclusion as *not-necessary*, but one which proves that it is *not probable*.

With the nature of *eikos* thus determined by Aristotle it appears that we have a rational basis for the whole domain of probable argumentation such as we possess it in rhetoric. For in *eikos* whose content expresses that which is generally (but not necessarily) the truth one possesses grounds for reasoned inference from any particular *eikos* to what is quite probably (but not necessarily) the fact in any given situation. In *eikos* we have, or may formulate, a *protasis endoxos*, as *eikos* is called in the *Prior Analytics* at 70a 3. Such premises are then used in the rhetorical syllogism. *Eikos* expresses a reasonable and stable aspect of the real order and as a source for the rhetorical syllogism we find that the rhetorical *pragmateia* is built upon sound, though probable, reasoning and that *pistis* is underpinned by the real order.

In his analysis of *eikos* Aristotle validates probable truth and reasoning from probable sources: there is another way to apprehend that which is. It is not the way of first philosophy which works through absolute, unconditioned, and necessary principles to certain knowledge and certain truth. This second way works through premises (*eikota*) which may be false. But insofar as these premises express that which is generally true it is legitimate to conclude to the probability that, all being equal, such and such is the fact in this concrete instance. An inference from *eikos* does not conclude to an unconditioned truth; but it does present an eminently reasonable guaranty that the conclusion represents the objective fact.

There appears to be an important point here. This Aristotelian explanation of *eikos* seems to move against such Platonic criticism as would reject the validity of rhetoric on the grounds that the only knowledge is knowledge of the absolute and the unconditioned (e. g. *Rep.* 510e-511d). Any knowledge derived from the world of sense data was neither knowledge nor a knowledge of the real. For Plato sense data can be incentives to knowledge. Aristotle accepts the world of sense experience as the world of the real. Indeed he specifies *eikos*, as we have seen, by this reality and in this he is opposed to Plato. For Aristotle the fact that something generally happens this way, or is this way, is genuine ground for the mind to think that such is the actual fact. In brief there is a foundation in the world of reality (v. *Rhetoric B* 25, 02b 15: ἢ ὄντων ἢ δοκούντων) which validates the mind thinking and knowing as it does. Plato specifies *eikos* differently. It appears to be more subjective than objective as we find it in the *Phaedrus* 272c; 259e; 260. *Eikos* is that which the generality of men think, or may think, and as such it carries persuasive force to the mind.[11] Aristotle's *eikos* and the knowledge which comes from it is rooted in the real order and it is this existential aspect of it which makes it a legitimate source for further knowledge. This character of *eikos* is further underlined by Aristotle when he indicates the kind of *eikota* to be used in rhetorical discourse: they will be determined by the *eide*, i.e. the special topics of the subject under discussion (*B* 1, 77b 18 ff.) and they will be *eikota* which are precisely determined and clearly accepted by men (*B* 22, 95b 31 ff.). Both qualifications simply re-state the fact that the *eikos* is so substantially and obviously grounded in the real order that the majority of men accept it as a totally acceptable representation of the truth.

The second source for argumentation by enthymeme is Aristotle's *semeion*, sign. What can be discovered about it does bear out Aristotle's comment in the *Analytics* that *eikos* and *semeion* are not the same. Indeed without turning to the *Analytics* there seems to be no question about a difference in the first mention of *eikos* and *semeion* in the *Rhetoric* at *A* 2, 57a 30-33, specifically the phrase at 57a 33: "consequently each of these (*eikos* and *semeion*) corresponds exactly to each of the aforementioned [i.e. contingent reality and necessary reality]." In this phrase *eikos* is obviously referred to in: τὰ δὲ πλεῖστα ὡς ἐπὶ τὸ πολύ (31-2) and *semeion* in: τὰ μὲν ἀναγκαῖα (31). The nature of this difference becomes clearer with a study of the statements on *semeion* in the *Rhetoric* and the *Analytics*. In the *Rhetoric* there is a description and a division of *semeion* but the *Prior Analytics* (70a 7-9) offers a descriptive definition of the term: "Whenever by the fact that one thing exists something else exists, or by the fact of its coming-to-be something else has come-to-be prior to it or consequent upon it, the first is a sign of the other's becoming or existing." What we have here is a very definite and firm relationship between two realities in the order of existence which leads from the knowledge of one to a knowledge of the other. From what Aristotle says sign is a relationship between two realities which has its foundation in the nature of these realities and exists objectively as soon as one of the realities exists.[12] The relationship between sign and signate leads the mind from the known to the unknown because of this one to one correspondence. Aristotle's signs in the *Rhetoric* and elsewhere are usually natural signs, entities which involve in their being the being of something else. There is a real relation which has its ground in the *esse* of the sign. It is the relationship of formal causality: present in the sign is the knowability of the signate, or we can say that the signate is in the sign in another mode of existence (*in alio esse*).

Owing to this relationship *semeion* for Aristotle possesses a stronger demonstrative force than *eikos*. This can be seen clearly in his discussion of *semeion* in the *Prior Analytics* 70a 11-b 6 by means of the three syllogistic figures; for the figures of the syllogism (prescinding from their effective probative power which is not the point here) by the very way in which Aristotle has constructed them implicate an internal necessity, *an intrinsic relationship,* between premises and conclusion. Further in his introduction to this passage he remarks that the whole thrust of *semeion* is to be a demonstrative premise, that is, a proposition which leads to more than a probable conclusion: σημεῖον δὲ βούλεται εἶναι πρότασις ἀποδεικτική (70a 6-7). It does not completely achieve this goal in every instance because of the fact that there are different kinds of sign. This difference is specified in the *Analytics* passage by the qualifying phrase: ἢ ἀναγκαία ἢ ἔνδοξος which corresponds to the distinction in the *Rhetoric A* 2, 57b 3-5 between the necessary *semeion* called τεκμήριον and the non-necessary *semeion* called σημεῖον ἀνώνυμον. The *tekmerion* contains within itself an element of necessity in relation to the signate (the πρότασις ἀποδεικτικὴ ἀναγκαία of the *Analytics* passage), whereas the *semeion anonymon* indicates the signate only with probability (πρότασις ἀποδεικτικὴ ἔνδοξος). Thus it is that we find the *Analytics* passage differentiating between the probative force of each sign by way of the middle term in each of the first three figures of the syllogism.[13] The point of the presentation in the *Analytics* would seem to be that *semeion* by its very nature, as opposed to the nature of *eikos*, has within itself a strong demonstrative power. Sign argues almost immediately and directly to signate. Whether or not this potency to demonstrate the signate will be realized is determined by the fact that not all *semeion* is the same. *Tekmerion* and sign *enthymeme* built upon it is apodeictic in the more strict sense of the word with respect to its signate. Such an *enthymeme* infers a necessary conclusion and cannot be refuted even though the conclusion states only the fact and not the reasoned fact (the reasoned fact is the conclusion of the fully apodeictic syllogism in Aristotle, *An. Post.* 75a 31-34). *Semeion anonymon*, on the other hand, and any sign *enthymeme* constructed on it can only give a probable conclusion with respect to its signate, that is, a very strong likelihood grounded in the experience of reality.

In either case, however, it is clear that in fact and in concept the *semeion* is something other than *eikos*. Because of the inner structure of the *semeion* it leads of and by itself to the probable or necessary truth of the thing signified, and so possesses a peculiar force for the demonstration of this signate. Anaximenes[14] presents us with a fairly clear notion of what Aristotle appears to have intended by *semeion:* "A sign is one thing of something else, not any one thing of any other thing, nor everything of everything [else]. Rather a sign is that which usually comes to be prior to, or simultaneously with, or subsequent to the thing [of which it is a sign]. That which has come to be is a sign not only of that which has come to be but also of that which has not, just as that which has not come to be is a sign not only of that which is not but also of that which is. One class of signs effects belief, the other effects knowledge; the best sign, however, is that which causes knowledge."

When we turn to the two kinds of *semeion* there is a noticeable difference in the kind of knowledge they lead to. The non-necessary *semeion* carries with it a general but non-constant relationship between itself and its signate. In an effort to demonstrate this relationship in the *Analytics* (70a 3 ff.) by identifying the non-necessary sign with the middle term in the second and third figure syllogism Aristotle is able to develop both the idea of relation and the idea of non-necessary relation. He does this specifically by using non-necessary sign in the second and third figure syllogism in a way whereby the correct form is violated with the result that the conclusion is invalid and refutable, e. g. *Rhet. A* 2, 57b 10-14 (for third figure); b18-21 (for second figure); see also *B* 24, 01b 9-15, *B* 25, 03a 2-5, *An. Pr.* 70a 16-24, 30-37.

Obviously the *semeion anonymon* is not strictly apodeictic and will only give a probable conclusion which is a probable truth. This is also true of *eikos*. The difference should be somewhat clear by now. The *semeion* (whether necessary or not) as used by Aristotle is radicated in the nature of the subject in such a way that it establishes a *relationship* of the subject to something else. *Eikos* is a general probability, again grounded in reality as man experiences and knows it; but the *eikos* exists in and by itself *without any formal relation* to an other. If one were to stress the similarity of *semeion anonymon* and *eikos* as sources of probable argumentation this might be said: the *semeion anonymon* could provide the basis for a general probable proposition (an *eikos*), as can be seen at *B* 6, 84a 5-7: 'those who continually speak of their accomplishments are boastful'. Indeed at *B* 19, 92b 25 f. Aristotle apparently makes a *semeion anonymon* into an *eikos*. This kind of proposition based on a *semeion anonymon* reminds one of Anaximenes' type of sign which creates the most persuasive opinion (τὸ δόξαν πιθανωτάτην ἐργαζόμενον). By and large one could agree that "where the general principle implied is not irrefragable [i. e. a *semeion anonymon* is used] but true for the most part, it is hard to distinguish the συλλογισμὸς ἐκ σημείου from a συλλογισμὸς ἐξ εἰκότος" (H. JOSEPH, An Introduction to Logic, Oxford 1916, p. 350, n. 1). If one compares *B* 25, 02b 15-31, a statement on the character of argument from *semeion* and *eikos* with *A* 5, 61a 28 (the expression here is used a number of times in *A* 4-14, e. g. *A* 9, 66b 23-24, *A* 9,67b 26-35) one can see that τιμή at 61a 28 can be used as a *semeion anonymon* argument to demonstrate "one who does good", or changed into an *eikos*: "those who do good are held in honor".

The necessary sign, or *tekmerion*, is of interest because of the dimension it gives to the subject-matter of rhetorical discourse, restricted as this subject-matter usually is to the field of probability. The necessary sign indicates a constant and unchanging relationship between sign and signate such that evidence for the sign guarantees the fact of the signate. This *tekmerion* implies unchanging entities in the sense in which Aristotle speaks of *anagkaion* in *Metaphysics* 1026b 27-30, a statement which expresses the contrast set forth in the *Rhetoric* at *A* 2, 57a 30-b 10. This *tekmerion-anagkaion* relationship is underlined further by the identification of the *tekmerion* with the middle term of the first figure syllogism; this figure is the usual locus of the strictly scientific syllogism which uses necessary subject-matter and concludes to *episteme*.[15] As Aristotle says in the *Analytics* (70b 2 f.): τὸ γὰρ τεκμήριον τὸ εἰδέναι ποιοῦν φασιν εἶναι, which recalls Anaximenes' comment on sign: κάλλιστον δὲ τὸ εἰδέναι ποιοῦν. The *Analytics* passage is picked up at *Rhetoric A* 2, 57b 8 where we are told that with a *tekmerion* men assume that their conclusion is δεδειγμένον καὶ πεπαρασμένον which Anonymus explains by the words τετελειωμένον διὰ προτάσεων ἀκριβῶν καὶ ἀληθῶν, a rather accepted expression for scientific demonstration.

Tekmerion, then, introduces into the field of rhetorical discourse subject matter which falls not under the probable but the certain and unconditioned. There should be no difficulty with this fact if rhetoric is understood as the art of the *logos*, of human discourse on human problems. If one is to discuss any problem rationally and reasonably—and from Aristotle's comments throughout the *Rhetoric* he expects this—there will be need to employ on occasion the special principles of that subject which in themselves are generally of an absolute and unchanging character. To speak intelligently on a problem which involves, for example, the nature of government, or law, or justice demands of necessity the introduction of certain *anagkaia*. There is no justification in the *Rhetoric* to force the discipline into a kind of case study as THROM seems to do (Die Thesis, Paderborn 1932, p. 12 ff.), or to decide that rhetorical argument is "persuasive rather than demonstrative" (G. LLOYD, *Polarity and Analogy*, Cambridge 1966, p. 406). There is no reason whatsoever that in the effort to achieve *pistis* with respect to the probability or improbability of an issue one may not entertain certain and necessary truth in the move toward the final objective. When Socrates, for example, in the *Phaedrus* desires to achieve the conviction (*pistis*) among his audience that the soul is immortal he argues among other things from knowledge that Plato would accept as certain and necessary truth: the theory of forms.

In noting the relationship between *tekmerion* and *anagkaion*, the *anagkaion* which for Aristotle leads to *episteme*, there is no intention of identifying *tekmerion* (πρότασις ἀποδεικτικὴ ἀναγκαία) with the πρότασις ἀποδεικτική of the

Prior Analytics 24a 22 ff. whose function is more fully described in the *Posterior Analytics* 71b 9 ff. as the instrument of strict scientific apodeixis: a demonstration of both the fact and the reasoned fact. None of the statements in our analysis here would lead to that conclusion. On the other hand *tekmerion* by reason of its necessary relation to its signate does possess the qualities requisite to give certain knowledge at least of the fact of the existence of the other. Thus is it ordinarily used by Aristotle and thus it is analyzed here. The *tekmerion* is capable of demonstrating with certainty the *fact* in the conclusion (*ratio cognoscendi*), not with certainty the *reasoned fact (ratio essendi)*. From Aristotle's examples of *tekmerion* and his statements about *tekmerion* this is surely his intention.

In presenting to us the sources for reasoning by enthymeme Aristotle appears to have remained consistent to his analysis of the rhetorical *pragmateia* as something larger and more significant than the mere art of persuasion. For *eikos* and *semeion anonymon* representing contingent and probable reality possess the formality of the kind of inference we find in his *Dialectics*. The *tekmerion* as necessary and unconditioned possesses in part the character of scientific reasoning as it is met in the *Analytics*.

The Topics

When Aristotle has presented us with the sources of the enthymeme, *eikota* and *semeia*, and told us that they are the premises of enthymematic reasoning (*A* 3, 59a 7-10) the question which immediately arises is where does the rhetor turn for the material which will provide him with such *eikota* and *semeia*. The answer is: the topics. Aristotle states clearly at *A* 2, 58a 10-35, and later at *Γ* 1, 03b 13-14 that the topics supply the material of enthymemes. If we inquire what Aristotle meant by the topics in the *Rhetoric* the answer is not as readily obvious. By way of a general and fairly safe answer we can say that the topics are sources, or *loci*, both particular and general, to which one must have recourse in constructing probable argumentation by enthymeme in an effort to effect *pistis*. The more, however, that one attempts to understand the meaning of these particular and general topics the more substantial are the difficulties met in the actual statements made by Aristotle in the text of the *Rhetoric*. And yet the effort to specify and discover the meaning of his comments opens the way to a reasonable understanding of the topics and the nature of the methodology of the Aristotelian topics. Certainly it is true that his observations on the *topoi* in the *Rhetoric* assume a coherent and consistent character. And the methodology outlined in the *Rhetoric* for the enthymeme seems quite capable of a legitimate extension to the methodology offered in the *Topics*.

By way of introduction it can be said that while the influence of the Aristotelian *topoi* has been extensive in our western tradition, particularly in literature, it does seem that their methodology has not been fully understood. A number of factors have contributed to this: the absence in Aristotle of a forthright and formal discussion of what he has in mind,[16] the neglect of the methodology after Aristotle,[17] a partially misdirected emphasis given to the method by Cicero, one of the first to concern himself with the topics,[18] and the continuation of the Ciceronian interpretation by Quintilian with whom it passed into the Middle Ages and the stream of our western tradition.

The rather truncated form in which the topics have come to us has been rather unfortunate since there has been lost along the way the far richer method of discourse on the human problem which they provide. Seen as mere static, stock 'commonplaces,' stylized sources for discussion on all kinds of subject-matter they have lost the vital, dynamic character given to them by Aristotle, a character extremely fruitful for intelligent, mature discussion of the innumerable significant problems which face man. Indeed their genesis within an intellectual environment which included among other things discussions on φύσις and νόμος and related problems of the First Sophistic, on the nature of justice, goodness, virtue, reality, etc., of the Platonic dialogues, on education and political science of Isocrates' discourses, seems to give a clue to their nature.

In his understanding of τόπος, it would seem that Aristotle was attempting to validate a mode of intelligent discussion in the area of probable knowledge comparable (but not equal) to that enjoyed in the area of scientific knowledge (i. e. the certain knowledge of metaphysics) and, even more than that, to enlarge where possible the subject of scientific knowledge. And in this last sense the topical method would not only be a propaideutic for *scientia*[19] but also an assistant discipline.

Even though this idea of the *topoi* as a formal discipline and an integrated methodology concerned with both the form and the content of discussion in the field of probable knowledge was lost shortly after Aristotle, as it would seem, it is interesting to note that in one form or another the *topoi* have influenced our western tradition. Understood in a rather static sense as 'rhetorical invention' they have enjoyed a dominant, and one would have to say a frequently creative, role in the literature of the West. CURTIUS gives abundant evidence for this but he has missed, it appears, the vitality of their contribution. This quality was seen by R. TUVE in her study of one phase of English poetry.[20] She notes with insight that it was in the area of the topics that the faculty of the imagination was thought to be most active: "Thinking of the adjuncts of something has provided the pattern for innumerable short poems, and for innumerable longish images within poems . . ." And there is surely no need to comment upon the importance of the imaginative faculty or the pervasive presence of metaphor and image in all significant poetry. Vico had an idea similar to Miss TUVE's in mind when he wrote *De nostri temporis studiorum ratione*, but he was more concerned with the possible exclusion of the whole area of probable knowledge. Apparently he feared that the rejection of the topical method would encourage that attitude of mind which does not examine all the possible aspects of a problem. In our own day this neglect of 'problem thinking' (as opposed to 'system thinking') could well limit the quest for truth. No subject is fully exhausted until intelligent queries can no longer be raised. The critical examination of subject-matter was one phase of the topical method. Another aspect of the method as Aristotle worked it out was the inferential phase, i.e. how one may legitimately advance by deductive reasoning the material gathered by the *topoi*. And here we have the *topoi* as sources of inference. Relatively little has been done with these latter topics, but R. WEAVER[21] has developed from them a way of analysis whose application to prose literature could bring to light the currents of thought influential in various periods of our western tradition. In the course of a discerning study of the topical argumentation of Burke and Lincoln he remarks: "the reasoner reveals his philosophical position by the source of argument which appears most often in his major premise because the major premise tells us how he is thinking about the world".[22]

Aristotle in his topical methodology combined both of the elements just mentioned. His dominant concern in the topical method appears to be that of problem thinking, but thinking informed by intelligent procedure. It does seem that in the whole area of the problematic, the probable, and the contingent, it is his desire to enable one, as far as this is possible, to reason as intelligently, as accurately, and as precisely as one can do in the areas of certain, scientific knowledge. Such reasoning becomes possible when one is in a position to examine the material of the problem with precision in order to determine it with all the accuracy permissible. After this one must be able to develop and enlarge this material by discursive reasoning to further conclusions. The kind of formal reasoning used, since one is engaged with the contingent and the probable, will generally be that which relies upon forms and principles of discursive reasoning which are usually considered to be, and are accepted as self-evident principles. The topics in the language of the *Rhetoric* and the explanation given there are the method devised to supply both the content for the critical examination of the subject and general inferential statements which would present legitimate forms for deductive reasoning. For the moment and on the basis of what is found in the text let us call the first the "particular topics", or the various aspects under which a given subject may be studied in order to arrive at a clearer understanding of it. The second type of topic can be called "general topics", or forms of inference in which to develop this understanding to further conclusions.

In the *Rhetoric* Aristotle uses the topical methodology both as a logic of invention and as a logic of inference. He presents us with a method which is more properly dynamic (cf. *Top.* 100a) rather than static. In the second sense we have a mere listing of likely materials readily usable in discussion, or, as the *topoi* have been called, "opinion surveys".[23] For Aristotle the *topoi* are the methodology of Dialectics, the area of probable knowledge, just as in the *Analytics* we are given a methodology for the area of certain knowledge, *scientia*.

In view of the fact that any methodology concerned with language must occupy itself with the form and content of statements (propositions, to use Aristotle's word),[24] it is possible to see where misinterpretation has arisen. Many commentators, from Cicero on,[25] have fastened upon the content (the particular topics) and then reduced the topics to the mere mechanics of invention, i.e. ways and means of developing and enlarging upon a theme. In more recent studies,[26] though not exclusively, the formal element has been stressed. While this captures the axiomatic character of the general topics, it neglects entirely the non-axiomatic, non-propositional character of the particular topics as they are found in the *Topics* and the *Rhetoric*.

In other words, the τόποι, which are the sources for intelligent discussion and reasoning in dialectic and rhetoric (*A* 2, 58a 10-35; *B* 1, 77b 16-24), are concerned with both the material and formal element in such discussion. As sources for the content of discussion (the ordinary meaning of *loci communes*: persons, places, things, properties, accidents, etc., the περιστάσεις or aspects of the subject pertinent to discussion) they ultimately provide the material by means of which general or particular propositions are enunciated. As sources for the forms of reasoning in discussion (*A* 2, 58a 12-17) they are axiomatic forms, or modes of inference, in which syllogistic (or what is called 'enthymematic' in the *Rhetoric*) reasoning naturally expresses itself. Neither aspect can be neglected. For, granted that the τόποι are concerned with propositions (a point obvious to one acquainted with the *Topics* and the *Rhetoric*), it must not be forgotten that propositions consist of terms which must be clearly defined and determined before they can be used in meaningful discussion, or in intelligent, convincing, although probable, inference. There must be a precise apprehension of the subject as far as is possible, and there must be reasonable, inferential modes in which to develop the subject further. In the methodology of the topics Aristotle was apparently concerned with both ideas.

In what follows an attempt will be made to justify this distinction from the *Rhetoric*. It is generally admitted[27] that we must go to the *Rhetoric* for a relatively clear explanation of the term τόπος and more than this, one can clearly show from the *Rhetoric* a definite distinction in the τόποι and how Aristotle has developed this idea of the τόποι.

The idea of τόποι, as far as one can decide historically, does not seem to originate with Aristotle. On the other hand he does seem to have isolated and formulated the technique or method which was at work in the collections of τόποι which were probably on hand. His apparent purpose was to arrive at the general method underlying discussion (*T*. 100a 18 f.; 102b 35-103a 5), not to burden the mind with the kind of lists of specific subject-headings and arguments for various occasions, which had probably been collected. And in this is the genius of his topical method.

When we turn to the pre-Aristotelian τόπος to make a brief review of the history of the idea, we find nothing quite similar to the meaning Aristotle gives to the term.[28] The ordinary use of the word is primarily one of local designation and we find this common in Plato[29] and Isocrates; and in the latter it is very frequently conjoined with χώρα.

There are, however, four passages in Isocrates which are germane to one aspect of the Aristotelian idea of τόπος as the place to go for material concerning one's subject, or for a clarification of it—the Aristotelian ὑπάρχοντα.[30] In *Philip* 109 the τόπος is the ἀγαθὰ τῆς ψυχῆς, a topic peculiar (τόπος ἴδιος) to Heracles, and one, as Isocrates says, πολλῶν μὲν ἐπαίνων καὶ καλῶν πράξεων γέμοντα. These ἀγαθά (see also *Helen* 38) are τῇ ψυχῇ πρόσοντα, which is again an echo of the ὑπάρχοντα idea of Aristotle.[31] In *Panathenaicus* 111 we have τόπος as material for discussion, and the same use in *Helen* 4.[32]

Demosthenes[33] gives further evidence that τόπος was used in his time and quite apparently with reference to the particular topics. RADERMACHER[34] gives rather substantial evidence that not only were such ἴδιοι τόποι known and used, but that writers frequently called them καιρούς rather than τόπους before Aristotle's time. These καιροί for the most part concerned themselves with determining the nature of, and examining in detail, not merely such words and ideas as the good, the useful, the right, the beautiful, the possible,[35] but also other ideas such as war, government, peace, etc.[36]

Such is the more direct evidence which is found on the pre-Aristotelian use of the word τόπος in a way that is at all similar to Aristotle's. Indirect evidence for the pre-Aristotelian existence of the idea in the manner in which Aristotle understood it is twofold: the testimony of Aristotle himself and later writers, and the fairly abundant evidence of Aristotle's τόποι at work in various pre-Aristotelian writers.

In the *Rhetoric* Aristotle cites on a number of occasions previous authors or technographers who have employed the particular *topos* of which he is speaking.[37] One conclusion that may be drawn from this is that the methodology of the topics as Aristotle understood it was being used, even if the term τόπος was not employed to identify it. And actually in the *Topics* 105b 11 ff. Aristotle suggests the listing of key ideas on life, on the good, a procedure which we have reason to believe was introduced by earlier rhetoricians. For Cicero[38] and Quintilian[39] mention Protagoras and Gorgias as those who were the first to present such 'communes locos',[40] while Doxopater[41] speaks of a tradition which has Corax devising τοὺς τῶν προοιμίων τόπους.

Were one, however, to question this commonly accepted tradition, it still remains true that the actual use of Aristotle's method of particular and general topics is convincing. Aside from Aristotle's illustrations of his topics by citations from earlier writers, the general topics have been exemplified from these earlier writers rather frequently by SPENGEL in his commentary[42] and by PALMER.[43] The particular topics have not been so fortunate, quite possibly because they were not considered τόποι.[44]. Why this should be, is strange in view of the fact that the Aristotelian τόπος was certainly understood in the sense of 'particular topics' by

Cicero, Quintilian and Plutarch[45] among others. Furthermore we find Gorgias continually using such particular topics in his *Palamedes*[46] and in 22 we find some of them mentioned: τὸν τόπον, τὸν χρόνον, πότε, ποῦ, πῶς. Aristotle himself when speaking of the particular topics connected with honor speaks of the importance of τὸ ποῦ and τὸ πότε, or as he calls them, A 5, 61a 33 f.: οἱ τόποι καὶ οἱ καιροί (cf. A 9, 68a 12-13: τὰ ἐκ τῶν χρόνων καὶ τῶν καιρῶν). We also get both of these in the *Phaedrus* 272a with a slightly different reference. In the *Meno* we find the particular topics for ἀρετή.[47] And this same process can be seen at work in Prodicus' efforts at definition, or the specification of a term, e. g. pleasure.[48] Further citation does not seem necessary, for, as RADERMACHER says (and he is speaking of what have thus far been called here 'particular topics'): "Non potest esse dubium quin de sedibus argumentorum, quae τελικὰ κεφάλαια vocantur, velut de iusto, utili, honesto, pulchro, possibili in scholis sophistarum iam ante Aristotelem sit disputatum".[49]

It would seem, then, that the idea of both particular topics and general topics, or topics to supply one with the material for propositions, as well as topics to supply one with ways of putting this material in a form of inference, was operative prior to Aristotle. Further it does appear that collections of τόποι were made which were concerned for the most part with material and with lines of argument specific to a definite, limited problem or case.[50] These would be the materials and the arguments to be used when a similar problem arose. The process as can be seen is rather static and similar to the study of case law. Aristotle's contribution was to derive and describe the method at work,[51] and he may have kept the name τόποι for the method since it describes the process: these are the places from which originate both the material and the formal elements in all dialectical and rhetorical discussion.

A moment's thought brings before one very distinctly the realization that if you are going to discuss a subject with another in an intelligently informed, but not necessarily scientific, way (e. g. A 2, 55b 27-34, A 2, 58a 23-26, A 4, 59b 5-15) you must know what you are talking about and to whom you are talking. This is certainly one of the purposes of rhetorical study and Aristotle leaves no doubt throughout his work that this is his objective. Indeed he expresses himself quite explicitly on the matter of being informed on the subject at B 22, 96a 4 ff. (which is a re-statement of A 4, 59b 33-37): "Well, then, first of all we must understand that it is necessary to have control of either all or some of the facts of the subject (τὰ τούτῳ ὑπάρχοντα) about which one must speak or reason—whether it be by political reasoning or by any other kind; for without control of any of the facts you could draw no conclusions. My meaning is this: how, for example, could we advise the Athenians as to whether they should engage in war if we have no idea of the nature of their power—whether a naval or land force, or both, and its size, and then the character of their revenues . . ." In other places, as we have seen, he states just as clearly the need of being informed about one's audience and one's relation to the audience (i. e. *ethos* and *pathos*); see, for example, the end of the present passage, *B* 22, 96b 31-34.

An art of rhetoric must, among other things, tell you how to come upon this information. For Aristotle the sources for such information are the *topoi*. But when we look at the text of the *Rhetoric* we begin to realize that Aristotle has something more in mind by *topoi* than mere sources for information about the subject and the audience. The topics also present one with the ways in which to use the information. In an analysis of rhetoric built primarily upon the enthymeme and thus upon his theory of deductive reasoning Aristotle gives in the topics sources for propositional statements and sources for the use of these statements in inferential forms. The *Rhetoric* introduces a distinction among *topoi* and further gives a clue to the nature of the methodology which Aristotle has in mind. A similar division does not exist in the *Topics* but it appears to be operative there. This last point might well be argued, and while the recent work of DePATER on the *Topics* does not apparently accept the explanation of this distinction as it will be presented here the author must accept the fact of the distinction between particular (εἴδη) and general (κοινοί) topics.[52] Our objective here is not the methodology of Aristotle's *Topics* but the methodology of the *Rhetoric*. I am still inclined to believe that the function of the topics in the *Rhetoric* can also be found at work in the *Topics*, as I will attempt to indicate briefly at the end of this chapter. On the other hand if one accepts DePATER's very competent analysis as valid for the *Topics* it must still be acknowledged that it does not work for the *Rhetoric*. There can be no question that Aristotle in the *Rhetoric* bases rhetorical argumentation by syllogism on the topics as sources, and distinguishes these topics into particular topics and general topics. If we question the text on the character of these sources the only answer we find in the *Rhetoric* is quite clear: the particular topics offer the material for propositional statements (Aristotle's προτάἑεις of, for example, *A* 2, 58a 31, *B* 1, 77b 18) about a subject, i.e. what can be said about a subject with respect to its logical comprehension and with respect to its emotional context relative to an other in discussion. The general topics offer forms of inference into which this material may be put so that one may reason by syllogism.

The whole question of particular and general topics is introduced at *A* 2, 58a 2-7. We are told here: "there is a distinction of major importance with respect to enthymemes—although it is almost universally disregarded—a distinction similar to that which is true of dialectical syllogism. For some enthymemes belong properly to rhetoric, as some syllogisms belong properly to dialectic; other enthymemes are peculiar to other arts and faculties (*dynameis*), either existent or still to be formulated".[53]

A possible commentary on this passage is, perhaps, *SE* 170 a 20-b 11. The best, as Aristotle himself suggests (*A* 2, 58a 9-10) may be the section which immediately follows in the text: *A* 2, 58a 10-28. Here Aristotle says that the dialectical and rhetorical syllogisms (10-11) are those formed on the basis of the *topoi*.[54] These *topoi* are then divided into the κοινοί (12) which would represent sources for enthymemes κατὰ τὴν ῥητορικὴν . . .καὶ . . . διαλεκτικὴν μέθοδον (5-6), and ἴδια (17) which are the sources κατ' ἄλλας τέχνας καὶ δυνάμεις (6-7). The ἴδια are then specified further: at 27 they are called εἴδη which is repeated at 30, 31 (εἴδη) and 33 (εἰδῶν).

The question is whether or not these ἴδια which are contrasted with οἱ κοινοί, e.g. *A* 2, 58a 12 *versus* 17, are also τόποι as the κοινοί are. By way of introduction let us note that no student of the *Rhetoric*, to my knowledge, has ever questioned the fact that Aristotle is talking about "topics" in *A* 4 to *B* 17. If this is so, then the ἴδια which in our text here are interchangeable with εἴδη are τόποι. For in *A* 4-*B* 17 Aristotle is unmistakeably speaking of what he promises to speak at *A* 2, 58a 32-33, namely "the particular elements, which are all those that come from statements peculiar to each species and class; for example, there are statements about physics from which it is not possible to construct an enthymeme or a syllogism about ethics" (*A* 2, 58a 17-19). Furthermore the statement at *A* 2, 58a 10-11 says that the rhetorical syllogism (like the dialectical) is built upon the topics: i.e. τοὺς τόπους without any qualification. He then introduces a qualification at 12: οἱ κοινοί which is rather senselessly confusing if κοινοί equals τόποι in the sense that the *only* τόποι are κοινοὶ τόποι. In other words if *topos* is a genus without any species there is no need at all to introduce confusion by using κοινοί. One could perhaps accept this idiosyncratic writing if κοινοί were not immediately set in contrast with ἴδια at 17 and both of them brought together in a contrasting statement at 21-28 with κἀκεῖνα (21) of necessity referring to οἱ κοινοί (12) and ταῦτα (23) to ἴδια (17) because the statement at 21-26 so clearly restates that at 12-20. In view of this close contrast and juxtaposition of κοινοί and ἴδια one must attend to the further parallelism in 27-28. Thus there can be little question that if we can understand τόπων with κοινῶν, we can understand it with ἰδίων.[55] And when in c. 22 of book *B* (96a 4-b 21) Aristotle summarizes the analysis he has made of these εἴδη (or ἴδια) in *A* 4-*B* 17 he concludes at 96b 20-21: "This, then, is one method, the first method of selecting sources—the topical (οὗτος ὁ τοπικός)."

We come, then, to the conclusion of our passage at *A* 2, 58a 10- 28 with the understanding that the sources of the enthymeme are "the topics" (e.g. *A* 2, 58a 10-12). At 29-32 Aristotle says that with respect to these sources of the enthymeme (ἐξ ὧν ληπτέον) a distinction must be made in the *Rhetoric*, as in the *Topics*, between the εἴδη i.e. "propositions proper to each subject" (31), and the τόπους i.e. "elements common alike to all subjects". It seems quite clear that, while both are *topoi*, the particular *topoi* are called εἴδη and the general *topoi* are given the name τόποι. However, as we will see, he also uses the term τόποι for the εἴδη.

Aristotle then proposes to discuss the εἴδη (32-33), or particular topics, and it is in his presentation of them that a distinction between them and the κοινοί becomes quite apparent.[56] The *eidos*, or particular topic, could be called a "material topic"[57] in the sense that it offers the matter (ὕλη) for the propositions. It presents one with sources, or focal points, to be examined in order that one may derive all the material pertinent to the subject, i. e. the ὑπάρχοντα of the subject which are necessary for an intelligent statement which carries meaning to the auditor. These εἴδη belong to the subject in itself and in all of its diverse relations. They represent the varied particular aspects of an individual subject which can throw light upon the subject for the audience and for the field of knowledge which it represents.[58]

To understand the point of view presented here one has merely to read Aristotle's discussion of the εἴδη for deliberative (cc. 4-8), epideictic (c. 9), and forensic oratory (cc. 10-14) in Book *A* or those for *pathos* (cc. 2-11) and *ethos* (cc. 1, 12-17) in Book *B*.

While a detailed analysis of these particular topics in *A-B* might be valuable in itself it would be neither to the purpose nor particularly helpful to engage upon it here. In order to correct some misunderstanding possibly occasioned by De-PATER'S study, however, a further word is necessary. The explanation of the εἴδη (which DePATER recognizes as particular topics) given by him simply will not explain the particular topics as we find them in the *Rhetoric*. In the *Rhetoric* these εἴδη are all specifics with an occasional principle (usually an accepted general opinion, or a general topic) used from which the specifics, namely, the ὑπάρχοντα, can be drawn.[59] It would be tedious, as I have indicated, to catalogue the process. It begins immediately in c. 4 of book *A* at 59b 19 where we learn that the deliberative speaker must know—and I am citing directly from c. 4—the extent of the State's resources, its expenses, its power, the wars it has waged, its conduct of them, the kind of food produced at home, the State's legislation, forms of government. And so it continues in each chapter through c. 17 of book *B*. Every now and then Aristotle will cite a definition, or a principle which is generally accepted, or a general topic, and from it develop specifics, e. g. in *A* 5, 60b 14-18: "Let happiness, then, be well-being combined with virtue, or independence of life, or . . ." This, then, enables him to cite the specifics of *eudaemonia*: "noble birth, good friends, wealth, etc.", each of which he then examines in further detail to the end of the chapter at 62a 14. If one wishes to take the statement on happiness as a definition, then Aristotle is using his general topic VII (*B* 23, 98a 15) to develop specific aspects of *eudaemonia*. The same procedure is followed in *A* 6 where in the course of his analysis he uses at 62b 30-31 his general topic I (*B* 23, 97a 7) from opposites in order to develop specifics. We have the same kind of particulars in *A* 8, 9. When we turn to *pathos* in book *B* we find that in c. 2 we have descriptions of the angry person, a process which is well expressed at 79a 29: "These, then, are the moods of men who are prone to anger". The same approach takes place in *B* 3 with respect to gentleness. In *B* 12 where he begins the analysis of *ethos* we have simply a detailed statement of the characteristics of the young; in *B* 13 of the old.

In all of these instances it would not be possible to apply DePATER's definition of the particular topic, the *eidos*, e.g. "le lieu est une formule de recherche et de preuve à la fois. Cela vaut pour la *Rhétorique* non moins que pour les *Topiques*".[60]

There is, however, in a chapter like 7 of book *A*, a use on the part of Aristotle of an assumed general principle (as has been noted), or accepted opinion, or a general *topos*, in order to derive the special elements, the ὑπάρχοντα, of a subject. This is a function which I find the general topics fulfilling frequently in the *Topics* as I mention toward the close of this chapter. This general principle (or accepted opinion, or general *topos*) does function as a "formule de recherche" and can be employed with a force "probatif". Some instances of this in the sections cited above are: *A*: 5, 60b 14 ff. a generalized definition; 6, 62b 30 f. a *topos*; 7, 63b 5 ff. a precisive use of the logical force of "more or less" throughout the section; 9, 66a 33-34 and 36-b1 a generally accepted statement; *B*: 2, 77a 31-33 a statement of what anger is; 3, 80a 7-8 the same for gentleness; cc. 12 and 13 of *B* contain all specific characteristics.

These instances would illustrate the character of the general *topos* as an "acte de l'inventio" and also as "probatif" (Les Topiques, pp. 109, 106) but they are not εἴδη, particular topics. There is certainly no reason to expect *only* εἴδη in *A* 4-*B* 17, particularly in view of the fact that the general topics frequently function as a method whereby one may establish the focal points (particular topics) for an informed understanding of the subject.

Obviously in any intelligent discussion of a subject the bulk of one's argument will be built around the particular topics; and it is this, as far as I can see, and nothing else, that Aristotle has in mind when he says that most enthymemes will come from the εἴδη (*A* 2, 58a 26-28). Finally in this explanation of the particular and general topics there is assuredly no reason to conclude that "les lieux propres et les lieux communs . . . *doivent* figurer tous deux dans le même argument" (Les Topiques, p. 98).

The εἴδη, then, express specific facts or characteristics relative to the subject-matter. As has been said it is difficult to avoid the conclusion that Aristotle considers them τόποι. He sums up his discussion of them with the words: ὥστε ἐξ ὧν δεῖ φέρειν τὰ ἐνθυμήματα τόπων (*B* 22, 96b 31-32). The same idea is repeated at *Γ* 19, 19b 15-29. And at *B* 3, 80b 30-31 he says of the εἴδη that he has been discussing relative to *pathos*: ἐκ τούτων τῶν τόπων.[61] As particular topics the *eide* are the sources to which one has recourse to develop both an understanding of the subject and the way in which to present it to a particular audience. Aristotle says quite simply at *B* 22, 96a 4-b 19: to reason intelligently upon a subject you must reason ἐκ τῶν περὶ ἕκαστον ὑπαρχόντων (b 2).[62] As a matter of fact this whole passage at *B* 22, 96a 4-b 21 illustrates how the *eide* provide information on the subject and are considered to be *topoi*.[63] Since the material derived from the *eide* as sources will usually appear as an enunciation on the subject, it follows that the *eide* supply us with particular propositions which can be used in enthymematic reasoning on the subject. In this sense the *eide* are the sources of particular propositions or statements on the subject under discussion (*A* 2, 58a 31). Yet the kind of statement which they provide does not directly implicate the ultimate and essential truths about the subject, although it may approach them. The *eide* as used in rhetoric are not concerned with a scientific analysis of the subject. This is the only conclusion which can be drawn from *A* 2, 58a 23-26. Here we are told that the more detail with which the *eide* are selected the more will the analysis move toward the first principles of the subject and so toward an *episteme* of the subject; and this is not the domain of either dialectic or rhetoric. Indeed a study of the *eide* in *A-B* will reveal that one could hardly construct a science of government, criminal law, or psychology from the *eide* presented. Rather the purpose of the particular topics we find is to enable one to speak intelligently, but not scientifically, upon the subject under discussion. Enthymematic reasoning based upon the particular topics is valid only for the subject to which the *eide* belong (*A* 2, 58a 17-21).

In this respect the εἴδη differ, as topics, from the κοινοὶ τόποι.[64] The latter transcend the various subjects which rhetoric may treat. They are valid for all subjects (*A* 2, 58a 12-17), and they exemplify in a particular way the nature of rhetoric as *dynamis* in its ability to occupy itself with the suasive in any subject (*A* 2, 55b 31-34 with 25-27).

This brings us to a very fundamental characteristic of the κοινοὶ τόποι emphatically stressed by Aristotle (*A* 2, 58a 2-7), namely, that these κοινοὶ τόποι are universal and transcend all the fields of knowledge to which rhetoric may legitimately apply itself (*A* 2, 58a 10-14); and Aristotle makes his meaning even more specific by referring at a14 to one of the *koinoi topoi* which he later discusses in c. 23 of book *B* at 97b 12 ff. Here, then, we have a kind of topic which is essentially different from the εἴδη. Particular topics are confined to and closely related to their own specific subject-matter (58a 17-18) and are valid sources of information on that matter alone (18-19). The κοινοί, on the contrary, have no such substrate (22) and are valid sources for enthymematic reasoning upon any subject (15-16). Hence it is that, no matter how much a particular topic is universalized, the result will never be a κοινοὶ τόπος as Aristotle understands that term in the *Rhetoric*. For an ἴδιος τόπος is always specific in its nature and confined to one subject: general or particular.[65]

Any topic, and such are the εἴδη, which is grounded in the particular subject-matter of a specific branch of learning and is productive of knowledge in that area (*A* 2, 58a 17-26) cannot transcend this discipline and include others. But the κοινοί transcend the individual disciplines. This difference in the topics translates itself into what have been called here 'particular topics' (εἴδη), or sources of information upon the subject-matter to be discussed, and 'general topics' (κοινοὶ τόποι), or sources for modes of reasoning by enthymeme: forms of inference most suitable for the enthymeme.[66]

A closer study of what Aristotle has to say of these κοινοί in the passage under discussion (A 2, 58a 2-7) and in chapter 23 of Book B appears to justify this division. In the first place the κοινοί are universal and belong properly to rhetoric (A 2, 58a 2-7, 12-17) in so far as rhetoric is a δύναμις περὶ ἔκαστον τοῦ θεωρῆσαι τὸ ἐνδεχόμενον πιθανόν (A 2, 55b 25-26) and in so far as it is not ἐπιστήμη.[67] Thus rhetoric does not possess any peculiar ὑποκείμενον (A 2, 55b 31-34), and neither do the κοινοὶ τόποι (A 2, 58a 21-23). And so we can understand why Aristotle, for whom Rhetoric is a *dynamis* just as Dialectic, lays stress upon the μεγίστη διαφορά in the section A 2, 58a 2 ff. which is so frequently discussed by the commentators. This 'difference' resides for him in the fact that there are enthymemes peculiar to rhetoric as a discipline: κατὰ τὴν ῥητορικὴν μέθοδον. If rhetoric possesses no particular subject-matter of its own, such enthymemes could only be syllogistic forms derived from universal propositional statements, which are modes for probable argumentation and reasoning. As he says in the *Sophistici Elenchi* (172a 29-b 1): there are certain general principles common to all the sciences which even the unlettered can use. In themselves they are known to everyone, for they are natural ways in which the mind thinks. Such in a way are the κοινοὶ τόποι. As general axiomatic propositions they are valid forms of inference by themselves. Further, they may also be applied to the subject-matter presented by the εἴδη to permit one to reason by enthymeme with this material.[68]

It would appear, then, that the κοινοὶ τόποι are logical modes of inference which generally obtain the matter for their inference from the εἴδη.[69] And as further confirmation that they are general, formal topics, i.e. forms of reasoning, it should be noted that study of the twenty-eight κοινοὶ τόποι in c. 23 of Book B shows that they are universal[70] and that they apparently fall into one of three inferential and logical patterns.[71]

a) antecedent-consequent, or cause-effect: VII, XI, XIII, XIV, XVII, XIX, XXIII, XXIV.
b) more-less: IV, V, VI, XX, XXV, XXVII.
c) some form of relation: I, II, III, VIII, IX, X, XII, XV, XVI, XVIII, XXI, XXII, XXVI, XXVIII.

One could undoubtedly argue about the terms used for classification, or the distribution of the κοινοί among them. The point of interest, however, is that, no matter how they are classified, these κοινοὶ τόποι reduce themselves to modes of inference.[72] They always assume a form of reasoning which leads the mind from one thing to another. Expressed quite simply they would resolve themselves into the proposition: if one, then the other. And this last statement acquires new significance when, knowing the close relation between the rhetorical syllogism (enthymeme) and the κοινοὶ τόποι[73], one reads: 'All Aristotelian syllogisms are implications of the type "if α and β, then γ . . ." '.[74] If, further, consideration is given to Aristotle's identification of these κοινοὶ τόποι with the στοιχεῖα rhetorical syllogisms, there appears to be no doubt that for Aristotle the general topic is a form of inference and represents the source of enthymemes: κατὰ τὴν ῥητορικὴν μέθοδον.

At B 22, 96b 20-22 Aristotle summarizes his discussion of the εἴδη and makes a transition to the section on the κοινοὶ τόποι in chapter 23. He introduces the new subject with the words "let us now speak of the στοιχεῖα of enthymemes." From A 2, 58a 31-2 one would expect him to say as commentators hasten to point out: let us speak of the τόπους τοὺς κοινοὺς ὁμοίως πάντων. Having used στοιχεῖα somewhat unexpectedly, Aristotle immediately clarifies the word with στοιχεῖον δὲ λέγω καὶ τόπον ἐνθυμήματος τὸ αὐτό. And lest there be any doubt that by τόπος here he means the κοινοὶ τόποι, he says that these τόποι are καθόλου περὶ ἁπάντων. Thus one can be fairly certain that the τόποι here are the same as the general topics of A 2, 58a 32: τοὺς κοινοὺς ὁμοίως πάντων.

Aristotle has now specified these κοινοὶ τόποι as στοιχεῖα. But what is meant by calling them στοιχεῖα? At B 26, 03a 17-18 we read: "By *stoicheion* and *topos* I mean the same thing; for a *stoicheion* and *topos* is a general class under which many enthymemes fall." The Greek here, εἰς δ πολλὰ ἐνθυμήματα ἐμπίπτει, describes στοιχεῖον (and so τόπος) as a larger category which contains many enthymemes. This at once recalls Theophrastus' definition of τόπος as ἀρχή τις ἢ στοιχεῖον . . . τῇ περιγραφῇ μὲν ὡρισμένος (i.e. of determinate form) . . . τοῖς δὲ καθ᾿ ἕκαστα ἀόριστος (i.e. indeterminate with respect to the individual matter to which it is applied).[75] Of this definition BOCHEŒSKI writes: "pour Théophraste le τόπος est une formule logique légitime qui sert à former les prémisses de déduction . . .".[76] But this is precisely what the *koinoi topoi* are: forms of inference by enthymeme, any one of which may offer a form for inference on various subjects. As WAITZ says of a passage in the *Analytics* 84b 21 which is parallel to B 26, 03a 17-18: "In *Topics* στοιχεῖα vocat quae alio nomine τόπους appellat, universa quaedam argumenta, ex quibus cum veritatis quadam specie aliquid vel probetur vel refellatur".[77]

Before concluding a word should perhaps be said about the *Topics*. First of all it should be noted that this formal distinction between *eide* and *koinoi topoi* is not found, as such, in the work although Aristotle states at *Rhetoric* A 2, 58a 29-30 that the distinction is also present in the *Topics*. Certainly a passage like that at 105b 12-18 strongly implies kinds of particular topics: "we should also make selections from written 'handbooks of arguments' and should make outlines of each and every subject, setting them down under separate headings, as, for example, 'on good', or 'on life'; and the list 'on good' should be on 'all good' beginning with the essence of good". The idea of both the particular and general *topos* appears to be at work in the *Topics*. For Aristotle is concerned with determining as accurately as possible the meaning of things by specifying the various ways in which this meaning can be understood; these specific meanings would be the *eide*. The topics as we generally find them are the principles by which to examine a subject and they frequently employ the same kind of reasoning which we find proper to the *koinoi topoi* in the *Rhetoric*.[78]

In the *Topics* Aristotle says that a problem can be considered from four primary aspects: definition, property, genus, accident (101b 15ff.). The effort in Books 2-7 is to examine the nature of these categories and what must follow with respect to a thing, if it comes under one of them. This examination is done by the τόποι, and the analysis is determined by the very nature of the category. For example: there are certain ways (τόποι) in which one can further determine the nature of a genus and consequently certain statements which can only be made about it—and they are not valid for an accident. They are ways—determined by reality—in which one must think about the subject. This kind of analysis is a vital, logical one, grounded in the metaphysical reality of the subject, and one engages in it in order to discover as far as possible the true nature of the subject. This was what was meant by saying that these particular topics are not mere mechanical lists of terms to be tried on a subject, no Procrustean bed to which the subject is fitted, rather we have here a method of analysis originating in the ontological reality of the subject.[79]

In the *Rhetoric*, however, as I understand Aristotle's effort, he enlarges the methodology of the particular topics owing to his awareness that anything—particularly anything in the area of the probable which is the primary subject-matter of rhetoric—may be conditioned and altered by its situation. In other words, the time, the place, the circumstances, the character, the emotional involvement, may vitally affect the total meaning of a thing in a given situation. Thus he introduced these elements to assist one toward a more precise discrimination of a subject when one is speaking to an other in the area of the problematic. Although the concern of the *Topics* is a methodology directed to a more critical testing and determining of things like substance, genus, relations, opinions, still we find less technical elements such as time (111b 24 ff.), circumstances (118a) which are quantitative and qualitative aspects that alter the meaning of terms like ambition, or covetousness (146b 20 ff.). We also find attention paid to the character of the persons involved in discussion, e.g. their qualities of intellect and emotion (141a 26 ff., 156b 18 ff., 161a 29-b10). As Aristotle says rather well on this point (141b 36-142a 2): "Different things happen to be more intelligible to different people and the same things are not, as it happens, more intelligible to all; consequently a different definition would have to be given to each one, if indeed the definition must be constructed from what is more intelligible to each individual".

As for the *koinoi topoi* they frequently appear in the *Topics* as the method whereby one may establish the special focal points (particular topics) from which a subject may be studied. In this use they appear in the same form and fulfil the same function, as modes of inference, which they have in the *Rhetoric*. That is to say, they are ways in which the mind naturally and readily reasons, and they are independent, in a way, of the subject to which they are applied, and may be said to be imposed as forms upon this material in order to clarify and determine it further.[80] Thus it is that we will at times find the general topics functioning in the *Topics* as a method to help in the determination of various particular topics to which one should have recourse.[81]

It is only in the *Rhetoric*, however, that a clear distinction between particular and general topics appears, and its presence would seem indisputable. This distinction may be ignored, but if the texts cited in this chapter are studied, one is forced either to reject the unity of the *Rhetoric*, or to question the text as one that has been confused by later editors, or to seek an interpretation of the text. The attempt here has been to offer a tentative interpretation which keeps in mind the character of the topics as they are met in the *Topics*; further, it is an interpretation which appears to be demanded by the text of the *Rhetoric* as we possess it, and it seems to express the method Aristotle had in mind when he proposed a way of rational discourse for the whole area of the contingent and the probable. In summary, then, it is proposed:

a) that the εἴδη are particular topics concerned with the specific content and meaning of the subject under discussion. They enable one to acquire the factual information pertinent to the matter which in turn permits one to make intelligent statements upon the subject;

b) that the κοινοὶ τόποι are general topics, i. e. forms of inference into which syllogistic, or enthymematic, reasoning naturally falls. As modes of reasoning they may be used for the εἴδη various subjects which specifically differ (A 2, 58a 13-14: διαφερόντων εἴδει), and when they are applied to the εἴδει they effect syllogistic or enthymematic argumentation.[82]

Notes

[1]ROSS is speaking of the *Rhetoric* passage; aside from the fact that he does not explain how *paradeigma* can be a source for the enthymeme, his comment on "types of enthymeme" could be confusing. It appears more correct to speak of ἐνθύμημα as the type just as φιλοσόφημα etc. (T. 162a 15ff.) might be called types of syllogism. Any difference in enthymemes would then be found in the modality of the premises, an explanation which Ross would admit.

[2]This is not to minimize the problem which SPENGEL sees (commentary s. 1402b 13) although I do not know what justification he has for his statement: "nunc et παράδειγμα in numero enthymematum referre licet." COPE seems somewhat confused in his paraphrase as far as I understand him by διὰ παραδείγματος. If he means to correlate it with διὰ τεκμηρίου (b19) and διὰ σημείων (b21) which he interprets correctly his English translation does not reveal it.

[3]ROSS, op. cit., p. 50; a good illustration of my statement is an Anonymus commenting on B 25, 03a 5 (*Commentaria Graeca*, vol. 21, p. 155.29 ff.) in which he takes an example of Aristotle and shows how a syllogism may be formed from the example. I would not agree with VATER, Animadversiones, p. 17, and I find his objection answered at *Prior Analytics* 68b 38. SOLMSEN, Die Entwicklung, p. 23, n. 4 would agree on the process.

[4]See also *Nicomachean Ethics* 1139b 27-28; ROSS, op. cit., commentary on *Prior Analytics* 68b 27-28. MARX's inability to see this enables him to interpret B 25, 02b 14 ff. as a reversion to

Isocratean teaching and so further proof of confusion in the editing of the *Rhetoric* ("Aristoteles' Rhetorik", p. 323).

[5]E. HAVET, op. cit., p. 57.

[6]J. H. McBURNEY in "The Place of the Enthymeme in Rhetorical Theory", Speech Monographs 3, 1936, pp. 49-74; E. MADDEN, The Enthymeme: Crossroads of Logic, Rhetoric, and Metaphysics, The Philosophical Review 51, 1952, pp. 368-376.

[7]Op. cit., pp. 499-500; see also S. SIMONSON, A Definitive Note on the Enthymeme, AJP66, 1945, p. 303.

[8]C. RITTER, Platon II, Munich 1923, p. 40 f. with certain qualifications of his opening phrases has pointed out the thrust of Aristotelian rhetoric in his comments on the Phaedrus: "Nun ist es unmöglich, die Masse wissenschaftlich zu belehren und zur vollen Erkenntnis der Wahrheit zu führen; wissenschaftliche Gründe sind ihr nicht faßbar und so ist sie nur durch einen Schein der Wahrheit, die 'Wahrscheinlichkeit' bestimmbar. Eben darum kann sich die Philosophie nicht mit der Masse abgeben und hat neben ihr die Rhetorik einen wichtigen Platz. Sie soll die wissenschaftlichen Beweise, die sich gleichsam an einen abstrakten Verstand wenden, in der Weise umformen, daß sie auf die Anlagen, Stimmungen, zufälligen Erfahrungen des einzelnen, an die sich anknüpfen läßt, Rücksicht nimmt. Sie wäre dann eine Technik des erziehenden Unterrichts. Und gründen muß sie sich nicht bloß im allgemeinen auf Psychologie, sondern auf psychologische Beobachtung der Individuen. So muß sie sich der Philosophie unterordnen und von ihr sich die Richtung und die allgemeinen Grundsätze vorschreiben lassen, die wichtiger sind als jene Einzelregeln rhetorischer Lehrbücher." Aside from the fact that Aristotle through the introduction of the syllogism into rhetoric has surely given the grounds for such a union of analytical and dialectical reasoning in the rhetorical *pragmateia*, it is time to recognize that far from being separate and unrelated methodologies the *Topics* and the *Analytics* are disciplines that are both necessary to each other and complement each other. This is well demonstrated by WEIL (La place de la logique. . .RMM 56, 1951, 283-315) who makes the rather telling point that if the *Analytics* replaced the *Topics* Theophrastus was clearly unaware of this move on the part of his teacher.

[9]At *An. Pr.* 32b 5-10 Aristotle puts forward an explanation of ἐνδέχεσθαι which aptly describes the situation in which *eikos* is legitimate: "that which generally happens but falls short of necessity. . .or in general what belongs to a thing naturally." COPE in his Introduction, p. 163 interprets the *Rhetoric* passage on *eikos* differently and in a way difficult to justify from the Greek text.

[10]Ordinarily "knowledge" is a correct translation of ἐπιστήμη and it means a knowledge of the *ousia* which is knowledge that is certain, absolute, and of the universal. However the word "knowledge" is an analogous one for Aristotle and *episteme* as defined above would be the primary analogate. He also recognized other kinds of knowledge one of which is *doxa*, and admitted different degrees of knowing as the treatises on ethics, the topics, and rhetoric itself reveal. In Aristotle one knows the concrete reality of things but not with exactitude since the real can be incomplete or imperfect, or, as we have been saying, "for the most part so". This knowing is engaged with things that can be other than they are and thus for him *eikos* is a perfectly legitimate starting point of knowledge. Just as the word *episteme* is used analogously by Aristotle so, too, is *apodeixis*. Ordinarily it means strict scientific demonstration of which he speaks in the *Metaphysics*. In our own treatise the noun or adjective is frequently used in an analogous sense: *A* 1, 55a 5-7; *A* 2, 56a 3-4 with which compare *A* 8, 66a 8-10; *A* 2, 58a 1; *B* 20, 94a 9-10; *B* 22, 96a 34-b 11; *B* 24, 01b 7 ff. where there is an interesting nexus implied between enthymeme and *apodeixis*; *Γ* 17, 17b 21 ff.; *Γ* 17, 18a 5, 39-40.

[11]In 272d 8-e 1 Plato makes *eikos* and the persuasive equal. It may be that this concept of *eikos* is not Plato's but an earlier view, see 273a; DUFOUR, Aristote Rhétorique Tome 1er, Paris 1932, p. 10 interprets it as Plato's attack on the theory of probability of Tisias and Corax. It may also

be that we have here a criticism of the social relativism of some of the Sophists who accepted the popular concepts of justice, courage, etc. These concepts, while suasive, are of little value toward understanding since they cannot be submitted to critical evaluation. An instance of *eikos* as simply "plausibility" can be seen at *Phaedo* 92d. Since the passages cited do not misrepresent Plato's views on *eikos* I do not intend to become more involved than this with the place of the probable in Plato's thought. Certainly Plato cannot accept an *episteme* of the non-exact (thus the problem of becoming always remains troublesome). Aristotle, however, does admit that the reality of things is given by the senses and that the objects so known can be incomplete and imperfect; consequently he acknowledged that concrete knowing (which comes through the senses and forms the major part of man's knowing) is occupied with that which can be otherwise, or the probable. As for the character of these *eikota* in the *Rhetoric* perhaps the following should be noted here: *Eikota* (and *semeia*) for Aristotle are drawn from the particular topics. Aristotle does not usually formulate these topics as *eikota*; an example, however, of how it is done is found in Thucydides I.121.2ff.: here Aristotle's particular topics on war and peace for the deliberative speaker (*A* 4, 59b 33-60a 5) are used by the Corinthians as *eikota* that they will be successful. (On *semeia* we find Aristotle at *A* 9, 66b 23-67a 5 using as the σημεῖα τῆς ἀρετῆς: actions of a good man, actions of a just man, etc.) One further point: while Aristotle does not usually formulate the topics as *eikota* or *semeia* he states explicitly at *A* 3, 59a 8 that the *eikota* and *semeia* are the rhetorical *protaseis*.

[12] An understanding of the relationship, particularly a non-necessary relation, which is present between sign and signate may be found in the *Sophistici Elenchi* 167b 1-8 where Aristotle speaks of the nature of consequent and signs. The citations under the so-called περὶ σημείων in V. ROSE, Aristoteles Pseudepigraphus, Lipsiae 1913 pp. 243 ff. indicate that placing the ground of sign in the realities themselves was in the Aristotelian tradition; related to this is R.A. MARKUS' comment in "St. Augustine on Signs", Phronesis 2, 1957, p. 61. TRENDELENBURG, Elementa Logices Aristoteleae III, Berlin 1845, p. 106 has a definition of Aristotelian sign: "externum est indicium, quod si ita rei est proprium ut ex nulla alia re existere potuerit, necessarium est; si aliis aeque accidat, dubium."

[13] The distinction we find in the *Rhetoric* between *semeia* is recognized in the *Analytics*. In 70b 1-6 *semeion* is identified with the middle term in the second and third figure syllogisms and this is the *semeion anonymon* of *Rhetoric A* 2, 57b 10- 25. *Tekmerion*, on the other hand, is identified in the same passage with the middle term in the first figure syllogism and this is the *tekmerion* of *Rhetoric A* 2, 57b 3-10. On this quesiton see ROSS, op. cit., p. 501; MAIER, Die Syllogistik, p. 482, n. 2; WAITZ, Organon, p. 538; SOLMSEN, Die Entwicklung, p. 22, n. 3 believes that we have in the *Rhetoric* an identity of *tekmerion* with the first figure syllogism, a point about which Aristotle was still doubtful in the *Analytics*. COPE, Introduction, p. 163 has a strange remark: "the distinctive name τεκμήριον does not occur in the *Analytics*".

[14] See M. FUHRMANN, Anaximenis Ars Rhetorica, Lipsiae 1966, c. 12, 1430b 30-38.

[15] Aristotle's example of such a necessary sign, *A* 2, 57b 15-16 is almost identical with his example in *An. Pr.* 70a 13-16 which is, as he says, in the first figure and which he calls *tekmerion* at 70b 1-2. Further it is quite possible that *syllogismos* at *A* 2, 57b 5-6 is the first figure syllogism (see SOLMSEN, Die Entwicklung, p. 14, n. 1). The fact that the *tekmerion* is irrefutable, *A* 22, 57b 16-17, also points in the same direction, e.g. *An. Pr.* 70a 28-30.

[16] The Port-Royal logicians rejected the *Topics* as "des livres étrangement confus." BOCHEŒSKI, La logique de Théophraste, Fribourg 1947, p. 122, claims that Aristotle never gave us the meaning of τόπος, while SOLMSEN, Die Entwicklung, p. 164 maintains that *B* 26, 03a 18-19 is Aristotle's only genuine statement on the essential character of the term.

[17] Theophrastus, of course, wrote on the topics, and apparently Straton continued the work (D. Laert. Straton 5.3). Collections of τόποι for prooemia and epilogues apparently existed in the 4th century (RE suppl. VII (1940) p. 1066). For the general trend in rhetoric between Aristotle

and Cicero see ibid. 1071-1089; and on the topics see VOLKMANN, Die Rhetorik der Griechen und Römer, Leipzig 1885, pp. 199 ff., 299 ff., 322 ff.

[18] He himself found Aristotle's work somewhat obscure (Topica 1); W. WALLIES, Die griechischen Ausleger der aristotelischen Topik, Berlin 1891, p. 4, and E. THIONVILLE, De la théorie des lieux communs, Paris 1855, p. 9 would agree with this, for they believe that Cicero's work in this field has nothing more in common with Aristotle's than its title. This is too severe, just as VIEHWEG, Topik und Jurisprudenz, Munich 1953, p. 10, is a bit too sanguine in his opinion that Cicero's work will help us to understand the Aristotelian topics. The diversity of Cicero's remarks, however, implies at times that he may have seen into the nature of Aristotle's topics; on this question see B. RIPOSATI, Studi sui 'Topica' di Cicerone, Milan 1947; his bibliography, pp. 15-30, is a good one for a study of the general problem.

[19] Top. 101a 34 ff.

[20] R. TUVE, Elizabethan and Metaphysical Imagery, Chicago 1947, c. XI, p. 3.

[21] R. WEAVER, The Ethics of Rhetoric, Chicago 1953, cc. 3, 4.

[22] Ibid., p. 55.

[23] K. BURKE, A Rhetoric of Motives, New York 1950, p. 56. On 57 f. he does see a difference in the topics: there are the 'commonplaces' just mentioned, and then 'another kind of "topic"'; this other kind, from his description of it, is actually the general topic as presented in this chapter.

[24] For Aristotle the topics are the sources for the προτάσεις and, as A 2, 58a 10-35 and B 1, 77b 16-24 would indicate, this means sources for both their content and form.

[25] THIONVILLE, op. cit., c. vi, traces briefly the development from Cicero to Marmontel. R. NADEAU gives some attention to this area in "Hermogenes on 'Stock Issues' in Deliberative Speaking," Speech Monographs 25.1, 1958, pp. 59-66.

[26] SOLMSEN, op. cit., pp. 163-6; RIPOSATI, op. cit., pp. 21 ff.; E. HAMBRUCH, Logische Regeln der platonischen Schule in der aristotelischen Topik, Berlin 1904, p. 31; THIONVILLE, op. cit., pp. 30 ff.

[27] VIEHWEG, op. cit., p. 9; SOLMSEN, op. cit., pp. 163-4; THIONVILLE, op. cit., pp. 30 f.; and most recently J. BRUNSCHWIG in his edition of Aristote Topiques I, Paris 1967.

[28] As SOLMSEN, op. cit., p. 156 remarks: the Aristotelian idea is something new; he discusses the term in general 151-175; see also F. SCHUPP, Zur Geschichte der Beweistopik in der älteren griechischen Gerichtsrede, Wiener Studien 45, 1926-7, pp. 17-28, 173-85.

[29] See AST, Lexicon Platonicum sub τόπος; this is also true of all the pertinent references in DIELS, Die Fragmente der Vorsokratiker⁶, Berlin 1952, with the exception of the Cicero and Quintilian citations which will be seen later.

[30] See Top. 105b 12-18 for the idea, and 112a 24 ff. and Rhet. B22, 96a 32-b9 where Aristotle says that what he was trying to do in the Topics was to determine the ὑπάρχοντα.

[31] SOLMSEN, op. cit., p. 167 mentions these two references and he tries to connect the Helen citation with his idea of the Aristotelian τόπος as 'Formprinzip', or a propositional, axiomatic topos. This appears no more possible here than THIONVILLE's attempt, op. cit., pp. 55-77 to formulate many of the τόποι in the Topics as propositional, axiomatic statements, a process of which he must say: "j'ai dû parfois interpréter, parfois changer la forme" (p. 63).

[32] In Panathenaicus 88 the use is ambiguous; it may mean the subject previously under discussion, but it more probably indicates the place in his speech at which he digressed.

[33] In Aristogeiton 76 (ed. DINDORF-BLASS, Teubner 1888).

[34] L. RADERMACHER, Artium Scriptores, Vienna 1951, see the notes on pp. 48-9, 224.

[35] What later rhetoricians called the τελικὰ κεφάλαια, see RADERMACHER, op. cit., p. 224 note to 62.

[36] See the scholiast to Thucydides 3.9.1 (ed. HUDE, Teubner 1927) where we find Thucydides doing this very thing for δημηγορία; or see Anaximenes c. 19 (ed. FUHRMANN) where

various meanings of δίκαιον and ἄδικον are given. Syrianus examines συμφέρον in this manner and introduces the examination thus: ἐξετάσομεν δὲ τὸ συμφέρον διὰ τόπων ἑπτὰ (RADERMACHER, op. cit., p. 227). I mention Syrianus here since RADERMACHER in his note is of the opinion that the τόποι may be quite old.

[37]E.g. B 23, 99a 15-7, 00a 4-5, 00b 15-7; B 24, 02a 17; and see RADERMACHER, op. cit., p. 221 note to 48.

[38]Brutus 12.46.8 (ed. G. FRIEDRICH, Teubner 1893).

[39]Institutiones Oratoriae 3.1.12 (ed. L. RADERMACHER—V. BUCHHEIT, Teubner 1959).

[40]SOLMSEN, op. cit., pp. 167-8 discusses the Cicero text.

[41]RADERMACHER, op. cit., p. 34.

[42]E.g. and 1398a 30 ff. and see note of RADERMACHER, op. cit., pp. 57 and 223 note to 52; and comment of SOLMSEN, op. cit., p. 166.

[43]G. PALMER, The ΤΟΠΟΙ of Aristotle's Rhetoric as Exemplified in the Orators (Diss. Univ. of Chicago 1934).

[44]MARX, Aristoteles' Rhetorik, BSG 52, 1900, p. 281 ff. does not consider the εἴδη (i.e. ἴδιοι τόποι) to be topics, he speaks of enthymemes from topoi and idiai protaseis; SOLMSEN does not admit eide either, op. cit., pp. 17, 34 ff., 165 and note 3.

[45]Quaest. conviv. 616c-d (ed. BERNARDAKIS); Plutarch remarks that to appreciate the social position of dinner guests who differ in so many ways — ἡλικίᾳ, δυνάμει, χρείᾳ, οἰκειότητι — one would need τοὺς ᾿Αριστοτέλους τόπους. These are particular topics. We also find such particular topics in the scholiast on the Staseis of Hermogenes (Rhetores Graeci, ed. WALZ, vol. IV. 352. 5 ff.); the scholiast calls them τόποι and finds them used in a work by Lysias.

[46]RADERMACHER, op. cit., pp. 59 ff.

[47]RADERMACHER, op. cit., p. 49 number 27 with note.

[48]Ibid. pp. 68 f., numbers 7-11 with notes.

[49]Ibid. p. 226 note to 62.

[50]NAVARRE, Essai sur la Rhétorique grecque, Paris 1900, speaks of collections of τόποι that were made, pp. 60 ff., 124 ff., 166-74.

[51]As NAVARRE, ibid., p. 166, says in comparing the treatment of ἤθη in the Rhetoric and in the Παρασκευαί attributed to Lysias: "l'ouvrage de Lysias n'était pas un traité théorique, mais un re cueil de modèles (τόποι γεγυμνασμένοι)." As far as can be judged (see Navarre, pp. 166-174) these collected topoi appear to be concerned with stock offense and defense tactics for typical situations, not for an intelligent discussion of the problem, which was what Aristotle had in mind: Top. 101a 25 ff., Rhet. A 1, 54a 11 ff. In the SE 183b 36 ff. Aristotle himself criticizes the formulaic quality of these collections.

[52]W. S. DePATER, Les Topiques d'Aristote et la Dialectique platonicienne, Fribourg 1965, pp. 92-150; "La fonction du lieu et de l'instrument dans les Topiques" in Aristotle on Dialectic: The Topics, ed. G.E.L. OWEN, Oxford 1968, pp. 164-188. A statement like the following in Les Topiques pp. 101-102 cannot be defended in the light of any number of passages in the Rhetoric: "Selon Aristote, toutes deux [i.e. rhetoric and dialectic] ne sont que des facultés pour fournir des arguments, sans qu'une connaissance spécialisée sur l'objet de l'argument soit présupposée. . ."; B 22, 96a 4 ff. is but one example which states the contrary.

[53]In the interpretation of this text I agree with MAIER, Die Syllogistik des Aristoteles II.1, Tübingen 1900, p. 497, note 1. SPENGEL in his Commentary (1867 edition) p. 71, and SOLMSEN op. cit. p. 15 note 1 substantially agree. The minor variant readings admitted by SPENGEL together with VATER (Animadversiones ad Aristotelis librum primum Rhetoricorum, Halle 1794, are not substantial, once the correct antithesis of the sentence is understood: μέν setting off 4-6 against the δέ of 6-7. In the light of the context 9-28 this gives the idea of

general and particular topics. Such a distinction is also seen in Anonymus, *Commentaria in Aristotelem Graeca*, vol. 21, p. 6.27 and in Stephanus, ibid., p. 267. 1-23. I would not accept their identification of the general topics.

[54]SOLMSEN, op. cit., p. 15 note 4 appears more correct on the meaning of περὶ ὧν than COPE-SANDYS, Cambridge 1877, I. p. 49.

[55]The neuter case, ἴδια, is noted by SPENGEL in his commentary sub linea. I do not see any insurmountable problem in it in the light of the neuter κἀκεῖνα (21) referring to κοινοὶ τόποι. See also ROEMER, Zur Kritik der *Rhetorik* des Aristoteles, *RhM* 39, 1884, p. 506 on similar uses of the neuter at *B* 21, 95a 11 and *A* 2, 55b 35. MAIER's note, op. cit., pp. 497-8 does not appear correct in its exclusion of the idea of τόπος from the ἴδια. This would also be true for SOLMSEN, op. cit. pp. 14ff.; MARX, op. cit. pp. 281 note 2, 283 and 296 (if I read him correctly) would understand ἐνθυμήματα or εἴδη with ἴδια; the first is not possible; the second is, on the basis of the text, unlikely. More recently DePATER, Les Topiques pp. 118-122 has attempted an exegesis of this passage. He reaches the conclusion that the passage discriminates between εἴδη i.e. τόποι ἴδιοι and τόποι κοινοί; cf. also his note 266.

[56]Thus SÜSS, Ethos, Leipzig-Berlin 1910, p. 170 would seem wrong in saying that Aristotle has not given us any sharp and satisfactory division between εἴδη and τόποι.

[57]SPENGEL, Über das Studium der Rhetorik bei den Alten, Munich 1842, pp. 22 ff. makes such a distinction. It may appear a quibble, but "sources for material" seems better than "material proofs" ("materielle Beweise"). For it would appear that the 'proof' is the enthymeme and that the *eide* offer material for inferential argument by syllogism, or enthymeme; whereas the *koinoi topoi* present forms for inference by syllogism. There would be no objection to calling the *koinoi topoi* which are sources for formal reasoning by syllogism, or enthymeme, "formelle Beweise" as SPENGEL does.

[58]See *B* 22, 96b 11-19 on the use of ἴδια; and Stephanus, *Commentaria in A. Graeca*, vol. 21, p. 268. 12-15.

[59]This process appears remarkably similar to that presented in *Topics* 105b 12-16 (see p. 132 *infra*); cf. also 10-12 on working with accepted statements or principles.

[60]W. DE PATER, Les Topiques, p. 117; cf. also 106-107, 109, 115. He is speaking of the *eide* and, as he says at 122: "le lieu propre est une proposition probative exprimant une connaissance spécialisée, une formule d'inférence, composée de constantes extra-logiques, et qu'il est, en même temps, une formule de recherche"; or, as he suggests at 124, neither Aristotle's texts nor examples suggest any difference of function between *eidos* and *koinos topos*, they are "tous deux, des formules de recherche et d'inférence".

[61]MARX admits that there are what he calls *eide* (i.e. *idiai protaseis*) for deliberative, forensic, epideictic oratory, but only *topoi* for the πάθη and ἤθη. This forces him to say on 1396b 28-34 that a "Redaktor" has confused the words and incorrectly brought them together, op. cit., pp. 287, 299, 307. SOLMSEN, on the other hand, op. cit., p. 170, note 2 with his interpretation of *topos*, has a far different problem: he cannot understand how any of these εἴδη can be called τόποι by Aristotle: it is "prinzipwidrig".

[62]The note of COPE-SANDYS, op. cit., II. pp. 228-9 indicates what is had in mind here. These εἴδη are always specific to the subject but may be particular or general, see *B* 22, 96b 11-19, with which compare Isocrates, *Philip* 109. This idea I find present in the *Topics*, e.g. 105b 12-8; one can discuss the idea of 'good' in itself, or that which constitutes 'the good' in this specific subject.

[63]*B* 22, 96b 28-34 undoubtedly refers to the section on the εἴδη in Books *A* and *B*, and they are called τόποι here. This is made more probable still by the contrast between τρόπος at *B* 22, 96b 20 and 97a 1. Here Aristotle contrasts the method already presented in the first two books, of securing source material for enthymemes (a method called τοπικός, see SPENGEL in his

commentary *sub* 1396b 20) with the method which he now intends to take up, namely the method of the κοινοὶ τόποι (cf. *supra* pp. 40-42). See also RICCOBONO, Paraphrasis in Rhetoricam Aristotelis, London 1822, p. 206, who writes on *B* 22, 96b 28 ff. and *A* 2, 58a 12 ff.: "Constat igitur locos accipi aut latius aut strictius. Primo modo loci comprehendunt etiam formas [his translation for εἴδη]. . .Secundo modo distinguuntur a formis."

[64]See Stephanus, *Commentaria Graeca*, vol. 21, p. 267 34 ff.

[65]See note 62.

[66]E. HAVET, Etude sur la rhétorique d'Aristote, Paris 1846, p. 34, expresses the distinction precisely: "En un mot, les τόποι ne sont que des formes logiques, . . . τὰ εἴδη, au contraire, ce sont les observations, les faits ou les idées, qui font la matière du raisonnement, et sans lesquels les formes sont vides." In essence the idea of a distinction is found in THROM, Die Thesis, Paderborn 1932, pp. 42-6; Jebb in an appendix to book II of his translation of the *Rhetoric* (ed. SANDYS, Cambridge 1909); LANE COOPER, The Rhetoric of Aristotle, New York 1932, p. xxiv.

[67]*A* 2, 55b 25-34; *A* 4, 59b 12-16. SPENGEL's long note in his commentary on 1355b 26 acquires, it seems, a greater significance in the light of this relation between rhetoric as a *dynamis* and the κοινοὶ τόποι.

[68]Aristotle at *B* 23, 97a 23 ff. gives an example. Here we have the κοινὸς τόπος from correlative terms. As we know, in true correlatives what is predicable of one is generally predicable of the other. As a general axiomatic proposition (assuming A and B to be correlatives) we may say: If A is x, then B is x. Aristotle applies this general form to the question of taxes (26-7). But he calls attention to the fact that it cannot be used indiscriminately and that before it can be applied to a subject (justice is his example) one must carefully determine the meaning of the terms (29 ff.). Such a determination must come from the εἴδη before the κοινὸς τόπος of correlative terms can be used.

[69]SPENGEL apparently has this in mind when he writes that the function of rhetoric is to work up the special proofs of the εἴδη and combine them with the formal to make the subject of discussion universally understood, Über das Studium, p. 22 (n. 51): ". . .ihr [der Rhetorik] liegt ob, die Beweise, welche die einzelne Wissenschaft gibt, zu verarbeiten, mit den formellen zu verbinden, und den Gegenstand zur allgemeinen Kenntnis zu bringen."

[70]SPENGEL in his commentary *sub* 1397a 1 maintains that some are not universal, i.e. common to all rhetorical argument; also COPE, An Introduction to Aristotle's Rhetoric, London 1867, p. 129.

[71]The Roman numerals refer to Roemer's numbering in his text.

[72]SOLMSEN, op. cit., p. 163 and note 5 says well: "Die als Beispiele beigebrachten ἐνθυμήματα der Rhetorik sind durchaus in sich geschlossene Gedankengänge. . .und verhalten sich zu den τόποι, die sie illustrieren, in der Tat wie die πολλά zum formbestimmenden ἕν." This idea of the topics as inferential or logical forms has been developed, as I have recently noticed, into a concept of the topics as "inference-warrants", i.e. "rules for constructing arguments once terms are given in some relation" (O. BIRD, The Tradition of the Logical Topics: Aristotle to Ockham, *JHI* 23 (1962) 307-323).

[73]Cf. supra p. 124, and *A* 2, 58a 10-17.

[74]J. LUKASIEWICZ, Aristotle's Syllogistic, Oxford 1951, p. 20, see also p. 2.

[75]And see Alexander, *Commentaria graeca*, vol. II.2, p. 5. 21-28.

[76]BOCHEŒSKI, op. cit., p. 122. BOCHEŒSKI (and also SOLMSEN) does not think that the Theophrastean τόπος is the same as the Aristotelian. THROM, op. cit., p. 43 and THIONVILLE, op. cit., pp. 30-35 consider it Aristotelian. And BONITZ and ROSS on Met. 1014b note that τόπος as στοιχεῖον would be "an argument applicable to a variety of subjects." *Top.* 163b 18-164a 2 appears to express a similar idea.

[77]WAITZ, op. cit., p. 362.

[78]I believe that THIONVILLE, op. cit., p. 74 sees this process at work but does not recognize it.

[79]In the *Topics* many of the *topoi* are principles for analysis, criticism, and evaluation of terms, all within the framework of the four categories. For instance at 132a 22-24 it is by these *topoi* (διὰ τῶνδε σκεπτέον, ἐκ τῶνδε θεωρητέον) that we determine a thing as a property. Another summary expression of the method appears at 153a 6-28, on definition: to be a true definition a *genus* and *differentia* must be present, and to ascertain whether these are present certain *topoi* must be examined. In this regard SOLMSEN's observation (op. cit., p. 156) on the origin of the *topoi* is interesting. He sees the genesis of the Aristotelian *topoi* in the attempt to specify one's subject, and traces their probable origin to the elenctic dialectic of the Socratic-early Platonic τί ἐστι questions. In general it does seem true (and a passage like *Top.* 152b 6-153a 5 would appear to strengthen this) that Aristotle is concerned with specifying the meaning of terms, and a meaning grounded in the metaphysical reality. In this sense his method may well have had in mind what HAMBRUCH (op. cit., p. 29) says was the aim of one of Plato's dialectical methods: "die Bildung eines festgefügten und wohlgegliederten Begriffsystems. . ."

[80]In this regard HAMBRUCH's attempt to discover the genesis of the methodology of Aristotle's topics appears valid in its general outline. He finds it (op. cit., pp. 8-17) in the logical-metaphysical rules for Platonic διαίρεσις e.g. ἅμα καὶ πρότερον φύσει, πρός τι ὄντα, μᾶλλον καὶ ἧττον. This last rule is called the κοινὸς τόπος of the more-less in the *Rhetoric* and is set down in this axiomatic form (B 23, 97b 12-24): τοῦτο γάρ ἐστιν, εἰ ᾧ μᾶλλον ἂν ὑπάρχοι μὴ ὑπάρχει , δῆλον ὅτι οὐδ᾽ ᾧ ἧττον. As I see it, HAMBRUCH's rules are the same fundamental sort of rules which were discovered independently to be at work in the general topics (see *supra* pp. 130 ff.).

[81]E.g. in 114b 38 ff. he uses κοινὸς τόπος IV; in 116a-b, XI, XIII, XVII; in 119a 37 ff. I and II are employed, and they are described as: μάλιστα δ᾽ ἐπίκαιροι καὶ κοινοὶ τῶν τόπων; in 124 a 15 ff. we find III, and in 154a 12-22 he speaks of the general effectiveness of these topics that are τοὺς μάλιστα κοινούς.

[82] In terms of this distinction it is interesting to note that if a rough analogy is drawn between rhetoric as a part of practical philosophy and *scientia* as a part of speculative philosophy we seem to have something of a parallel between the principal elements leading to ἐπιστήμη in one instance, and to πίστις in the other:

i) ἀρχαί
$$\begin{bmatrix} \text{κοιναί — ἀξιώματα} \\ \text{ἴδιαι — θέσεις} \begin{bmatrix} \text{ὁρισμοί} \\ \text{ὑποθέσεις} \end{bmatrix} \end{bmatrix}$$
through which syllogism and induction effect knowledge

ii) ἀρχαί
$$\begin{bmatrix} \text{κοιναί — τόποι} \\ \text{ἴδιαι — εἴδη} \end{bmatrix}$$
through which enthymeme and example effect belief

Furthermore it would follow that there is not in the *Rhetoric* a double enthymeme theory as MARX, op. cit., pp. 281ff. and SOLMSEN, op. cit., pp. 14 f. would suggest, but rather a single theory which considers the enthymeme a unit composed of εἴδη and κοινοὶ τόποι.

CONCLUSION

Any critical study of the *Rhetoric* quickly reveals that Aristotle's analysis develops its form with the enthymeme as the master structural idea. The basic building blocks of the art are the audience, the speaker, subject-matter open to deliberation and judgment, and the source material both logical and psychological which will enable the audience under the informed direction of the speaker (or writer) to attain the truth as best it can be reached on an open problem. For Aristotle these structural elements of rhetorical discourse are subject to a methodology and it is, as has been seen, the methodology of discursive reasoning through induction and deduction. As far as the *Rhetoric* is concerned deduction by means of the enthymeme is the dominant method. In the light of this evidence it is extremely difficult to avoid the conclusion that the enthymeme cast in such a role is totally ineffective as method if it does not incorporate these essential structural elements. The task before us is to discover whether it does or does not do so.

It is more than clear that rhetoric, viewed as Aristotle views it, must be an integrated act in which person speaks to person for this is both the beginning and the end of the whole operation. Furthermore, the very grounds for initiating such discourse, as outlined by Aristotle, necessarily implicate, if the action is to be successful, the three critical areas which he calls the *pisteis entechnoi*. For in discourse on any problem these *pisteis* are the substantial elements which enable a person to lead an other toward belief or conviction. These *pisteis* are *pragma*, the logical and factual presentation of the subject-matter, those rational probabilities, opinions, truths about the subject which translate it to the mind as reasonable; *ethos*, the element of the personal, the person of the speaker and the auditor, his style, so to speak, as it is affected by and flows into the subject-matter; and finally *pathos*, the interplay of feeling, sensibility, emotions in relation to the subject of discourse. These are the intellectual and psychological forces which come into action in the effort to establish conviction. For, as Aristotle says (*B* 1, 78a 7-9), there are other grounds for belief besides the rational argument (ἀποδείξεων). Rhetorical discourse ideally should integrate these three elements which lead to conviction. If the enthymeme is the major methodological instrument for such discourse, then it should integrate them as well.

As a structural form the enthymeme is certainly well adapted to do so. Just as the scientific syllogism organizes the sources of knowledge, so the rhetorical syllogism can organize the sources of conviction. If we ask ourselves what the scientific syllogism is we find that basically it is an instrument for the acquisition of knowledge which takes apparently separate and independent concepts and puts them into a structure which leads to new knowledge. In the same way the enthymeme gives structure to the sources which contribute to belief or conviction. In both instances the scientific syllogism and the rhetorical syllogism, as structural form, stand apart from their sources. They are a technique which utilizes the sources, a method for discursive reasoning. If the speculative reason alone is at work the sources will be concerned with reason alone; if the practical reason is operating the sources will be different. There is a recognition of such a difference at *Rhetoric Γ* 16, 17a 19-20: "Thus mathematical discourses possess no *ethos* since they have no *proairesis*", and *De Anima* 433a 14-15: "mind which calculates to an end, that is the practical mind; it differs from the speculative mind by its *telos*". As has been said previously the only permanent element in "syllogism" is its structure as a form of inference. Its apodeictic, dialectical, rhetorical character is determined by its content, or the source material it uses. In so far as Aristotle usually thinks of syllogism as the apodeictic syllogism, that is to say the inferential form using epistemonic source material, it may be that he calls the enthymeme quite early in the *Rhetoric* (*A* 1, 55a 8) "a kind of, a sort of syllogism".

When Aristotle calls the enthymeme σῶμα τῆς πίστεως (*A* 1, 54a 15) it certainly appears that it is in this sense of inferential form, something which is able to contain and give form to the *pisteis*. Since the *pisteis* as source material are three in number it is clear that the enthymeme as the body must contain all three.[1] There is certainly no ground on which to assume that this phrase refers to the enthymeme as the third of the three *pisteis*, that is to say the logical proof of the subject, with the underlying idea rightly rejected by VATER: "*robur et nervum fidei faciendae, ut enthymema fit* πίστις *potentissima, sicuti robur militaris; ceterae autem fidei faciendae rationes sint minus efficaces, ut arma*".[2] This idea is simply not in the Greek word. Rather σῶμα means the body, the whole in which a thing is contained.[3] As that which incorporates the *pisteis* the enthymeme as structural form should contain and give organization to the material which establishes belief in rhetorical discourse, namely, *pragma* (the logical explanation of the subject), *ethos*, and *pathos*.

Textually it appears impossible to establish the enthymeme as the third *pistis*, i.e. the rational demonstration of the subject. We have already seen that Aristotle never calls the enthymeme the third *pistis*, and, further, that a distinction clearly exists between the sources (the *pisteis entechnoi*) used by the enthymeme and the enthymeme as an inferential form (together with *paradeigma* called the *pisteis apodeiktikai*). Further evidence of that clear separation is found at *Γ* 1, 03b 6-15. Here in a summary of what has been achieved thus far in the treatise Aristotle says that he has discussed the three *pisteis* and he indicates that these are *pathos*, *ethos*, and a probative explanation of the subject (e.g. ἀποδεδεῖχθαι 10-12). He continues the statement with the remark that he has also discussed the enthymeme and its topics (13-14). If one insists that enthymeme is the third *pistis* and consequently that he is referring to enthymeme in the word ἀποδεδεῖχθαι (12) then Aristotle is talking in circles. For he states rather confusingly: "*pathos, ethos*, and 'the enthymeme' have been discussed . . . and the enthymeme has also been discussed".

To rest one's evidence for this identification of enthymeme with the third *pistis* on a phrase at *A* 1, 55a 7 where Aristotle calls the enthymeme κυριώτατον τῶν πίστεων is to forget that *pistis* here refers to the two modes of inferential reasoning, deduction and induction, which he calls the κοιναὶ πίστεις at *B* 20, 93a 24 and the πίστεις ἀποδεικτικαί at *A* 2, 58a 1. There is no question of "logical proof" being the "most decisive, or master, proof", although the statement does have an Aristotelian ring to it and for that reason apparently has an attractive quality. Yet it would indeed be rather foolish for Aristotle to say such a thing of rhetorical discourse directed as it is to move an other toward belief and conviction when he remarks in the *Ethics* (1139a 35-6) that pure reason moves nothing. Further, the tenuous character of such evidence becomes clear when one notes that just a page later in the *Rhetoric* (*A* 2, 56a 13) Aristotle says of *ethos*: σχεδὸν . . . κυριωτάτην ἔχει πίστιν. The enthymeme, then, as "the most decisive" of the proofs means, if anything, that deductive reasoning by the enthymeme is superior to inductive reasoning by *paradeigma*, a judgment completely in accord with his general attitude on the two kinds of inferential reasoning.

As we will see shortly all rhetorical demonstration which is directed toward achieving judgment from the auditor in the area of human action demands specifically a presentation which confronts both the intellect and the appetitive faculties, or *reason, ethos* and *pathos*. Consequently the instruments of such demonstration, whether they be inductive or deductive, must integrate these elements. Since, however, there has been persistent insistence that Aristotle is primarily concerned with rational proof of one's subject and that the enthymeme as the syllogism of rhetoric is the deductive instrument of that rational proof we must carry this matter somewhat further.

As far as I can see the strongest evidence in the *Rhetoric* for the enthymeme as the third *pistis entechnos* is a passage at Γ 17, 18a 1-b 4. Here it appears that enthymeme is identified with logical proof of one's statement (i. e. *apodeixis*) and separated from *ethos* and *pathos*.[4] In some ways the text does seem insurmountable, and visions of Marx' editor of Γ (see p. 50) begin to take shape before the mind's eye. Unfortunately, however, what is said in part of this passage (e. g. 18a 1-5) was said earlier at *A* 9, 68a 29-33 and the word *apodeixis* was also used, namely, that *paradeigmata* are best for deliberative discourse, enthymemes for judicial. It is of interest to note that this passage at *A* 9 is one of the only three times that ἐνθύμημα is used between *A* 4 and *B* 17 inclusively, a section in which Aristotle discusses the particular topics (*eide*) of enthymemes. His usual phrase throughout is *pistis* such as can be found at *A* 7, 65b 19-21. The other instances are at *A* 15, 76a 32 and *B* 1, 77b 19. In the *A* 15 passage we can see something of the difficulty of making an absolute identification of enthymeme and *apodeixis* to represent the exclusively logical demonstration of the subject. Here (76a 29-32) Aristotle says that in presenting the character of a witness "we must speak from the same topics from which we take our enthymemes". The presumption in this statement is that enthymemes can be derived from topics concerned with *ethos*. There is a somewhat similar difficulty in the *B* 1, 77b 16-24 statement. In the text we are told that from the topics presented (i. e. book *A*) come our "enthymemes" on each genre of rhetoric. This is quite understandable since we are and have been looking throughout the book for the sources of enthymemes. But at b23 Aristotle (in the ordinary interpretation of this passage) seems to explain "enthymeme" by the words [λόγος] ἀποδεικτικός . . . καὶ πιστός, and once more the enthymeme appears to be *apodeixis*, or logical demonstration (cf. also 78a 8 ἀποδείξεων). Again, however, it can be asked whether *apodeiktikos* here means anything more than *logos* which arises from the actual presentation of the case. This was the general quest of *A*, a presentation grounded in the *pisteis pragmatikai*. *Apodeiktikos* is found in a similar use at *A* 8, 66a 9-10 where we are told that our "*pisteis* come not only δι' ἀποδεικτικοῦ λόγου ἀλλὰ καὶ δι' ἠθικοῦ".

In other words can we be absolutely certain that in every instance in which Aristotle uses some form of *apodeixis* he necessarily means rational demonstration by syllogism? Can not *apodeixis* mean also the rational character of discourse in the instances cited in contradistinction to the emotional or ethical character? Indeed, in one of the only three passages between *A* 4-*B* 17 where Aristotle uses *syllogismos* (*A* 6, 62b 30; 10, 68b 2; 11, 71b 9), and where he could have used *enthymema* (or *apodeixis* if one insists upon the absolute identity of the two), Aristotle clearly states that the sources of this syllogism in rhetorical discourse are more than merely logical in character. For we read at *A* 10, 68b 1-5: "With respect to accusation and defense one should next state from how many and what kind of propositions the syllogisms must be constructed. It is necessary, in fact, to consider three things, first, for what reasons and for how many reasons men act wrongly, secondly, in what state of mind they are, thirdly, their character and disposition." The presence here among the sources of actual evidence (*pragma*) as well as *pathos* (cf. also 68b 25-26) and *ethos* is more than clear. Equally clear is it that all are the substance for inference by syllogism.

When we turn to our passage at *Γ* 17, 18a 12-17 we read: "wherever you are trying to arouse emotion don't use an enthymeme; for it will either expel the emotion or will be used to no avail. Simultaneous movements expel each other, and they either destroy or weaken each other. Nor must one seek any enthymeme at the moment when making the *logos* ethical; for *apodeixis* has neither *ethos* nor moral purpose". We have here what appears to be an explicit identification of enthymeme with *apodeixis*; and so the enthymeme is apparently the logical proof of one's subject-matter. This viewpoint is presumably repeated at 18a 32-b 2.

Aristotle does seem to speak of the enthymeme as logical demonstration by syllogism of the subject-matter in contradistinction to proof derived from *ethos* and *pathos*. To decide whether or not he is in fact saying this can only be done within the context of his comments on rhetorical discourse as I have just tried to illustrate, not in the study of an isolated statement.

But if we take the statement here does it submit to an explanation? It must be said immediately that there is no problem in the identification of enthymeme with *apodeixis* for Aristotle actually calls the enthymeme the *apodeixis* of rhetoric (*A* 1, 55a 6). *Apodeixis* usually refers to scientific demonstration by syllogism, but in a more extended sense and one met in the *Rhetoric* means demonstration by syllogism which is for Aristotle a form of rational inference. We should note next that in our passage at *Γ* 17 Aristotle clearly desires to emphasize proof by *pathos*. He separates it distinctly from logical proof. We have already seen in chapter I that Aristotle recognizes that any of the three *pisteis entechnoi* (*pragma, ethos, pathos*) can be used independently to effect belief or conviction. In our section this acceptance of separate ways of proof is present,[5] and with this compartmentalized approach uppermost in his mind Aristotle could readily designate logical proof in our passage by the one word so firmly tied to such proof: *apodeixis* and its rhetorical correlative enthymeme. It is not impossible—though perhaps unfortunate—that when Aristotle wishes to speak of winning conviction by *reason* as opposed to winning conviction by *pathos* or *ethos* he employs the word enthymeme which he has already called ἀπόδειξις ῥητορική (*A* 1, 55a 6). It does not seem that we must inevitably conclude from *Γ*17 that the enthymeme is, and can only be, the logical demonstration of the subject by syllogistic inference.

In conclusion attention should be directed to the fact that when we find the verb form ἀποδεικνύναι (it is used once between *A* 4-*B* 17 at *B* 4, 82a 17) it can mean simply "demonstration by syllogism".[6] For example its use in *B* 22, 96a 35 together with δεικνύναι b 2, 10 is at the most "demonstration by syllogism". It would be difficult for it to be *exclusively rational* demonstration by syllogism since *B* 22, 96a 34-b 19 is the conclusion to a 4-34. And in a 4-34 we cannot escape the fact that the "demonstration" includes not simply a knowledge of the facts of the case but of those facts which carry an emotional appeal and reflect the *ethos* of the people addressed, e.g. what is specifically necessary to convince the Athenians that war is necessary. Aristotle is speaking here about the choice of material for argumentation, and as he says (*Topics* 105b 15) such selection should begin with the subject itself (ἀπὸ τοῦ τί ἐστιν). In rhetorical discourse the subject is of necessity specified by something more than its mere logical analysis.[7]

However if any corrective to the interpretation of the enthymeme as the third *pistis* and exclusively logical proof is needed it can be found first of all in Aristotle's statements on maxim, γνώμη (*B* 21, 94a 18-95a 34). From his description (94a 22-29) maxim can be called a general truth embodying a moral or practical precept concerning human action.[8] There are four kinds: (A) maxim with its reason given

(e. g. no man is free for he is either a slave of money or chance); this kind of maxim is either (1) part of an enthymeme, or, (2) enthymematic, but not part of an enthymeme; (B) maxim without its reason added (e. g. no man is completely happy); this is either (3) well-known gnomic statement and so familiar, or, (4) eminently clear from the mere enunciation. Our attention naturally gravitates to the first two types because of their relation to enthymeme. It is a very intimate relation since Aristotle says (B 21, 94a 26-29): "Consequently since enthymemes are syllogisms concerned with such subject-matter maxims are more or less the conclusions of enthymemes or the premises with the syllogistic form removed".[9] This statement is general and is true for all kinds of maxim. If it is pressed we can legitimately conclude that premises or conclusions of an enthymeme are often gnomic in character. As such the enthymeme would obviously be something substantively different from bare logical proof. Again, however, from what Aristotle tells us about the enthymeme and maxim there is no need to conclude that maxim *must be* "part of an enthymeme". There can be enthymeme without gnomic statement. The *Anonymi Scholia*[10] explain it well: "the enthymeme differs from the non-apodeictic maxim [i. e. those without the reason added] in that this last is a simple declaration and the enthymeme is a syllogism so to speak; it differs from the apodeictic maxim [i. e. those with the reason added] as the parts differ from a whole, for the enthymeme is contained within the maxim". In Aristotle, however, a close relationship is established between enthymeme and maxim and we read at B 20, 93a 25 that maxim is not to be included among the *koinai pisteis* (enthymeme and *paradeigma*) because "it is part of enthymeme".[11] As an illustration of this relation we have in our section two maxims which become enthymemes (B 21, 94a 29 ff.), and at Γ 17, 18b 33-38 we have in Aristotle's own words an enthymeme which becomes a maxim with the reason added. This exchange between maxim and enthymeme is also true of maxim which Aristotle says is particularly esteemed by the auditors and which he calls "enthymematic" (B 21, 94b 19-20). It is not "part of an enthymeme" but stands by itself. Since it carries in its statement the reason for its truth, e. g. "mortal as you are cherish not an immortal anger" (94b 21-22) it can be easily presented in a syllogistic form and so is called "enthymematic".[12] Such a ready interchange of maxim and enthymeme obviously raises substantial questions about the purely logical character of enthymematic argumentation.

We know from Aristotle's explanation (B 21, 94a 22-26) that maxim is a general proposition, or assertion, relative to moral action and human conduct.[13] As such it will of necessity implicate the constituent elements of moral action which includes *ethos* and *pathos*. The maxim is concerned with human action and particularly with *proairesis* in human action (B 21, 95a 28 ff.; b12 ff.). In addition to this maxim is an instrument for making discourse ethical (b 13) and for the delineation of *ethos* in the speaker (B 21, 95a 2-5, 23; b 15-18; Γ 17, 18a 17-18). It also is related to *pathos* in discourse, both subjectively on the speaker's part (95a 24-25) and objectively with respect to the audience (95b 10 ff.). A quick glance at the maxims cited by Aristotle reveals, for example, emotional states reflecting fear, patriotism, courage, anger.[14] Maxim functions clearly on two levels: the intellectual and the appetitive. In Aristotle's words the listeners "delight if the speaker happens to express in a general way their specific convictions" (95b 2-5). Thus maxim is a statement of reason together with emotional and associative overtones which influence the person, the appetitive as well as the rational part of him. Aeschines (3.135) expresses it rather well: "I believe that we learn the *gnomai* of poets carefully when we are children for this reason, that we may use them when we are men".

In maxim, then, which is so closely connected with enthymeme, we have argumentation which aims quite directly at the emotional and appetitive side of man. The conclusion which we must draw from this is that the enthymeme cannot be exclusively rational and intellectual. Nor can it be called the third *pistis*, namely the logical proof of the subject. It can not even be identified with the third *pistis* as the rational explanation of the subject-matter. We come back again to the idea that the enthymeme is something which stands apart from the three *pisteis*: *ethos*, *pathos*, *rational explanation*. It gives them form as argumentation incorporating them in rhetorical demonstration. For an assured corollary of Aristotle's comments on maxim is that the enthymeme works not merely upon the intellect but also upon the affective part of man. The enthymeme employs both reason, emotion, *ethos*, and directs itself in its argumentation to the whole man. This should not be startling when we realize that it is the primary methodological tool in a *techne* which aims ultimately at effecting in others a judgment and decision with a view to action.

To recall and slightly enlarge upon some of the statements in c. I we know that any kind of argumentation or demonstration which concerns itself with effecting judgment and decision in this area must take into consideration all the factors which make decision possible. Aristotle is always quite clear in the *Rhetoric* that its *telos* is a judgment of some sort, an evaluation to be made by the auditor. When we consider man as someone to be disposed toward *praxis* we soon discover that for Aristotle something more than an informed mind is needed. We learn in the *Nicomachean Ethics* (1098a 3 ff.) that man's nature directed to action involves a twofold element: intellect and appetition. Intellect is directive, appetition is subject to direction, capable of obeying rule. But both are necessary. This nature is more carefully analysed at 1102a 27 ff. and we find that man's soul, as the principle of responsible human action, calls upon two factors in order to act: reason and appetition, *nous* and *orexis*.[15] It is interesting to see this analysis reflected in the *Rhetoric* at A 11, 70a 13-27, particularly at 25-27: "rational desires are those men form upon conviction for they desire to see and possess many things after hearing of them and being convinced about them". If we take a closer look at man's nature as the principle of *praxis* we arrive at this general picture of it. From the appetitive side man's soul consists of πάθη (emotions, feelings), δυνάμεις (psychical capacities for experiencing such feelings), ἕξεις (acquired dispositions with respect to the feelings) 1105b 19-21. Fundamentally these are the elements which enter into human *praxis*.[16] If we advance somewhat further there appears to exist in man's soul a dominant appetitive faculty. βούλησις fits the role rather well although Aristotle is admittedly not particularly clear on this. βούλησις is an appetency for the *telos* (1111b 26; 1113a 11 15; b 3) and for the good (1113a 14-24; *Rhet. A* 10, 69a 3: βούλησις ἀγαθοῦ ὄρεξις). It is "rational wish" and it corresponds well with that part of the rational soul which Aristotle describes in 1102b 25-6 as λόγου μετέχειν.[17] βούλησις, then, would be the faculty which can exercise control over ἐπιθυμία with which it forms substantially the orectic soul. This dominance by the rational part of the soul, i.e. the part which obeys reason (1102b 26), permits one to understand how intentional habits (ἕξεις) are formed in the soul. For there is definitely something in the orectic soul "contrary to reason and opposed to it" (1102b 24) which can be controlled since ἕξεις is that "by which we are well or badly disposed with respect to the πάθη" (1105b 26; see also 1106a 2-3). βούλησις is consistent with this rational control of the πάθη in accord with the rule set by *phronesis*.[18] It is then possible to understand why such ἕξεις when they are "praiseworthy" (1103a 9) can be called "virtues". For *arete* (1106b 36 ff.), as a state of soul apt to exercise deliberate choice under reason, implies a higher rational appetitive faculty controlling first the πάθη and then action.[19] With this in mind we can understand why such ἕξεις in man may be good or bad, and how it is that these stabile dispositions, dispositions in which βούλησις is the controlling factor, manifest a person's *ethos* or character as we see it in *Poetics* 1450a 5, b 8. *Ethos*, then, would represent the appetitive soul as it is firmly disposed in one way or another, a disposition produced by a dominant appetitive faculty under the control of reason: λόγου μετέχειν.[20] With this understanding of *ethos* it becomes possible to comprehend VAHLEN'S translation of ἦθος in the *Poetics* as "Wille", e. g. "Dort sind διάνοια und ἦθος Intelligenz und Charakter, Verstand und Wille, zusammengefaßt als die beiden Seiten, in denen die geistige Qualität des Menschen überhaupt aufgeht...", as well as BUTCHER'S interpretation: "*Ethos*, as explained by Aristotle, is the moral element in character. It reveals a certain state or direction of the will".[21] Since πάθη play a prominent part in the orectic soul and are capable of influence (1106a 4-5; 1111a 22-25, b1-3) we can understand that the dominant appetitive faculty seeks to acquire a constant disposition with respect to them. Thus whenever Aristotle speaks of the "good disposition" (*arete*) he tells us that it is concerned with the πάθη.

   This, then, is the appetitive part of the psyche concerned with *praxis*. If we now consider the role of reason in *praxis* we may apprehend the final process better. In 1112a 18-1113a 14 Aristotle describes the intellectual process. Reason starts from an assumed or desired *telos* and considers the means necessary to achieve it through deliberation. This activity terminates at the first means necessary and there it stops since neither deliberation nor reason can give the end. Something else must come in to initiate this final action. This is the most damaging criticism of those who would insist that Aristotle identifies rhetorical demonstration with reason alone. Such demonstration would be sterile. When reason has done its work then an evaluation (*krisis*) and a choice must be made. Deliberate choice, *proairesis*, must step in (1113a 2-14). This is the appetitive part of the psyche, "*orexis* assenting to the result of deliberation", or, as Aristotle explains it (1113a 15-b 2; see also 1111 b 5 ff.), "deliberate desire of things in our power". Again this is reflected rather well in the *Rhetoric A* 10, 68b 9-12: "men do willingly all that they do with knowledge and without constraint. Thus while all voluntary acts are not the object of deliberate choice (προαιρούμενοι) all that men deliberately choose they do with knowledge; for no one is ignorant of that which he deliberately chooses (προαιρεῖται)".

Praxis, then, is the result of appetition (ὄρεξις) and reason (νοῦς) in two ways: a) remotely in so far as they inaugurate and enter into the process, b) proximately in so far as they constitute *proairesis* which is the efficient cause of action (1139a 31-33). Further the orectic soul, as we have seen, includes feelings, emotions, and stabile dispositions with respect to them. These form the threshold from which the orectic soul steps into action under the guidance of reason.[22]

We are thus confronted with the fact that *pathos*, *ethos*, and *reason* are intimately united in *praxis*. In rhetoric which prepares for *praxis* we should expect to find them closely united, particularly in the enthymeme which for Aristotle is the heart of the rhetorical process. Deliberation occupies itself with matters within our power and of consequence to us. In rhetorical discourse the audience must be brought not only to knowledge of the subject but knowledge as relevant and significant for they are either indifferent, opposed, or in partial agreement. They will ultimately decide to act or not after deliberate choice, and *proairesis* is always reason and appetition moving together as Aristotle says at 1113a 11-12: "for coming to a decision after deliberation we desire in accord with our deliberation". The whole person acts and we find this again in the *Rhetoric* at *A* 10, 68b 32-69a 7. Confining ourselves to that part of the text immediately pertinent to the analysis here we read that πάντες δὴ πάντα πράττουσι . . . δι᾽ αὐτούς . . . δι᾽ ὄρεξιν . . . τὰ μὲν διὰ λογιστικὴν ὄρεξιν τὰ δὲ δι᾽ ἄλογον, sc. ὀργὴν καὶ ἐπιθυμίαν: "all men perform all actions . . . which are owing to themselves . . . through appetition . . . some through appetition guided by reason others without the guidance of reason . . . in anger and lust". In the *De Motu Animalium* 700 b 15-24 we read in part: "For all living things both move and are moved with a view to some object . . . the end in view. We perceive that what moves the living creature is intellect (διάνοια), imagination, deliberate choice, will (βούλησις) and appetite. All these are reducible to mind and appetition (ταῦτα δὲ πάντα ἀνάγεται εἰς νοῦν καὶ ὄρεξιν)". In the *Poetics* 1449b 35 ff. (cf. p. 27 f. *supra*) we are told quite explicitly that drama is an imitation of *praxis* and demands the causes of *praxis*: *ethos* and *dianoia*.[23] Since, as we have seen, *ethos* implicates the play of the emotions *praxis* in drama is the result of the interaction of *ethos*, *pathos* and *dianoia*. It is the externalization of an inward psychical process which develops from the interaction of feelings and reason and is carried forward to its conclusion by the will. "Action, to be dramatic, must be exhibited in its development and in its results; it must stand in reciprocal and causal relation to certain mental states. We desire to see the feelings out of which it grows, the motive force of will which carries it to its conclusion; and, again, to trace the effect of the deed accomplished on the mind of the doer—the emotions there generated as they become in turn new factors of action . . .".[24] It is clear that the emotions qualify and condition man's action both from the appetitive and the intellectual side in so far as they affect reason which is guiding *proairesis*. As Aristotle says at *Rhet. B* 1, 78a 20-21: "The emotions are those things through which men alter and change their decisions". Human action must, then, be determined by *ethos, pathos*, and *nous*.

If the whole person acts, then it is the whole person to whom discourse in rhetoric must be directed. One can say *a priori* that anything, such as the enthymeme, which for Aristotle embodies the rhetorical technique must consider *intellect, ethos* (that is to say stabile dispositions with respect to one's appetitive state), and *pathos* (emotions which enter into and influence human action).

If we return now to the *Rhetoric* and give attention to some statements in the text we find further evidence that Aristotle did not intend the enthymeme, as the rhetorical mode of demonstration, to be exclusively rational, but to incorporate *ethos* and *pathos* as well as *reason*. At *B* 1, 77b 16-24 Aristotle notes that we have been given in the first book δόξαι καὶ προτάσεις (18) which are useful for proving (19). In other words we have at our disposal at the moment generally accepted opinions and propositional statements for logical statements on the subject-matter in each of the three branches of rhetoric (20). From these opinions and propositions enthymemes are formed (19). However, Aristotle continues, rhetoric is directed toward judgment (21) and this demands that the *logos* (23) present not merely the logical aspect of the subject-matter but also give attention to *ethos* and *pathos* (23-24), since they, too, affect judgment (25 ff.). It is not unnatural to expect that he would now present us with such "generally accepted opinions and propositions" on *ethos* and *pathos* and this he tells us (78a 28-30) is his plan: "and so just as we drew up a list of premises in the case of the earlier material, let us now also do this on the material before us and analyse it in the same way". When we come to the conclusion of the analysis of *ethos* and *pathos* in the second book we read at *B* 18, 91b 25-29: "and with respect to all the kinds of rhetoric generally accepted opinions and propositional statements have been selected from which those who engage in deliberative, epideictic and forensic rhetoric take their proofs, and further still those opinions and propositions have also been determined from which it is possible to make the *logos* ethical".[25] Even were the advocates of the enthymeme as exclusively rational demonstration to confine themselves to cc. 4-14 of book *A* together with the summation of these chapters at *B* 1, 77b 16-24 their argument would be incomplete and inadequate. For in the course of these chapters Aristotle manifests an awareness of the role of *ethos* and *pathos* in demonstration. For example he explicitly remarks of judicial oratory (*A* 9, 68b 1 ff.) that with regard to the number and nature of the premises of rhetorical syllogisms we must not only consider the reasons why men act but also their emotional attitudes and their characters. These elements also enter into the rhetorical syllogism. In view of the fact that as yet there is no formal discussion of *ethos* and *pathos* one would rightly expect such a discussion and Aristotle promises it at 68b 25-26.

These text statements on δόξαι καὶ προτάσεις coalesce and we can see a larger meaning when they are taken together with the seminal statement which is the preface to the entire discussion. At *A* 1, 59a 6-10 we read: "It is clear from what has been said that we must have first of all premises on such matters; for *tekmeria*, *eikota* and *semeia* are the premises of rhetoric; while in general a syllogism is built upon premises, the enthymeme is a syllogism built upon the premises just mentioned". This statement is a preface to a study of precisely such particular premises from c. 4 of book *A* to c. 17 of book *B*. At the end of the study we find the same statement substantially at *B* 18, 91 b 24-29 and again at *B* 22, 96b 28-34. This last immediately precedes his discussion of the general sources for the enthymeme and states in part: "for premises have already been singled out with respect to each branch of rhetoric so that the sources from which one must draw enthymemes on the good or bad, honorable or dishonorable, just or unjust are on hand, and in like manner the sources for *ethos*, *pathos* and the habits have been selected and are on hand for us".[26] We cannot forget that Aristotle refers in these last two passages to his discussion from *A* 4 to *B* 17 which presents the particular topics. These topics are the sources for *eikota, semeia*, and *tekmeria*. The *eikota, semeia, tekmeria*, however, are the premises which form rhetorical enthymemes.

It appears rather difficult to escape the fact that the enthymeme as the primary instrument of rhetorical argumentation and demonstration brings together reason and appetition in its effort to make a judgment possible. This understanding of the enthymeme was not entirely unknown to the ancients. Planudes in a discussion of enthymeme in which he defines it as a condensed syllogism, incomplete with respect to one of its propositions, goes on to cite Neocles: "Neocles says that the syllogism is put together from premises and a conclusion; but the enthymeme as compared with the epicheireme is produced in a condensed form with one proposition of *ethos* and *pathos*, and sometimes *ethos* and *pathos* are commingled".[27]

Aristotle's achievement is expressed well by Cicero (*De Orat.* 2. 160): "*Atque inter hunc Aristotelem, cuius . . . legi . . . et illos, in quibus ipse sua quaedam de eadem arte dixit, et hos germanos huius artis magistros hoc mihi visum est interesse, quod ille eadem acie mentis, qua rerum omnium vim naturamque viderat, haec quoque aspexit quae ad dicendi artem, . . .*". The major difference between the Aristotelian analysis and that of others is that Aristotle recognized the organic character of discourse. Knowing that men are moved to judgment by the concomitant action of reason and appetition he argued that discourse must be unified in both its argumentation and its language. *Reason, ethos*, and *pathos* not only permeate the language of discourse but are also unified in its argumentation, particularly in the enthymeme. The movement toward conviction (*pistis*) and so toward judgment (*krisis*) is an integral action and implicates reason (*nous*) and appetition (*orexis*) working together. The *logos* in both its expression and argumentation must fuse these elements. Aristotle's view of discourse is organic not separatist. This last which we can find in a statement attributed to Theodectes: "to make the exordium with a view to winning good will, the narration with a view to plausibility, the confirmation with a view to persuasion, the peroration with a view to anger or pity" (cf. H. RABE, Prolegomenon Sylloge, Teubner 1931, p. 216) is an interpretation which has come down into modern rhetorical theory where we find parts of the discourse given over to logical proof, parts to emotional appeal.

With some qualifications Aristotle's attitude toward discourse is more correctly represented in an article of F. SOLMSEN, "Aristotle and Cicero on the Orator's Playing upon the Feelings". SOLMSEN believes that he has recovered the Aristotelian theory of rhetoric in Cicero's *De Oratore* 2. 27.115, where Cicero's view of rhetorical discourse is that of a unified *logos*. With a slight change of the schema given we have Aristotle's theory well expressed. The *ratio dicendi* (the discourse) represents in itself a concurrence of (a) *ratio probandi* (*pragma*, i. e. logical analysis of subject), (b) *ratio conciliandi* (*ethos*), (c) *ratio commovendi* (*pathos*). SOLMSEN concludes that Aristotle "rather thinks of the λόγος as a whole and thinks of it as being made πιστός and becoming effective by the combined and simultaneous application of the three πίστεις: ἀπόδειξις, τὸ ἦθος τοῦ λέγοντος and τὰ πάθη".[28]

Aristotle has created a superb synthesis. He has fully justified rhetoric for the most Platonic Platonist. Rhetoric is not philosophy nor is it a mere technical game. It is the use of language in an artistic way, language which brings together in its effort to communicate knowledge and understanding to an other the elements essential to that understanding: reason and appetition.

Notes

[1] A reading of *A* 1, 54a 11-16 together with 54b 19-22 and 55a 3-5, *A* 2, 55b 35-39 with their stress on the entechnic *pisteis* indicates that the enthymeme must be involved somehow with these three sources.

[2] VATER, Animadversiones, p. 5. While he does not appear to say what is being said in this analysis he does discern the import of Aristotle's statements, e.g. "Ad enthymema autem referuntur omnia quibus argumentatio efficitur. Qui versatus est in ταῖς ἐντέχνοις πίστεσι est ἐνθυμηματικός . . ."

[3] I. CASAUBON, Animadversiones in Athenaei Deipnosophistas, Lyon 1600, on II.6, p. 54 gives instances of *soma* in this sense. VATER, Animadversiones, p. 5 cites *Meteor.* II.4 in same sense; he also approves Maioragius' translation of our phrase σῶμα τῆς πίστεως as "ipsa

natura et substantia"; in his comments here VATER appears to understand *soma* as I take it, i.e. literally, not metaphorically.

[4]It is not possible to refrain from saying here that were we to pursue the not uncommon way of explaining problems in the text we could say that in the light of the evidence already produced Aristotle simply could not have made these statements and that these passages represent the kind of misunderstanding and interpolation characteristic of the *Rhetoric* in general and particularly of the third book. In fact this has been done for the first passage (Γ 17, 18a 12 ff.), see SOLMSEN, Drei Rekonstruktionen, Hermes 67, 1932, p. 149.

[5]Our passage appears in a section of the third book which has been said to be from a treatise on "the parts of speech" (μόρια λόγου). This was a fairly traditional approach to rhetoric according to which certain parts of speech were concerned exclusively with logical proof, others with proof by *pathos*, others with proof by *ethos*; see K. BARWICK, Die Gliederung der rhetorischen τέχνη und die horazische Epistula ad Pisones, Hermes 57, 1922, pp. 11ff. A number of scholars believe that Aristotle was strongly influenced in this part of the third book by just such an approach, e.g. SPENGEL, τεχνῶν συναγωγή, Leipzig 1828, p. 159, MARX, Aristoteles Rhetorik, pp. 245 ff., SÜSS, Ethos, pp. 193 ff., SOLMSEN, Drei Rekonstruktionen, pp. 146ff.

[6]At times cognates of *apodeixis* appear quite similar to uses of δεικνύναι i.e. "universe demonstrandi, exponendi, explicandi vim habet" (BONITZ); the idea of explanation, exposition of the subject-matter rather than its demonstration.

[7]In the area of formal rhetoric a cursory examination of the argumentation of the Attic orators makes this clear; for a general conspectus of such argumentation see M. LAVENCY, La technique des lieux communs de la rhétorique grecque, LEC 35, 1965, pp. 113-126.

[8]There is a perceptive analysis of the word by Planudes in *Rhetores Graeci* (ed. WALZ) vol. 5, p. 422.3-16 in which he locates its role in the sphere of human action and its purpose "to teach the kind of action something is or ought to be"; also in vol. 7, pt. 2, p. 765.11-766.4 there is an intelligent discussion of Aristotle's division from the *Anonymi Scholia*. Anaximenes in c. 11 on maxim considers only classes 1 and 2 and his discussion is quite informative about Aristotle's division.

[9]In the light of such an explicit statement there should be no necessity to say that the relationship is *not* based on form, i.e. the enthymeme and maxim are related because they express their thought in a shortened syllogistic form. The relationship is grounded in the subject-matter of each.

[10]See note 8.

[11]This does not mean that *gnomai* cannot be used alone; obviously those without the reason added are so used, and those with the reason given may be. If they do not have the syllogistic form they are not part of an enthymeme but possess the potential to be made into enthymemes.

[12]Anonymus, *Commentaria Graeca*, vol. 21, p. 127.5 says as much in a rather vague and elusive comment which leaves his testimony somewhat questionable.

[13]See Gregory in *Rhetores Graeci* (ed. WALZ) vol. 7, pt. 2, p. 1154.15 who gives the explanation of Theophrastus: "a general assertion in the area of what one must do", or the *Auctor ad Her.* 4.24 and HORNA, RE suppl. VI (1935) p. 75, on the passage in Aristotle "ihr Zweck das sittliche oder lebenskluge Verhalten des Menschen zu regeln", and RHYS ROBERTS, Demetrius on Style, Cambridge 1902, p. 272.

[14]Anonymus, *Comm. Graeca*, vol. 21, p. 129.3 ff., grasps the role of *pathos* in *gnome* although he misrepresents Aristotle at *B* 21, 95b 10 ff. in saying that the purpose of gnomologia is to pander to what you suspect the audience's feelings to be.

[15]See 1139a 17-b 13; we read at 21f.: "what affirmation and negation are in thought, pursuit and flight are in appetition". See *De An.* 432b 26-433b 30; at 433a 9: "these two, then, appear to be the sources of movement, *orexis* and *nous*".

[16]We are not including αἴσθησις (1139a 17-19) since it is not immediately relevant to the problem under discussion.

[17]In cc. 9-11 of the *De Anima* βούλησις is rational wish; on this see R.D. HICKS, Aristotle *De Anima*, Cambridge 1907, s. 432b 5. At 411a 28 (and see 414b 2) βούλησις is a species of *orexis* which is opposed to ἐπιθυμία as rational to irrational desire and this same relationship is present at *Rhet. A* 10, 69a 1-3 where βούλησις concerns action which results from ὄρεξις λογιστική as opposed to ὄρεξις ἄλογος.

[18]*Phronesis* determines the *true* response demanded by the situation; as Aristotle says of the "good" man (1106b 36ff.): "Virtue is a stabile disposition having to do with deliberate choice consisting in a mean that is relative to us, a mean determined by a rational principle and by that rational principle by which the *phronimos* man would determine it"; see H. JOACHIM, Aristotle, The Nicomachean Ethics, Oxford 1951, pp. 85-89; L.H.G. GREENWOOD, Aristotle, Nicomachean Ethics, Cambridge 1909, p. 37.

[19]Aristotle mentions a number of times that *arete* is concerned with πάθη and πράξεις, e.g. 1104b 13-14; 1106b 16-17, 24-25.

[20]See 1138b 35-1139a 3 where *ethos* is connected with the *aretai ethikai*; and 1138b 18-20 where there is a volitional faculty of some kind (also 1109b 30 ff.); and 1110a 12, 19 where we see some such faculty at work.

[21]J. VAHLEN, Aristoteles' Lehre von der Rangfolge der Teile der Tragödie, Symbola Philologorum Bonnensium, Lipsiae 1867, p. 172, n. 43; S.H. BUTCHER, Aristotle's Theory of Poetry and Fine Art[3], London 1902, p. 339; see Isocrates, *Antidosis* 276-280 on the importance of *ethos* as *pistis*.

[22]GREENWOOD, Aristotle, p. 40, "Action we learn is caused by προαίρεσις or purpose, which is, as the *Ethics* has already shown, a combination of reasoning with ὄρεξις or desire. Therefore the goodness or badness of action must depend on the goodness or badness of both reasoning and desire. The reasoning that has to do with action is, like other reasoning, only a means to an end. But whereas other reasoning attains its end, which is truth, if it is good in itself, reasoning that has to do with action does not necessarily attain its end by being good in itself, but only by also harmonizing with good desire: indeed it cannot in practise ever be called good in itself, because it is in practise inseparable from desire, and the goodness of its relation to that desire is, as it were, an essential part of its own goodness."

[23]*De Anima* 433a 1-b 30 explains this in more detail and includes the emotions more specifically.

[24]BUTCHER, Aristotle's Theory, p. 347.

[25]It is not usual to take *B* 18, 91b 27 in this way with δόξαι καὶ προτάσεις as the antecedent; in the light of *B* 1, 77b 16 ff., 78a 28ff., *B* 22, 96b 28 ff., however, it is more than justified.

[26]The Greek itself seems clear; a check on a few translations reveals the following. SANDYS and FREESE agree; SANDYS translates: "so that we have already ascertained the topics from which enthymemes are to be drawn about good or evil, . . .characters, feelings, moral states". BONAFOUS, La Rhétorique d'Aristote, Paris, 1856, p. 249 concurs. SCHRADER in his third edition of the *Rhetoric* (1672), whom MURETUS apparently follows in his edition of 1685, puts a period after ἄδικον (b33) and starts a new sentence. This, however, does not change the meaning from the above translations. On the Greek itself COPE, Commentary, vol. II pp. 233-234 has a note. SOLMSEN, Die Entwicklung, pp. 233 ff. acknowledges that the discussion on *pathos* in book *B* cc. 2-11 parallels the discussion in *A* cc. 4-15 in its concern for what SOLMSEN calls the *idiai protaseis* of enthymemes which in this study are called the *eide*. SOLMSEN also calls attention to *B* 1, 78a 28 (p. 148 above) and claims that here Aristotle wishes to emphasize the parallelism. It is unclear whether SOLMSEN would draw the conclusion from this that since *pathos* is a source for his *idiai protaseis* of enthymeme *pathos* should be as much a part of enthymeme as *reason*. He does make note of, but also rejects (p.

224, n. 1) BRANDIS' theory of the "πάθη-Lehre. . .als einen Teil der Enthymemtheorie". Those who maintain that the *Rhetoric* as we have it represents a conflation of two theories: purely rational demonstration, *ethos-pathos* argumentation which did not succeed too well, must ask themselves in the light of a passage like this (*B* 22, 96b 28-34) whether or not the synthesis of *reason-pathos-ethos* was not Aristotle's starting point.

[27]Planudes in *Rhetores Graeci* (ed. Walz) vol. 5, pp. 403.10-404.2. Neocles is probably the technographer of the first-second century A.D. The Greek reads: Νεοκλῆς δέ φησιν, ὅτι ὁ μὲν συλλογισμὸς ἐκ λημμάτων καὶ ἐπιφορᾶς συνέστηκε τὸ δὲ ἐνθύμημα παρὰ τὸ ἐπιχείρημα συνειλημμένως ἐκφέρεται καθ᾽ ἕν ἀξίωμα ἤθους καὶ πάθους, ἐσθ᾽ ὅτε συναναμεμιγμένων.

[28]See p. 393 of the article in Classical Philology 33, 1938, pp. 390-404. What has been said in this study of the enthymeme and the idea of *praxis* lends strong confirmation to this interpretation. At the same time it would be difficult to make the correlation which SOLMSEN makes, i.e. *ratio probandi* (*apodeixis* which is then subdivided into *pisteis atechnoi* and *pisteis entechnoi*). For it seems clear that *ethos* and *pathos* are *pisteis entechnoi*.

WILLIAM GRIMALDI– REINTERPRETING ARISTOTLE

James Kinneavy

I would like to begin this discussion by affirming quite categorically that I believe that the work which William Grimaldi has done in Aristotelian rhetoric is both critically important at the present time and of the highest level of scholarship. There has not been a comprehensive commentary on Aristotle's *Rhetoric* for over a hundred years, and Grimaldi's commentary and his accompanying studies have already established him as the outstanding scholar of the century in this area. I agree with Grimaldi in the importance he attaches to the study of rhetoric and I also agree that the study of rhetoric is much larger than the teaching of freshman composition in departments of English, or the concern with advertising, or propaganda. In other words, our agreements are much more comprehensive and important than our disagreements. It is against the background of this statement that I wish the following discussion to be made.

Grimaldi first began to attract the attention of students in rhetoric with a series of articles he published in classical journals back in the 1950s. Some of these were eventually anthologized in *Studies in the Philosophy of Aristotle's Rhetoric*, published by *Hermes* in 1972. In this work and in his recent commentary on the first book of Aristotle's *Rhetoric*, he established a basic thesis underlying his interpretation of Aristotle: classical rhetoric is a general theory of language for serious human communication, and as such, it should be taken much more seriously than it currently is. As he says in the first chapter of *Studies*, "Any effort to understand Aristotle's *Art of Rhetoric* must begin with its place within his philosophy. For rhetoric functions as a method of communication, spoken or written, between people as they seek to determine truth or fallacy in real situations" (18). He repeats this idea in several instances: "Rhetoric is the art which presents man with the

161

structure for language, and, by way of structure, enables language to become an effective medium whereby man apprehends reality" (8). He acknowledges that this is not the usual view of either Aristotelian or classical rhetoric generally: "This is a different view of rhetoric than that which is commonly put forward. While it is certainly true of Aristotle's *Rhetoric* there is reason to believe that the *Rhetoric*, in this respect, gives expression to what was substantially the Greek view" (8).

By contrast, many modern views simply equate rhetoric to manipulative persuasion, or advertising, or just a study of techniques of writing. Grimaldi repudiates these views, saying,

> If one were to argue that, on the contrary, the object of Aristotle's treatise is ultimately an analysis of the nature of human discourse in all areas of human knowledge, the argument would be received with suspicion (1).
>
> . . .
>
> This stance on the part of these men [the Greeks] becomes more readily understandable when we realize that for the Greeks rhetorical study was a method of education and consequently a responsible activity. To equate this *paideusis*, as has been done, with public relations, advertising, or even with college textbooks on English composition is an admission that we have little or no idea of what the Greeks were about (1; see also 6).

Consequently, rhetoric is as extensive as serious discourse. It is, as he laconically defines it at one place, "the study of language for significant discourse" (14). It is therefore a very general discipline: "Aristotle's point of departure on the nature of rhetoric begins with the idea that rhetoric is quite simply the art of language," he says (1; see also 55, 66). As such, it extends into all the disciplines: "rhetoric. . .is the artful use of language in the various disciplines, to achieve effective communication" (55). For this reason, it encompasses the sciences and literature, as well as philosophy:

> In other words. . .rhetoric is general and touches all areas of human knowledge wherein man attempts to convey understanding to another whether it be philosophy, literature, or the physical sciences (54).

Citations like these could be multiplied. But it is sufficiently clear from these that Grimaldi has indeed attempted to rescue classical rhetoric from the general disregard in which it is held. Indeed, from the ridiculous he has elevated it to the sublime. It is involved any time humans attempt serious communication. It is also clear, that, as with Derrida, de Man, Feyerabend, and others, the traditional taxonomies of the liberal arts have been seriously dislodged.

It is the thesis of this paper that such an interpretation of Aristotleian rhetoric is too expansive. Whether it is desirable at the present time to define twentieth-century rhetoric in such broad terms is not the issue. The issue is whether such an interpretation is historically valid. Is that what Aristotle and the ancients meant by rhetoric? The arguments of this paper contend that it isn't. First, the meaning of rhetoric in Aristotle will be examined. Then the meaning of rhetoric in general in antiquity, both from direct evidence of the time and from the testimony of scholars, will be presented.

I. THE MEANING OF RHETORIC IN ARISTOTLE

It is difficult to see how rhetoric in Aristotle can be defined as a general theory of language when the evidence of the canon is so clear. From his earliest statements in the *Gryllus* to the last work on both the *Rhetoric* and the *Poetics*, Aristotle carefully distinguished rhetoric from other arts of language.

The first statement in the *Rhetoric* distinguishes rhetoric from dialectic and is usually interpreted to mean that the two constitute two opposite and sister arts, to use the terminology of Cope (A, 2), each with its own nature, its own logic, and its own style, although they share the ability to be applied to any subject whatsoever. But Grimaldi immediately turns the statement into an opportunity to distinguish the two from a quite different point of view:

> rhetoric is a methodology of discourse, the method by which to speak on any subject. Dialect is the method by which to investigate the nature of any subject, the art of logical inquiry: "Dialect is a process of examination which leads the way toward the first principles of all disciplines" (*Top.* 101b 3-4).

In my opinion, this distinction not only takes away from rhetoric its own heuristic function with regard to the truth in general, which Aristotle alludes to in the second chapter and which the epistemic rhetoricians, as they are called, make so much of, but it also deprives poetry, dialectic, and science of any verbal aspect. As Grimaldi says, speaking of rhetoric's ability to treat of any subject: "Further, it attends to all the aspects of that subject which admit of verbal presentation and which are necessary to make the subject understandable and acceptable to an other" (*Studies,* 3).

This certainly surprises any student of poetics, who has always thought that verbal issues are at least as much the concern of poetry as of rhetoric. And, of course, Aristotle gave considerable attention to lexical issues in poetry. On the other hand, this position also ignores the communicative function of science, of dialectic, and of poetry. Yet Aristotle had insisted that dialectic was concerned with the audience, as he says in the *Topics*:

> Now so far as the selection of his ground is concerned the problem is one alike for the philosopher and the dialectician; but how to go on to arrange his points and frame his questions concerns the dialectician only: for in every problem of that kind a reference to another party is involved (155b 7-11).

In fact, Aristotle could not have so easily have forgotten the very roots of the word dialectic—*dia lexis*, through language.

It seems dangerous to reduce rhetoric to simply verbal issues—in fact, Ramus had already fallen into this trap. Let us look rather at the general assumptions of history, that rhetoric is a discipline parallel to poetry, to dialectic, to science, and indeed to sophistic. Aristotle then can be construed as devoting a book or part of a book to each: the *Prior* and *Posterior Analytics* to science, the *Topics* to dialectic, the *Rhetoric* to persuasion, the *Poetics* to literature, and *Of Sophistical Refutations* to sophistic. Each of these has its own nature, heuristic, and style. This is the traditional interpretation of the canon, and I believe that it is preferable to the one which would follow if Grimaldi's view were applied to the entire canon.

On his view, only dialectic would have a logic. Science would be a process of arranging the logic which dialectic found successful, rhetoric would be the verbal rendition of science, and it is not at all clear what poetry would be. By contrast, it is clear in the canon that science has a logic; that dialectic has a different logic; that rhetoric has an invention type of logic for persuasion involving in addition to the inductive parallels of induction and deduction a logic of character and a logic of emotion; that literature has also its own logic ("There should be nothing irrational [*alogon*] in the incidents themselves, and if there is an irrationality, it should be outside the tragedy," *Poetics*, 1456b6), and that sophistic also has its own logic, which is fallacious and which is examined in *De Sophisticis Elenchis*.

Epistemological Basis of the Distinctions

These logics are necessarily distinct, for the language arts have different purposes deriving from their epistemological bases. Science is demonstrative in the realm of the certain; dialectic is exploratory in the area of the probable; rhetoric is persuasive in the area of the probable; and poetry is pleasurable in the area of the internally probable. Neither the purposes nor the epistemological levels are fundamentally compatible, although there are clearly overlaps. These distinctions are Platonic and Aristotle continued them and built them into his entire construct of the mental psyche, particularly as described in the sixth book of the *Ethics*. To equate all serious discourse to rhetoric is to conflate nearly all of Aristotle's intellectual virtues, with their careful distinctions of intuitive thought from discursive thought, of both thinking which eventuates in doing in morality, and of all of these from thinking which eventuates in making in rhetoric and poetic. These distinctions continued on into the tradition—all the way through the Middle Ages into Islamic and Christian thought (see La Driere, 1948).

Possibly the most dramatic difference between rhetorical thinking and scientific thinking (both in the area of the probable, it might be noted) can be seen in the differences in the scientific definitions given of many things in the *Ethics* and in the rhetorical definitions given of these same things in the *Rhetoric*, definitions to be used for "persuasion." Cope has carefully contrasted these definitions, especially that for pleasure, noting that the definition given to be used in rhetorical thinking and writing is a definition which Aristotle had gone to a good deal of trouble to prove wrong in the *Ethics* (Cope, *Introduction*, 234-39). The same is true of his definition of happiness in I, 5 versus the careful scientific definition in the *Ethics*, as well as of the definition of virtue "according to opinion," as Aristotle says in I, 9 versus its scientific definition in the *Ethics*, which expressly disproves the rhetorical definition here posited (see Cope, I, 159-60). Brandis, Spengel, and Cope all agree that the rhetorical definitions, prefaced by "Let us assume," are not to be taken as serious definitions. It is "as if it were a matter of indifference whether they are right or not, provided that they are so generally acceptable as to be certain to satisfy the audience" (Cope, I, 73). It is difficult to justify this view of rhetoric with Grimaldi's which equates rhetoric to serious discourse.

Aristotle's View of Style

It is also clear in the canon that poetry and rhetoric have their own styles, although each can use the techniques of the other. The styles of science and dialectic are not as neatly outlined as those of rhetoric and poetry. But the tradition tells much about Aristotle's careful distinctions of scientific style from rhetorical and literary style. An impressive array of classical scholars, Werner Jaeger, Ingemar Düring, H. Bloch, and John Patrick Lynch (references below) have all contributed to our knowledge of this aspect of Aristotle and his school. He founded, according to Düring, "a new mode of expression, scientific prose" (*AABT*, 360), which repudiated the kind of writing represented by Plato's dialogue, which Aristotle called "half-way between poetry and prose" (Diogenes Laertius, III, 37), and favored a systematic collection on a theme "without literary ambitions" (Düring, "Notes," 58-59). This type of treatise, a *synagoge*, is characteristic of the style of the Aristotelien treatises and the Peripatetic school (see Lynch, 89). The in-school lectures, the *pragmateiai*, were not protected by literary proprietorship and were revised by student and lecturer alike, and no doubt are what we read when we study the extant treatises called Aristotelian (see Lynch, 89-90).

We must remember when we read Aristotle's treatises that he had made a conscious and deliberate choice to exclude emotional and stylistic exuberance in order to address the subject matter itself. Scientific discourse is "logos pros ta pragmata," language directed to the subject matter itself. As he says in *De Sophisticis Elenchis*, "Didactic arguments are those that reason from the principles appropriate to each subject and not from the opinions held by the answerer" (165bl; see further *Rhet.*, 1357b36, esp. 1367b9; 1358a8; 1359b15; 1391bll ff.; *Topics*, 155b7-11).

Aristotle had earlier displayed his rhetorical and his epistolary style. In terms that seem strange to us, Cicero speaks of Aristotle's "golden flame of oratory" in the dialogues (see Ruch, 47). Similarly, Jaeger reminds us that Aristotle had the reputation of having the ideal epistolary style in antiquity (*Aristotle*, 311), a reputation which had obviously died by the time of Plutarch, who says of Aristotle's works on metaphysics that they are "...written in a style which makes them useless for ordinary teaching, and instructive only in the way of memoranda for those who have been already conversant in that sort of learning" ("Alexander," 543).

The canon, the epistemology, the heuristic of each language art, and the radical differences in style from one language art to the other all argue for a careful distinction of rhetoric from other language arts in Aristotle. Yet each language art is a serious undertaking. To reduce all of them to rhetoric is to violate the canon, the description of the intellectual virtues, the various logical heuristics peculiar to each discipline, and the consequent styles.

Aristotle's Definition of Rhetoric and Subsequent Views of Rhetoric in Antiquity

Richard Volkmann, in his famous treatise on Greek and Roman rhetoric, has made one of the more serious attempts to gauge the meanings of rhetoric in antiquity (*Die Rhetorik der Griechen und Römer*, 1-15), and the extent of influence of each. His careful conclusion is that the Aristotelian definition was adopted by Hermagoras and that it became the usual definition of the Greek rhetoricians throughout the Roman empire (*Die Rhetorik*, 13-14). The reason for this influence is undoubtedly the predominant role which Hermagoras played in both Greek and Roman stasis rhetorics, one of the three major genres of rhetorical treatises in antiquity—a point to which we will return later. Another important reason for this Aristotelian hegemony is the thoroughness of Aristotle's analysis. Cicero, for instance, who is philosophically a disciple of Isocrates, finds it useful to adopt the terminology, the distinctions, and in effect the system of Aristotle.

The spread of the Aristotelian definition was assisted by its compatibility both with the Homeric domination of the educational scene at the lower levels and with the view of rhetoric by the various schools of Hellenistic rhetoric. Let us turn to these two facets of the question by considering them in the context of what other competitive views of serious discourse there were in antiquity that challenged the view proposed by Grimaldi.

II. COMPETITIVE VIEWS OF SERIOUS DISCOURSE IN ANTIQUITY

The Overwhelming Case for Poetry in Greece and Rome

Anyone who talks about serious discourse in antiquity in Western civilization has to contend with the towering figure of Homer. One realistic way of assessing his influence is to look at papyri remains. One study by Pinner gives a complete survey of papyri remains from Greco-Roman Egypt. Of the approximately 600 remains,

315 were from the *Iliad* and 80 were from the *Odyssey*; these were followed in descending order by Demosthenes, Euripides, Menander, Plato, Thucydides, Xenophon, Isocrates, Hesiod, Pindar, Sophocles, Herodotus, Aristophanes, Sappho, Theocritus, Bacchylides (Oldfather, 27-28). In other words, almost two-thirds of the remains are Homeric; and of the 16 listed authors, ten are poets or dramatists, three are historians, two are rhetoricians or orators, and one is a philosopher. Oldfather remarks, in passing, that Aristotle was "hardly represented and the towering Aeschylus not at all" (28). Pinner also suggests another criterion of importance when he quotes Martial as saying that the most popular authors at Rome for gifts in order were: Homer, Virgil, Cicero, Livy, and Ovid (43). Three of the five are poets, one is a historian, and one is an orator and rhetorician.

The remains studied by Pinner were from general remains and excluded the school editions of any of these authors. The school situation, at both the elementary and secondary equivalents, further supports the hegemony of Homer, for Homer, more than anyone else, was memorized, recited, and interpreted at these levels of school throughout antiquity (see Gerhardsson, Rengstorf). The general scene and the school scene at the lower levels in the Hellenic and Hellenistic periods certainly support Shelley's contention that poets are the unacknowledged legislators of the world and that Homer was the teacher of all Greece. Homer was taken more seriously than any author in antiquity. And rhetoricians are far down the line in importance. This may be the most serious challenge to Grimaldi's thesis.

The situation in higher education will emerge from the next two sections. Let us first look at the case for philosophy and then at the case for rhetoric.

The Case for Philosophy—The Long Conflict Between Poetry and Philosophy

The conflict between philosophy and rhetoric, started by Plato, and continued by some of the major philosophical names and schools in antiquity, provides another dimension for assessing the validity of Grimaldi's position that in antiquity rhetoric was simply "the study of language for significant discourse" (14), and in particular Grimaldi's position that rhetoric "is general and touches all areas of human knowledge wherein many attempts to convey understanding to another whether it be philosophy, literature, or the physical sciences" (*Studies*, 54).

The first representatives of rhetoric in the conflict were the sophists, and we are traditionally well aware of their dismissal as serious thinkers by Plato, Aristotle, Thucydides, and others—a view which has been challenged by Hegel and Grote in the last century and by such writers as Untersteiner, Kerferd, and Guthrie in this century (see bibliography for references). We know of Plato's position—many of the sophists are Socrates's opponents and give their names to some of Plato's major dialogues: Gorgias, Protagoras, Hippias. Aristotle was almost as negative: "the sophist is one who makes money from apparent and not real wisdom" (*De*

Sophisticis Elenchis, 165a22-23; see also *Metaphysics*, 1004b25ff.). Gomperz, studying Cleon's condemnation of the sophists in a speech early in the Peloponnesian war, contends that for Thucydides, Gorgias was the prototypical rhetorician, a ". . .case in which the rhetorical element is displayed at a maximum and the content element a minimum, the type of Sophist, who is only a rhetor and hardly a thinker at all" ("Sophistik und Rhetorik," 35). This was Thucydides' view of Sophists generally (see Gomperz, 33). Whether we today agree or not, this view of the Sophists as mere rhetoricians prevailed in antiquity, as Kerferd remarks (*The Sophistic Movement*, 36).

Opposition to rhetoric on the part of one or several philosophic movements continued almost without interruption from the time of the First Sophistic in the fifth century B.C. through the Second Sophistic in the first through fourth centuries A.D. The feud between the two was particularly intense from 165 B.C. till 80 B.C.

The four major Hellenistic schools took varying views of rhetoric. The Epicureans were the most serious in their opposition to rhetoric, especially political and legal rhetoric, since it had to do with public life, which Epicurus had repudiated. There were a few who wrote on rhetoric, including Epicurus himself and Philodemus of Gadara (see Von Arnim, 73-76; Kennedy, 300-1).

Some Platonists continued Plato's aversion to rhetoric. Thus Carneades, founder of the Third Academy, was one of the Platonists who expressly opposed rhetoric, despite an epistemology which rejected the certainty of Plato's *episteme* and favored only probability (see Kennedy, *The Art of Persuasion in Greece*, 328, and *The Art of Rhetoric in the Roman World*, 53-54).

The Stoics were the only philosophical school which included rhetoric under logic as a part of philosophy. But Chrisippus and Cleanthes, two Stoics who uncharacteristically wrote on rhetoric, defined it as the art of speaking well, which they opposed to the science which was the way of speaking rightly (*eu legein* and *orthos legein*, which Quintilian translated *bene dicendi* and *recte dicendi*, see Volkmann, 10). This attitude supports the view of some Stoics, such as Sopater, who leaned in the direction of a purely stylistic view of rhetoric (Volkmann, 12). Both positions, of course, question the serious position of rhetoric.

Aristotelians, of the fourth philosophical school, were more favorable to rhetoric and more influential on its future development (Kennedy, *The Art of Persuasion in Greece*, 322). Yet even some Aristotelians opposed rhetoric. In the controversy between the philosophers and the rhetoricians, Critolaus the Peripatetic joined Carneades the Academic and Diogenes the Stoic to attempt to vindicate philosophy in the conflict against rhetoric and journeyed to Rome to do so in 155 B.C. (Kennedy, *The Art of Persuasion in Greece*, 272). Usually, however, the Peripatetics followed Aristotle's distinctions, which were discussed above, and considered rhetoric a serious discipline, but one coordinate to science, dialectic, and poetry, each with its own separate and serious function. In any case, the Peripatetics certainly did not subsume all serious discourse under rhetoric.

The case for philosophy, whether Hellenic or Hellenistic, and in the case of the latter, whether Epicurean, Stoic, Platonist, or Aristotelian, continually poses a major alternative to rhetoric as the dominant art of serious discourse in antiquity.

The declining years of Hellenistic culture saw the rise of the Second Sophistic, which is generally considered to have flourished in the second to fourth centuries A.D. More even than in the First Sophistic, the writers of the Second Sophistic regarded declamation and the display of rhetorical powers as their most important activity, as Kennedy has said (560), though sometimes some of the second sophists, such as Dio of Prusa, Lucian, and Apuleius become important literarily. Dio of Prusa, however, is famous for his "Encomium of Hair" and for his "Trojan Discourse," in which he attempts to prove that the Trojans won the war. Even his most famous work, his Olympic speech, is conceded by Kennedy to be more sophistic than philosophical (576). Other important names in the Second Sophistic were Philostratus and Eunapius (these were also the historians of the movement), Herodes Atticus and Libanius (the teacher of St. Basil, St. Gregory of Nazienzen, and St. John Chrysostom).

One of the reasons for the dominance of the epideictic in rhetoric in the Second Sophistic was the absence of any motivation to the real political speech in the period of the emperors. Rhetoric declines in periods of tyranny, as Tacitus explains at length in his "Dialogue on Orators," and for this reason Tacitus turns from rhetoric to history in his later years. The "Dialogue" was written in the early period of the Second Sophistic—the "Dialogue" was probably written in A.D. 101.

Religion did allow a serious alternative to politics in this period. But the sophistic spirit also invaded the pulpit. Speaking on this issue, St. John Chrysostom wrote:

> This has turned the Churches upside down, because you do not desire to hear a discourse calculated to lead you to compunction, but one that may delight you from the sound and composition of the words, as though you were listening to singers and minstrels. . .Just such is our case, when we vainly busy ourselves about beautiful expressions, and the composition and harmony of our sentences, in order that we may please, not profit; (when) we make it our aim to be admired, not to instruct ("Hom. XXX on Acts XIII, 2;" 60,225. Cited in Armeringer, 26).

He opposed applause for sermons even when he received it and he blames the audience as well as the competitive preachers: "For the public are accustomed to listen not for profit, but for pleasure, sitting like critics of tragedies, and of musical entertainments" ("On the Priesthood," 48, 675,7; cited by Armeringer, 26).

It is difficult to make a case for rhetoric as serious discourse—either political, legal, philosophical, or religious—in the Second Sophistic. It is possible to make a serious case for some literary writers who were also sophists—Apuleius and Lucian, especially.

The Case for Rhetoric

It is possible to make a fairly plausible case for rhetoric as a serious art in antiquity, possibly as the most popular serious art in antiquity from the standpoint of higher education. Let us examine this case from two separate perspectives, first from that of the educational system and second from that of the two most important names in this tradition—Isocrates and Cicero.

The core of the educational system in antiquity was the two-year educational experience preparing the young man for his civic duties of voter in the assembly, of possible executive in the city council, and of juror in the courts. This educational experience was called the *ephebia*, and it usually took place in the center of the civic life in the polis, the *gymnasion*. The *ephebia*, as an educational experience, and the *gymnasion*, as a cultural site, were at the center of more than 350 city states in the Mediterranean area, from Gibraltar to the eastern end of the Greek and Roman empires (see Kinneavy, *The Greek Rhetorical Origins of the Christian Concept Of Faith*, ms. 3-29, on the Greek cities). The *ephebia* was by far the most influential factor in higher education in antiquity from the fourth century B.C. till the fourth century A.D.

The two major subjects that were taught in these free and autonomous city states were philosophy and rhetoric. As Marrou says, speaking specifically about the *ephebia*, ". . .the program consisted essentially in the two disciplines characteristic of higher education, those taught by the philosophers on one hand and by the rhetoricians on the other" (Marrou, *Histoire de l'education dans l'antiquite*, 124).

Despite the presence of philosophy and other subjects in the *ephebia*, the major thrust of higher education in antiquity was rhetoric. As Marrou says,

> Hellenistic culture was above all a rhetorical culture, and its typical literary form was the public lecture.
>
> . . .
>
> For a thousand years—possibly two—from Demetrius of Phaleron to Ennodius (later still at Byzantium), this was the standard type of teaching in all higher education (Marrou, *History*, 267).

Marrou maintains that in the educational system rhetoric outranked philosophy in importance in higher education.

> For the vast majority of students [in Greece], higher education meant taking lessons from the rhetor, learning the art of eloquence from him.
> This fact must be emphasized from the start. On the level of history, Plato had been defeated; posterity had not accepted his educational ideals. The victor, generally speaking, was Isocrates, and Isocrates became the educator first of Greece and then of the whole ancient world. . .Rhetoric is the specific object of Greek education and the highest Greek culture (Marrou, *History*, 194).

This statement of Marrou, more than any other single assertion which I have found, would seem to support Grimaldi's thesis. Yet three qualifications must be made in this regard. Even though Marrou maintains that rhetoric dominated higher education in antiquity, he nowhere contends that all serious discourse was generated by rhetoric. Second, the papyri remains of the period, as we have seen above, do not support this claim for rhetoric. Third, the rhetoric textbooks used in the schools do not make any monolithic claims for rhetoric as the province of all serious discourse.

The Notion of Rhetoric in the Textbooks

There were three types of Greek rhetorics used in the schools: comprehensive rhetorics attempting to cover the entire field of rhetoric (such as Aristotle's); *stasis* rhetorics confined to the consideration of the types of stands which could be taken on issues, mainly legal (such as Hermagoras's); and stylistic rhetorics considering mainly the four virtues of style, the three levels of style, and the many figures of speech and of sound (most influential seem to have been those of Theophrastus and of Demetrius, see Kennedy, *The Art of Persuasion in Greece*, 273-90).

By far the most important of the comprehensive rhetorics is that of Aristotle, then the *Rhetorica ad Alexandrum*. Both define rhetoric as the art of persuasion, but the author of the second treatise takes a much more narrow view of rhetoric than does Aristotle, although Aristotle himself considered rhetoric only "a subordinate, and comparatively unimportant branch" of politics (Cope, *Introduction*, 404; 402-6 are all relevant).

The *stasis* rhetorics were dominated by Hermagoras, who, as Volkmann has illustrated, draws his definition of rhetoric from Aristotle and passes it on to antiquity generally (see above). Thus the comprehensive and the *stasis* rhetorics, making up about two-thirds of the extant Greek rhetorics in Spengel's collection, follow the Aristotelian definition of rhetoric, with its limitations and recognitions of other important areas of discourse. The stylistic rhetorics were, according to Kennedy, heavily influenced by Theophrastus and Demetrius, the former an immediate disciple of Aristotle and the second probably a Peripatetic. Many of them also follow in the same tradition.

The textbooks, therefore, do not allow for a large discourse theory of rhetoric in antiquity. In general, they speak of a dominance of the Aristotelian notion of rhetoric.

A Discourse Theory of Rhetoric: Isocrates and Cicero

If there are any figures in antiquity who have the view of rhetoric which Grimaldi finds typical of antiquity, they would have to be Isocrates and Cicero. There is no doubt that Isocrates speaks of rhetoric as the source of most of our blessings; . . because there has been implanted in us the power to persuade each other and to make clear to each other whatever we desire. . . we have come together and founded cities and made laws and invented arts; and, generally speaking there is no institution devised by man which the power of speech has not helped us to establish ("Antidosis," 253-54).

The entire section of the "Antidosis" from which this quotation is taken is called by Marrou, Isocrates's hymn to *logos* (*History*, 122). Isocrates frequently equates rhetoric to philosophy (e.g., "Antidosis," 266, 270). What enables him almost to reduce culture to rhetoric is his disparaging views of arts, sciences, and specialties (see "Antidosis," 84). He does not despise poetry, however; in fact, he threatened all his life to write a treatise on poetics but never got around to it ("Panathenaicus," 33). Besides poetry, his *paideia* also includes history and mathematics (see Marrou, *History*, 125).

The differentiation of poetry and astronomy and geometry and possibly history from rhetoric would seem to dilute somewhat the purity of Isocrates's view of rhetoric as equivalent to all serious discourse.

Cicero, in his view of rhetoric, is probably closer to Isocrates than to any other Greek rhetorician. A. D. Leeman discusses the almost total communication theory which Cicero sometimes seems to equate to rhetoric. Speaking of *De Oratore*, Leeman says:

> In Book III we read what amounts to the following: "eloquence is one, whatever the subject it deals with may be, whatever the circumstances in which it operates may be, whatever the intention of the speaker may be, whatever the audience he addresses may be: few people or many, strange people or friends. . .or oneself" [III, 22-24]. In this remarkable statement Cicero opens the way for a conception of rhetoric including every kind of human utterance, and ultimately for a general theory of human communication ("The Variety of Classical Rhetoric," 43).

On the other hand, Leeman points out that Cicero often made the common distinctions of antiquity, differentiating the three prose genres of rhetoric, philosophy, and historiography, and separating them from poetry. Quintilian, he says, also makes the same distinctions. If this is true, then both Cicero and Isocrates are somewhat ambivalent. In some exuberant passages, they seem to subsume all serious discourse under rhetoric. But, more systematically, they recognize poetry and then the usual prose genres of antiquity.

Conclusion

The coverage of the concept of rhetoric in Aristotle and in antiquity in this paper has not, of course, been exhaustive, but it has attempted to be somewhat comprehensive, covering the topic from several different perspectives. A few conclusions do seem fairly strong. First, in Aristotle the canon clearly differentiates rhetoric from science, from dialectic, from poetry, and from sophistic. Each of these has its own heuristic, its own organizational techniques, and its own style. The epistemology of Aristotle rigidly forbids the reduction of the arts of discourse to one heuristic (dialectic) and to one verbal art (rhetoric). The different styles which Aristotle wrote about and practiced follow the same differentiations. Second, Aristotle's definition of rhetoric, largely because of the influence of Hermagoras, passed into general currency and seems to have been the dominant notion of rhetoric in antiquity. This view is supported by a look at the three types of extant textbooks in Greek rhetoric. And the Aristotelian view of rhetoric, in his own work and in the Peripatetic school, always differentiated rhetoric from philosophy, from poetry, and from other verbal arts. Third, there are too many other major competitive views of serious discourse in antiquity to allow for rhetoric to be accepted as the one matrix of the art of serious discourse. Poetry, among both Greeks and Romans, has to be regarded as the dominating discourse in antiquity, if we judge by papyri remains and other types of evidence. A strong case has to be made for philosophy, which from the fifth century B.C. till the first century A.D. continually challenged rhetoric and frequently dismissed it as trivial and incapable of important thought. None of the four major philosophies of the Hellenistic period took the view that rhetoric was *the* serious art of discourse. Three of the four, at some periods, denied it any seriousness at all. Both the First and the Second Sophistic movements were usually looked on as being trivial and inconsequential.

The case for rhetoric as *the* serious art of discourse is seen most vividly in Isocrates and Cicero. Even these two, however, in their more systematic moments, follow the usual tradition of antiquity, which recognized poetry and the three prose genres of rhetoric, history, and philosophy. Grimaldi, I believe, can be forgiven for his own Ciceronian and Isocratean exuberance—but in his prosaic moments, I believe he will have to recognize that rhetoric was only one of the serious discourses in antiquity.

Department of English
University of Texas

References

Aristotle, "De Sophisticis Elenchis." *The Works of Aristotle*, vol. 1. Trans. W. A. Pickard-Cambridge. Great Books of the Western World, no. 9, ed. Robert Maynard Hutchins. Chicago, Ill.: Encyclopaedia Britannica, Inc., 1954, 227-53.

—. "Rhetoric." *The Works of Aristotle*, vol. 2. Trans. W. Rhys Roberts. Great Books of the Western World, no. 9, ed. Hutchins. Chicago, Ill.: Encyclopaedia Britannica, Inc., 1954, 503-671.

—. "Topics." *The Works of Aristotle*, vol. 1. Trans. W. A. Pickard-Cambridge. Great Books of the Western World, no. 9, ed. Hutchins. Chicago, Ill.: Encyclopaedia Britannica, 1954, 143-223.

Armeringer, Thomas E., O.F.M. *The Stylistic Influence of the Second Sophistic on the Panegyrical Sermons of St. John Chrysostom: A Study in Greek Rhetoric*. Washington, D.C.: Catholic University of America, 1921.

Bloch, H. "Studies in Historical Literature of the Fourth Century B.C.," *Harvard Studies in Classical Philology*, Suppl. 1, *Athenian Studies Presented to W. S. Ferguson* (1940), 303-76.

Cope, Edward Meredith. *An Introduction to Aristotle's Rhetoric with Analysis, Notes, and Appendices.* London: Macmillan and Co., 1867, repr. Dubuque, Iowa: Wm. C. Brown, n.d.

—. *The Rhetoric of Aristotle with a Commentary*, vols. 1-3. Rev. ed. John Edwin Sandys. Cambridge: At the University Press, 1877.

Düring, Ingemar. *Aristotle in the Ancient Bibliographical Tradition. Studia Graeca et Latina Gothoburgensia* 5. Göteborg, 1957.

—. "Notes on the Transmission of Aristotle's Writings," *Göteborgs högskolas ärsskrift* 56 (1950): 37-70.

Gerhardsson, Birger. *Memory and Manuscript: Oral Transmission and Written Transmission in Rabbinic Judaism and Early Christianity.* Lund: C.W.K. Gleerup, 1961.

Gomperz, Heinrich. "Sophistik und Rhetorik." In Carl Joachim Classen, *Sophistik. Wege der Forschung*, vol. XLXXXVII. Dramstadt: Wissenschaftliche Buchgesellschaft, 1976, 21-38.

Grimaldi, William M.A., S.J. *Aristotle, Rhetoric I: A Commentary.* New York: Fordham University Press, 1980.

—. *Studies in the Philosophy of Aristotle's Rhetoric.* Einzelschriften, Heft 25, *Hermes : Zeitschrift für klassische Philologie.* Wiesbaden: Franz Steiner Verlag, 1972.

Grote, G. *A History of Greece from the Earliest Period to the Close of the Generation Contemporary with Alexander the Great.* 10 vols. 6th ed., vol. 7. London, 1888.

—. *Plato and the Other Companions of Sokrates.* 3 vols. 3d ed. London, 1875.

Guthrie, W.K.C. *A History of Greek Philosophy. Vol. III: The Fifth Century Enlightenment.* Cambridge: At the University Press, 1969.

Isocrates. *Isocrates.* Trans. George Norlin. 3 vols. The Loeb Classical Library. Cambridge, Mass.: Harvard University Press, 1954.

Jaeger, Werner. *Aristotle: Fundamentals of the History of His Development.* Trans. Richard Robinson. Oxford: At the University Press, 1948.

Kennedy, George. *The Art of Persuasion in Greece.* Princeton, N.J.: Princeton University Press, 1963.

—. *The Art of Rhetoric in the Roman World.* Princeton, N.J.: Princeton University Press, 1972.

Kerferd, G.B. *The Sophistic Movement.* Cambridge: Cambridge University Press, 1981.

Kinneavy, James L. *The Greek Rhetorical Origins of the Christian Concept of Faith.* New York: Oxford University Press, 1986 (forthcoming).

La Driere, James Craig. "Rhetoric and 'Merely Verbal Art'." In *English Institute Essays, 1948*, ed. D. A. Robertson, Jr. New York: Columbia University Press, 1949, 134-52.

Diogenes Laertius. *Lives of Eminent Philosophers.* Trans. R. D. Hicks, M.A. 2 vols. Cambridge, Mass.: Harvard University Press, 1942.

Leeman, A. D. "The Variety of Classical Rhetoric." In Brian Vickers, ed. *Rhetoric Revalued.* Medieval and Renaissance Texts & Studies, vol. 19. Binghamton, N.Y.: State University of New York at Binghamton. Center for Medieval and Early Renaissance Studies, 1982. 41-46.

Lynch, John Patrick. *Aristotle's School: A Study of a Greek Educational Institution.* Berkeley: Univ. of California Press, 1972.

Marrou, Henri I. *Histoire de l'education dans l'antiquite.* 6th ed., rev. and enlarged. Paris: Editions du Seuil, 1965.

—. *A History of Education in Antiquity.* Trans. George Lamb. London: Sheed and Ward, 1956.

Oldfather, Charles Henry. "The Greek Literary Texts from Greco-Roman Egypt: A Study in the History of Civilization." *University of Wisconsin Studies in the Social Sciences and History*, 9 (1923), 1-104.

Pinner, H. L. *The World of Books in Classical Antiquity.* Leiden: A. W. Sijthoff, 1948.

Plutarch. *Lives of the Noble Greeks and Romans*. The Dryden Translation. Great Books of the Western World, 14. Ed. Robert Maynard Hutchins. Chicago, Ill.: Encyclopaedia Britannica, 1952.

Rengstorf, Karl Heinrich. *"Didasko*, etc." *Theological Dictionary of the New Testament*, ed. Gerhard Kittel. Trans. and ed. in English, Geoffrey W. Bromiley. Grand Rapids, Mich.: William B. Eerdmans Pub. Co., 1964-1976.

Ruch, Michel. *Le preambule dans les oeuvres philosophiques de Ciceron*. Paris: Les Belles Lettres, 1958.

Spengel, Leonardi, ed. *Rhetores Graeci*. 3 vols. Leipzig: B. G. Teubner, 1883; repr. Frankfurt/Main: Minerva, 1966.

—. *Aristotelis Ars rhetorica*. 2 vols. Leipzig: B. G. Teubner, 1867.

Tacitus. *Dialogue on Orators*. Trans. Herbert W. Benario. Indianapolis, Ind.: Library of Liberal Arts, 1967.

Untersteiner, Mario. *The Sophists*. Trans. Kathleen Freeman. Oxford: Basil Blackwell, 1954.

Volkmann, Richard. *Die Rhetorik der Griechen und Römer in systematischen Übersicht*. Leipzig: B. G. Teubner, 1885; repr. Hildesheim: Georg Olms Verlagsbuchandlung, 1963.

von Arnim, Hans. *Leben und Werke des Dio von Prusa*. Berlin, 1898.

Theoretical Issues

ARISTOTLE'S ENTHYMEME REVISITED

Lloyd F. Bitzer

Aristotle has said that enthymemes are "the substance of rhetorical persuasion."[1] In view of the importance he has given the enthymeme, we might reasonably expect to find it carefully defined. However, although there are many hints as to its nature, the reader of Aristotle's *Rhetoric* will find no unambiguous statement defining the enthymeme. The problem is perplexing to one of the ablest of Aristotelian scholars, W. D. Ross, who writes, "The enthymeme is discussed in many passages in the *Rhetoric*, and it is impossible to extract from them a completely consistent theory of its nature."[2]

The problem is no less perplexing to scholars in rhetorical theory. Some of them have attempted to formulate clear definitions of the enthymeme, based on Aristotle's descriptions. The most notable recent attempt of this sort is James H. McBurney's.[3] Other attempts include definitions by Lane Cooper,[4] Charles Sears Baldwin,[5] Thomas De Quincey,[6] and E. M. Cope.[7] With the exception of Cooper, each attempts to define the enthymeme by showing how it differs from the dialectical or the scientific syllogism. My purpose in this paper is to point out some difficulties in the interpretations given by these men and to suggest a possible definition which does not run counter to Aristotle's descriptions. Since Aristotle's statements, however, seem to permit some variety of interpretation of the enthymeme, further criticism and exploration seem justified.

Consider first Lane Cooper's remarks about the enthymeme. He notes the difficulty of determining Aristotle's meaning and suggests that we simply look at good speeches in order to understand what an enthymeme is. "The arguments good speakers actually use in persuasion are enthymemes," he says, and that "is the answer to our question, 'What is an enthymeme?'"[8] Cooper defines the enthymeme, not by stating its characteristics and telling how it differs from other kinds of arguments, but by pointing to where it may be found—in persuasive speeches actually made by good speakers. This notion is important in a respect I will try to indicate later; for the moment, however, Cooper's definition is put aside because it does not help us understand precisely what the enthymeme is. It does not tell what characteristics make the enthymeme the substance of rhetorical persuasion.

Baldwin is more specific. He approaches definition of the enthymeme by contrasting it with the syllogism. He holds that by enthymeme Aristotle

> means concrete proof, proof applicable to human affairs, such argument as is actually available in current discussions. The enthymeme is not inferior to the syllogism; it is merely different.[9]

Baldwin later says that "abstract deduction is summed up in the syllogism; concrete deduction, in the enthymeme."[10] Apparently he believes that the enthymeme is quite different from the syllogism and that the mark of difference is its concreteness.

Both Cope and De Quincey argue that the essential feature of the enthymeme is its foundation in probability and that this feature separates it from the regular syllogism. De Quincey writes:

> An enthymeme differs from a syllogism. . .; the difference is essential, and in the nature of the matter: that of the syllogism proper being certain and apodeictic; that of the enthymeme simply probable, and drawn from the province of opinion.[11]

In *An Introduction to Aristotle's Rhetoric*, Cope rather cautiously says the same: "It appears. . . that the only essential difference between the two is that the one leads to a necessary and universal, the other only to a probable conclusion." [12] Later, however, it will be noted that Cope changes his opinion in a startling way.

McBurney defines the enthymeme

> as a syllogism, drawn from probable causes, signs (certain and fallible) and examples. As a syllogism drawn from these materials. . .the enthymeme starts from these materials. . .the enthymeme starts from probable premises (probable in a *material sense*) and lacks *formal validity* in certain of the types explained.[13]

The essential part of this definition is the statement that enthymemes are drawn from probabilities and signs.[14] McBurney emphasizes two other important features of enthymemes—the basis of the premises in probability and the lack of formal validity in many enthymematic types. On these two points, he says:

> Both dialectic and rhetoric are differentiated from scientific demonstration in the fact that they deal with probabilities and do not attempt apodeictic proof in the sense that it appears in scientific demonstration.[15]

> Perhaps no other passages in Aristotle bring out more forcibly the point that several forms of the enthymeme are formally deficient than these explanations dealing with the refutation of enthymemes. This is an exceedingly important point, that is almost

universally overlooked. Many rhetorical arguments which are perfectly legitimate in reasoned discourse and which may establish high degrees of probability, are formally deficient; i. e., they cannot be thrown into a formally valid syllogism. Many enthymemes which are wholly acceptable from the standpoint of cogent speech are formally deficient from the point of view of the apodeictic syllogism.[16]

Thus, except for Cooper, these writers among them hold that the enthymeme is distinctive on account of (1) its basis in probability, (2) its concreteness, and (3) its usual formal deficiency. Too, they hold that the definition of the enthymeme usually found in textbooks on logic is totally inadequate. That definition, which will be discussed later, makes the enthymeme simply a syllogism having a suppressed premise or conclusion. The task now is to show how the definitions offered by Cope and De Quincey, Baldwin, and McBurney may not adequately distinguish the enthymeme from the other kinds of syllogism (demonstrative and dialectical), although the definitions do undoubtedly name characteristics which enthymemes usually possess.[17]

Cope and De Quincey try to distinguish between the syllogism and the enthymeme on the grounds that the enthymeme always must be probable, whereas the syllogism always must be certain and necessary. But a major fault attends these definitions. They fail to take account of those descriptions of the enthymeme in which Aristotle expressly states that sometimes the enthymeme does begin with certain and necessary propositions and that sometimes the conclusion is necessary. At 1357^a30-32 Aristotle says,

> It is evident, therefore, that the propositions forming the basis of enthymemes, though some of them may be 'necessary,' will most of them be only usually true. [18]

And at 1356^b14-17 he writes,

> When it is shown that, certain propositions being true, a further and quite distinct proposition must also be true in consequence, *whether invariably* or *usually*, this is called syllogism in dialectic, enthymeme in rhetoric. [Italics mine.][19]

Also, at 1396^a2-4 he says, "We should also base our arguments upon probabilities as well as upon certainties."[20] From these statements, it seems clear that there is no sharp distinction between syllogism and enthymeme on the basis of probability since the propositions of enthymemes may be certain and necessary.[21]

McBurney recognizes as the essential part of the enthymeme's definition the same description Aristotle gives in the *Prior Analytics*: "Now an enthymeme is a syllogism starting from probabilities or signs."[22] He shares with Cope and De Quincey the view that the premises of enthymemes are merely probable;[23] in addition, he seems to hold that the usual formal deficiency of most enthymemes is an important identifying feature. Yet I think it can be shown that neither of these features absolutely distinguishes the enthymeme.

First, McBurney correctly observes that both dialectic and rhetoric deal with probabilities, with the contingent. As Aristotle often repeats, neither discipline deals with "things that could not have been, and cannot now or in the future be."[24] Neither do these disciplines treat subjects which are invariable.[25] Therefore, McBurney is correct in his statement, "Both dialectic and rhetoric are differentiated from scientific demonstration in the fact that they deal with probabilities. . . ."[26] But he infers (without sufficient warrant, I believe) that the premises upon which enthymemes are built must therefore be probable. He says, for example (continuing the sentence just quoted), that dialectic and rhetoric "do not attempt apodeictic proof in the sense that it appears in scientific demonstration." However, Aristotle indicates that there is one kind of enthymeme that meets the conditions for scientific demonstration. At 1402[b]18-19 he says, "Enthymemes based upon Infallible Signs are those which argue from the inevitable and invariable." Further, at 1403[a]10-17 he says:

> It will be impossible to refute Infallible Signs, and Enthymemes resting on them, by showing in any way that they do not form a valid logical proof. . . . All we can do is to show that the fact alleged does not exist. If there is no doubt that it does, and that it is an Infallible Sign, refutation now becomes impossible: *for this is equivalent to a demonstration which is clear in every respect.* [Italics mine.][27]

Therefore, whenever we find enthymemes based on infallible signs, we have before us truly demonstrative arguments, resting on inevitable and invariable premises. Such arguments, proper in both rhetoric and science, are (or may be) both materially certain and formally valid.

Further, there is some doubt about the belief, implicit in McBurney's interpretation, that scientific demonstration must always begin with universal and necessary premises. Ross points out that Aristotle is willing to construct a science upon premises that are "for the most part true." He writes:

> It is noteworthy that, while Aristotle conceives of demonstration in the strict sense as proceeding from premises that are necessarily true to conclusions that are necessarily true, he recognizes demonstration (in a less strict sense, of course) as capable of proceeding from premises for the most part true to similar conclusions.[28]

It is clear, then, that scientific syllogisms may be constructed out of highly probable premises and that enthymemes may be constructed out of certain and necessary premises. From this it follows that we cannot claim probability of premises or probability of conclusions as the essential characteristic of enthymemes.

McBurney's second point of emphasis is that many enthymemes are formally invalid, but that they still constitute rhetorical proof. He finds this significant as a distinguishing feature between enthymemes and scientific syllogisms. His point loses its significance, however, when we note that a great many scientific syllogisms are also invalid. For example, of the sixty-four possible first-figure syllogisms, only four are valid. Yet in ordinary talk we often infer successfully from several of the invalid forms. If it is true that enthymemes are usually formally deficient, it is equally true that many dialectical and scientific syllogisms, as used in ordinary discourse, are formally deficient. Hence, formal deficiency may characterize both the enthymeme and the syllogism.

Baldwin's treatment of the enthymeme—the enthymeme is concrete whereas the syllogism is abstract—is also questionable. Many syllogisms have particulars as the subjects of their conclusions, and many enthymemes have abstract ideas as the subjects of their conclusions. The classic example of the syllogism has "Socrates is mortal" as its conclusion. It could hardly have a more concrete subject. Also, an enthymeme with "Let justice be done" as its conclusion could hardly have a less concrete subject.

Perhaps Baldwin's statement that enthymemes are concrete means that such arguments, when successful, always require a specific human commitment or action. But concreteness in this sense is not peculiar to the enthymeme alone, since dialectical syllogisms sometimes require commitment to conclusions and action in accordance with those conclusions. Indeed, Aristotle says that dialectical inquiry "contributes either to choice and avoidance, or to truth and knowledge."[29] If the conclusions of dialectical arguments contribute to truth and knowledge, then intellectual commitment to conclusions is required of those who accept premises. If the conclusions contribute to choice and avoidance, then acts of choice and avoidance are logically required. Therefore, concreteness is not an essential feature of the enthymeme, although, as Baldwin suggests, most enthymemes probably are concrete.

In summary, the following points may be made about the enthymeme. (1) The enthymeme is a species of syllogism which differs in some way from the demonstrative and the dialectical syllogism. (2) The essential difference is not to be found in the probability of its premises, because Aristotle's statements indicate that (a) some enthymemes have as their premises propositions based on "the inevitable and invariable," and (b) some scientific syllogisms may have as their premises propositions that are "for the most part true." (3) Neither is the essential difference to be found in the formal deficiency of enthymemes, because (a) Aristotle holds that some enthymemes (those based on infallible signs) are equivalent to strict demonstrations. Furthermore, (b) in ordinary discourse we often infer successfully by using formally deficient dialectical or demonstrative syllogisms. (4) Finally, the essential difference is not to be found in the concreteness of enthymemes, because (a) this feature does not always characterize enthymemes and (b) it sometimes characterizes other kinds of syllogism.

It is no doubt true that most enthymemes are probable, formally deficient, and concrete. Since not all enthymemes exhibit these features, however, it is impossible to claim any or all of them as the distinctive mark of the enthymeme. Precisely what, then, is the difference between the enthymeme and the demonstrative or dialectical syllogism? If we answer this question, we may be in a good position to formulate a consistent definition of the enthymeme. In the following paragraphs I wish to suggest an interpretation which I believe is in agreement with Aristotle's statements.

In the *Prior Analytics* Aristotle distinguishes between two kinds of premises—the demonstrative and the dialectical. Because his distinction provides an important clue to interpretation of the enthymeme, I quote the passage in full.

> The demonstrative premiss differs from the dialectical, because the demonstrative premiss is the assertion of one of two contradictory statements (the demonstrator does not ask for his premisses, but lays them down), whereas the dialectical premiss depends on the adversary's choice between two contradictories. But this will make no difference to the production of a syllogism in either case; for both the demonstrator and the dialectician argue syllogistically after stating that something does or does not belong to something else. Therefore, a syllogistic premiss without qualification will be an affirmation or denial of something concerning something else in the way we have described; it will be demonstrative, if it is true and obtained through the first principles of its science; while a dialectical premiss is the giving of a choice between two contradictories, when a man is proceeding by question, but when he is syllogizing it is the assertion of that which is apparent and generally admitted, as has been said in the *Topics*.[30]

In this passage there are two features which distinguish demonstrative premises and syllogisms from dialectical premises and syllogisms. First, the demonstrator *asserts*, or *lays-down*, his premises without regard to the wishes of any opponent. On the other hand, the dialectician *asks for* his premises. Instead of laying them down, he seeks the consent of his adversary about them; he gives his adversary "a choice between two contradictories." The first and most important distinction, then, is that the demonstrator lays down his premises, whereas the dialectician asks for his premises.[31] Second, the main requirement for demonstrative syllogizing is that a premise be "true and obtained through the first principles of its science." On the other hand, the main requirement for dialectical syllogizing is that a premise be apparent and generally admitted.

We should note here that, although the premises of dialectic and rhetoric need not be true and need not be obtained through the principles of some science, it is quite possible that some of them are of this character. Scientific propositions—such as Newton's laws—are often popularized and made part of the class of statements from which the orator draws his premises—the class of statements which are apparent and generally admitted. Also, the orator may use special lines of argument which properly belong to other disciplines, including the sciences.[32]

Several statements in the *Rhetoric* indicate that enthymemes differ from demonstrative syllogisms in the same way that demonstrative premises differ from dialectical premises. At 1355[a]27-28 Aristotle says, "We must use as our modes of persuasion and argument, notions possessed by everybody." Also, at 1395[b]31-1396[a]4 he writes:

> We must not, therefore, start from any and every accepted opinion, but only from those we have defined—those accepted by our judges or by those whose authority they recognize. . . . We should also base our arguments upon probabilities as well as upon certainties.

And at $1402^a33\text{-}34$ he says: "The materials of [rhetorical] syllogisms are the ordinary opinions of men." The practitioner of rhetoric, then, does not lay down premises, but like the dialectician he asks for them. The premises he asks for are notions already possessed by his audience.

We have, then, two kinds of syllogism, demonstrative and dialectical-rhetorical. One important difference—perhaps the essential difference—between the two lies in how premises are secured. In demonstration they are laid down; in dialectic and rhetoric they are asked for. We need now to distinguish between the dialectical syllogism and the enthymeme.

The difference between the dialectical syllogism and the enthymeme is partly the consequence of a difference in the functions or purposes of the arts. Dialectic, says Aristotle, "is a process of criticism," and criticism is its chief function.[33] On the other hand, rhetoric discovers the available means of persuasion, and persuasion is the chief function of rhetorical discourse. Both dialectic and rhetoric ask for their premises (which may or may not be certain and necessary); but they ask for premises with different ends in view. Dialectic must ask for premises because criticism cannot begin until the parties involved agree on some propositions. Rhetoric must ask for premises—must begin with premises held by the audience—because persuasion cannot take place unless the audience views a conclusion as required by the premises it subscribes to.

The dialectical syllogism differs from the enthymeme also according to the kind of response made by the respondent and by the audience when each is asked for premises. The nature of this difference will be noted shortly. For the moment, let us distinguish among the three species of syllogism in the following way: (1) Demonstrative syllogisms are those in which premises are laid down in order to establish scientific conclusions; (2) Dialectical syllogisms are those in which premises are asked for in order to achieve criticism; (3) Rhetorical syllogisms, or enthymemes, are those in which premises are asked for in order to achieve persuasion.

It was stated near the beginning of this paper that recent theorists, including E. M. Cope, have tended to reject the definition of the enthymeme as a syllogism having one or more suppressed premises. In his *Introduction to Aristotle's Rhetoric*, Cope holds that the essential difference between the syllogism and the enthymeme is that the former "leads to a necessary and universal, the other only to a probable conclusion." He holds also that the definition of the enthymeme as a syllogism having a suppressed premise, is totally inadequate, since the suppression of a premise is not essential to the enthymeme. These views are presented in the text on pages 102 and 103. In a lengthy footnote on page 103, however, Cope alters his view drastically:

> The view of the distinctive characteristic of rhetoric given in the text was adopted mainly in deference to the decided opinion expressed by Sir W. Hamilton. I am now however convinced that he is wrong, and return to the opinion which I have myself previously formed upon the question. If the only difference between the rhetorical enthymeme and the syllogism lay in the probability of the one and the certainty of the other, it would leave no distinction remaining between the dialectical syllogism and the rhetorical enthymeme: besides which the position is not true of the dialectical syllogism, whose materials and conclusions are all probable and nothing more. Plainly the difference between the two latter is one of form. The syllogism is complete in all its parts; the enthymeme incomplete; one of the premises or the conclusion is invariably wanting.

Thereafter, in the text, Cope refers to the enthymeme as an "imperfect syllogism"[34] and reiterates the view expressed in the footnote quoted above. For example, at one place he writes:

> The enthymeme is deduced from a few premises. . . and often (always, I believe; else what remains to distinguish it from the dialectical syllogism?) consists of fewer propositions (including the conclusion) than the primary or normal syllogism.[35]

Cope's change of opinion seems to have been prompted chiefly by his recognition that, given his earlier definition, he could not distinguish between the dialectical syllogism and the enthymeme. Earlier he had said that the enthymeme leads to a probable conclusion, whereas the syllogism leads to a necessary conclusion. However, he observed that the dialectical syllogism also leads to probable conclusions. Therefore, the enthymeme is confounded with the dialectical syllogism. In order to separate the two, he returned to the position he had previously repudiated—that the enthymeme is an incomplete syllogism. In justifying this latter view, he writes that there is no need for the rhetorician to state all his premises,

> because if any of these is already well known—and the propositions of the rhetorician are well known, being popular and current maxims and opinions, and generally accepted rules and principles, which he uses for the major premises of his arguments—there is no occasion to state it at all; the listener will supply it for himself.[36]

There are two difficulties in Cope's revised definition of the enthymeme, provided we consider the enthymeme as the chief instrument of rhetorical persuasion. First, if we understand the enthymeme as simply a syllogism having one or more suppressed premises or a suppressed conclusion, then we have to maintain that whenever Socrates omits a premise or whenever he lets his adversary draw the necessary conclusion, he is at that moment practicing rhetoric instead of dialectic, regardless of how concise and rigorous his argument. We must also maintain that whenever an orator fully states his premises and conclusion, he is at that moment practicing something other than rhetoric.[37] Because of these difficulties, it seems to me that the definition of the enthymeme as an incomplete syllogism must be rejected, unless we use the term "incomplete syllogism" in a special sense.

The second difficulty in Cope's definition is the inadequacy of the reason he gives to support it. He holds that the orator need not state all his premises because the listener already knows most of them and will supply them for himself. Undoubtedly this is a good practical reason which adequately explains why most enthymemes do in fact have suppressed premises. But is this reason strong enough to explain Aristotle's claim that the enthymeme is the substance of rhetorical persuasion? It seems to me that the reason is not strong enough, because rhetorical persuasion can occur whether an orator vocalizes both or only one of his premises. The success or failure of rhetorical persuasion does not turn upon the suppression of a premise but upon something more fundamental, which I will try to point out shortly.

If we use the term, "incomplete syllogism" in a special sense, however, I believe it expresses very nearly what Aristotle means by the enthymeme and avoids the difficulties which attend Cope's definition. Let us understand the term in this sense: To say that the enthymeme is an "incomplete syllogism"—that is, a syllogism having one or more suppressed premises—means that the speaker does not *lay down* his premises but lets his audience supply them out of its stock of opinion and knowledge. This does not mean that premises are never verbalized, although to verbalize them often amounts to redundancy and poor rhetorical taste. Whether or not premises are verbalized is of no logical importance. What is of great rhetorical importance, however, is that the premises of enthymemes be supplied by the audience.

The same thought may be expressed in a different way. An orator or a dialectician can *plan* a rhetorical or dialectical argument while sitting at the desk in his study, but he cannot really *complete* it by himself, because some of the materials from which he builds arguments are absent. The missing materials of rhetorical arguments are the premises which the audience brings with it and supplies at the proper moment provided the orator is skillful. The missing materials of dialectical arguments are the premises which the respondent supplies when he chooses between contradictories. The relationship of practitioner of rhetoric to audience and of practitioner of dialectic to respondent is precisely the same: In either case, the successful building of arguments depends on cooperative interaction between the practitioner and his hearers.

But we must note an important difference between the forms of interaction which occur in rhetoric and in dialectic—a difference which further clarifies the distinction between the dialectical syllogism and the enthymeme. In dialectic, the interaction between speaker and respondent takes the form of question and answer, and the respondent vocally contributes premises for the construction of dialectical syllogisms. The aim of dialectic is criticism—often the aim is criticism of the respondent's own position, since arguments are formed from premises supplied by the respondent, dialectical arguments have the virtue of being self-critical. Probably there is no more effective way of appraising one's own opinions than the activity of dialectic because when one assumes the role of respondent and answers the dialectician, one supplies premises from which damaging conclusions may be drawn. The respondent in fact builds a case for or against his own position; he criticizes himself.

The interaction between speaker and audience must have a different form in rhetoric, however, because continuous discourse by the speaker does not allow him to obtain premises from his audience through question and answer. The speaker uses a form of interaction which has its "counterpart" in dialectic, but instead of using question and answer to achieve interaction, he uses the enthymeme, which accomplishes for rhetoric what the method of question and answer accomplishes for dialectic. The speaker draws the premises for his proofs from propositions which members of his audience would supply if he were to proceed by question and answer, and the syllogisms produced in this way by speaker and audience are enthymemes.

The point to be emphasized, then, is that enthymemes occur only when speaker and audience jointly produce them. Because they are jointly produced, enthymemes intimately unite speaker and audience and provide the strongest possible proofs. The aim of rhetorical discourse is persuasion; since rhetorical arguments, or enthymemes, are formed out of premises supplied by the audience, they have the virtue of being self-persuasive. Owing to the skill of the speaker, *the audience itself helps construct the proofs by which it is persuaded.* I believe this is the reason Aristotle calls enthymemes the "substance of rhetorical persuasion," and it may be the reason for Lane Cooper's remark that we will find enthymemes in the actual speeches of good speakers.[38]

In this paper I have examined three common interpretations of the enthymeme. One interpretation emphasizes the content of its propositions and holds that the distinctive feature of the enthymeme is the material probability of premises and conclusions. A second interpretation emphasizes its formal structure and holds that the enthymeme is distinctive because usually it is formally deficient. The third interpretation emphasizes its relationship to human affairs and holds that the distinctive feature of the enthymeme is its concrete relationship to human thought and conduct. These interpretations were rejected because each failed to separate the enthymeme from other kinds of syllogism. Each failed to name a truly distinguishing feature.

I have suggested a fourth interpretation which emphasizes the manner of construction of the enthymeme rather than content, form, or relation. In addition to avoiding the difficulties which attend the other interpretations, I think this view succeeds in focusing upon the unique function of the enthymeme in rhetorical persuasion. This view holds that the enthymeme succeeds as an instrument of rational persuasion because its premises are always drawn from the audience.

Accordingly, I offer the following as a tentative and exploratory definition. The enthymeme is a syllogism based on probabilities, signs, and examples, whose function is rhetorical persuasion. Its successful construction is accomplished through the joint efforts of speaker and audience, and this is its essential character.

Notes

[1]*Rhetorica* 1354[a]14-15. Unless otherwise indicated, references are to the Rhys Roberts translation of Aristotle's *Rhetorica* in Vol. XI of *The Works of Aristotle*, ed. W. D. Ross (Oxford, 1946).

[2]W. D. Ross, *Aristotle's Prior and Posterior Analytics* (Oxford, 1949), p. 409.

[3]James H. McBurney, "The Place of the Enthymeme in Rhetorical Theory," *SM*, III (1936), 49-74.

[4]*The Rhetoric of Aristotle,* translated and with Introduction by Lane Cooper (New York, 1932).

[5]Charles Sears Baldwin, *Ancient Rhetoric and Poetic* (New York, 1924).

[6]Thomas De Quincey, "Rhetoric," *The Collected Writings of Thomas De Quincey*, ed. David Masson (Edinburgh, 1890), X.

[7]Edward M. Cope, *An Introduction to Aristotle's Rhetoric* (London, 1867).

[8]Cooper, p. xxvii.

[9]Baldwin, p. 9.

[10]Baldwin, p. 13.

[11]De Quincey, p. 90.

[12]Cope, p. 102.

[13]McBurney, p. 58.

[14]McBurney, p. 66.

[15]McBurney, p. 52.

[16]McBurney, p. 65.

[17]It is important to note that these authors recognize that the enthymeme is a species of syllogism. When they contrast the enthymeme and the "syllogism," they mean by the latter either the dialectical or demonstrative syllogism. Therefore, the question is not, How does the enthymeme differ from the syllogism? Properly speaking, the question is, How does the enthymeme, which is one type of syllogism, differ from the dialectical and the demonstrative syllogism? Aristotle clearly holds that the enthymeme is a kind, or species, of syllogism. At 1355[a]6-8 he refers to the enthymeme as "a sort of syllogism"; and at 1356[b]3-5 he says, "the enthymeme is a syllogism, and the apparent enthymeme is an apparent syllogism. I call the enthymeme a rhetorical syllogism."

[18]Lane Cooper translates this passage as follows: "Let us grant that only a few of the premises of rhetorical deduction are necessarily admitted, and that the majority of cases. . .may lie this way or that." The translation by Freese (Aristotle, *The "Art" of Rhetoric*, Cambridge, Mass., 1939) reads as follows: "Few of the propositions of the rhetorical syllogism are necessary, for most of the things which we judge and examine can be other than they are."

[19]Cope's translation of this passage may account for his view that probability of premises and conclusion is the essential feature of the enthymeme. Cope's understanding of the passage is substantially different, commencing with the italicized portion: ". . .either universal or general and probable, is called in the former case a syllogism, in the latter an enthymeme." He follows immediately with: "So that it appears from this. . .that the only *essential* difference between the two is that the one leads to a necessary and universal, the other only to a probable conclusion" (Cope, 102). Translations by Cooper, Freese, and Jebb agree with Roberts, however. "To conclude from certain assumptions that something else follows from those assumptions (something distinct from them, yet dependent upon their existing) either universally or as a rule—this in Dialectic is called a syllogism, and in Rhetoric an en-

thymeme."—Cooper. "When, certain things being posited, something different results by reason of them, alongside of them, from their being true, either universally or in most cases, such a conclusion in Dialectic is called a syllogism, in Rhetoric an enthymeme."—Freese. "When certain things exist, and something else comes to pass through them, distinct from them but due to their existing, either as an universal or as an ordinary result, this is called in Dialectic, a Syllogism, as in Rhetoric it is called an Enthymeme."—Jebb, *The Rhetoric of Aristotle* (Cambridge, 1909).

[20]Cooper's translation reads: "And he must argue not only from necessary truths, but from probable truths as well." Freese's translation reads: "Conclusions should not be drawn from necessary premises alone, but also from those which are only true as a rule."

[21]Grote's explanation of the enthymeme indicates that some rhetorical arguments may begin with propositions which are universal and necessary and may produce conclusions which are universally true: "The Enthymeme is a syllogism from Probabilities or Signs; the two being not exactly the same. Probabilities are propositions commonly accepted, and true in the greater number of cases; such as, Envious men hate those whom they envy, Persons who are beloved look with affection on those who love them. We call it a Sign, when one fact is the antecedent or consequent of another, and therefore serves as mark or evidence thereof. The conjunction may be either constant, or frequent, or merely occasional: if constant, we obtain for the major premise of our syllogism a proposition approaching that which is universally or necessarily true. . . . The constant conjunction will furnish us with a Syllogism or Enthymeme in the First figure. . . . We can then get a conclusion both affirmative and universally true." See George Grote, *Aristotle* (London, 1880), pp. 202-203.

Cope's position remains a puzzle. At several places he recognizes that enthymemes sometimes include universal and necessary propositions, yet he holds that the probability of premises and conclusion is the essential feature of the enthymeme. For example, in *The Rhetoric of Aristotle* (ed. John Edwin Sandys, Cambridge, 1877), he says, "The certain sign, the necessary concomitant, is the only *necessary* argument admitted in Rhetoric: its ordinary materials are. . .only probable." (See p. 225; also p. 271, Introduction.) We will note later that Cope removes some confusion by altering his position substantially.

[22]*Prior Analytics* 70^{a}9-11. Aristotle expands this definition in the *Rhetoric* (1402^{b}12-14) to include examples along with probabilities and the two kinds of signs, fallible and complete proofs.

[23]Walter J. Ong, S.J., has recently expressed a similar view. In *Ramus, Method, and the Decay of Dialogue* (Cambridge, Mass., 1958), Father Ong writes that Aristotle always understands the enthymeme as a "syllogism defective in the sense that it moves from premises at least one of which is only probable, to a merely probable conclusion" (p. 187).

[24]*Rhetorica* 1357^{a}1-7.

[25]*Topics* 104^{a}3-8.

[26]McBurney, p. 52.

[27]Jebb's translation of this passage reads: "Infallible Signs,and the Enthymemes taken from them, will not admit of refutation on the ground that the reasoning is not strict. . . .It remains to show that the alleged fact does not exist. If it is shown that it *does* exist, and that it is an Infallible Sign, then there is no further possibility of refutation; for this amounts to a manifest demonstration."

[28]Ross, p. 74. See also *Posterior Analytics*, Book II, Ch. 30.

[29]*Topics* 104^{b}1-3.

[30]*Prior Analytics* 24^{a}21-24^{b}12.

[31]Cope writes that the philosopher, or investigator, proceeds without regard to any respondent; "the man of science is not allowed to choose which side of an alternative he will take." However, the dialectician "depends upon the concessions of his opponent" (Introduction, pp. 75, 78).

[32]"In proportion as a speaker uses specific arguments, he is deserting the province of rhetoric; but in view of the comparatively small number of general arguments available Aristotle allows the speaker to use specific arguments as well" (Ross, *Aristotle*, p. 271).

[33]*Topics* 101^b2-4.

[34]Cope, *Introduction*, p. 105.

[35]Cope, *Introduction*, pp. 157-58.

[36]Cope, *Introduction*, p. 158.

[37]Cope's position leads him directly to this consequence. Note especially the last line of this quotation from his *Rhetoric of Aristotle*, p. 221: "I will repeat here, that the enthymeme differs from the strict dialectical syllogism only in *form*. The materials of the two are the same, *probable* matter, and of unlimited extent . . . The difference between the two is simply this, that the dialectician rigorously maintains the form of the syllogism, with its three propositions, major and minor premiss and conclusion: the rhetorician *never* expresses all three—if he did, his enthymeme would become a regular syllogism."

[38]It may be worthwhile to note that this interpretation of the enthymeme— and of the whole sphere of rhetorical discourse—provides a sound theoretical justification for that kind of speech criticism which studies the audience and relevant aspects of its context as carefully as it studies the speaker and his preserved speeches. According to this interpretation, a recorded speech is only partially a speech. The complete speech is the actual speech which occurs when speaker and audience interact, either cooperatively or not. Therefore, a sound speech criticism of past speeches must reconstruct the actual speech, and this requires detailed study of the particular audience to determine the premises it would or would not have supplied.

SOME ARISTOTELIAN AND STOIC INFLUENCES ON THE THEORY OF STASES

Ray Nadeau

The earliest formal system of stases, or issues, that has come down to us is found in the work of Hermagoras of Temnos (second century B.C.), who considered political questions under two heads, those relating to *reasoned discourse* and those relating to *law and customs*. Under the first, Hermagoras listed the four stases of conjecture, definition, quality, and objection or substitution; under the second, he discussed four types of legal questions without, so far as we know, using the term *stasis* in connection with them. The system of Hermagoras, reconstructed through sixty quotations from secondary sources,[1] is the first specific and detailed theory on the analysis of stases. Not too much information is available, unfortunately, about the pre-Hermagorean history of stases, and this paper undertakes to suggest some early influences on Hermagoras and, through him, on later theory.

In a 1950 article on "Stasis," Otto Dieter traced the physical origins of that term and concluded with a definition of it as the ". . . station, or standing still, which necessarily must occur momentarily in-between opposite 'changes' and in-between contrary motions, movements, processes, functions, or forces in action."[2] Prior to arriving at that thorough definition, Professor Dieter showed through an analysis of early works, primarily those of Aristotle, that physical changes, motions, et cetera, are of four kinds and four kinds only. To cite one of several quotations: "For the thing being changed always changes in respect to substance or to quantity or to quality or to place."[3] Dieter then demonstrated that stases of the foregoing physical motions are *analogous*[4] to the four rhetorical stases of Hermagoras and others. That there is anything more than an analogy between the physical and rhetorical stases Dieter does not suggest, and I can find no evidence that Hermagoras (or anybody else) used the physical stases as a basis for constructing a system of rhetorical stases.

In this current study, I am supporting the theory that the actual *analytical method* of the rhetorical stases was developed from and reflects characteristic uses by the ancients of (1) the four Aristotelian predicables of genus, definition, property, and coincident, and uses of (2) the four Stoic categories of body, of a particular kind, in a particular state, in a particular relation. Although this theory is not new,[5] it has never been fully explored or elaborated; this I propose to do.

At this point, it will be useful to review the generally accepted meanings of the stases of Hermagoras. In his system, στάσις στοχασμός means *stasis of conjecture* on, for instance, whether an act took place; ὅρος means stasis of *definition* which states what a thing is through its essence or essential qualities; ποιότης means quality of non-essential kinds as distinguished from essential qualities noted in a definition; μετάληψις means an *objection* to a charge, or *substitution* of a plea, on technical grounds not directly concerned with the act itself. Stated in another way, arguments pro and con on whether an act took place result in stasis of conjecture; arguments about its essential qualities (e.g., felony or misdemeanor) result in stasis of definition; arguments about its non-essential attributes (e.g., extenuating circumstances) result in stasis of quality; and procedural arguments on such matters as jurisdiction result in stasis of objection (e.g., "You cannot charge me with murder for secretly killing a man who was later tried in absentia and sentenced to death by the courts."[6]).

Since the foregoing are basic rhetorical stases, how did the system and the terms come into being? No less an authority than Quintilian says, in reference to the Aristotelian categories of substance (οὐσία), quantity (ποσόν), quality (ποιόν), and relation (πρός τι), that these "first four seem to concern the stases. He uses the word *seem*[7] with reason because some difficulties stand in the way of a direct relationship between these categories and the four rhetorical stases.

For one, does ποσόν mean definition in the sense of the later rhetorical stasis of ὅρος? According to Cope three Aristotelian "stases" (ἀμφισβητήσεις) appear in the familiar quotation "ὅτι ἐστι ..., ὅτι ποιόν, ἤ ὅτι ποσόν ...".[8] This last term of quantity is "what was afterwards called the ὁρικὴ στάσις, and by Cicero and the Latin rhetoricians 'nomen' or 'finitio.'"[9] How Cope arrives at his conclusion is not clear. The passage quoted by him means "that the action took place, that it has quality, or that it has quantity. . . ." Just as strong a case, if not stronger, could be made for interpreting ποιόν as definition and ποσόν as non-essential quality; further, the latter interpretation would be strengthened by the Aristotelian order of words, assuming that they are in logical order. To be accepted as a parallel, equivalent, or antecedent form of ὅρος, the term ποσόν should have the meaning of essential quality; however, the basic Aristotelian example of the term is simply "two cubits" or "three cubits."[10] Aristotle also goes on to distinguish between discrete quantity (e.g., number) and continuous quantity (e.g., lines, space, time).[11] It is difficult to see how these "quantities" would be used primarily in definitions.

A man is no less a man for his being five or seven feet tall. Thus, the instances in which ποσόν could be interpreted as essential quality only would seem to be limited; its classical meaning is generally less ambitious and just as easily related to non-essential attributes.

For another difficulty, does ποιόν mean *non-essential quality* as opposed to essential quality? The Aristotelian category of quality is a term embracing both concepts; very early in his treatment of the first of many senses (τῶν πλεοναχῶς λεγομένων)[12] of quality, Aristotle distinguishes between ἕξις and διάθεσις – the first is a thing "more lasting and stable,"[13] e.g. justice; the second is "easily moved and more quickly changed,"[14] e.g. health. In other words, ἕξις is a relatively permanent condition differing from the relatively transient and alterable διάθεσις; the first could have a bearing on the essence of a thing, and the second would normally have a bearing on temporary non-essential quality. To move on to Aristotle's examples for another kind of quality, that of figure and form, he uses *square* and *triangle* as examples.[15] *These do not admit of variation in degree*, for "those things to which the definition of a triangle . . . is applicable are all equally triangular. . . ."[16] Carrying this idea a step farther, it is easy to see how this kind of quality, the shape of a thing, might be a part of its essence (definition). For instance, a ball is round. "Round" is not a quantity; it is a quality but an essential one not in the class of non-essential qualities like, in this instance, rubber, sponge, or plastic. My point is that here again, in the ποιόν (or ποιότης) of Aristotle, we have a term covering an essential attribute of a thing *or* a non-essential attribute *or* both; although non-quantitative, the term can be definitive and/or qualitative in the "non-essential" sense.

As for the other two categories of οὐσία and πρός τι, as well as for ποσόν and ποιόν, a fact which is sometimes overlooked is that the categories of Aristotle were predications "out of context" (κατὰ μηδεμίαν συμπλοκὴν).[17] Thus, a particular concept like *ten miles long* is in the category of quantity, but it has that status whether, or not, it is ever predicated of a particular thing. All predicates fall to one or more of the categories or classes of existences; yet the categories themselves are only a division of terms out of construction.

Accordingly, in reviewing some of the difficulties standing in the way of a direct relationship between the Aristotelian categories and the rhetorical stases, we see that, separately and together, the two terms of ποσόν and ποιόν encompass both essential and non-essential qualities; as categories in the Aristotelian system, *neither is a synonym* for the rhetorical stasis of ὅρος (essential quality or definition) or for ποιότης (non-essential quality). We also note that no one of the categories was intended to be anything but a general class of existence.

If the rhetorical stases are not directly related to the first four Aristotelian categories, what more probable sources of the stasis theory and of its terms can we suggest? We can suggest that both the theory and its terms are more directly related to early ways of examining matter. For our purposes here, we are talking about matter from the standpoint of Aristotle's fourth aspect of *being*[18] as exemplified by the ten varieties of categories and by the predicables below. In this aspect, substance is not really in question—it is a person or thing already isolated for observation but not yet defined, qualified, or related to other persons or things. Without attempting complete analysis of the metaphysical problems involved in distinguishing between Aristotelian and Stoic views on matter, it is enough to say that, at this level of examination, the "substance without quality" (ὑποκείμενον) of the Stoics is, for all practical purposes, a term equal to the categorical οὐσία of Aristotle.[19] We have previously shown, however, that each Aristotelian category was a judgment in isolation; as applied to a specific subject, a category, predicate, or judgment must be, according to Aristotle in his *Topics*, either the definition, or the genus, or the differentia, or a property, or a coincident of that subject.[20] These *predicables*, then, are the relations in which a predicate may stand to a subject *in actual practice*. They constitute a *plan of inquiry*[21] which enables us more easily to attack any subject proposed. Later in his *Topics*, Aristotle reduces the number of predicables to four by ranking the differentia with genus (γένος) which answers the question, "What is the object before you?"; then, he distinguishes definition (ὅρος) as giving the essence and property (ἴδιον) as including non-essential qualities belonging to a particular thing alone. Thus, with the coincident (συμβεβηκός), an accidental quality which is none of the foregoing and yet belongs to a thing, we have a list of *four basic judgments* which Aristotle considers *appropriate in upholding proposi-tions*.[22] It is true that he is here dealing with dialectic, but the same modus operandi is certainly applicable to rhetoric.

In their attitude toward the study of matter, the Stoics had a similar fourfold plan for arriving at necessary basic judgments. Influenced by the Peripatetics but uninterested in out-of-context predications, the practical Stoics moved directly to an in-service system of classifying persons and things under the following "categories": substance (ὑποκείμενον), essential quality (ποιόν), non-essential disposition or quality (πὼς ἔχον), and coincidental, accidental, or relational quality (πρὸς τι πὼς ἔχον).[23] The Stoic categories are different from the Aristotelian predicables in form but the meanings of the terms are much the same.

We are now in a position to note that the predicables and the Stoic categories cover about the same ground as these rhetorical stases: conjecture about existence or substance (στοχασμός), definition (ὅρος), non-essential quality (ποιότης), and objection (μετάληψις), the latter being a motion or demurrer of a coincidental or accidental relation to the "thing" itself. All three of these systems (Aristotelian predicables, Stoic categories, rhetorical stases) are practical relations in which predicates may stand to subjects. All three represent the characteristic mode of the ancients for studying a matter from the standpoint of (1) its state of being, e.g. physician, (2) its definition, e.g. a licensed practitioner of medicine, (3) its quality, property, or non-essential attributes, e.g. tall, blond, athletic, and (4) its coincidents, relations, or properties which may or may not belong to a body without changing its essence, e.g. father. It seems reasonable to me, therefore, to regard the four rhetorical stases as developing from the four standard steps used by both the Peripatetics and the Stoics in studying matter and, in the *Topics* of Aristotle at least, in stating propositions.

From what sources do we get the specific rhetorical terms is the next question. Since, in rhetoric, the ancients were dealing with an inexact art of speculation rather than with physical matter, it is not unexpected to find them falling back on an adjectival form of an old word for conjecture, στοχάζομαι *to conjecture about* or *to guess at a thing*. In Plato's *Philebus*, the art of persuasion (ἡ τοῦ πείθειν [58a]) is listed among arts like music, medicine, and agriculture as being subject to the powers of guessing (ταῖς τῆς στοχαστικης . . . δυνάμεσιν [55e]) Plato also uses the word στοχασμός in reference to attaining harmony in music "by guesswork based on practice" (μελέτης στοχασμῷ [56a]). Later, he adds that music is full of guesswork (στοχάσεως [62c]). In Plato's *Gorgias*, he has Socrates saying, "I do not say with knowledge but by speculation (στοχασαμένη [464c]) in talking about the art of flattery and its divisions."

In his *Rhetoric*, Aristotle uses the adverbial στοχαστικῶς (1355a) in a context of weighing matters *by conjecture* and, later (1395b), he has στοχάζεσθαι in the sense of the speaker's need *to guess at* the opinions of others. In 1357a and b, as well as elsewhere in the *Rhetoric* and in the *Prior Analytics*, we find Aristotle demonstrating that, in rhetoric, we are dealing with εἰκότα (probabilities or propositions generally true) and with the second two degrees of σημεῖα (usual or indefinite signs—propositions that seem to be true) as distinguished from τεκμήρια or signs in the first degree of σημεῖα (definite, invariable, inescapable, irrefutable, and conclusive signs—propositions that are always true). Probabilities and signs of the usual or indefinite degrees are used deductively in the form of enthymemes to reach conclusions that are never more than probable.[24] In the inductive process, παραδείγματα(examples) are assembled to arrive at conclusions which cannot be certain because the induction is incomplete. The customary instruments of proof in rhetoric, then, are the example and the so-called rhetorical syllogism or enthymeme, both of which require judgment or conjecture from incomplete, uncertain evidence.

Use of στοχάζομαι in one form or another by Xenophon,[25] Isocrates,[26] and others, further attests to use of this word to describe common practice among the ancients of drawing inferences *by conjecture*, primarily from probabilities and uncertain signs, in rhetoric and the other conjectural arts. It is not surprising then, to find στοχασμός coming into technical use as the first rhetorical stasis to denote inference *by conjecture* as to whether or not an act took place. We should hardly expect to see οὐσία, γένος, or ὑποκείμενον, in this sense, since all three terms carry the implication that the "thing," as yet undifferentiated and unqualified, already exists.

Once a thing is in hand, man turns to its definition (ὅρος), a word which to the ancients (and to us) meant designation of the *essence* of a thing, that is, essential qualities which make a thing what it is and nothing else. For example, "A theatre is a structure used primarily for presenting dramatic performances." Both the Aristotelian ὅρος and the Stoic ποιόν (qualified entity) have this meaning of essential quality. (I have already stated objections to interpreting ποσόν, the second Aristotelian category, in this way only.) The word ὅρος is the one we find as the second Aristotelian predicable and as the second rhetorical stasis; it is used in exactly the same way in both instances as a second analytical step.

The third step in practical analysis, Peripatetic or Stoic, is the determination of *non-essential qualities* of external variety, i.e. attributes peculiar to the thing and not to the class. It is in this sense that Aristotle uses ἴδιον as the third predicable; in the same sense, the Stoics use πὼς ἔχον (in a particular state) as their third category. Neither of these is identical in form to the third rhetorical stasis of ποιότης but, in at least one sense, the latter word was regarded by the Stoics as being a more restricted form of quality than their definitive ποιόν;[27] the word was also used by them in combination with the feminine form of ἴδιον as in ἰδία ποιότης. In that phrase, or alone, ποιότης was, to the Stoics, a term equivalent to πὼς ἔχον [28] and both of these terms, along with Aristotle's predicable ἴδιον, had *particular non-essential* quality as a meaning.

Coincidental non-essential attributes of relation are the fourth concern of the ancients in analyses of the kind under consideration. Aristotle uses the predicable συμβεβηκός in this connection, and the Stoics use the category of πρός τι πὼς ἔχον. The fourth rhetorical term is μετάληψις (objection), a word already defined in this paper. In his *Prior Analytics*, Aristotle uses the participle μεταλαμβανόμενον in comment on a proposition substituted for original theses.[29] In his *Rhetoric*, elements of the same idea are discussed in 1375b, but no form of the word is actually used. However, I submit that μετάληψις, which later rhetoricians like Hermagoras used as a fourth complementary step in a quadripartite system of analysis, falls readily into the pattern of the four predicables and of the four Stoic categories. In Hermagoras' day, it may have been substituted for the more general πρός τι simply because it was the typical and specific relational action to which speakers resorted in objections of all kinds not directly concerned with the "case" itself. That μετάληψις was a conscious substitution for πρός τι is suggested, at least, by retention of the latter term in the systems of Posidonius (c. 135-51/50 B.C.) and of Theodorus (fl. 33 B.C.).[30]

Here let us interject the following table and use it as the base for a summary of conclusions:

First, we see no direct relationship between the Aristotelian categories and the rhetorical stases because (1) neither ποσόν nor ποιόν can be interpreted to mean *exclusively* either definition or non-essential quality, and (2) no category was, in

Systems—	Substance– quality undefined	Definition– essential quality	Quality– non-essential quality	Relation– coincidental quality
Categories,			ποσόν	
Aristotelian	οὐσία		ποιόν	πρός τι
Predicables,				
Aristotelian	γένος	ὅρος	ἴδιον	συμβεβηκός
Categories,				πρός τι
Stoic	ὑποκείμενον	ποιόν	πὼς ἔχον	πὼς ἔχον
Stases,				
Rhetorical	στοχασμός	ὅρος	ποιότης	μετάληψις

any case, intended by Aristotle to be anything but a state of existence outside of specific context.

Secondly, we see the Aristotelian predicables and the Stoic categories as the characteristic four-fold approach of the Peripatetics and Stoics to the study of primary substance. We see, also, that the terms differ but their meanings are similar.

Thirdly, we see the conjectural activity of the first rhetorical stasis as typical of any investigation conducted through an inexact art in contrast to a physical science. We expect the word used (στοχασμός) to be a step short of the existence already implied in such words as οὐσία, γένος, and ὑποκείμενον. We see the second rhetorical stasis of definition coinciding in form and meaning with the second Aristotelian predicable and in meaning with the second Stoic category. We see the third stasis of quality coinciding in meaning with the third predicable and with the third Stoic category. We see the rhetorical μετάληψις as a reasonable substitution for the more general πρός τι; the former is not like the other relational terms in form or in meaning but it does cover legal action of a coincidental, accidental, and relational kind.

Finally, we recognize the physical origins of the word *stasis* and the appropriateness of the analogy between the physical stases and the rhetorical stases; we also understand Quintilian's comment to the effect that the first four categories *seem* to concern the stases, for they do so appear to concern them; we conclude, however, that the rhetorical stases stem more reasonably and directly from the traditional four-fold analysis of matter as seen in actual and customary Peripatetic and Stoic practice—not intrinsically a part of this analytical process itself, although borrowing terminology from it, the stases are seen as temporary halts or blocks set up and standing in the way of any one major (or subordinate) step in the analysis.

Notes

[1]Georg Thiele, *Hermagoras* (Strassburg: Trübner, 1893), pp. 2-16. A complete outline of the Hermagorean system appears on p. 85.

[2]Otto A. Dieter, "Stasis," *Speech Monographs,* XVII (November, 1950), 369.

[3]Aristotle, *Physics*, 200b 33.

[4]Dieter, *op. cit.,* p. 356.

[5]Both Thiele and Jaeneke note influences of Aristotelian and Stoic logic and dialectic without pointing them up in the way undertaken in this article. Cf. Thiele, *op. cit.,* p. 177 ff., and Gualtherus Jaeneke, *De Statuum Doctrina Ab Hermogene Tradita* (Leipzig; Robert Noske, 1904), p. 43 ff. Among others commenting on these influences: Richard Volkmann, *Die Rhetorik der Griechen und Römer* (Leipzig: Teubner, 1885), p. 56 et passim, M. L. Clarke *Rhetoric at Rome* (London: Cohen & West, 1953), p. 8, and the Loeb edition of the *Rhetorica ad Herennium*, trans. Harry Caplan (Cambridge: Harvard University Press, 1954), p. 32, note c. The number of writers who show general Peripatetic influences on the Stoics is legion.

[6]Hermogenes, *On Stases*, 53. Quotation is my paraphrase of situation described in this passage. For comment on the forensic emphasis in Hermagoras, see Friedrich Solmsen, "The Aristotelian Tradition in Ancient Rhetoric," *American Journal of Philology*, LXII (1941), 177.

[7]Italics mine. The Loeb edition of Quintilian, H. E. Butler's translation, gives only "concern" for "pertinere. . . videntur." If Quintilian had meant only "concern," he would have used "pertinent" alone. See Quint. iii.6.24. For a survey of the history of categories, see Adolph Trendelenburg, *Geschichte der Kategorienlehre* (Vol. I, *Historische Beiträge zur Philosophie*: Berlin; Bethge, 1846), pp. 1-364. This volume traces categories from Aristotle through Hegel; Stoic forms are discussed at some length, pp. 217-31.

[8]Aristotle, *Rhetoric,* 1417b.

[9]E. M. Cope, *An Introduction to Aristotle's Rhetoric* (London: Macmillan, 1867), p. 398.

[10]Aristotle, *Categories*, 1b 28.

[11]*Ibid.,* 4b 20 ff.

[12]*Ibid.,* 8b 26.

[13]*Ibid.,* 8b 28.

[14]*Ibid.,* 8b 35-36.

[15]*Ibid.,* 10a 14.

[16]*Ibid.,* 11a 7-8.

[17]*Ibid.,* 1b 25.

[18]For a discussion of Aristotle's four principal aspects of *Entia*, things or matters, see George Grote, *Aristotle* (London: John Murray, 1872), 1, pp. 85-93.

[19]E. Vernon Arnold, *Roman Stoicism* (Cambridge, England; University Press, 1911), p. 165. Here, and elsewhere in the same volume, Arnold discusses the differences between Aristotelian and Stoic views on the theory of causes, matter, etc.

[20]Aristotle, *Topics*, 101b 17-25.

[21]*Ibid.,* 101a 29.

[22]*Ibid.,* 101a 29 and 101b 4. Later logicians used a list omitting *definition* and adding *species* (εἶδος) to make up the following series: genus, species, differentia, property, and accident; this list passed into Europe through Porphyry (b. 233 A.D.) and Boethius (fl. 500 A.D.). For the history of this development, see H.W.B. Joseph, *An Introduction to Logic* (Oxford: Clarendon Press, 1916), pp. 66-75.

[23]The following works are among those providing interpretations of the Stoic categories: Eduard Zeller, *The Stoics, Epicureans, and Sceptics*, trans. O. J. Reichel (London: Longmans, Green, 1870), p. 95 ff.; E. Vernon Arnold, *op. cit.,* pp. 164-69; Max Pohlenz, *Die Stoa* (Göttingen: Vandenhoech & Ruprecht, 1948), pp. 69-75; Émile Bréhier, *Chrysippe et l'ancien Stoicisme*

(Paris: Presses Universitaires de France, 1951), p. 132 ff.; Benson Mates, *Stoic Logic* (Vol. XXVI, *U. of California Publications in Philosophy:* Berkeley; University of California Press, 1953), p. 18 ff.; and Margaret E. Reesor, "The Stoic Categories," *American Journal of Philology*, LXXVII (January, 1957), 63-82.

[24] Analogies between rhetoric and medicine occur very frequently in Philodemus' *Rhetoric*, written about 78 B.C. The De Lacys believe that it is "probable that the rhetoricians took the conjectural method from medicine; for even in the early Hippocratic work *On Ancient Medicine* (9), the use of conjecture is discussed. . . ." See P.H. and E.A. De Lacy, *Philodemus: On Methods of Inference* (Philadelphia: American Philological Association, 1941), pp. 131-37. See also *The Rhetorica of Philodemus*, trans. H. M. Hubbell (New Haven; Yale University Press, 1920), Suppl. 12, 13, 14, 16, 27, 32.

[25] The materials in the enthymeme *may* be "necessary" but, with few exceptions, they are only probable. Cf. Aristotle, *Rhet.* 1357a.

[26] *Memorabilia*, 11.2.5.

[27] Isocrates, 1.50.

[28] Reesor, *op. cit.,* p. 80.

[29] *Pr. Anal.*, 41a 29.

[30] For Posidonius' system, see Francis Striller, *De Stoicorum Studiis Rhetoricis* (Vol. 1, *Breslauer Philogische Abhandlungen:* Warsaw; Koebner, 1886), p. 15. For Theodorus, see C. W. Piderit, *De Apollodoro. . .et Theodoro. . .Rhetoribus* (Marburg; Elwert, 1842), p. 32.

THE MEANING OF *HEURISTIC* IN ARISTOTLE'S *RHETORIC* AND ITS IMPLICATIONS FOR CONTEMPORARY RHETORICAL THEORY

Richard Leo Enos
Janice M. Lauer

A side of the coin which is rarely alluded to is the fact that the formal study of rhetoric began and flourished in Greece at a time when there was confidence in the human intellect and in man's ability to formulate his problems.

-William M. A. Grimaldi, "Studies in the Philosophy of Aristotle's Rhetoric"

The study of heuristics has been a topic of concern in the field of rhetoric and composition. Yet this study is not new but rather one of renewal. Although there is no doubt that the meaning of heuristic has grown in sophistication and importance, its centrality to rhetoric and composition comes as no new phenomenon. This essay encourages a reexamination of the meaning of *heuristic* in Aristotle's *Rhetoric* in an effort to reenvision not only the invention processes inherent in his notion of rhetoric but also the *Rhetoric* itself. Specifically, this essay argues that Aristotle used the term *heuristic* to capture the way meaning is cocreated between rhetor and audience and how, through this process of interaction, participatory meaning is shared. In short, this essay provides an explanation of the place of *heuristic* in Aristotle's *Rhetoric* by showing its endemic operation between rhetor and audience in constructing probable knowledge. A sensitivity to the heuristic processes of

Aristotelian rhetoric will provide a richer understanding of his notion of persuasion.

Heuristic originates in the Greek term εὑρίσκω, meaning "to find out or discover." The Latinized form of the term is *inventio*, which became a principal canon in the study of classical rhetoric. The term *heuristic* came to mean the *technai* or techniques within the *techne* of rhetoric that served to create effective discourse.[1] Much of the traditional scholarly attention to the study of Aristotle's proofs has stressed the ways in which meaning is articulated to others. Yet such treatments provide an incomplete interpretation of Aristotelian rhetoric, since Aristotle's meaning of *heuristic* entails an epistemic process not explicated by theoreticians. By the term *epistemic*, we do not mean philosophical or scientific knowledge but rather productive knowledge for social ends. Aristotle himself made distinctions between a formal *episteme*, such as physics, whose end is interpretation of the physical world, and a formal *techne* or knowledge whose end is in the user.[2] An understanding of this term *heuristic* is central to interpreting one of the basic components of Aristotle's *Rhetoric* and, of shared importance, the very process by which meaning is created through language.

Today researchers have an array of systematic approaches to rhetoric, and several rhetorical theories facilitate invention through heuristic procedures, presenting strategies for creating, organizing, classifying, and articulating one's thoughts and sentiments.[3] Aristotle's notion of heuristic has long been seen as a framework for structuring preexisting ideas, causing us to restrict his notion of invention to a collection of methods for categorizing and explicating. Since this view of his heuristic as a set of formulaic arguments currently overshadows it as heuristic process, many tend to view his inventional strategies as cookie-cutter schemata and thus do not come to grips with the notions, presumptions, and presuppositions of Hellenic thought (Enos, "Notions, Presumptions").[4] Reconsideration of Aristotle's notion of heuristic reveals both another dimension of classical invention and an important feature of Aristotle's *Rhetoric*. Heuristic is not only an instrument for inventing techniques to articulate to others but is also a *techne* enabling the rhetor and audience to cocreate meaning.[5]

If theories of rhetoric are to be sensitive accounts of how people compose and understand discourse, all aspects of the processes need to be explicated, particularly those most fundamental to the thinking of the rhetor and the audience. Students of classical theory learn about such concepts as *topoi, stasis, pistis, example* and *enthymeme*. The problem comes with conceptions of their purpose. Do the heuristic processes of classical rhetoric actually help "invent" discourse and generate probable knowledge, or do they only "translate" meaning to others through forms compatible with rhetor and audience? For Aristotle, rhetoric was concerned with conceptualization through discourse. His heuristic strategies were central to discovering not only how one should express thoughts and sentiments to others but also how one creates judgments meaningful to rhetor and auditor. There is little doubt that probable judgment, or κρίσις, is, as William Grimaldi argues, the "one primary objective of rhetorical methodology" (*Aristotle* 350). Considering Aristotle's concept of heuristic as a method of generating probable knowledge for oneself and others reveals the implications of that concept.

Aristotle himself gives us insight into heuristic as creating meaning within the rhetor and cocreating meaning within the audience in the beginning of the *Rhetoric* when he discusses *pisteis* (πίστεις), or "proofs." These *pisteis* included atechnic or inartistic (ἄτεχνοι) proofs such as oaths and witnesses and entechnic or artistic (ἔντεχνοι) proofs.[6]

> On the [matter] of proofs, some are non-systemic [atechnic] and others are systemic [entechnic]. By "non-systemic", I mean those which have not been tracked out by us but [known] beforehand, such as witnesses, tortures, written contracts and such, but "systemic" [entechnic] are all those which can be composed through a method and [also] through our own ability. Consequently, we are bound to use the former but the latter are invented by us. (1.2.2. [1355b])[7]

Several points of significance emerge from this passage. First, proofs are a matter of choice; among these proofs the inartistic, atechnic ones are already established and need no composing but are merely exposition within the discourse. Yet there are also entechnic proofs that the rhetor may choose to compose through rhetoric, for Aristotle claims that rhetoric can construct the existence of these proofs "through a method and [also] through our own ability." The next sentence opens the meaning to interpretation, for Aristotle says, "Consequently, we are bound to use the former but the latter are invented by us." The standard interpretation of this result clause is that "the former" are the atechnic (inartistic) proofs, which are already in existence, and that "the latter" are the entechnic (artistic) proofs, which are invented and constitute rhetoric's *techne*.[8]

However, another interpretation could modify the meaning of this critical passage and provide a point for expanding Aristotle's notion of heuristic as an epistemic process. Aristotle says, "consequently, we are bound to use the former but the latter are invented by us," immediately after saying that artistic proofs "can be composed through a method and [also] through our own ability." Based on this statement, the "consequently" clause could apply not only to the distinctions between atechnic and entechnic proofs but also to the distinctions within entechnic proofs; that is, rhetors can create meaning by advancing proofs similar to topics with which others are familiar as well as by inventing new proofs. Rhetoric, then, has two kinds of heuristics that can actually generate a way of constructing social knowledge.

The passage discussed above is the only point in the *Rhetoric* where Aristotle uses the verb for *heuristic* (εὑρεῖν) in such a manner. As a verb, it indicates a process, and that process explains how rhetoric's *techne* can be used as a generative power to create probable knowledge. The first kind of heuristic is the entechnic proofs, the topics, which aid the rhetor in creating meaning. These heuristic procedures, *pisteis*, or proofs are at the surface socially shared instruments. Aristotle's use of the term for *heuristic* is quite specific: εὑρεῖν is a second, aorist infinitive active indicating completed action. Thus the verb in context should read "are invented by us." The first meaning of this phrase, then, is that the *topoi* are generative codifications for proofs that have already been invented by successful rhetors.

For example, the twenty-eight *topoi*, as Grimaldi has viewed them, fall into three general inferential patterns: antecedent-consequent, cause-effect; more-less; and relation (*Aristotle* 356). Normally, *topoi* are characterized as "places" and, in that sense, connote a static quality. Taken with the meaning of heuristic advanced here, however, we can better capture the meaning of *topoi* as heuristics having the potentially dynamic characteristic of energizing thought by shaping meaning. *Topoi*, then, may appear as dormant "places" but can also energize ideas through the socially shared understanding of such modes of relational thought. In this sense, *heuristic* captures the meaning of Aristotle's *Rhetoric* as an instrumental activity of invention through shared discourse. Such a perspective gives us a window to view not only how ancient Greeks tried to share thoughts and sentiments with others but also how they came to artistically conceive of discursive meaning itself.

The second application of the phrase "invented by us" refers to entirely new proofs generated by the rhetor. For example, Jesus Christ invented new proofs for making judgments about social action. Through language he fashioned arguments for reaching human decisions, for creating social knowledge as members of a community. The Gospel offered new reasons for making moral and social decisions. James L. Kinneavy's detailed account of *pistis* in the New Testament reveals that Christian faith itself, rooted in the notion of rhetorical *pistis*, constituted a set of new proofs by which to live. So new were the arguments that both Matthew (7.28) and Luke (4.22) record that the multitude were sometimes baffled and perplexed. George A. Kennedy asserts that Christ's efforts at articulating new faith-proofs occasionally left listeners "astonished" (69). These proofs were not existing *topoi* but were invented within a faith community.

These two kinds of heuristics entail Aristotle's conception of rhetoric as a "power [δύναμις] for observing [θεωρῆσαι] the available means of persuasion."[9] While Aristotle sees rhetoric as an art or *techne*, he is careful in this opening passage of the *Rhetoric* also to characterize it as a power or capacity (δύναμις). As Grimaldi indicates in his commentary on book 1 of the *Rhetoric*, these two terms are not inconsistent but compatible, for method and ability coexist as interactive components of rhetoric (*Aristotle* 5). This interplay between ability and *techne* can be seen at work in two kinds of rhetorical education. For example, at some law or business schools students study endless cases from which they "create" or learn indirectly the way professionals think; that is, the heuristics are not explicitly taught but rather tacitly realized through the repetition of discrete cases. Students learn the heuristics of legal or business thinking "through their own ability." In other circumstances, students are taught explicit heuristic procedures, the entechnic proofs for creating meaning, but these proofs generate new meaning only when the students "through their own ability" use them in legal and business situations to cocreate judgments with audiences.

Aristotle also speaks of the role of observation in this heuristic process. Θεωρῆσαι is a term used by Aristotle to capture how one "observes" a proof; that is, the evidence is available but must be made meaningful to others through rhetoric. This "observing" is akin to Sherlock Holmes "observing" in a London flat a residue of venom from a poisonous Indian snake that triggers his interpretation of the mysterious death of the unfortunate victim. The evidence exists; Holmes does not create it, but his keen investigation enables him to create its meaning within his discourse community. In other words, Aristotle holds not that rhetoric creates all reality but rather that it creates the meaning of that reality. This distinction can also be found in Kenneth Burke's view of motion-action.

Moreover, our interpretation, while advancing the heuristic function of Aristotle's rhetoric, does not deny the persuasive function: to articulate preexisting knowledge through effective expression, by using the atechnic proofs and the preestablished entechnic proofs to structure and present previously created knowledge. The difficulty is that some rhetoricians believe these to be the limits of Aristotelian invention. Yet for those who compose discourse, it is essential to differentiate between invention as a formulaic system for communicating existing knowledge and as heuristics to create new meaning. From this perspective, rhetoric can not only be a way of arguing but can also generate its own way of knowing, its own kind of epistemic processes. All such ways of knowing are grounded in and predicated on the rhetor's construct of the audience and its participation in the meaningfulness of the discourse. In short, all rhetorical situations can be inventional situations between rhetor and audience.[10]

Consequently, Aristotle's *technai* have this heuristic power. Take the example as a case in point; it not only articulates a proof but is also an invention instrument within the rhetor invoking an interpretive pattern with the audience (Perelman and Olbrechts-Tyteca 350-57). Similarly, the enthymeme is not only a form for showing purpose or result but is also a fundamental apodictic modality for generating premises of shared values that can enable the audience to participate in the discursive thinking of the rhetor.[11] In the same way, such strategies as metaphor, *topoi*, and *stasis* must be reconsidered for this deeper meaning of heuristic.

How does this interpretation situate Aristotle in current discussions in composition theory? To what extent does it address charges of logocentrism or the issue of writing as a social act? Does it speak to the controversy over *techne* or contribute to the debate on heuristics? And what are its implications for teaching? Derrida's charge of logocentrism against Plato has been extended by others (e.g., Knoblauch and Brannon) to all classical rhetoricians, including Aristotle. Our interpretation in this essay counters this charge, arguing that Aristotle describes a *rhetorical* kind of

thinking in which meaning is made through discourse in the realm of the probable.[12]
This conception is radically different from one holding that Aristotelian rhetorical
invention entails silent ratiocination in which meaning is drawn naked from the
mind and clothed in words for readers or in which thoughts conceived through
dialectic or demonstrative reasoning are transferred to rhetoric for packaging.
Viewing Aristotelian invention as heuristic removes it from "psophistry," which
Jasper Neel describes as rhetors replacing "their own knowledge with their ability
to generate a desired opinion in someone else" (90). He argues that psophistry
"teaches students nothing more than to persuade an audience—the success or failure
depends on the effect writing has on the intended audience" (137). In contrast to
psophistry, Aristotelian rhetoric, according to our interpretation, encourages genuine writing (Neel calls this "sophistry") in which writers and readers persuade
themselves of the probability of judgments.

We do *not* maintain, however, that Aristotle views discourse as the only process
for creating knowledge. In his treatises on demonstrative and dialectical thinking,
he considers empirical investigation and syllogistic reasoning as processes of
thinking that are not necessarily discursive.[13] We cannot, therefore, place him on
the extreme left of any of the continua of rhetoric-as-epistemic positions described
by Michael Leff, James Berlin, Barry Brummett, or Richard Fulkerson. Aristotle
does not consider language as the creator of all meaning and all reality; he stands
closer to Kenneth Burke or Thomas B. Farrell, who consider language the major
meaning-making symbol system.

Our interpretation argues that Aristotle considers invention a social act. Rhetors
initiate discourse in contexts of social exigencies whose urgency and saliency are
reciprocally enacted by rhetors and their audiences; mutual needs and values
motivate the epistemic act. A meaningful rhetorical process begins in a moment
of converging forces, a situation in which members of the polis face an irresolute
but pressing problem that calls for new meaning and thus compels or occasions a
search to develop ever more probable courses of action or explanation. The rhetor
is driven toward understanding by the values and beliefs of the audience and the
culture, weaving new meaning with old, interlacing *ethos, pathos*, and *logos* in
discourse that makes probable knowledge. In Aristotelian rhetoric, discourse is
always intertextual and interactive, not the product of the muse, never created
apart from social problems. In Aristotle's invention, as we view it here, rhetors
persuade by establishing meaning within the framework of their audience's
cultural presuppositions, within the network of existing texts, guided by arts that
have already been developed by others. We therefore consider Aristotelian invention a complex social act.

Our interpretation addresses another composition issue—the role of techne in
the meaning-making act. As we have discussed, Aristotle's *technai* are instrumental
in creating social knowledge—the sharing of probable meaning. The entechnic
proofs facilitate this creation in several ways. Three of Aristotle's inventional arts

are central to the process of creating new meaning—the *common requisites*, the common topics, and the special topics. Aristotle's common requisites (e.g., possible/impossible: 1.3.7-9 [1359a]; Grimaldi, "Studies" 35-39) provide a taxonomy of viable rhetorical situations warranting inquiry. They operate at the initiation of discourse to insure a meaningful social act. The *common topics* (2.23.1-29 [1397a-1400b]) act as investigatory perspectives to prompt a dialogue of many voices, oral and textual, in order to go beyond the known. Already social in their existence as codifications of others' expert practice, they preclude univocal points of view because they enable rhetors and audiences to form meanings that might be otherwise overlooked. The topics as a heuristic set operate fully when rhetors and audiences are willing to reexamine, even to repudiate, entrenched judgments in order to forge new understandings. The third art, the *special topics* (1.2.20-22[1358a]; 1.4.20-1.14.20[1359b-75a]; Grimaldi, "Studies" 125-29), are detailed issues about political, judicial, or ceremonial subjects; they lead rhetors and audiences to test emerging understandings in light of specific, past knowledge and experience and a range of contextual evidence, engaging them in discourse as a fully human act, passionate, credible, and reasonable, not merely well reasoned and abstract.

Within the experienced rhetor, these arts are informed capacities, a *dynamis* distinct from *phronesis* (practical knowledge for determinate action) and *epistemic* (knowledge for its own sake), an interplay between unique gifts and common modes of investigation. In the learner, the arts are still somewhat explicit, closer to the treatises in which they are formulated, because the learner has not yet fully assimilated them. Through experience with audiences in actual situations, the rhetor as learner develops these *technai* into working strategies to guide the cocreating of meaning in unique circumstances. Rhetorical *techne* is always socially situated, contingent on time and circumstances (Atwill and Lauer). William Covino agrees with this interpretation, arguing, as we do here, that Aristotle sees the activity of rhetoric as "movements of the mind that impose no particular pattern upon inquiry," distinguishing rhetorical invention from "the enumeration of predetermined subjects" (28). He contends that the activity of rhetoric is "not the filling in of discursive forms; it is, rather, the formation of forms, via shifting among categories of understanding with a persistent whimsy, in order to create a temporary scaffold for constructions of even greater complexity" (28).

In our interpretation, the three arts—the common requisites, the common topics, and the special topics—are instrumental in creating social knowledge. They free rhetors from reinventing the wheel of investigatory alternatives in order to use these means to weave new knowledge. They mediate between rhetors' knowledge of the subject, premature judgments, and contextual constraints, guiding rhetors and audiences to problematize experience, cultural beliefs, and current theories to cocreate new meanings. The entire discourse process, a series of verbal acts—inner and outer dialogues, plans, drafts—constitutes Aristotelian rhetoric as an evolving interplay of images, ideas, values, and beliefs, whose power is channeled through art into what Neel calls "strong discourse" (210-11), which argues for desirable courses of action with consequences for society.

Aristotle presented a new way of thinking about rhetoric, one based on the assumption that "reasons" could be mutually created. Plato's concern that preference and attitudes had no rational basis was countered by Aristotle's method, one that provided a way for the rhetor and audience to share in the determination of meaning, to engage in creating meaning based on shared interpretive patterns. The meaning of heuristic argued here challenges those interpretations of the *Rhetoric* that consider Aristotle's view to be little more than managerial psychology and a packaging and labeling of content. Rather, we view Aristotle's *Rhetoric* as concerned with the creation of meaning socially, an interpretation of his concept of invention more compatible with contemporary rhetorical theory.

Notes

[1] For notions of *heuristic* that date back to Homer, see Enos, "Emerging Notions."

[2] See Atwill for a new interpretation of Aristotle's notion of productive knowledge.

[3] Bailey; Hughes; Wiethoff; Garver; Wallace; Young, Becker, and Pike; Clark and Delia, *"Topoi."* For a discussion of contemporary invention, see Young; Bramer.

[4] Corbett's objective in *Classical Rhetoric for the Modern Student* is to enable a student of composition to utilize *heuristic* processes to facilitate communicating one's meaning to others. In their discussion of arguments, Perelman and Olbrechts-Tyteca stress audience adherence rather than the development of the rhetor's own knowledge. Knoblauch and Brannon contend that classical rhetoric's "purpose of discourse . . . was simple . . .to convey the truth in a verbal dress" (23).

[5] Lauer reviews the two purposes of the topics in "Issues in Rhetorical Invention."

[6] Aristotle, *Rhetoric* 1.2.2 (1355b). For an excellent commentary of Aristotle's concept of "proofs" see Grimaldi, "Appendix: The Role of Πίστεις in Aristotle's Methodology," in his *Aristotle, Rhetoric 1: A Commentary* 349-56.

[7] The style of citation for classical sources varies widely. We have cited passages of the *Rhetoric* by two of the most popular forms. The reader should note, however, that neither format refers to line numbers but rather to sections and/or subdivisions.

[8] *Aristotelis Ars Rhetorica,* ed. Spengel, 1:5; 2:43. *The Rhetoric of Aristotle,* ed. Cope (rev. ed. John E. Sandys) 1:28; Cope, *Introduction* 27-36 (esp. 33), 150; Grimaldi, *Aristotle* 38.

[9] For an example contrasting the concept of "observing" with "inventing," see Aristotle, *Rhetoric* 1.2.1 (1355b).

[10] We wish to thank Margaret McCaffrey for her notion of and comment on "inventional situations."

[11] This point is consistent with Grimaldi's view but goes beyond the discussion of structuring arguments to the structuring of an epistemology; see Grimaldi, *Aristotle* 355. One of the best statements regarding this interactive and cocreative phenomenon appears in Bitzer. Gage sees Aristotle's enthymeme as epistemic.

[12] Nussbaum (240-51) argues that Aristotle's entire philosophical method is committed to *phainomena,* shared human beliefs and interpretations, often as revealed in linguistic usage—a method completely opposed to Plato's.

[13]One of the most enduring (and best) statements on the range of nondiscursive thought remains Langer's *Philosophy in a New Key*.

Works Cited

Atwill, Janet M. "Refiguring Rhetoric as Art: The Concept of *Techne* and the Humanist Paradigm." Diss. Purdue U, 1990.

Atwill, Janet M., and Janice Lauer. "Refiguring Rhetoric as Art: Aristotle's Concept of *Techne*." *Discourse Studies in Honor of James Kinneavy*. Ed. Rosalind J. Gabin. Potomac, MD: Scriptica Humanistica, forthcoming.

Bailey, Dudley. "A Plea for a Modern Set of Topoi." *College English* 26 (1964): 111-17.

Berlin, James. "Contemporary Composition: The Major Pedagogical Theories." *College English* 44 (1982): 765-77.

Bitzer, Lloyd. "Aristotle's Enthymeme Revisited." *Quarterly Journal of Speech* 45 (1959): 399-408.

Bramer, George R. "Right Rhetoric: Classical Roots for Contemporary Aims in Writing." *Rhetoric and Praxis: The Contributions of Classical Rhetoric to Practical Reasoning*. Ed. Jean D. Moss. Washington, DC: Catholic U of America P, 1986. 135-55.

Brummett, Barry. "Three Meanings of Epistemic Rhetoric." Speech Communication Association Annual Convention. San Antonio, Texas, 1979.

Burke, Kenneth. *A Rhetoric of Motives*. Berkeley and Los Angeles: U of California P, 1950.

Clark, Ruth Anne, and Jesse Delia. "*Topoi* and Rhetorical Competence." *Quarterly Journal of Speech* 65 (1979): 187-206.

Cope, Edward M. *An Introduction to Aristotle's* Rhetoric*: With Analyses, Notes, and Appendices*. London: Macmillan, 1867. Dubuque, IA: Wm. C. Brown Reprint Library, n.d.

—. *The Rhetoric of Aristotle*. Rev. and ed. John E. Sandys. 3 vols. Cambridge: Cambridge UP, 1877. Hildesheim: Georg Olms Verlag, 1970.

Corbett, Edward P. J. *Classical Rhetoric for the Modern Student*. 3d ed. New York: Oxford UP, 1990.

Covino, William. *The Art of Wondering: A Revisionist Return to the History of Rhetoric*. Portsmouth, NH: Boynton/Cook, 1988.

Enos, Richard Leo. "Emerging Notions of Heuristic, Eristic, and Protreptic Rhetoric in Homeric Discourse: Proto-literate Conniving, Wrangling and Reasoning." *Selected Papers from the 1981 Texas Writing Research Conference*. Ed. Maxine C. Hairston and Cynthia L. Selfe. Austin: Texas Writing Research Group, 1981. 44-64.

—. "Notions, Presumptions, and Presuppositions in Hellenic Discourse: Rhetorical Theory as Philological Evidence." *Philosophy and Rhetoric* 14 (1981): 173-84.

Farrell, Thomas B. "Knowledge, Consensus, and Rhetorical Theory." *Quarterly Journal of Speech* 62 (1976): 1-14.

Fulkerson, Richard. "On Theories of Rhetoric as Epistemic: A Bi-disciplinary View." *Old-speak/Newspeak: Rhetorical Transformations*. Ed. Charles Kneupper. Arlington, TX: Rhetoric Society of America, 1985. 194-207.

Gage, John. "An Adequate Epistemology for Composition: Classical and Modern Perspectives." *Essays on Classical Rhetoric and Modern Discourse*. Ed. Robert Connors, Lisa Ede, and Andrea Lunsford. Carbondale: Southern Illinois UP, 1984. 152-69.

Garver, Eugene. "Demystifying Classical Rhetoric." *Rhetoric Society Quarterly* 10 (1980): 75-82.

Grimaldi, William M. A. *Aristotle,* Rhetoric *1: A Commentary*. Bronx: Fordham UP, 1980.

—. "Studies in the Philosophy of Aristotle's Rhetoric." *Hermes: Zeitschrift für Klassische Philologie* 25. Wiesbaden: Franz Steiner Verlag GMBH, 1972.

Hughes, Richard E. "The Contemporaneity of Classical Rhetoric." *CCC* 16 (1965): 157-59.

Kennedy, George A. *New Testament Interpretation Through Rhetorical Criticism.* Chapel Hill: U of North Carolina P, 1984.

Kinneavy, James L. *Greek Rhetorical Origins of Christian Faith.* New York: Oxford UP, 1987.

Knoblauch, C. H., and L. Brannon. *Rhetorical Traditions and the Teaching of Writing.* Upper Montclair, NJ: Boynton/Cook, 1984.

Langer, S. *Philosophy in a New Key: A Study in the Symbolism of Reason, Rite, and Art.* 3d ed. Cambridge: Harvard UP, 1976.

Lauer, Janice. "Issues in Rhetorical Invention." *Essays on Classical Rhetoric and Modern Discourse.* Ed. Robert Connors, Lisa Ede, and Andrea Lunsford. Carbondale: Southern Illinois UP, 1984. 127-39.

Leff, Michael. "In Search of Ariadne's Thread: A Review of the Recent Literature on Rhetorical Theory." *Central States Speech Journal* 29 (1978): 73-91.

Neel, Jasper. *Plato, Derrida, and Writing.* Carbondale: Southern Illinois UP, 1988.

Nussbaum, Martha C. *The Fragility of Goodness: Luck and Ethics in Greek Tragedy and Philosophy.* Cambridge: Cambridge UP, 1986.

Perelman, Chaim, and L. Olbrechts-Tyteca. *The New Rhetoric: A Treatise on Argumentation.* Trans. J. Wilkinson and P. Weaver. Notre Dame, IN: U of Notre Dame P, 1966.

Spengel, Leonard. *Aristotelis Ars Rhetorica Lipsiae*: B. G. Teubner, 1867.

Wallace, Karl. "*Topoi* and the Problem of Invention." *Quarterly Journal of Speech* 58 (1972): 387-95.

Wiethoff, William. "A Classical Rhetoric for 'Powerful Argumentation.'" *Journal of the American Forensic Association* 17 (1980): 1-10.

Young, Richard E. "Recent Developments in Rhetorical Invention." *Teaching Composition: Twelve Bibliographic Essays.* Rev. ed. Gary Tate. Fort Worth: Texas Christian UP, 1987. 1-38.

Young, Richard E., Alton Becker, and Kenneth Pike. *Rhetoric: Discovery and Change.* New York: Harcourt, 1970.

Historical Perspectives

THE ARISTOTELIAN TRADITION IN ANCIENT RHETORIC

Friedrich Solmsen

Quintilian in the course of a somewhat sketchy but nevertheless invaluable account of the history of rhetorical theory informs us that after the first generations of rhetoricians had gradually built up the science of rhetoric it split up into two different types—the one represented by Isocrates and his school, the other by Aristotle, his pupils and, later, by other schools of philosophy like the Stoic.[1] In the next paragraph he mentions that a third type came into being with Hermagoras. We are at liberty to combine this piece of information with that found in Cicero's *De inventione*, where in the context of a similar historical sketch we learn that the rhetorical systems of the Aristotelian and Isocratean schools were fused into a new system by the later theorists *qui ab utrisque ea quae commode dici videbantur in suas artes transtulerunt*.[2] Taken together, these passages seem to provide something like a clue to the history of ancient rhetorical theory, for, even though Cicero may be considered slightly unfair to the originality of later writers on rhetoric, it will certainly be worth while to trace the transformations of the two original systems through the later stages of ancient rhetoric. I am ready to admit that modern writers on the development of ancient rhetoric[3] have good reasons for treating the material along rather different lines; yet by doing so they deprive themselves of the opportunity of appreciating the extent to which the two outstanding theorists left their mark on the subsequent phases of the system.

In this paper I have confined myself to tracing the Aristotelian or, rather, Peripatetic influence on the later theories, partly because this is nearer to the line of my own studies in the field of ancient rhetoric, and partly because it seems advisable to attack this subject first, since for the history of the Isocratean tradition we lack a starting point of the same solidity and authenticity as Aristotle's three

books on rhetoric.[4] I do not suggest that when the Aristotelian factor has been
brought to light the Isocratean may be found by a process of subtraction, but I hope
that the direction in which one must look for the Isocratean element will be more
obvious when the first half of the job of analysis has been done. Moreover, as a
result of the investigations of Hendrickson, Kroll, Barwick, Hinks, and Stroux the
material to be used in the reconstruction of the Aristotelian tradition seems to lie
more ready at hand than the corresponding material for the Isocratean.[5] Thanks are
due in particular to Professor Stroux for throwing light on the relation between
Aristotle's system and that of his Peripatetic disciples,[6] for his conclusions show
(in remarkable agreement with those reached in different fields of the Peripatetic
philosophy) that Aristotle's pupils and successors, while keeping alive the master's
ideas wherever they could do so with a good conscience, made it their object to fill
out gaps which he had left (and frequently indicated as such), to arrange the material
more systematically under certain basic categories, and to increase the amount of
empirical data to be fitted into the framework of these categories.

Before we enter into an analysis of later *artes* it seems necessary to form as clear
a notion as possible of those factors in Aristotle's own *Rhetoric* which are sufficiently original and characteristic to justify our singling them out as his peculiar
contributions to the rhetorical system. It would be an impossible (and for our
purpose a fruitless) undertaking if we tried to enumerate all those more or less
significant details which are or may be new in his work and we must content
ourselves with pointing out the basic and truly epoch-making methodical ideas
through which he made of the rhetorical system something very different from what
it had been before. I am aware that in distinguishing between essential and
inessential features in his work subjectivity cannot be altogether avoided; yet the
following account may not be far from the mark:

1. Aristotle breaks emphatically with the traditional method of organizing the
rhetorical material under the heading of the *partes orationis* (μόρια λόγου):
proem, narration, etc. We gather from Plato's *Phaedrus* and from Aristotle himself[7]
that some teachers of rhetoric had gone very far in dividing the oration into its parts
and subdividing these parts into their various species; but, if it is true that the
Isocratean school recognized only four parts—proem, narration, proofs, and epilogue—,[8] we may regard this as a reaction against the other rhetoricians who, as I
have said, went much further. To maintain that the Isocrateans organized their entire
material under these headings would be hazardous, but there can be no doubt that
this school has left its mark on the theory of the proem, the narration, and the rest,
and there are few Hellenistic rhetoricians who do not echo certain fundamental
Isocratean precepts for them (e. g. that the narration should avoid unnecessary
length, be ἐναργές, πιθανόν, ἡδύ, κτλ). Although we are not dealing with the
Isocratean tradition, we have to bear these facts in mind in order to understand
Aristotle against the right background.

Aristotle is no less scornful than Plato in castigating the superficiality of this approach and the lack of a clear conception of the essential functions of a speech which it betrays.[9] In his *Poetics* Aristotle looks on tragedy as a *totum et unum* and concentrates on those features which are essential to tragedy as such, i. e. to the idea of tragedy: plot, characters, and the other like elements. The external (or quantitative) parts of a tragedy such as the prologue and episodes he relegates to one chapter (12) and treats them as a matter of secondary importance.[10] Similarly in the *Rhetoric* he assigns the "parts of a speech" their place in the third main section of the work where he discusses "disposition,"[11] but organizes the whole material under categories representing essential qualities or functions of any speech. In every speech the orator must seek to prove his point, to produce a definite emotional reaction in his audience, to convey an impression of the speaker's character. Also, every speech must have a definite style and a disposition; it is here that the "parts" get their due, yet even here only the really essential and more or less indispensable ones.[12] Thus, in opposition to the old τέχνη where the material was arranged under "proem," "narration," "proofs," "epilogue," or even more parts, a new type comes into existence, consisting of three main parts: Proofs (or material content), Style, and Disposition. The "proofs" in the alternative system; "proofs" are no longer a part but a function of the speech, and Aristotle's "proofs" are subdivided into the theories of the rhetorical argument, of the emotions (πάθη), and of the speaker's character (ἤθη), since these three factors should combine to make the speech effective. We may note that Aristotle draws attention to a further factor worthy of the same standing in the system as "proofs," "style," and "disposition," namely the delivery (ὑπόκριϐις), yet he refrains from actually working this out.[13]

This entirely new approach to rhetoric is, like the new approach to poetry, obviously based on Aristotle's conception of a thing's organic unity as implying a principle of structure and being different from a mere accumulation of its parts. We know this conception from the *Metaphysics*[14] where it is an integral phase of Aristotle's notion of an entity.

2. The system of "proofs" (πίστεις) may be called the core of Aristotle's *Rhetoric*. As we have seen, the "proofs" are subdivided into three kinds: the rhetorical argument, the arousing of emotions, and the speaker's character. In dealing with the first Aristotle again makes a new departure: He bases the theory of the rhetorical argument on his logic, that is on his dialectic and analytics. The "enthymeme" which with other rhetoricians had been merely a particular way of formulating a thought (in other words, a concept of a stylistic rather than logical complexion)[15] turns with him into the rhetorical syllogism and has to be constructed in close analogy to the logical syllogism, even though in formulating it one of the premises may, if self-evident, be omitted. Similarly the rhetorical παράδειγμα is made to correspond to the logical induction (ἐπαγωγή).[16]

Moreover, such traditional types of "evidence" as σημεῖον, εἰκός, τεκμήριον which in all probability had never before received a logical foundation are by

Aristotle reinterpreted as representing certain definite types of syllogisms.[17] To be sure, some of them have to be regarded as somewhat lax and inconclusive, but the fact that matters is that in *Rhet. A* 2 Aristotle looks at them from the perspective of his new theory of the logical syllogism as set forth in the *Analytica Priora*.

The τόποι had before Aristotle been ready-made arguments or commonplaces "into which they expected the speeches of both parties to fall most frequently."[18] They referred invariably to particular subjects in the sense that the orator had his ready-made commonplaces for either enhancing or minimizing, say, the trustworthiness of the witnesses, the importance of the oaths to be sworn in court, etc. Aristotle compares this instruction to a procedure by which instead of learning the art of making shoes the apprentice receives a great number of ready-made shoes without any suggestion as to how to make them.[19]

He replaces this method by an altogether different system of τόποι, conceiving the τόπος as a "type" or "form" of argument of which you need grasp only the basic structural idea to apply it forthwith to discussions about any and every subject. Once you have grasped the τόπος of the "More and Less" you will be able to argue: If not even the gods know everything, human beings will certainly not know everything; or, Whoever beats his father will certainly also beat his neighbors, or to form any other argument of the same kind, always proceeding from the less likely thing (which has nevertheless occurred) to the more likely.[20] What matters in this system is the "form" of the argument, this being perfectly independent of any particular subject-matter or content. Aristotle in II, 2 enumerates twenty-eight τόποι or "forms" of arguments and in addition nine of paralogisms.[21] Here too we find him constructing the rhetorical argument after the model of his logic, this time that of his *Topics* where he provides τόποι (of the same kind) for purely logical discussions. Obviously this new Aristotelian concept of the τόπος presupposes a new capacity for abstracting from the material content and for grasping the καθόλου or ἓν ἐπὶ πολλῶν. This is an ability which the previous teachers of rhetoric had lacked; in fact I venture the suggestion that before Plato and Aristotle the Greeks had generally lacked this capacity for abstracting. Whether or not Aristotle's τόποι are more practical than the ready-made cliches of Antiphon, Protagoras, and others is a question which we need not discuss, for, although Aristotle would probably claim superiority for his method in the field of practical application also, yet his primary objective is to elevate rhetoric to a subject of philosophical dignity and standing.

In other chapters Aristotle provides premises for the rhetorical syllogisms.[22] These premises appear in the form of general propositions about the "good" ("a thing which everybody seeks to attain is good"), the "useful," the "beautiful," the "just," the "possible," and their opposites. We have to reckon with the possibility that at Aristotle's time other teachers of rhetoric had also adopted the course of providing their pupils with general propositions as to what was "good," "just," and, more particularly, of enumerating good, just, desirable things.[23] This may be regarded as a step in the same direction, and yet an important difference lies in the fact that behind Aristotle's procedure there is a definite logical conception of the nature of the rhetorical argument. His general propositions are really intended to be major premises in a rhetorical syllogism.

3. We have already referred to the important position of the three πίστεις or means of persuasion in Aristotle's system. It was Aristotle who set up the argumentation, the playing upon the feelings, and the speaker's character as the three factors essential for the effectiveness of a speech. We know that both earlier and contemporary rhetoricians included some practical suggestions for the arousing of pity, indignation, good will, etc. in their treatment of the "parts of the speech," especially of proem and epilogue. Aristotle's innovation consists not only in his granting to πάθη and ἤθη a status on a par with the arguments and thereby elevating them to first-rate factors but also in his careful analysis of the nature of the various emotions and of the conditions under which they may be either aroused or allayed.[24] The chapters B 12-17 are certainly a very interesting essay on "social psychology," if this term may be used for a theory of the customary reactions of certain social groups or age-groups (the young, the old, the rich, the noble, etc.). It must be admitted, however, that we are completely in the dark as to the position of the ἤθη in the conventional rhetorical system before Aristotle.[25]

4. Aristotle distinguishes between three different kinds of speeches, the political speech, the forensic speech, and the laudation. The first deals with the ἀγαθόν, the second with the δίκαιον, the third with the καλόν; in other words they are related to three cardinal values. He arrives at these *tria genera causarum* (as they are technically called) by a deductive reasoning which is Platonic in form and method.[26] Yet it is also possible to regard the concentration on these three species as the logical result of the development of the rhetorical theory and practice in the course of the fourth century and to suggest that in spite of his deductive efforts the result was for Aristotle something like a foregone conclusion. In these circumstances we welcome the testimony of Quintilian who tells us that the adoption of this tripartite scheme by later theorists at large was due to Aristotle's influence.[27] It may have been his authority rather than his originality which determined developments in this phase of the rhetorical system.

5. In the field of style or diction Aristotle went a long way towards fixing the "virtues of style," i.e. the qualities which a good speech or, more generally, a good piece of prose ought to possess. He lays down three: clarity, ornateness, and appropriateness (the last being subdivided in accordance with the three πίστεις).[28] A considerable portion of his more specified propositions and suggestions is arranged under these categories, and there is also a chapter on Ἑλληνισμός,[29] the correct use of the Greek language; but the organization of the material under these headings is by no means complete, and it was left to Theophrastus to put the finishing touch to his master's work here and to reduce this whole part of rhetoric to a hard and fast system, along the following lines:[30]

"Virtues of style"
(ἀρεταὶ λέξως)

| (1) correct use of the language ('Ελληνισμός) | (2) clarity (σαφήνεαι) | (3) appropriateness (πρέπον) | (4) ornateness (κόσμος) (a) selection of words ἐκλογή) (b) composition of words (σύνθεσις) (c) figures (σχήματα) |

Further stylistic categories like ἀστεῖον, ψυχρόν, ὄγκος find a treatment in *Rhet. Γ*,[31] and although Aristotle may not have been the first to use them he is likely to have been original in constituting their main types and organizing the material which comes under them. Yet we are not in a position to define the degree of his originality here; and, as we lack material for a comparison, any attempt to detect new departures in his theory of the metaphor[32] or other phases of the rhetorical ornament would necessarily lead to guesswork. In a few points his dependence on the Isocratean tradition or, more particularly, the Theodectean τέχνη appears obvious.[33]

It may be well to add a few other points even though they are slightly less important. In *A* 2 (1355 b 35) and *A* 15 (1375 a 22) Aristotle differentiates between those "proofs" which the orator has to provide by himself and those which do not depend on him but may be "used" by him to his best advantage. The former are those which we have already discussed, namely the argumentation, the speaker's character, the arousing of emotions (pp. 38, 42, *supra*); the other class consists of the witnesses, oaths sworn by the parties before the jury, the laws which are relevant to the case in hand, documents such as contracts, etc.[34] It is obvious that the orator cannot "invent" this material; he can at best "use" or, to put it less euphemistically, twist it according to his purpose, and Aristotle in fact tells him how to do this. He refers to these "proofs" as ἄτεχνοι πίστεις, contrasting them with the other kind of proofs which he calls ἔντεχνοι πίστεις. It should be noted that the author of the *Rhetorica ad Alexandrum* draws a similar distinction although he does not use the same terms.[35]

The definition of the sentence period as a "sentence which has beginning and end in itself" and a certain definite extension in all probability originated with Aristotle.[36] His point is that what he calls "beginning and end in itself" should be secured through the rhythm. Also his famous distinction between λέξις εἰρομένη and λέξις κατεστραμμένη rests on the fact that the former lacks this quality of having beginning and end definitely marked. On the other hand it is not essential for Aristotle's conception of the period that it should consist of several κῶλα.

Among the new items which the Peripatetics after Aristotle added to the stock of his system two should certainly be mentioned. The Peripatetic theory of the rhetorical joke or the "laughable" (τὰ γελοῖα) has been reconstructed, mainly with the help of the so called *Tractatus Coislinianus*, "Demetrius," περὶ ἑρμηνείας, and Cicero's *De oratore*.[37] Two main sources of the "laughable" appear to have been distinguished; the theory is that it may lie either in the subject matter or in the verbal expression.

Theophrastus was the first to theorize on ὑπόκρισις, the oratorical delivery. Aristotle had suggested[38] that in working out this part of the system particular attention should be paid to the voice and its modulation, but Theophrastus may have gone further and may have included *gestus* and the expression of the orator's face (though we cannot say this with certainty since we do not know how closely later authors, especially Cicero, followed him).[39]

I should hesitate to credit Aristotle with any of the notions or precepts of the second part of book Γ (chaps. 13-19), since there are good reasons for assuming that Aristotle in that section is reproducing a system of the alternative "Isocratean" type. I have suggested elsewhere[40] that the τέχνη from which he borrows was that of his friend Theodectes. To be sure, Aristotle does not reproduce his source mechanically and there are passages in which he evidently expresses disagreement with the author from whom he derived most of his material.[41] Nevertheless, chaps. 13-19 represent a system of the μόρια λόγου type and, so far from being characteristic of Aristotle's own approach to rhetoric, may rather be regarded as the first stage in the process of fusion between the two rival traditions.

On the basis of the foregoing analysis it should now be possible to form an opinion about the way in which the *ratio Aristotelia* has left its mark upon the later rhetorical systems.

1. (corresponding to section 1, page 182 *supra*). In a paper published in *Hermes*[42] Professor Barwick pointed out that the extant *artes* of the Hellenistic and Imperial era fall into two groups according to the way in which their authors divide and arrange their material. Although we have to reckon with a considerable amount of mutual borrowing, mixing, and combining between the two types, the basic forms emerge with certainty. The one type consists of a discussion of proem, narration, proofs, epilogue, and usually one or several more "parts" of the speech,[43] whereas the other type is usually a quinquepartite system including *inventio*, *dispositio*, *elocutio*, *actio*, and *memoria*. It is not difficult to recognize in the former type a continuation of the system which had been in vogue before Plato and Aristotle and which as we know was severely criticized by both of them. The other is described by Quintilian as that of the *plurimi maximique auctores*,[44] and I think that we have every right to consider these *plurimi maximique auctores* as following in the footsteps of Aristotle. The first three sections certainly correspond to his

three: Proofs, Style, Disposition, εὕρεσις (inventio) being merely a new name for that part of the system in which, as in Aristotle's πίστεις, the material content of the speech is discussed.[45] The fourth part, ὑπόκρισις or *actio*, had, as we have seen (p. 39, *supra*), been postulated by Aristotle as a necessary supplement to his tripartite division. It was supplied in accordance with the master's suggestion by his faithful pupil Theophrastus.[46] The problem which remains and which cannot be solved with certainty is this: Who was the first rhetorician to add *memoria* (μνήμη) to the Peripatetic system? All that we may say is that this addition must have been made between Theophrastus and those authors from whom Cicero and the *Auctor ad Herennium* borrow the structure of their *artes*, since when they wrote this quinquepartite scheme must have been firmly established.[47] Yet, although the inclusion of *memoria* (μνήμη) had as far as we know never been contemplated by Aristotle or Theophrastus, the fact remains that the *plurimi maximique auctores* have their place in the Peripatetic tradition.

Cicero's *De inventione* was meant to cover the first part of this quinquepartite scheme, explicit references to which it contains.[48] Thirty years later Cicero adopted the same division of the rhetorical system for *De oratore*, dealing in book II with *inventio, dispositio, memoria*, in book III with *elocutio* and *actio*.[49] Quintilian's *Institutio* is also based on the Peripatetic scheme; here the *inventio* is treated in III, 4-VI, *dispositio* in VII,[50] *elocutio* in VIII-XI, 1, *memoria* in XI, 2, *pronuntiatio* (which *a plerisque actio dicitur*) in XI, 3. Fortunatianus, Julius Victor, Martianus Capella, and, on the Greek side, Longinus are the other extant authors whose *artes* show the same structure.[51]

We must add at once, however, that scarcely any *ars* presents the Peripatetic system in its true and uncontaminated form. Compromises with the alternative system are a regular and normal feature. Cicero in his *De inventione* and the *Auctor ad Herennium* in his (closely corresponding) section on *inventio* so far from reproducing an Aristotelian or Peripatetic theory of the πίστεις actually deal with the "parts of the speech": *prooemium, narratio, partitio, confirmatio, refutatio, epilogus*.[52] This at least is true in the discussion of the forensic branch (*genus iuridiciale*) which receives far more attention and much fuller treatment than either of the other branches (see p. 282 *supra*). In the description of these others (which is rather sketchy) the "parts" have not been adopted as a basis,[53] and we are entitled to conclude that the *inventio* of these two *genera causarum* (the laudation and the political oration) has suffered less interference from an alternative system, whether "Isocratean" or Hermagorean. The different fate of these branches is, however, certainly not due to a greater respect for them in their true Peripatetic form but rather to a neglect of them and to a general concentration of interest on the *genus iuridiciale*. Quintilian also organizes his material for the *inventio* of the forensic speech under headings representing the *partes* (*exordium, narratio, egressio, propositio, partitio* in IV; *probatio* including *refutatio* in V; *peroratio* in VI, 1) but refrains from following the same method in his discussion of the two other branches, which is, again, much shorter.[54] A further instance of εὕρεσις (*inventio*) based on the parts of the speech is to be found in Longinus' τέχνη.[55]

Wherever the *inventio* consists of a discussion of the *partes* the material available for the " proofs" would naturally find its place under *probatio* (or *confirmatio*, which is only another name for the same part). As a result this "part" by far exceeds the others in bulk. Theoretically this material might still be good Aristotelian or Peripatetic theory; to what extent it actually is we shall have to discuss under 2. It is clear, however, that the use of the "parts of the speech" as the principle of structure and organization in the section on *inventio* constitutes an important departure from the original Peripatetic system; in fact we have to regard it as a "contamination" with the alternative Isocratean tradition.[56] The only major work that shows no signs of this contamination is Cicero's *De oratore*.[57] The fusion of the two systems must have taken place some time prior to Cicero's *De inventione* and the *Auctor ad Herennium*, and it is not difficult to imagine that practical reasons determined influential teachers of rhetoric to blend the two rival systems in the manner which we have discussed. Cicero's *unum quoddam genus est conflatum a posterioribus* is certainly borne out.

We remember that Aristotle himself had borrowed from the alternative system and discussed the "parts of the speech" under τάξις, that is to say in the section on *dispositio*. The later rhetoricians who use the "parts" in the *inventio* cannot, of course, discuss them again in the *dispositio*. Thus they must in the *dispositio* confine themselves to some remarks concerning the length of each of these parts, the sequence of the points to be made, and other subjects of minor importance.[58] With them, therefore, the *dispositio* tends to assume the form of *Addenda* to the *inventio*, and this may be the reason (or perhaps one of several reasons, as we cannot trace this development with certainty) why the rhetoricians preferred to deal with *dispositio* immediately after *inventio* instead of discussing *elocutio* between them—which would have been in keeping with the original Peripatetic order.

Martianus Capella obviously knew both traditions and was anxious to give each of them its due; in his book on rhetoric (V) he first presents us with a discussion on the lines of the quinquepartite system, refraining from any reference to the *partes* in the *inventio* (although he makes extensive use of the *status*) and treating the *dispositio* very briefly (30), yet after finishing this he adds a full treatment of the alternative system beginning with the proem and ending with the epilogue (44-53). This is a unique procedure, and it is interesting to see that in the "Aristotelian" part of the book he preserves some elements of that tradition which the majority of rhetorical theorists no longer know.[59] Another curious fact is that he deals with argumentation in both parts of the book but treats it differently.

2. (see p. 183 *supra*). Aristotle, as we have seen, provided a new basis for the theory of the rhetorical argument by constructing the enthymeme in closest analogy to his logical syllogism. Thus any theory of the argument in a later system that shows a distinctly syllogistic complexion would naturally come under suspicion of

Aristotelian influence even though in the details it may be found to diverge from Aristotle. A theory of the kind is in fact included in not a few of the later systems, but it must be mentioned at once that the customary name for the rhetorical argumentation which corresponds to the syllogism is no longer "enthymeme" but "epicheireme"; at least this is the term used by Cicero and Quintilian, and there is every probability that Hermagoras too preferred this name. The difference, however, between "enthymeme" and "epicheireme" is not of a purely terminological nature.[60] For, while Aristotle's enthymeme (like his syllogism) consists of two premises and a conclusion, but may under certain circumstances be reduced to a single premise and the conclusion,[61] the epicheireme has a more complicated form. Its normal type includes no less than four premises and the tendency of the rhetoricians is to regard epicheiremes consisting of less than five sentences as a reduction of this normal type. We learn, however, from Cicero's De inventione[62] that another school of thought, which he considers important enough to justify a lengthy discussion of its view, clung to the old tripartite Aristotelian syllogism; and Quintilian actually reverts to this view, after duly informing us that other authors regard four or five or even six parts of the epicheireme as normal.[63]

In comparing Aristotle's enthymeme with the normal form of the epicheireme we easily realize what accounts for the difference: whereas Aristotle took the premises for granted the later theorists consider it necessary to prove each of them before combining them in the final conclusion. This is again stated in so many words by Cicero,[64] who points out that the controversy between the champions of the quinquepartite form of the epicheireme and those of the tripartite form reduces itself to one simple question: If it is necessary to argue in support of one's premises should these arguments be regarded as having an existence independent of these premises and as forming separate parts of the epicheireme or rather as an integral part of the premises which they support. We need not go into the details of this discussion, but we may confidently assume that the epicheireme with its five parts is an outgrowth or extension of the Aristotelian syllogism. In fact Cicero assures us that this form was favored by *omnes ab Aristotele et Theophrasto profecti* and passed from these men to the rhetoricians.[65] The authors of late *artes* waver between the enthymeme and the epicheireme and show a considerable variety with regard to the definition as well as the place of each of these terms.[66] Some authors include both, describing the enthymeme as a reduced, the epicheireme as an extended form of the syllogism. We should admit that this description is reasonable and in keeping with the historical origin of these forms.

In *De inventione* the "epicheireme" is treated on a par with "Socratic" induction.[67] Cicero's Latin name for the epicheireme is *ratiocinatio*, and the distinction in his system between *ratiocinatio* and induction obviously echoes Aristotle's distinction between enthymeme and paradeigma, i. e. between syllogism and induction (ἐπαγωγή). But in *De inventione* the theory of *inductio* and *ratiocinatio* is preceded by a discussion not only of the material of the argument but also of *necessaria* and *probabilis argumentatio, complexio, enumeratio, simplex conclusio, signum, credibile, comparabile*, etc.[68] It is not suggested (and it would be difficult to believe) that all these forms should be fitted into the syllogistic procedure or resolved into the epicheireme. Post-Aristotelian rhetoricians obviously added a great amount of material to the old Peripatetic stock. As a result, those writers of *artes* who were anxious to include as much as they could of the new material found it increasingly difficult (if they attempted it at all) to bring order, system, and unity into the great variety of argumentative forms. It cannot be our aim to unravel the various threads and to write the history of the *locus de argumentatione*. Let us rather note with gratitude that Quintilian is more restrained than some others since he concentrates on the *loci argumentorum*, the *exempla* (for which he refers us to Socrates and Aristotle, see p. 288 *supra*), the epicheireme, and, of course, on the refutation of these forms.[69] Yet he too separates *signa* as well as *credibilia* (σημεία and εἰκότα) from the syllogistic procedure as represented by the epicheireme. For him they are not even *argumenta*, though he reports that others regarded them as a class of the *argumenta*.[70] To class them under *argumentum*, however, is by no means the same (for a rhetorician of the Hellenistic or Imperial era) as to regard them as a form of the epicheireme and to describe them along syllogistic lines. Altogether our evidence suggests that hardly any later author followed Aristotle in his very interesting attempt to understand *signa, credibilia*, etc. (i.e. τεκμήρια, εἰκότα, σημεῖα) as imperfect and not fully cogent syllogisms.[71] We have to remember that τεκμήρια, σημεῖα, εἰκότα had their place and function even before Aristotle in the legal and (more or less technical) rhetorical practice. They were simply "evidences." Traces of blood are "evidence" of a murder; the fact that someone has been seen on the spot is evidence that he has committed the murder. Early rhetoricians distinguished different types of such "evidence," using the words which they found in common use. It was left to Aristotle to force τεκμήρια, σημεῖα, εἰκότα into the strait-jacket of his syllogism; but, as in the later systems we find them discussed without any reference to the syllogistic epicheireme, we are obviously entitled to infer that Hellenistic authorities considered it wiser not to follow him in this point. We may say that the *signa*, etc. come to the fore again in their Pre-Aristotelian form even though in passing through the hands of rhetoricians they have naturally become somewhat more technical.

The distinction between *necessaria argumentatio* and *probabilis argumentatio*[72] may also be traced back to Aristotle; yet we observe again that Aristotle explained the difference between them from the point of view of the syllogism, whereas later writers discuss them without reference to the syllogistic principle. For the rest, it goes without saying that the theory of the *refutatio* had to keep pace with that of the *argumentatio* and became in the same degree more elaborate and complicated.

Aristotle also bequeathed to the later rhetoricians a new conception of the τόπος. As we have seen, his new approach sprang from the idea that instead of providing a great number of ready-made arguments (one and all applying to quite definite and specific subjects or situations) the teacher of rhetoric ought to concentrate on general forms or types of arguments (see pp. 183 *supra*). To judge from the Roman authors, the question how general a way one should adopt in dealing with the arguments continued to occupy the rhetoricians, and remarks to the effect that it is unnecessary or impossible to provide ready-made arguments for every possible subject on which an orator may have to speak are found in Cicero and Quintilian.[73] We have again to note that in *De oratore* Cicero keeps very close to what he, with perfect right as it seems to me at least, considers Aristotle's idea. The *loci* or *sedes argumentorum* enumerated in II, 163-173 are of the Aristotelian type even though they are not materially identical with Aristotle's τόποι.[74] They are not connected with any definite subject-matter, and yet they are applicable to every subject. On the other hand, certain sections of *De inventione* contain *loci* of a more specific type.[75] We read there that arguments may be drawn from circumstances connected either with the person or with the fact under discussion and find a good deal of information about those circumstances which may serve as a basis for impressive arguments. Although it is true that Aristotle investigated the motives leading to crimes and the psychological conditions favoring their perpetration,[76] the discussion of "circumstances" in *De inventione* has little in common with his theory. The Greek word for circumstance is περίστασις, and there is evidence that this term played an important role in Hermagoras' system of the *status* (στάσεις).[77] For this reason (and others) scholars have assumed that the elaborate theory of the circumstances in the form in which we find it in Cicero's *De inventione* and in later *artes* is closely connected with that of the *status* and owes much to Hermagoras and to the Stoics who inspired him. It may be wise to leave the matter at that without indulging in further guesses about the inventor. Nor should I stress the fact that material of the same kind is found in τέχναι of the fourth century B. C., notably in the *Rhetorica ad Alexandrum* under εἰκός.[78]

Quintilian has *loci* of the general as well as of the more specialized type.[79] Even in discussing the πίστεις ἄτεχνοι (witnesses, documents, etc.) he proceeds along rather general lines, although here if anywhere the traditional practice was to provide ready-made arguments, and even Aristotle had condescended to lay down in concrete terms arguments both for the strengthening and for the minimizing of witnesses, etc. We may wonder, however, whether Quintilian's teacher Domitius Afer, who wrote two books on this subject,[80] also confined himself to general points of view and excluded the customary clichés altogether. A remark like the following in Quintilian (V, 10, 20): *locos apello non ut vulgo nune intelliguntur in luxuriem et adulterium et similia, sed sedes argumentorum* shows that the Pre-Aristotelian type of "commonplace" survived and that Aristotle killed this as little as the traditional conception of σημεῖα, εἰκότα, etc., or the practice of organizing the material under the "parts of the speech." The rhetoricians of the better type, however, appear to leave these commonplaces alone.

Among the rhetoricians of the Imperial era the Anonymus Seguerianus stands out as reproducing most closely the Aristotelian conception and division of the πίστεις:

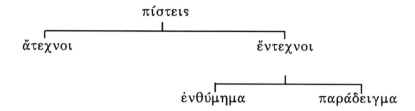

Also, following Alexander Numenius, he defines the relation between the τόπος and the epicheireme in the true Aristotelian spirit: τόπος. . . ἐστὶν . . . ἀφορμὴ ἐπιχειρήματος ἤ ἀφορμὴ πίστεως ἤ ὅθεν ἄν τις ὁρμώμενος ἐπιχείρημα εὕροι.

His system has rightly been used as evidence for a revival of the Aristotelian system in earlier phases of the Imperial epoch,[81] and this revival among the Greeks is in some way comparable to that on the Roman side for which Cicero is responsible. No other Greek rhetorician, however, appears to be affected by this revival in the same degree as the Anonymus.

Reverting to the τόποι or *loci*, we are justified in saying that they are an almost regular feature in the later *artes* where they appear in different forms; in some authors they are conceived as points of view of a general type useful for the argumentation irrespective of its subject. This appears to be the closest approximation to Aristotle's original conception. Yet other authors confine their *loci* to a more specified use either by connecting them with the "circumstances" or by dividing them, according to a scheme which seems to have been rather popular, into *loci ante rem* (that is *loci* to be used in discussing what happened before the fact, e. g. before the murder), *in re, circa rem, post rem*. Yet, even in this form they are still "types" of arguments, not ready-made cliches; in other words they are very different from the "commonplaces" of the rhetorical tradition before Aristotle.[82] To maintain that it is due to Aristotle that no Hellenistic or Imperial *ars* (of which we know) consists merely of an enumeration of such commonplaces would be a gross overstatement of his influence; for the tendency to give rhetorical precepts a more general form is probably characteristic of the fourth century B. C., as the evidence of Theodectes and the *Rhetorica ad Alexandrum* shows. We should also beware of underestimating the extent to which the τόποι were affected and their original idea modified by their close connection (in most of the later systems) with Hermagoras' status. And yet, in spite of these considerations, I suggest that whoever among the late writers of *artes* thinks in terms of "types" of arguments and not in terms of concrete, ready-made arguments is in some measure indebted to Aristotle and to his philosophical treatment of the rhetorical "proofs."

Propositions comparable to the "premises" put forward by Aristotle (see p. 183f. *supra*) occur in the sections on the political speech and the laudation, which are on the whole less affected by the innovations of Post-Aristotelian theorists.[83] The old values which had been allotted to the political speech and the laudation (καλόν, συμθέρον, ἀγαθόν = *honesta, utilia, bona*) continue to dominate them and we feel on familiar Aristotelian ground in reading general propositions referring to *honestas* or *utilitas*, for example, as well as enumerations of specific *honesta, utilia*, etc. It should be noted, however, that these propositions are no longer characterized as premises for rhetorical syllogisms and that propositions of the kind are also found in the *Rhetorica ad Alexandrum*. Yet the propositions there are less general than Aristotle's, and it was Aristotle after all who had taught how to define the values as well as the "goods" classed under them. In the *Auctor ad Herennium* the sections dealing with the *laudatio* and the political speech include precepts concerning the arrangement and disposition of material in these types of speeches.[84] Evidently this is a concession to the alternative, "Isocratean," τέχνη.

Generally speaking, Post-Aristotelian theories of the rhetorical argumentation show a curious mixture of Aristotelian and un-Aristotelian features; and we have to admit that the latter have, on the whole, attained a dominating position. Even the most casual glance at the sections on *confirmatio* (or *argumentatio*) in the works collected in Halm's *Rhetores Latini Minores* would satisfy anyone that Hermagoras with his reorganization of the material under the *constitutiones* carried the day over alternative theories and tendencies.[85] His four basic status and the distinction between λογικὰ and νομικὰ ζητήματα provided the groundwork for almost all later *artes*. In addition, there is that considerable variety of arguments to be drawn from the place, the time, the motives, and other circumstances of the fact under discussion. Naturally Hermagoras' theory too suffered many alterations; it appears to have been the ambition of every rhetorician to make some new departure in this field, at the very least by selecting and arranging the traditional material differently from his predecessors. The result is that the *inventio* in most of the late *artes* reduces to the verge of despair anyone who attempts something in the nature of an historical analysis. I shall be satisfied if I have come near the truth at least with regard to the outlines of the development, and I am under no illusion about the ample chances of error in this field. The Isocratean school does not seem to have left a deep mark on this part of the system but it looks as though some Pre-Aristotelian concepts have been carried along in the stream of the tradition and may occasionally even come to the surface, though on the whole they are buried under the various layers of later origin and it is not easy to recognize them.

3. (corresponding to section 3, page 183 *supra*). It may be a matter for wonder that Aristotle's theory of the three "proofs" (or, rather, means of carrying one's point) did not become a mainstay of the later systems; but our evidence for the

Hellenistic centuries (which is more definite and explicit than usual[86]) suggests that the inclusion of ἦθος and πάθος—the speaker's character and the art of playing upon the feelings—was abandoned by the Hellenistic rhetoricians.[87] How soon after Aristotle this happened it is difficult to say, but one of the usual taunts of the philosophers against the rhetoricians in the late Hellenistic centuries seems to have been this very point—that the rhetoricians had given up the analysis *more Aristoteleo* of character and emotions. The Stoics, as is well known, generally disapproved of the arousing of emotions, and Hermagoras was influenced by them. In view of his enormous influence on the later rhetorical systems I should think that he was responsible (though not necessarily alone responsible) for the facts that *inventio* was reduced to a theory of the arguments and that the other two factors disappeared. Naturally, practical suggestions for the arousing of this and that definite emotion continued to find their place in the sections on proem and epilogue. To rescue the theory of πάθος from such a dubious existence and, in a spirit of loyalty to Aristotle, to restore it to its old dignity were again left to Cicero. In *De inventione*[88] Cicero still follows the Hellenistic tradition in confining the arousing of emotions to proem and epilogue and refuses to recognize this as one of the principal functions of the orator. Yet in his maturer works we find him assigning to the orator the threefold task *probare, delectare*, and *permovere;*[89] and this new conviction, which must have grown out of his practical experience, is reflected in a readmission of ἦθη and πάθη to a position on a par with the rhetorical argument. ἦθος, however, means to him something slightly different from what it had been to Aristotle, it now denotes the *leniores affectus*, a lesser degree of πάθος.[90]

It is probably the result of Cicero's authority that Quintilian too makes an attempt to give the theory of *affectus* its due; but it is a rather unfortunate attempt, the execution being poor because of the dearth of material.[91] He says in so many words that he found no more information in his (Hellenistic and early Imperial) sources, and he obviously did not see his way back to the original Aristotelian theory. In later times Martianus Capella on the Roman and Minucianus on the Greek side return to Aristotle's tripartite system of πίστεις, and certain other rhetoricians also take the πάθη into account.[92] In fact Professor Hendrickson[93] has found a considerable body of evidence for a theory that assigned to the orator a twofold function (instead of the old threefold one) and divided rhetorical productions or prose in general into works designed to teach and convince and those of a more emotional complexion. This theory also goes back to the Peripatetic school and may in the last analysis have grown out of an Aristotelian distinction between two types of style.[94]

4. (corresponding to section 4, page 185 *supra*). With regard to the *tria genera causarum* (the forensic speech, the political speech, and the laudation) we have Quintilian's very valuable testimony: *nec dubie prope omnes utique summae apud antiquos auctoritatis scriptores Aristotelem secuti . . . hac partitione contenti fuerunt.*[95] The Aristotelian division was in fact adopted by the Stoics,[96] and we

find it reproduced in the *Auctor ad Herennium*, Cicero, Quintilian, Fortunatianus, and Martianus Capella. On the Greek side, Alexander is particularly close to Aristotle's wording and idea; the rhetorician Menander characterizes his theory of the ἐπιδεικτικόν as covering a third of the whole field, and a glance at Rabe's *Prolegomenon Sylloge* will satisfy us that the division persisted even among the Byzantines.[97] On the other hand, both Cicero and Quintilian indulge in some criticism, and the latter informs us that the division was opposed by the *maximus temporum nostrorum auctor*.[98] It was in fact an obvious disadvantage that a good part of the potential field of rhetoric remained outside the division, and remarks to this effect are found in Cicero's *De oratore* and Quintilian. Moreover, the term which Aristotle had used as the common denominator of eulogy and invective, τὸ ἐπιδεικτικόν, lent itself to different interpretations, misunderstandings, and, on the basis of these misunderstandings, again to criticism; this has recently been interestingly shown by Mr. Hinks.[99] The alternative procedure, however, that we notice is an almost exclusive concentration on one of these three genera—the forensic. This tendency which was probably widespread in Hellenistic centuries is, as far as we can judge, typically represented by Hermagoras, whose new system (of the *status*) fits only the forensic branch while the other two are condemned to a rather obscure existence in a corner.[100]

The effect of this development may be studied in *De inventione*, where the system of the *status*, though suitable only for the forensic kind, has yet in principle at least been made the basis for the whole section on the content of the speech (*inventio*). In the *Rhetorica ad Herennium* too the forensic branch receives preferential treatment, and some of the later rhetoricians forget the others altogether. Hermogenes ignored Aristotle's classification. His own λόγος πολιτικός embraces in effect the forensic and the deliberative—that is political—branch, and his division into λόγος ἁπλῶς πολιτικός and λόγος ἁπλῶς πανηγυρικός would cover the whole Aristotelian field if his λόγος πανηγυρικός were not something very different from Aristotle's ἐπιδεικτικόν. (To say that the deliberative branch "takes revenge" for the neglect to which it was commonly exposed, "by finding a new and disruptive place within the theory of *status* itself,"[101] is not quite fair to Hermogenes who is constantly thinking of deliberative—political—speeches and tries to fit them into all his *status*.)

5. (corresponding to section 5, page 185 *supra*). The history of the Aristotelian (or Theophrastean) "virtues" of style in later rhetorical theory has been admirably written by Professor Stroux.[102] The fourth book of the *Rhetorica ad Herennium* shows how completely the Theophrastean scheme had been destroyed, and in what a chaotic condition the theory of style found itself before Cicero in *De oratore* decided to go back to the *auctores et inventores harum sane minutarum rerum*, that is to revive the old Peripatetic doctrine. In the third book of *De oratore* a theory of rhetorical diction (*elocutio*) is put forward which in its outlines and organization corresponds exactly to Theophrastus' scheme (see *supra*, p. 186).[103] It is no

exaggeration to maintain that but for this revival modern scholars would not have been able to reconstruct the original system. And yet, if Cicero when he wrote *De inventione* had carried out his intention of reproducing the entire Hellenistic system, the section on *elocutio* would in all probability show the same close resemblance to that in the *Rhetorica ad Herennium* as does the part which he actually worked out. As he stopped before arriving at *elocutio* his development from "Asianism" to "classicism" can be traced only in his stylistic practice, and it is only to the later phase that we have a corresponding "classical" theory in *De oratore*. In *Orator*, Cicero is preoccupied with the three "characters"; yet in that work too the Peripatetic basis is unmistakable.[104]

Quintilian, who devotes three and a half books to *elocutio*,[105] follows Cicero in arranging the material under the four "virtues" and Fortunatianus, Julius Victor, Martianus Capella, and Cassiodorus proceed in principle on the same lines. In the field of diction, however, a huge amount of new material had accumulated since Theophrastus' time. Innumerable new "figures," the whole array of τρόποι, and many other recent pieces of theory were claiming a place in this phase of the system, so that we need not wonder that, while the general outlines of the Peripatetic scheme are preserved intact in writers like Quintilian and the others just mentioned, the content of a section like the *ornatus continuae orationis* (i. e. κόσμος in the σύνθεσις) differs considerably from what Aristotle, Theophrastus, and other Peripatetic writers would have discussed under this heading. In fact, as far as the material (as distinct from its organization) is concerned, we find a closer reproduction of the old Peripatetic doctrine in "Demetrius," περὶ ἑρμηνείας, although this author, unlike Quintilian, has broken up the Peripatetic structure.[106]

On the Greek side no revival of the old Peripatetic scheme seems to have taken place. On the contrary, Stroux has ingeniously shown that writers like Dionysius tend to make the *ornatus* supreme and to give it a monopoly of *elocutio*,[107] thus abandoning the fundamental idea of the Peripatetic school for which *ornatus* (κόσμος) ranked with the three other "virtues": correct language, clarity, and appropriateness to subject matter. Since this is the theory which the Romans beginning with Cicero revive, we note an important divergence between them and their Greek colleagues, who think of style primarily as an "ornament" and tend to ignore the instructive and informative function of language (guaranteed by σαφήνεια)[108] as well as the requirement of a proper relation between style and subject matter, etc. (τὸ πρέπον.)

The so-called Atticistic movement is to a large extent controlled by the κριτικοί who either believe in a multitude of stylistic "ideas" to be used in the appraisal and emulation of the great models or put the main emphasis on the three (or, eventually, more) stylistic "characters." The origin of this stock-in-trade of the later systems does not concern us here. It suffices for our purpose to note that the Peripatetic school is no longer considered responsible for its introduction and that the essential difference between this approach to style and that along the line of "virtues" has come to be recognized.[109] It lies, above everything else, in the fact that, while the Peripatetic believers in virtues theorize on style in a general way and provide precepts applicable to every speech (or even every piece of prose), the writers on χαρακτῆρες divide the whole literature of the past into three or four different types and proceed to describe the peculiarities of each of these. In other words, the theorists of the former type recognize only a distinction between good style and bad style, whereas those of the latter know and approve of four different styles and disapprove of another four.

I am far from minimizing this important difference, and yet it is equally important to understand that both the writers dealing with stylistic "ideas" and those discussing the "characters" draw to a very large extent on material provided for the "virtues" and, in fact, on the virtues themselves.[110] Thus they too are indebted to the Peripatetics. Dionysius' "ideas" are, from the historical point of view, a rather variegated affair, and yet the Peripatetic stock is clearly discernible (more so, as it seems to me at least, than in Hermogenes' περὶ ιδεῶν). It is true that, besides τὸ σαφές, τὸ πρέπον, etc., we also find the Isocratean ἡδύ, πιθανόν, ἐναργές, but we shall see presently that later Peripatetics had found a way of combining these with the original Aristotelian "virtues", and we should bear in mind that Peripatetic writers like Demetrius of Phaleron had been liberal enough to theorize e.g. on χάρις. It has also been pointed out that Dionysius in discriminating between good and bad style makes frequent use of the Peripatetic principle of the "mean" (μεσότης) between two extremes, which helps him also in establishing the supremacy of his εὔκρατος ἁρμονία, the middle style.[111] As regards the writers on χαρακτῆρες, the Peripatetic basis of Pseudo-Longinus and "Demetrius," περὶ ἑρμηνείας is obvious enough. Three of the "sources of sublimity" (πηγαὶ τοῦ ὕψους) in "Longinus" are identical with the sub-headings of Theophrastus' κόσμος, namely the right choice of words (ἐκλογὴ τῶν ὀνομάτων), the dignified composition of words (σύνθεσις τῶν ὀνομάτων), and the "figures" (σχήματα).[112] "Demetrius" makes an even more extensive use of Peripatetic material. In discussing the ἰσχνὸς χαρακτήρ (the *tenue genus dicendi*) he declares that in this character σαφῆ δεῖ εἶναι τὴν λέξιν and proceeds to expound such precepts as the Peripatetics from Aristotle onwards provided for clarity, one of their "virtues" (σαφήνεια): use the common words, avoid ambiguities, leave the words in their natural order, use plenty of particles, etc.[113] Another Peripatetic virtue, *ornatus*, provides him with material on metaphors, images, new words, compound words, allegories, etc., which he uses in his description of the sublime or magnificent character. He also draws on this material, though in a somewhat different manner, in his sections on the two remaining "characters."[114] Again, in theorizing on the "composition of words" in the various characters and in selecting the figures suitable for each of them he proceeds for the most part by dividing up between them the Peripatetic material for σύνθεσις ὀνομάτων and σχήματα.

Instead of pursuing this subject further in detail, let us note that "Demetrius," who borrows and hands on so much Peripatetic material, shows very clearly that this material had suffered—obviously at the hands of the Peripatetics themselves—important modifications, especially through the addition to the old stock of some new categories which had previously been sponsored by the Isocrateans (we here notice again the *conflatio* of the two traditions). Theophrastus is known to have found room in his system of style for τὸ ἡδύ and τὸ μεγαλοπρεπές, two Isocratean requirements for the narration which Aristotle himself had rejected as unnecessary. From "Demetrius" we infer that τὸ πιθανόν and τὸ ἐναργές,[115] two other Isocratean "virtues" of the narration, were also admitted by the Peripatetics (after Aristotle's time) and even elevated to the position of a quality of style in general, whereas the Isocrateans had confined these to the narration, one of their four "parts of the speech." Among the more specialized subjects on which the Isocratean school had theorized and which now came to be absorbed in the Peripatetic system hiatus is probably the most important. Aristotle himself, though dealing at length with the period and its rhythm, had refrained from making any reference to hiatus. He probably knew that the Isocrateans prided themselves on avoiding collisions of vowels but considered it beneath his dignity to pay attention to this newfangled subtlety. His successors, however, did not share his prejudice.

Yet, although the later Peripatetics compromised with the rival school, they did not normally surrender vital and axiomatic features of their master's system. This may be gathered from the following two passages in "Demetrius" which are probably typical of the Peripatetic attitude to Isocratean propositions.[116]

"There are people who hold that we ought to talk about little things in a grand fashion (τὰ μικρὰ μεγάλως λέγειν; this has been taken as a reference to Isocrates and is in fact more likely to have been aimed at him than at Gorgias) and they regard this as proof of surpassing power. . . . Yet fitness must be observed whatever the subject be or, in other words, the style must be appropriate." This "fitness" is τὸ πρέπον, one of the Aristotelian "virtues" which is here played off against an Isocratean principle. Instead of τὰ μικρὰ μεγάλως λέγειν the Peripatetics formulate a new principle, with the help of Aristotle's πρέπον, namely τὰ μικρὰ μικρῶς λέγειν, τὰ δὲ μεγάλα μεγάλως.

The following passage refers to the question of hiatus: "With regard to hiatus different opinions have been held by different people. Isocrates and his followers avoided hiatus while others have admitted it whenever it chanced to occur and between all vowels (reading πάντα πᾶσιν instead of παντάπασιν). One ought, however, neither to make the composition noisy as it will be if the vowels are allowed inartistically to collide just as they fall together. . .nor shun the direct contact of such letters altogether." This is a good Peripatetic middle course for which several reasons are given, especially that common parlance (ἡ συνήθεια) does not hesitate to bring these letters into contact, in words like χιών, and that much music and euphony would be lost if hiatus were shunned everywhere.

We referred above (p. 185ff.) to certain other contributions and new departures made either by Aristotle himself or by his school and may now add a few brief remarks concerning their fate in later authors. Quintilian[117] records that the division of proofs into ἔντεχνοι and ἄτεχνοι was accepted by almost all writers on rhetoric (*illa partitio ab Aristotele tradita consensum fere omnium meruit*). This is borne out by the extant systems, especially by those constructed on the lines of the quinquepartite scheme.[118] A divergent attitude is taken by Cicero in *De inventione* where he does not recognize a distinction between these two kinds of proofs and polemizes against people holding that *quaestiones, testimonia*, etc. *artificio non indigere*.[119] Some rhetoricians, one may assume from this, considered that ἄτεχνα should find either no place at all or at least no technical treatment in the τέχνη. Cicero's own view (or, more probably, that of a Hellenistic rhetorician whom he follows) is that these proofs are a phase of one particular *status*, namely *coniectura*. Yet, in *De oratore* he has changed his mind and returns to the orthodox Aristotelian distinction between ἔντεχνα and ἄτεχνα,[120] including in the latter category even the *leges*. This is noteworthy since, as a rule, later rhetoricians diverged from Aristotle in excluding this item. Nor is it difficult to account for this; the devices which Aristotle in his discussion of the ἄτεχνοι πίστεις had provided for the interpretation of the law, the appeal to the lawgiver's intention as against the letter of the law, the defense of the letter against the supposed intention of the lawgiver, etc., have in the meantime received a place in a different part of the system. Hermagoras used material very similar to Aristotle's to build up his νομικαὶ στάσεις;[121] and, as the later rhetoricians adopted his system of στάσεις, it was logical for them no longer to include the νόμος with the rest of the ἄτεχνοι πίστεις.

As for the sentence period, my impression is that hardly any later rhetorician fully grasped the idea behind Aristotle's definition. The general tendency is to treat this subject more "empirically" and less philosophically. Instead of emphasizing (as Aristotle had done) that the period has a beginning and an end "in itself" and that it is the function of the rhythm to mark these, later writers stress the fact that the period consists of κῶλα and κόμματα, a point which Aristotle as we have seen did not regard as at all essential.[122] Cicero in *Orator* (where he quotes Aristotle in support of his plea for a rhythmical structure of the oration) comes nearer than anyone else perhaps to the original Aristotelian idea.[123]

The sections of "Demetrius" on χάρις and τὸ γελοῖον are, like almost everything else in his treatise, derived from a Peripatetic source; and Cicero's discussion of the rhetorical joke in *De oratore* II is based on the Peripatetic distinction between the laughable in the subject-matter and the laughable in verbal expression and certainly owes many of the more specific points also to Peripatetic theory. This has been shown by a comparison with the *Tractatus Coislinianus* the results of which seem valid, even though one might feel that Cicero's own contributions have been somewhat underrated. Quintilian in turn depends on Cicero. Since the Peripatetics, as far as we know, treated this subject in monographs, it was left to later authors (especially the Romans) to locate it in the system. Cicero as well as Quintilian decided to place it close to his propositions about the arousing of emotions, but Kroll rightly says that the place was never definitively fixed.[124]

We know so little of the Peripatetic theories concerning oratorical delivery that it is very difficult to define the extent to which later authors reproduce them. According to Kroll, Cicero followed Theophrastus closely both in *De oratore* and *Orator*;[125] this would mean that not only the precepts referring to the orator's voice (which Theophrastus certainly discussed) but also those covering his *gestus* and the movements of his body go back to Theophrastus. It is not easy to substantiate this suggestion. The best argument (which, however, Kroll would hardly use) is that it is generally Cicero's tendency, especially in *De oratore*, to revert to the Peripatetic authorities. And we have seen that the Peripatetics were responsible for the inclusion of ὑπόκρισις (*actio*) in the quinquepartite system.

The quinquepartite system is certainly the most comprehensive put forward in the history of ancient rhetoric, but even in characterizing it thus we are far from doing full justice to its importance. It is safe to say that through the quinquepartite system and through the tripartite scheme of "proofs" (arguments, emotions, speaker's character) Aristotle and his school provided the rhetoricians with a principle of organization based on the nature and functions of a public speech. This is the truly philosophical approach to rhetoric; and, though the Peripatetics did not actually kill the rather mechanical alternative system, they at least succeeded in breaking its monopoly. Next to this contribution, the theory of argumentation and the theory of style are the two major fields where Aristotle's methods and ideas have left their mark. Oratorical delivery is a somewhat less important subject; and the analysis of the emotions, though revived from time to time, never secured a definite and undisputed place in the system. While the history of the most important rival tradition, the Isocratean, still remains to be written, we have at least been able to observe how it weakened and to some extent undermined the Peripatetic position in the two most important sections of the rhetorical system, *inventio* and *elocutio*. To this extent Cicero's *unum quoddam genus est conflatum a posterioribus* is certainly borne out.[126] In the field of *inventio* an even more dangerous rival arose in the person of Hermagoras, and it is not too much to say that with the subtle, scholastic distinctions and the elaborate casuistry of his *status* he carried the day over Aristotle. Certain Aristotelian features survived, however, indicating that even Hermagoras' triumph was not complete and that on the whole the result was (here as well as in the fields of conflict between Aristotle and Isocrates) a compromise.

If it is asked (and I do not see why this should not be a perfectly legitimate question) who did most to keep alive or revive Aristotelian ideas and concepts, the answer can hardly be doubtful. I should not stress the fact that the quinquepartite system underlies *De oratore* (for this system was scarcely in danger of being eclipsed) but rather draw attention to the inclusion in this work of ἦθος and πάθος, the revival of Aristotle's conception of the *loci argumentorum*, the return to the four "virtues" of the diction, and the insistence on the old boundary between *inventio* and *dispositio*. And we may add as a point of a less technical nature, that Cicero regards a wide range of knowledge and philosophical speculation as prior conditions for successful oratory.[127] These facts lend substance to his claim that in *De oratore* he renewed the *ratio Aristotelia* (along with the *ratio Isocratea*),[128] and I cannot help wondering why the tendency among scholars has been either to ignore or to minimize the importance of this testimony.

Notes

[1] *Inst. orat.*, III, 1, 14f. Professor Harry Caplan has kindly read the manuscript of this paper which has profited by his suggestions.

[2] Cicero, *De invent.*, II, 8. Cf. G. L. Hendrickson, *A.J. P.*, XXVI (1905), p. 266.

[3] The long felt need for a truly historical treatment of ancient rhetoric has at last been met by Professor Kroll's very valuable article "Rhetorik" in Pauly-Wissowa-Kroll, *R. E.* (Suppl. VI).

[4] See, however, Harry M. Hubbell, *The Influence of Isocrates on Cicero, Dionysius and Aristides* (New Haven, 1913).

[5] In view of the absence of an authentic Isocratean τέχνη a thorough and at the same time cautious analysis of Isocrates' "speeches" from the technical point of view would seem necessary.

[6] Joh. Stroux, *De Theophrasti virtutibus dicendi* (Leipzig, 1912). For the relation between Aristotle and Theophrastus see especially pp. 29-42. Cf. on this point also H. Diels, *Abh. Berl. Akad.*, 1886, pp. 25ff. and G. L. Hendrickson, *A. J. P.*, XXV (1904), pp. 136f.

[7] See Plato, *Phaedrus* 266 d-267 d; Aristotle, *Rhet. A* 1, 1354 b 16-19. Cf. O. Navarre's admirable reconstruction of these systems (*Essai sur la rhétorique grecque* [Paris 1900], pp. 211-327) and see also Hendrickson, *A. J. P.* XXVI (1905), pp. 250f.

[8] Dionysius' testimony (*De Lys.* 16ff.) is borne out by what we know about Theodectes' τέχνη (see especially the evidence in Rose, *Aristotelis Fragmenta*, 133 or in Rabe's *Prolegg. Sylloge*, 32, 216).

[9] *Rhet. A* 1, 1354 b 16-1355 a 1; *Γ* 13, 1414 b 13-18; *Γ* 14, 1415 b 4-9. In this paper I take Aristotle's *Rhetoric* as a unity and a whole without going into the questions concerning the development of Aristotle's theories which I have treated elsewhere (*Die Entwicklung d. aristot. Logik und Rhetorik* [Berlin, 1929]). From the point of view of the Aristotelian "tradition" these questions seem irrelevant as there is no evidence that they ever bothered later rhetoricians.

[10] Cf. my paper on "The Origins and Methods of Aristotle's Poetics," in *Class. Quart.*, XXIX (1935), pp. 192-201.

[11] *Γ* 13-19.

[12] See especially *Rhet. A* 2, 1356 a 1-27 and *Γ* 1, 1403 b 6-18, 1404 a 8-12 and 13. It has been pointed out by Volkmann (*Rhetorik d. Griechen und Römer*, p. 17) that the *Rhetorica ad Alex.* may be divided into sections dealing with A) πράγματα, B) λέξις, and C) τάξις, but the fact is that its author does not seem to have been aware of this. He certainly makes no attempt to establish a rational division of his subject, still less to deduce the necessity of such a division. Whether or not rhetorical systems before Aristotle included anything comparable to *ad Alex.* 2- 7 and to what extent they had gone beyond organizing the entire material under the "parts of the speech" is a question which we can hardly attempt to answer. Aristotle's *Rhetoric* bears the mark of philosophical reasoning, whereas the average τέχνη developed out of practical

needs and practical habits. To divide the τέχνη into *proem, narration, proofs*, etc. is to follow the way in which anyone however untrained would state his case before a jury.

[13] Γ1, 1403 b 21-36.

[14] See e. g. *Metaph. Z* 17, especially 1041 b 11-33, where Aristotle insists on the difference between a syllable and the letters of which it consists. See also H 2. Cf. W. D. Ross, *Aristotle* (3rd edition, London, 1937), pp. 172f.

[15] The evidence for the meaning of the word ἐνθύμημα before Aristotle is not very definite, but on the basis of Isocrates, *Paneg.* 9, *Contra soph.* 16, *Euag.* 10 one may form the impression that any rather elaborate (and elaborately expressed) thought could be called by that name (cf. Navarre, *op. cit.*, p. 255); and I see no reason why Isocrates should not regard e. g. the famous opening passage of the *Panegyricus* as an enthymeme. Quintilian, V, 10, 1 records different meanings of the word and mentions that *plures* favored a notion of *enthymema* which is certainly not Aristotle's. The third variety which he mentions seems to have something in common with the description of the enthymeme found in *ad Alex.* 11. "Demetrius," περὶ ἑρμ. 30-33 finds it necessary to emphasize the fact that an enthymeme is not the same thing as a sentence period. See also Quintilian, VIII, 5, 9.

[16] The principal passages are *Rhet. A* 1, 1354 b 3-10; 2, 1356 a 35-b 25; 1357 b 26-36; 1358 a 1-35; *B* 20, 1393 a 24-27. See also *Anal. Pr. B* 23f. The necessity of basing rhetoric on dialectic had been emphasized by Plato (*Phaedrus* 265) but Plato did not think of dialectic in terms of syllogisms.

[17] The Attic orators make ample use of εἰκότα, σημεῖα, τεκμήρια (see Antiphon, V, 25, 28, 37, 38, 43, 61, 63 and compare the *indices* for the other orators; see also Thucydides, I, 1, 3; 2, 6; 3, 3; and *passim*). I should hesitate to believe that all of them would agree with the definitions given to *ad Alex.* 8, 10, 13. For Aristotle's syllogistic construction of these forms see *A* 2, 1357 a 22-b 25 and *Anal. Pr. B* 27.

[18] See Aristotle, *Soph. El.* 34, 183 b 36-184 a 1; Cicero, *Brut.* 46f. Cf. Navarre, *op. cit.*, pp. 124-132; Volkmann, *op. cit.*, p. 159, and my *Antiphonstudien* (Berlin, 1931), p. 39, n. 2; pp. 47, 65.

[19] *Soph. El.* 34, 183 b 36-184 a 8.

[20] See the τόπος τοῦ μᾶλλον καὶ ἧττον in *Rhet. B* 23 (1397 b).

[21] Cf. on Aristotle's τόποι Georgiana P. Palmer, *The τόποι of Aristotle's Rhetoric as exemplified in the Orators* (Diss. Chicago, 1934). I cannot fully agree with James H. McBurney's comments on the relation between the τόποι and the enthymeme (*Pap. Mich. Ac.*, XXI [1935], p. 493).

[22] Cf. especially chapters like *A* 6f., 9, *B* 19. *A* 10-19 may also with some justification be mentioned here. For the methodical idea behind the premises (and behind the τόποι) see *A* 2, 1358 a 1-*A* 3, 1359 a 5. See for comment on this section of the *Rhetoric* my book (see *supra* n. 9), pp. 13-27.

[23] *Ad Alex.* 2-6. Aristotle too has some chapters in which he enumerates τὰ ἀγαθά or τὰ καλά (*A* 5; *A* 6, 1362 b 10-28; *A* 9, 1366 a 34-b 22) and it might be argued that in these he is keeping closer to the procedure of the average, unphilosophical τέχναι.

[24] *Rhet. A* 2, 1356 a 1-33; *B* 1-18. See for a fuller discussion my paper in *C. P.*, XXXIII (1938), pp. 390-404.

[25] The most instructive passage is perhaps Aristotle, *Rhet. A* 2, 1356 a 10-13.

[26] *Rhet. A* 3, 1358 a 1-13, Aristotle proceeds along lines of a strictly dichotomous διαίρεσις; and, as this method is typical of Plato rather than of Aristotle, the division of the rhetorical λόγοι which we read here may well go back to the Academy (cf. Diog. Laert., 3, 93). The peculiar quality of Aristotle's procedure ought to have been taken into account by D. A. G. Hinks in his important article on the *tria genera causarum* in *Class. Quart.*, XXX (1936) pp. 170-176 because it explains some of the things which puzzle him and puzzled ancient rhetoricians.

[27]See Quintilian, III, 4, 1. The division into three γένη and their sub-division into six εἴδη are also found in the so called *Divis. Aristoteleae* §§ 93f. H. Mutschmann in his edition (p. xiii) remarks pertinently: *quae* εἴδη *Aristoteles a vulgari arte acceperat.* Professor Cherniss has drawn my attention to these passages.

[28]Cf. especially Γ 2, 1404 b 1-8. Γ 2 and 4 come definitely under κόσμος, 7 under πρέπον. Cf. Stroux, *op. cit.*, pp. 29-43. Stroux maintains that for Aristotle these virtues form a unity, but this is one of the few points in his book where one may not follow him.

[29]Γ 5.

[30]See Stroux, *op. cit.*, pp. 9-28.

[31]Γ 3, 6, 10.

[32]Γ 2, 1405 a 3ff.

[33]A definite reference to this work is found in Γ 9, 1410 b 3, but it is hard to believe that Aristotle should not have drawn on it also for his discussion of the sentence period in general, rhythm, and related subjects. Cf. p. 46 *infra.*

[34]A 15. In some of the earliest extant Attic orations the argumentation consists entirely in an elaborate twisting of the available ἄτεχνοι πίστεις. See my *Antiphonstudien* (Berlin, 1931).

[35]Chap. 8 *init.*

[36]See Γ 9 *passim*, especially 1409 a 35f. Cf. also Γ 8. Much light has been shed on these theories and some mistaken interpretations have been refuted by Josef Zehetmeier in his valuable dissertation on *Die Periodenlehre des Aristoteles* (München, 1930, printed also in *Philologus*, LXXXV [1930], pp. 192-208, 255-284, 414-436).

[37]Cf. E. Arndt, *De ridiculi doctr. rhet.* (Diss., Bonn, 1904) and Mary A. Grant, *The Ancient Theories of the Laughable* (Madison, 1924). See also Kroll, *R.-E., s. v.* "Rhetorik," 38f. Cf. *infra.*

[38]Γ 1, 1403 b 26-31.

[39]Kroll (*R. -E., s.v.* "Rhetorik" 36f.) is probably right in assuming that Cicero's discussion of the *actio* (*De orat.*, III, 213-225; *Orat.* 55-60) is a reliable basis for the reconstruction of Theophrastus' theory. See also Stroux, *op. cit.*, pp. 70f.

[40]*Hermes*, LXVII (1932), pp. 144-151. Cf. also Barwick, *Hermes*, LVII (1922), pp. l ff., 12.

[41]See especially Γ 14, 1415 a 24; Γ 16, 1416 b 30.

[42]*Hermes*, LVII (1922), pp. 1-11.

[43]This type is represented by Julius Severianus, Apsines, Rufus, and the Anonymus Seguerianus.

[44]Quintilian, III, 3, 1. Cf. Cicero *De invent.*, I, 9: *partes . . . quas plerique dixerunt.* Quintilian (*loc. cit.*) refers to attempts made by some rhetoricians to add *iudicium* to these five sections and mentions a number of writers who in some way or other diverged from the orthodox quinquepartite scheme. According to Diog. Laert., VII, 1, 43, the Stoics had εὕρεσις, φράσις, τάξις, ὑπόκρισις (see Striller, *De Stoicorum studiis rhet.* [Breslau, 1887], p. 35). I should gather from Diog., *loc. cit.* and Cicero, *De orat.*, I, 142 that the Stoics and other Hellenistic teachers tried to do justice to both traditions. In the end, a combination was brought about (see *infra*, pp. 48-50).

[45]See for πράγματα Γ 1, 1403 b 19, for εὕρεσις A 2, 1355 b 39 (cf. Plato, *Phaedrus* 263a). I cannot agree with Barwick's reconstruction of the history of this type of rhetorical system (*loc. cit.*, pp. 39-41) and think that Kroll's discussion (*R.-E., s. v.* "Rhetorik," 58f.) is more in keeping with the evidence at our disposal.

[46]Cf. Diog. Laert., V, 2, 48 and Stroux, *op. cit.*, p. 70. The Stoics evidently (see n. 44) adopted Theophrastus' system.

[47]For the place of μνήμη in the rhetorical system see Kroll, *R.-E., s. v.* "Rhetorik," 58f.

[48]See especially I, 9. The *Auctor ad Herennium* has all five sections.

[49]The *inventio* is discussed in II, 104-306, 333-349; *dispositio* in II, 307-332; *memoria* in II, 350-360; *elocutio* in III, 37-212; *actio* in III, 213-225.

[50]To be sure, there is a great deal of material in VII that we should hardly expect to find under *dispositio*, but we have to infer from the first and last sentences of the book that for Quintilian himself the book deals with *dispositio*. (Radermacher's recent explanation [*Gnomon*, 1939, p. 100] is not fully convincing.)

[51]See for an analysis of these authors (and for references to Cicero's *Orator*) Barwick, *loc. cit.*, p. 2.

[52]Cicero goes even a step further. He starts by giving a theory of the *status* (I, 10) for which Hermagoras had set the fashion.

[53]*De invent.*, II, 157 (see, however, 155, 177). Cf. *Auctor ad Herennium*, III, 2, 10.

[54]III, 7, 8.

[55]This may be gathered from *Rhet. Graec.* (ed. Spengel-Hammer), II, 182, 20; 208, 5.

[56]For the "Isocratean" system see *supra* p. 37.

[57]Cicero does, however, in *De oratore* make a concession to the Hermagorean doctrine of the *status*, the basic idea of which is embodied in II, 104. In *Part. orat.* the *status* bulk even larger.

[58]Cicero's treatment of *dispositio* in *De orat.*, II, 307-332 is again an exception since he has not anticipated the discussion of the *partes* under *inventio*. To deal with them under *dispositio* as he does was in keeping with the original Peripatetic procedure (i. e. with his *ratio Aristotelia*, see my remarks at the end of this article).

[59]I am referring to his inclusion of ἦθος and πάθος.

[60]For terminological problems cf. especially Quintilian, V, 10, lff. See also p. 170 *infra*.

[61]*Rhet. A* 2, 1357 a 16-21.

[62]*De invent.*, I, 57-66. The *Auctor ad Herennium* discusses the epicheireme along different lines and shows less interest in its syllogistic form. See on his discussion (II, 28-30) and on the epicheireme in general Kroll, *Sitzb. Wien. Akad.*, CCXVI, No. 2, pp. 4 - 17. For Hermagoras cf. Thiele, *Hermagoras* (Strassburg, 1893), p. 134.

[63]Quintilian, V, 13 (especially 5-9).

[64]*De invent.*, I, 60f.

[65]*Ibid.*, 61. Cf. Kroll, *op. cit.*, p. 16.

[66]Hermogenes describes the enthymeme (περὶ εὑρ., III, 8) as an argument to be used after the epicheireme and as reinforcing it. Apsines (ch. 10) and Minucianus (περὶ ἐπιχειρ., 2, 3) regard the enthymeme and the παράδειγμα as parts or forms of the epicheireme. For the theory mentioned in the text see especially Julius Victor, 9, 11; Fortunatianus, 2, 28; Cassiodorus, 12, 15. Cf. Dionysius Hal., *De Isaeo*, 16 where he observes that Lysias prefers enthymemes whereas Isaeus favors epicheiremes (Thiele, *op. cit.*, p. 135).

[67]*De invent.*, I, 51-56. For Aristotle see pp. 39 *supra*.

[68]I, 44-49.

[69]Quintilian, V, 10-14.

[70]*Ibid.*, V, 9, 1; 10, 11. Cf. Philodemus, *Rhet.*, I, 248, 369 (Sudhaus).

[71]See p. 40 *supra*. Cf. Kroll, *Philologus*, LXXXIX (1934), pp. 337, 340. Kroll rightly points out that the division of σημεῖα into such *ante factum, in facto, post factum*, which is frequently found in later writers, occurs as early as the *Rhet. ad Alex.* (ch. 13). Thus we get a glimpse of a tradition which continued in spite of Aristotle. Cf. further Volkmann, *op. cit.* (*supra*, note 12), p. 155.

[72]See e. g. Cicero, *De invent.*, 1, 44. Cf. Aristotle, *Rhet. A* 2, 1357 a 22-b 25.

[73]Cf. e. g. *De invent.*, II, 44f.; *De orat.*, II, 117, 130; Quintilian, II, 4, 27; V, 10, 100.

[74]See the references to Aristotle in *De orat.*, II, 152, 160. It is generally and probably rightly assumed that Cicero borrows the *loci* of the *De orat.* (and similarly those included in the *Topica* and the *Part. orat.*) from a contemporary Academic system which in turn shows Stoic

influence. See M. Wallies, *De Fontibus Topic. Ciceronis* (Diss. Halle, 1878); W. Kroll, *Rhein. Mus.*, LVIII (1903), p. 590; P. Sternkopf, *De M. Tulli Ciceronis Part. Orat.* (Diss. Münst., 1914), pp. 20f. From our point of view, however, the immediate source of Cicero's *loci* is less important than the fact that he reverts to Aristotle's method.

[75] *De invent.*, I, 34-43; II, 17-42 (the points of view mentioned in I, 41 *fin.*-42 are not very different from the *loci* of the *De orat.*). Cf. the shorter and somewhat different treatment of the material of the argumentation in *Ad Herennium*, II, 3-8. For the distinction between *persona* and *negotium* cf. Longinus, p. 182 (Spengel-Hammer) and Rufus, 27-29.

[76] *Rhet. A* 10-12.

[77] See especially Augustine, *De rhet.*, 7f. Cf. Thiele, *op. cit.*, pp. 37-44; Kroll, *R.-E., s. v.* "Rhetorik," 56. Cf. also Volkmann, *op. cit.*, p. 160.

[78] Ch. 8.

[79] The first set of *loci* in Quintilian, V, 10 (23-52) refers to *persona* and *res*, but in V, 10, 53 he proceeds to an enumeration of less specified *loci*, refusing to connect them with the *status* (as other rhetoricians did, see e. g. Neocles in the Anonymus Seguerianus, 170; cf. Sternkopf's judicious discussion, *op. cit.*, pp. 21f.). For the πίστεις ἄτεχνοι see Aristotle, *Rhet. A* 15, Quintilian, V, 1-7. Aristotle provides τόποι of a rather specific kind in his chapter on the διαβολή (Γ 15) in which he probably borrowed a great deal from Theodectes.

[80] See Quintilian, V, 7, 7. Cf. also Quintilian's remark in II, 4, 27.

[81] Anonymus Seguerianus, 144ff., 168f., 172ff. O. Angermann, *De Aristotele rhetorum auctore* (Diss. Leipzig, 1904), pp. 28-59, suggests that the Anonymus is indebted for the Aristotelian material in his τέχνη to Caecilius of Calacte, since the two authorities on whom he depends, Alexander Numenius and Neocles, may both have used Caecilius. Angermann comments on a number of "Aristotelian" passages in Quintilian which show a remarkable resemblance to the Aristotelian material in the Anonymus. His arguments for a common source of Quintilian, Alexander, and Neocles are, on the whole, convincing, though I cannot regard it as proved that this common source was Caecilius and that he was the rhetorician who returned to the genuine Aristotelian doctrine and passed it on to other rhetoricians of the Imperial time. Ofenloch's collection (*Caec. Calact. Fragmenta* [Leipzig, 1907]) is based on Angermann.

[82] For the first type see Apsines, 10 and Anonymus Seguerianus 169-181. Fortunatianus, II, 23, Julius Victor VI, 1-4, and Martianus Capella, 49 (contrast 21) have the fourfold division described in the text; but, while the *loci ante rem* are based on the περιστάσεις, those *circa rem* and *in re* are of a general logical complexion resembling those in Aristotle and the *De oratore*. For another combination of these types see Minucianus, 3 (p. 343, 24 Spengel-Hammer). For the τόποι in the mediaeval systems see Harry Caplan's very interesting discussion in *C. P.*, XXVIII (1933), p. 75. In this context attention may be drawn to some attempts to use Aristotle's categories as a basis for *inventio* (Quintilian, III, 6, 23; Longinus, pp. 179-181 [Spengel-Hammer]).

[83] See especially Cicero, *De invent.*, II, 157-178; *De orat.*, II, 342-349; *Ad Herennium*, III, 2-15; Quintilian, III, 7f.

[84] III, 7-9 and 15. It may be noted that the chapters on the *laudatio* frequently include references to Peripatetic divisions of the "goods," especially to the famous tripartite division (goods of the mind, of the body, external goods; see e. g. *Ad Herennium*, III, 10; Cicero, *De orat.*, II, 342; *Part orat.*, 38; Quintilian, III, 7, 12). For Stoic influence on Cicero, *De invent.*, II, 160ff. see Kroll, *Philologus*, XCI (1936), pp. 197-205.

[85] One naturally wonders whether Hermagoras' own system shows any signs of indebtedness to Aristotle. Unfortunately, the system has in spite of the careful studies of Thiele and W. Jäneke (*De statuum doctrine ab Hermogene tradita* [Diss. Leipzig, 1904]) not yet been reconstructed with sufficient certainty. It is true that Quintilian was in a position to point to certain *semina* of Hermagoras' theory in Aristotle's work (III, 6, 24, 49, 60). *Rhet. A* 1, 1354 a 26-31, *A* 13,

1378 b 38ff. are some of the passages which he may have had in mind, but those which come nearest to Hermagoras are found in the second part of book III (15, 1416 a 6-9; 16, 1416 b 20-22; 1416 b 39-1417 a 2) where Aristotle himself depends on the Isocratean tradition (see p. 46 *supra*). The value of these passages lies in the fact that they put us in mind of some practical facts which form a background also to Hermagoras' theory, but Quintilian's *fecit deinde velut propriam Hermagoras viam* (III, 1, 16) remains, after all, unassailable. See, however, for a different opinion Volkmann, *op. cit.*, pp. 31f.; Navarre, *op. cit. (supra*, note 7), p. 265.

[86] See Cicero, *De orat.*, I, 87, 201, Philodemus, *Rhet.*, I, 370 (Sudhaus). Cf. also Quintilian (p. 170 *infra*).

[87] See for details *C. P.*, XXXIII (1938), p. 396.

[88] See *De invent.*, I, 22, 100ff., 106ff.

[89] E. g. *De orat.*, II, 114, 128, 310; *Orator*, 69; *Brutus*, 158; *De opt. gen. or.*, 3.

[90] *De orat.*, II, 182-214. Cf. II, 115. See also *Orator*, 128-133. It must be admitted that Cicero's analysis of the emotions goes less deep and is less philosophic than Aristotle's. See for a fuller discussion of these points *C. P.*, XXXIII (1938), pp. 396-401. For Cicero's practical ψυχαγωγία see *T. A. P. A.*, LXIX (1938), pp. 542ff. where I have discussed the reasons why Cicero was more attracted by Aristotle's *Rhetoric* than by the Hellenistic systems. For the new notion of ἦθος see L. Voit, Δεινότης, *Ein antiker Stilbegriff* (Leipzig, 1934), pp. 135-140. Cf. Quintilian, VI, 2, 8.

[91] VI, 2. Cf. especially his remark VI, 2, 25.

[92] Martianus Capella, 28, 29; Minucianus, 1. Julius Severianus discusses the *affectus* at length and from various points of view, drawing to a large extent on Cicero's practice (ch. 21 represents a curious attempt to utilize the *loci argumentorum* in building up an analogous theory for the *affectus*). Apsines (306-329 [Spengel-Hammer]) and the Anonymus Seguerianus (222-239) treat τὰ πάθη in the context of the epilogue, and the latter has characteristically a reference (208) to "Aristotle in the θεοδεκτικαὶ τέχναι"; see p. 46 *supra*. It is certainly not the genuine Aristotelian tradition. For a reference to Aristotle's tripartite division of the πίστεις see Dionysius Hal., *De Lys.*, 19 *init.* I cannot include in this paper a discussion of the place of ἦθος in the theory of style.

[93] *A. J. P.*, XXVI (1905), pp. 249-267.

[94] *Rhet.* Γ 12, 1413 b 3 ff. Cf. Theophrastus' much quoted fragment (Ammonius, *In Arist. de interpret.*, p. 65, 31 [Berlin ed.]).

[95] III, 4, 1; cf. *ibid.*, 12.

[96] Cf. Diogenes Laert., VII, 42.

[97] See Alexander in *Rhet. Graec.* (ed. Spengel-Hammer), III, 1; Menander, *ibid.*, 331. For the rest of Rabe's index *s. v.* δικανικός, ἐπιδεικτικός, πανηγυρικός, συμβουλευτικός.

[98] Cf. especially Cicero, *De orat.*, II, 43-51 and 68; Quintilian, III, 4, 2.

[99] D. A. G. Hinks, "Tria Genera Causarum," *Class. Quart.* XXX (1936), pp. 170-176.

[100] Namely under the *status* called *qualitas* (ποιότης). Cf. Quintilian, III, 6, 56; Thiele, *op. cit.*, pp. 53f., 78 (see also p. 182 concerning Athenaeus); Kroll, *R.-E.*, *s. v.* "Rhetorik," 53.

[101] Hinks, *op. cit.*, p. 176.

[102] See p. 36 *supra*.

[103] See especially III, 148, 187. *Elocutio* is discussed in III, 37-212 (though the "excursuses" containing lofty philosophical speculations are, of course, foreign to the rhetorical theory and have to be considered as Cicero's own addition). See for the disposition of this part of the work III, 37. Cf. Stroux, *op. cit. (supra*, note 6), pp. 11-28, 54-56.

[104] It is apparent especially in the inclusion of πάθος and ἦθος (128), the reference to the four "virtues of style" as a standard of which the Atticists fall short (79), the use made of τὸ πρέπον

in defining, among other things, the proper sphere of each character (70ff.), and the reference to Aristotle and Theophrastus as authorities on period and rhythm (172, 228).

[105]VIII-XI, 1. See for Quintilian and the *virtutes dicendi* in later Roman rhetoricians Stroux, *op. cit.*, pp. 56-64. Cf. Fortunatianus, III, 8; Martianus Capella, 31 (Julius Victor, 20).

[106]See my paper in *Hermes*, LXVI (1931), pp. 241-267. The features of the σύνθεσις which the Peripatetic source of "Demetrius" had under κεκοσμημένον appear to have been rhythm, length of κῶλα, περιαγωγή, εὐφωνία, structure of the period, order and arrangement of the words, σύνδεσμοι, hiatus.

[107]Cf. Stroux, *op. cit.*, pp. 19, 23.

[108]Cf. Aristotle, *Rhet.*, Γ 2, 1404 b 2.

[109]See again Stroux, *op. cit.*, especially pp. 88-104 and Hendrickson's papers quoted *supra*, notes 2 and 6. For a more conservative view cf. Kroll, *R.-E.*, *s.v.* "Rhetorik," 35; Radermacher, *Gnomon*, XV (1939), p. 101. For the history of the problem see Stroux' first chapter.

[110]Cf. again Stroux, *op. cit.*, pp. 72-88 (for the material in Dionysius see especially pp. 73 f., 77f.), 104-126. I am confining myself in the following pages to a few significant illustrations of the process.

[111]See S. F. Bonner's recent article (*C.P.* XXXIII [1938], pp. 257-266) in which the author proceeds successfully on lines indicated by Hendrickson in *A.J.P.*, XXV (1904), pp. 125-146.

[112]See *De Subl.*, 8 *init.*, 16-29, 30-38, 39-43. Cf. Hans Stefan Schultz, *Der Aufbau der Schrift* περὶ ὕφους (Diss. Berlin, 1936), pp. 30 ff., 42, 44.

[113]"Demetrius," 191f., 196, 199ff. Cf. Cicero, *De orat.*, III, 48f.

[114]Cf. for a fuller treatment my paper in *Hermes*, LXVI (1931), pp. 244-249, 251, 253. The Peripatetic influence in this work is recognized also (at least in principle) by Rhys Roberts, *Demetrius on Style* (Cambridge, 1902), pp. 50-52 and *passim* in the notes, and by Radermacher on p. 12 of his edition (Leipzig, 1901).

[115]"Demetrius," 208-222.

[116]*Ibid.*, 120, 68-71.

[117]V, 1, 1.

[118]See, besides Cicero and Quintilian, Julius Victor, VI, 5, 6; Martianus Capella, 27, 43; Anonymus Seguerianus, 145 f.; Minucianus, 1.

[119]*De invent.*, II, 47; cf. Quintilian, V, 1, 2.

[120]*De orat.*, II, 116-119. Cf. *Part. orat.*, 6, 48, 117 (in 117 a particular ἄτεχνον, *testes*, is discussed under the heading *coniectura*, which is in keeping with Cicero's decision in *De invent.*, II, 47).

[121]See Thiele, *op. cit.*, pp. 78-84 and cf. Quintilian, III, 6, 61. It is possible, as Thiele points out, that Hermagoras' own term was νομικὰ ζητήματα (not στάσεις). A detailed comparison of Hermagoras' theory and Aristotle, *Rhet. A* 15, 1375 a 25-b 25 would seem to be a desideratum.

[122]"Demetrius," 10 is a typical passage. Cf. also Aristides, II, 507, 6 (Spengel); Anonymus Seguerianus, 242; Quintilian, IX, 4, 122ff., especially 125. See also Martianus Capella, 39. Cf. Zehetmeier, *op. cit.* (*supra*, note 36), *passim*, especially pp. 423 ff., 434.

[123]*Orator*, 228. Yet cf. 221.

[124]E. Arndt (*op cit.*, *supra*, note 37) deals with Cicero, *De orat.*, II, 217-289 (pp. 25-40) and Quintilian, VI, 3 (pp. 41-62). See also Roger Pack, *C.P.*, XXXIII (1938), pp. 405- 410, who proceeds more cautiously. Kroll, *R.-E.*, *s.v.* "Rhetorik," 38f., emphasizes that in the *Orator*, unlike the *De oratore*, Cicero connects the *ridiculum* with the *genus tenue* (see the notes in his commentary on *Orator*, 87-89); Kroll's identification of *facetiae* and *dicacitas* with χάρις and γέλως is not tenable and has been refuted by Miss Grant, *op. cit.* (note 37, *supra*), p. 103. See also *Ad Herennium*, I, 10 which has something in common with Cicero (Arndt, *op. cit.*, p. 38).

[125]*De orat.*, III, 213-225 (much that we read here must have originated with Cicero himself), *Orator*, 55-60. Cf. Kroll, *R.-E.*, *s.v.* "Rhetorik," 36; Stroux, *op. cit.*, p. 70.

[126]*De invent.*, II, 8. See *supra* p. 49 and p. 185.

[127] In stressing the need of philosophical penetration Cicero agrees with Plato's *Phaedrus*, whereas the emphasis put on extensive knowledge has parallels in Aristotle (see especially *Rhet. A* 4; *B* 22). Cf. Hans Schulte, *Orator, Untersuchungen über das Ciceronische Bildungsideal* (Frankfurt, 1935) and my review of this book in *A.J.P.*, LIX (1938), p. 106.

[128] *Ad Fam.*, I, 9, 23. See for literature *C.P.*, XXXIII (1938), p. 398 (add Kroll, *R.-E.*, *s.v.* "Rhetorik," 47-50).

PRINTINGS OF ARISTOTLE'S *RHETORIC* DURING THE FIFTEENTH AND SIXTEENTH CENTURIES

Paul D. Brandes*

This study applies the results of an updated and extended investigation of the printings of Aristotle's Rhetoric *between 1477 and 1599 to demonstrate the availability of the* Rhetoric *during the Renaissance. Four conclusions are drawn: (1) the* Rhetoric *was widely available, for at least 95 printings occurred during the period examined; (2) the repeated printings of Latin translations by five different humanists indicates a growing demand for the* Rhetoric; *(3) Victorius's efforts to reconstruct an authentic Greek text had a favorable influence on improving subsequent editions; and (4) the fact that most of the printings appeared in five continental cities indicates that the dissemination of the* Rhetoric *depended upon its purchase by private scholars and collectors.*

The purpose of this study is to apply the resources of an updated and extended investigation of the early printings and locations of Aristotle's *Rhetoric* to demonstrate the widespread availability of the work to scholars of the Renaissance. In so doing, the material will clarify the development of the *Rhetoric* from manuscript to book form.

This investigation makes two contributions. First, the researcher has verified, either by visit or by reliable correspondence, the availability of the *Rhetoric*. Therefore, these findings improve what had been reported by previous studies: (a) by expanding and verifying the number of editions printed and (b) by clarifying the

institutions that hold these editions. In the process of this research, many errors
have been corrected. Furthermore, libraries whose holdings had not been incorporated before were investigated, and the holdings of repositories suffering damage
from World War II were amended. Second, based on these investigations, this study
presents a perspective on the sweep of Greek and Latin editions of Aristotle's
Rhetoric available to scholars during the Renaissance.

The study has four limitations. First, the research was confined to editions in
Greek and Latin. Second, no inferences can be drawn either from where the books
were published or from where they are now housed as to their influence on learning
in that area. The editions examined frequently bear the bookplates of individuals,
but how the editions came to be housed where they are now held is generally
unknown. Third, inferences are not drawn concerning the uses to which the editions
were put. Fourth, there can be no guarantee that further editions of the *Rhetoric*
printed between 1475 and 1599 will not be discovered. Every lead furnished by
previous researchers and by the libraries contacted has been investigated.[1] But the
researcher is always in hopes that further data will appear. However, the expanded
and verified findings of this research permit us to establish how readily available
the *Rhetoric* was to scholars during the Renaissance.

Method

First, pertinent bibliographies and library catalogues were used to develop a
chronological list of editions.[2] When available, the location and call numbers of
such editions were noted. Equipped with this list, the researcher visited 66 libraries
where holdings had been listed or were likely to be found.[3] At the same time,
libraries listed in the *Primo Catalogo* (1962-), the *Index Aureliensis* (1962-), the
Gesamtkatalog der Wiegendrucke (1925-1940), the *Gesamtkatalog der Preussischen Bibliotheken* (1931-1939), and the *National Union Catalogue: Pre-1956
Imprints* (1968-1980) that could not be visited because of time and financial
restraints[4] were mailed forms seeking verification of their holdings.[5] Information
collected from on-site visits and mailings was catalogued (see Table 1). These
findings furnish the data for the following report on the availability of printed
editions of the *Rhetoric* during the late 15th and 16th centuries.

Early Latin Translations

The earliest printed edition is variously dated from 1475 to 1477. As no identification marks appear in the volume, the details must be inferred from printer's marks.
The *Bibliothèque Nationale*, which holds two of the four known copies of this
work,[6] attributes the edition to Paris printers Jean Stall and Pierre Caesar and
proposes a publication date of c. 1477. The volume reproduced the Latin translation
of the *Rhetoric* by George of Trebizond (Georgius Trapezuntius) (1395-c. 1473).[7]
According to Monfasani, Vaticanus Latin 4564 preserves the working copy of

TABLE 1

SAMPLE ENTRY SHOWING DATA ON THE 1523 EDITION

Date	Locations	Titles	Annotations	Documentation
1523	BN Rés.X275	TITLE IN INDEX:	in 4°	Gesamtk 6,6370
	BM 11340.k.1	Aristotelis Rhetoricorum ad Theodecten	a=15; b=26; g=18	
	Harv f.105.T1945.523g		chaps	Hoffman 336
	Bodl Byw.C.4.9	Libri III	Bk I=109r-118v;	Schwab 2946
	Munich 2° A.gr.C.24		Bk II=118v-128v;	
	Gennadius GC 3890	On folio 109r:Georgii	Bk III=128v-135v	NUC
	Camb U Lib	Trapezuntii in Tres	NUC listing for MWA	195,487,0139027
	F.152.b.2.2; Trinity	Rhetoricorum Aristotelis Libros ad Theodecten Tralatio	is false	+ 21,18,0403844
	Grylls.11.400		Includes Trapezuntius's	
	ViU *PA3484.C65		own R along with other Rs	Erickson(1975)does not list this edition
	1523	Venice: Aldus Manus,		
	NY Pub *KB+ Vienna 22.M.5 Basel B.C.II.14 Hntgton HEH 137910 Brown not catalogued	1523 (colophon)	Capital letters at beginnings of chaps are sometimes omitted e.g. in ViU copy, all are missing	

Trapezuntius's translation, which was begun as early as 1442 (1976, p. 57, note 131) and was probably completed between 1443 and 1446 (1976, p. 55). Judging from the number of manuscripts that have survived, the Trapezuntius translation was a likely choice for the printer because he would not have had much difficulty in obtaining a manuscript. This version was reprinted in 1504 in Venice and in 1515 in Paris. Its numerous printings later in the 16th century will be detailed below.

Another Latin translation used by early printers was the version by William of Moerbeck (?-between 1281-1300). Moerbeck's knowledge of Arabic and Greek plus his strategic location as Bishop of Corinth provided him access to manuscripts now seemingly lost. Therefore, his Latin version, completed in 1273, is somewhat at variance with leading Greek texts.[8] Again, inferring from the existing number of manuscripts of the Moerbeck translation,[9] it was not difficult for a printer to obtain copy. This version was first printed in Venice in 1481, but, because of confusion in catalogues, it is sometimes not attributed to Moerbeck or Aristotle.[10] It was reprinted in Leipzig in 1499 and again in Venice in 1515. The Leipzig edition is notable for apparently being the first issue of the *Rhetoric* from Eastern Europe.[11] The third printing of the Moerbeck translation in Venice in 1515 closely followed B.N. MS. N.A. Latin 1876, a 14th century manuscript from the Phillipps collection. Whereas the format of the printed edition alternated in two columns per folio the Latin translation of Moerbeck with a commentary by Egidio Colonna,[12] the format of the manuscript placed the Latin of Moerbeck in the middle of two peripheral columns, one on either side of the centered translation.

The Moerbeck version appears not to have been reprinted after 1515 until it was reissued in Frankfurt in 1968.[13]

The First Greek Edition

When Aldus Manus issued his Greek edition of Aristotle's works between 1495 and 1498, he did not include the *Rhetoric* or the *Poetics*, either because he could not locate suitable manuscripts or because he was saving them for a later publication that might be more profitable. It was not until 1508 that Aldus included the Greek text of the *Rhetoric* in a book entitled *Rhetores in hoc volumine habentur hi*. Earlier publications had been in Latin because there was a wider reading public for books in Latin than in Greek. Aldus evidently felt that combining the *Rhetoric* with other rhetorics would make the Greek printing saleable. The 1508 venture was seemingly successful enough for Aldus to issue his *Rhetorum Graecorum Orationes* in 1515. According to Kassel (1971, pp. 61-62), Aldus Manus used what are now Parisinus 2038 and Vaticanus 1580. The reasons why these particular MSS. were available to Manus are unknown.

Subsequent Editions of
the Trapezuntius Latin Translation

It was a relatively easy task for 16th century printers to reissue the Trapezuntius edition. Evidently a combination of a literary revival plus the desire of the wealthy to develop home libraries made sales profitable. At least 21 editions were issued between 1530 and 1581.[14] As the century progressed, new translations of the *Rhetoric* appeared, causing publishers to shift from Trapezuntius to a Latin translator who could boast he had consulted with the latest Greek editions and other contemporary sources. But it was the Trapezuntius edition that introduced much of the early Latin-reading public to Aristotle's *Rhetoric* and demonstrated that issuing the *Rhetoric* would be a successful venture for printers.

Greek Editions Preceding 1548

While the printers kept the public supplied with a steady sequence of Latin translations, Greek editions were being issued steadily but more cautiously. The first Greek edition printed after the 1508 Aldine and before the 1548 Victorius edition was issued at Basel in 1529, followed by eight other printings.[15] Of these nine Greek editions, two were more than reissues of the Manus version and deserve comment because of their individuality. The two volume set of Aristotle's works, edited by Desiderius Erasmus and Simon Grynaeus, published in Basel in 1531 and reissued in 1539, undoubtedly owed its widespread sale to the fame of its editors. Of the 1531 edition, thirty-two were located, not including those identified by previous researchers at Kiel, Bonn, and Berlin and reported by those libraries as destroyed. Twenty-six copies of the 1539 reissue were located, with Kiel reporting that its copy was lost in World War II, and Griefswald and Wurzburg certifying that their collections had contained copies that are now missing.[16] It seems possible to infer from the relatively large number of copies of the 1531 and 1539 editions still in existence that the Erasmus-Grynaeus version was widely disseminated.

The second Greek edition making a special contribution appeared in 1536 at Venice under the editorship of Joannis Francisco Trincavelli and was a crude first attempt to establish a Greek text superior to that of the 1508 Aldine edition. Trincavelli's methodology was to reprint the 1508 edition, noting variations in the margins. Kassel (1971, p. 99) determined that Trincavelli consulted Parisinus 1869 or one of its descendants. However, because of his inferior sources, Trincavelli's work fostered additional errors. But he did challenge the Aldine version and was therefore a forerunner to Victorius. The library in Munich has a copy of the Trincavelli, heavily annotated by Victorius.[17]

A Collated Greek Text:
Victorius's Three Editions of 1548, 1549, and 1579

The Greek edition of Victorius was printed at Florence in 1548 and at Basel in 1549. Victorius's letters indicate that he had contemplated an edition of the *Rhetoric* since April of 1542, and to prepare himself had been studying the *Ethics* and the *Poetics* (Niccolai, 1914, pp. 227-228). As Niccolai (1914, p. 227) pointed out, Barbaro's Latin translation, published posthumously in Venice in 1544, did not supply the need for a definitive text. Therefore, in his workroom in Florence, Victorius assembled a number of Greek manuscripts and printed editions of the *Rhetoric* and began his restoration of the Greek text.

Victorius had powerful friends to help him. Francesco Pucci and Cardinal Nicolas Ridolfi assisted him in locating manuscripts (Kassel, 1971, p. 100). Francesco Medici advised him on the interpretation of selected passages.[18] Victorius's most important find was what is now known as Parisinus MS. 1741 which, as Kassel pointed out, was in itself sufficient for Victorius to straighten out most of the corruptions that had entered the Greek text.[19] Victorius had other manuscripts available to him as well, including the Latin version of William of Moerbeck. He also used three MSS. now housed in the *Bayerische Staatsbibliothek* in Munich, bearing marginalia in his hand.[20] A note in Munich's L.imprs.c.n.mass. 87/la, Victorius's working copy of the 1508 Aldine edition, states that Victorius must also have had Vaticanus 2228 available to him.

Victorius's methodology was what you would expect. He clipped folios 161-234 from the Aldine edition and mounted them in the middle of blank pages so that he could write his emendations in the margins. The notes he supplied from both manuscripts and printed editions[21] are copious.[22]

A number of Victorius's sources were corrupt. Kassel's careful collations led him to conclude that the Aldine text was based upon two corrupt manuscripts. The Trincavelli edition, concluded Kassel (1971, pp. 98-99), also bore errors. Victorius himself realized that two of the Monacensis MSS. contained faults, and that Monacensis 175 was based upon Trincavelli. If we keep in mind that Victorius did not realize that dominant position that Parisinus 1741 should have assumed in his collations, we can comprehend better Victorius's puzzlement until it became clear to him that some of his sources were more authentic than others. Victorius was a careful scholar.[23] He knew he was breaking new ground. He deplored the errors of previous scribes and editors and wished not to add to the confusion. Kassel concluded that Victorius proceeded with "übergrossen, oft in Änstglichkeit ausartenden Vorsicht,"[24] avoiding conjecture and questioning each point carefully.

Even with its limitations, Victorius's critical edition of 1548 made changes in the Greek text that were to be honored repeatedly during the remainder of the 16th century. Editors customarily referenced their Greek and Latin editions to Victorius's readings. His interest in the *Rhetoric* continued, for a new edition was issued at Florence in 1579, accompanied for the first time by Victorius's own Latin translation.

Latin Translations of the
Second Half of the Sixteenth Century

A number of translators assisted in making Latin versions of the *Rhetoric* available between 1544 and 1599. Of these, five had three or more editions of their version published.[25] A brief examination of these five will assist us in understanding how the *Rhetoric* became available during the second half of the 16th century.[26]

Whereas Victorius not only held the chair of eloquence at Florence for almost 50 years but was also something of a politician and statesperson, the five popular translators who developed their editions between 1544 and 1599 were best known as rhetoricians and presumably developed their books to assist them in their teaching. Four were native Italians: Antonio Maioragio (1514-?) of Milan; Carlo Sigonio (1524-1584) of Modena, Venice, and Padua; Antonio Riccobono (1541-1599) of Padua; and Hermolao Barbaro (1454-1493) of Venice and Rome. The fifth, Marc Antoine Muret (1526-1585), who translated only the first two books of the *Rhetoric*, fled Paris to establish himself in Rome. These five translators accumulated a total of 37 printings of the *Rhetoric*, largely published in Venice, Lyon, Paris, and Basel. There were additional single issue translations in 1570 by Johann Sturm (1507-1589), principal of a preparatory school in Strasbourg, and in 1598, by Emilio Porto (c. 1550-1610) of the University of Lausanne. Thus, it was largely the humanist professors who concerned themselves with making the *Rhetoric* easily available in Latin. As Kristeller (1955, p. 40) noted, "Aristotle's *Rhetoric*, which in the Middle Ages had been neglected by the professional rhetoricians and treated by the scholastic philosophers as an appendix to the *Ethics* and *Politics*, became during the 16th century an important text for the humanist rhetoricians." Victorius, Maioragio, Sigonio, Riccobono, Barbaro, and Muret were prominent among those humanist professors who provided themselves and others with the *Rhetoric* as a viable text.

Greek Editions of Significance Between 1549-1599

The 1548 Victorius collation of the manuscripts had an immediate influence on later printings. As early as 1549, a Greek edition issued in Paris acknowledged that its text had been adjusted to allow for Victorius's readings, and the 1550 reissue of the Erasmus-Grynaeus Greek text acknowledged its indebtedness to Victorius. Seventeen printings of various Greek editions appeared during this latter half of the 16th century. Although this number does not match the flow of Latin translations discussed above, it demonstrates that there was a market for the Greek text. Early publishers were no different from their contemporaries; what was printed had to be profitable. Even the well-established publishers had not the reserve resources to take many risks. Seventeen printings by a variety of publishers is an indication that the *Rhetoric* in Greek remained available to scholars of the Renaissance.

Two Greek editions published during the second half of the 16th century deserve discussion. It can be argued pro and con that the present availability of certain editions can be interpreted as an indication of the popularity of a publication at the time it was issued. On the one hand, the most popular editions may have been worn out by constant use and therefore have not been preserved. On the other hand, the preservation of sizeable numbers of an edition in contemporary libraries can be interpreted as evidence that the edition was in wide use at the time. This researcher was impressed not only by the 50 copies of *Rhetoric* that had survived from the 10 volume Frankfurt edition of 1584-1596,[27] but also with the number of these editions that were well annotated in Greek and Latin, and showed signs of use.[28]

The massive Greek 1590 edition of two volumes of Aristotle's works has caused bibliographers confusion because volume one is sometimes credited to the publisher Jacobus Bubonius and sometimes to the publisher Guillelmus Laemarius. The library at Halle has both versions of volume one. The *Rhetoric*, however, located in volume two, is consistently credited to Bubonius. The copies of the 1590 edition at Braunsberg, Bonn, and Kiel were destroyed in World War II, but the Berlin copy survived, making a total of 31 extant copies.

Summary

It can be concluded that numerous 15th and 16th century Greek and Latin editions of Aristotle's *Rhetoric* were available to facilitate scholarship. The advent of the printing press, therefore, greatly increased the potential use of the *Rhetoric* during the Renaissance. Recorded for this study were 66 editions in Latin, 17 in Greek, and 12 in Greek and Latin, totaling 95 editions between the years 1477 and 1599.[29]

Furthermore, the continuing interest of printers in the *Rhetoric* suggests not only that there were copies available but that printers could make a profit from their ventures. The repeated printings of the Latin translations of Trapezuntius, Maioragio, Sigonio, Riccobono, Barbaro, and Muret would indicate a growing demand for the *Rhetoric* that encouraged early printers to keep the treatise in press.

Third, scholars had access to Victorius's contribution toward reconstructing an authentic Greek text. Although Victorius had sources that would have permitted establishing a better restoration than he achieved, his pioneer efforts at collation were a decided improvement over the Aldine text of 1508 and had a strong influence on subsequent issues of the *Rhetoric*, both in Greek and Latin. Only in the 19th and 20th centuries was Victorius's work superceded by the more definitive editions appearing in England and Germany.

The somewhat restricted areas where the *Rhetoric* was repeatedly published indicate that its dissemination depended upon its purchase by private scholars and collectors. Venice, Basel, Lyon, Paris, and Frankfurt were locations where the climate of the times encouraged printers to work. However, even assuming wide dissemination, the extent of the influence of the *Rhetoric* on instruction and scholarly thought during the 15th and 16th centuries is an area of research that has only been provisionally covered.[30]

Notes

[1]Research continues in an effort to locate editions to which there have been references but for which no copy can be located. For example, Hoffman in his *Lexicon bibliographicum* (1800, Vol. 1, p. 337) cited an edition of the *Rhetoric* published in Louvain in 1550. A letter dated 9 October 1984 from the *Centre Général de Documentation* of the *Université Catholique de Louvain* established that Hoffman confused a 1550 Fortunatianus edition published in Louvain

by Nannius with the *Rhetoric* of Aristotle, and concluded that no such 1550 Louvain edition of Aristotle's *Rhetoric* was ever published. On the other hand, the *Civica Biblioteca Queriniana* of Brescia forwarded reproductions of the title page and introduction to the 1584 Sigonio translation that had been cited by Hoffman (Vol. 1, p. 337) and Erickson (1975, p. 23), but for which no copies had been found in libraries visited or previously contacted by mail. Schwab (1896, entry #3009) identified 1565 and 1577 editions of the Barbaro translation, which this research has been unable to confirm. Of the 1565 edition, no trace has been found. Of the 1577 edition, Schwab possibly erred in attributing the 1577 Sigonio edition to Barbaro. Hoffman (1, 291), Schwab (#388), Schweiger (1, 51), and Chaix (146) note a 1596 two volume edition, as a reissue of the 1590 Greek folio edition. They also note a 1597 reissue of the same edition. A search by the University of Geneva did not produce a 1596 edition. However, there is a 1597 edition of the Riccobono translation attributed to the publisher Laemarius with "Lyon" on the title page. A letter from the *Bibliothèque de la Ville de Lyon* stated that the printer, Guillaume de Leymarie of Geneva and Morges, never worked in Lyon, but falsely attributed the place of publication of his books as Lyon. Since the 1597 Laemarius edition is in two volumes and does follow the 1590 edition also published by Laemarius, either there is a 1596 Riccobono edition issued from Geneva that this research has not yet located, or the 1597 Riccobono edition is what Schweiger (1930), Hoffman (1832), Schwab (1896), and Chaix (1966) had reference to, and one erred by adding a 1596 edition to which the other bibliographers conformed. Niccolai (p. 227) referred to a 1543 edition of Barbaro, but again this researcher has not been able to document such a publication. The earliest edition recorded for this study was dated 1544.

[2]The bibliographies and catalogues consulted are given here by short title or by name of author: For the incunabula: *Catalogue Général Bibliothèque Nationale; General Catalogue Printed Books, British Library*; Brunet; Coppinger; *Gesamtkatalog der Wiegendrucke*; Goff; Hain; *Indici/e Cataloghi*; Johnson & Scholderer; Mitarelli; *National Union Catalogue Pre-1956*; Pellechet; Pollard & Scholderer; Proctor; Renouard; and Schwab. For the 16th century editions, in addition to those above when applicable: Adams; Chaix; Chevalier; Cranz; Delisle; Englemann; Erickson (1975); Fabricci; *Gesamtkatalog der Preussischen Bibliothekin*: Hoffman; *Index Aureliensis*; Marshall; Murphy (1971); *Primo Catalogo*, and Schweiger.

[3]In Great Britain: Bodleian; British Library; Cambridge University Library and all college libraries, including access to Adams' notes in Trinity College Library; National Library of Scotland; on the continent, West Zone: *Université de Basel; Bibliothèque Nationale; Bibliothèque Mazarine*; Gennadius; *Universitäts Bibliothek Göttingen; Universitäts Bibliothek Heidelberg; Bayerische Staatsbibliothek; Bibliothèque Sainte-Genviève;* Vienna *Staatsbibliothek*; on the continent, East Zone: *Deutsche Staatsbibliothek* in East Berlin plus telephone calls to libraries in West Berlin; *Egyetemi Könyvtár; Magyar Tudományos Akadémia Könyvtár; Orszagos Széchényi Könyvtár;* and *Ráday Gyüjtémenye*, Budapest; *Biblioteka Jagiellońska*, Krakow; *Státní Védecká Kńihovna, Olomouc; Státní Kńihovna*, Prague; in the United States: Boston Public; Catholic University; University of Chicago; Columbia University; Duke University; Folger Library; Harvard University; University of Illinois; Indiana University; Library of Congress; University of Michigan; University of North Carolina; Northwestern University; Ohio State University; University of Pennsylvania; Princeton University; University of Virginia; and Yale University.

[4]Research in countries under domination by the U.S.S.R. is usually not impossible, but poses visa and permit problems that make travel difficult; e.g., the researcher had planned to visit both of the major libraries in Wroclaw (Breslau, see Note 5) while in Krakow, but, although the distances were short, the tourist bureau was unable to arrange train transportation, and flights between minor cities are non-existent. The Lenin State Library of the U.S.S.R. in Moscow was willing to search its union catalogue of foreign books housed in the Soviet Union to see if the books formerly at Königsberg were among its listing of consolidated libraries in the Soviet

Union, but a general search of U.S.S.R. holdings has not been possible. The degree of proficiency and recency of the *Primo Catalog* caused the researcher to expend what funds were available for foreign travel in libraries outside of Italy, particularly in German libraries where the cataloguing was interrupted by World War II and where war casualties to books were frequent.

[5]The letters sent to the libraries were accompanied by duplicates of the bibliographical entries as previously developed by the researcher. Replies to the mailing have been more than generous, and there have been one or two follow-up inquiries to most libraries. The rare book librarians who responded were meticulous in their comments, amendations, or corrections. Unfortunately, a number of libraries had their copies destroyed in World War II. This was particularly discouraging in Bonn, Kiel, Louvain-la-Neuve, and Braunsberg. A fire in Tours in 1940 appears to have seriously damaged its collection. Berlin, that had been a major Aristotelian repository, lost what is perhaps half of its holdings of the *Rhetoric*.

As Note 1 pointed out, special mailings continue the search for rare editions and for copies of editions referred to in the catalogues or bibliographies but for which no locations can be found. An attempt is also being made to clarify the holdings in the libraries at Wroclaw, Poland (formerly Breslau). Although a partial response has been received and although, while this researcher was in Krakow, the librarians at the *Jagiellońska* in Krakow spoke by telephone with the rare book librarians of the *Biblioteka Uniwersytecka* and the *Polska Akademia Nauk, Zaklad Narodowy im Ossolińskich* in Wroclaw, both of which have major Aristotelian holdings, complete information on their editions is still being sought.

[6]*Bibliothèque Nationale*, Rés.X.269 and Rés.X.637; Basel F.I.12; Bourges Incunable 179.

[7]Trapezuntius's translation of Aristotle's *Rhetoric* should not be confused with Trapezuntius's own five book rhetoric, written probably while Trapezuntius was a teacher in Venice between 1432-1434. Lacombe (1939, pp. 838, 925) refers to two existing MSS. of Trapezuntius's translation whereas Monfasani (1984, pp. 699-700) identified 23.

[8]Parisinus MS.1741 and Cantabrigiensis Ff.5.8. to mention the two oldest and probably most important Greek manuscripts of the *Rhetoric*. For a schemata of how the Greek manuscripts related to one another, see Kassel (1971, appendix). For a similar schemata showing the interrelationships of the Latin manuscripts, see Schneider (1971, p. 188).

[9]Lacombe (1956, p. 1348) acknowledged 98 extant manuscript copies.

[10]The work is sometimes attributed to "Farabi, Mohammad Abu-Nasr Al-" and occasionally referenced to Hermannus Alemannus. Such errors may have resulted from the cataloguers following too closely the contents of B.N. MS. Latin 16673 that does contain as its first entry a translation of the *Rhetoric* by Hermannus Alemannus (Boggess, 1971, 236-245). Apparently the printer had available to him three Paris manuscripts or their equivalents: MS. Latin 16673, MS. Latin 16097, and MS. Latin 7695.

[11]The next Eastern European edition was *Rhetoricorum liber primus* (Wittenberg, 1564). Unfortunately, the Berlin copy of this edition was lost in World War II, and there has not yet been an official confirmation of the copy that is supposedly in the *Biblioteka Uniwersytecka* in Wroclaw.

[12]See Murphy (1971, 33) and Murphy (1969).

[13]Aegidius Romanus (Egidio Colonna). (1515). *Commentaria in Rhetoricam Aristotelis*. Venice. Republished (1968). Frankfurt. Minerva GMBH.

[14]This research and Monfasani's findings (1984, 700-701), done independently of each other, concur. The methodology for this study lists independently the printings of 1561, sometimes attributed to the printer Frellonius and sometimes to the printer Vincentius, making the total 21 instead of the 20 listed by Monfasani.

[15]1530 (Paris); 1531 (Basel); 1536 (Venice); 1538 (Paris); 1539 (Basel); 1546 (Basel); 1546 (Venice); and 1547 (Strasbourg).

[16]The Wurzburg copy L.gr.f.108 has been missing since 1963, while the Griefswald copy is simply reported as being lost, presumably not in World War II but from other causes.

[17]*Bayerische Staatsbibliothek:* A.gr.b.626 (defective).

[18]"Finally, for the sake of completeness, it should be added that Victorius sought Francesco Medici's advice to correct various passages; to resolve doubts about the authenticity of certain parts, and to clarify obscure concepts and sentences" (Niccolai, p. 230).

[19]*"Mit dem Parisinus aber hatte der Editor das Instrument zur Hand, die aristotelische Schrift von zahllosen Verfälschungen zu befreiden. . ."* (Kassel, 1971, p. 100). "But, with the Paris manuscript, the editor had the instrument at hand to rescue Aristotle's text from its numerous errors."

[20]Monacensis 90; Monacensis 175; Monacensis 176.

[21]Niccolai (1912, p. 230) cited only the 1546 and 1549 editions as being in Victorius's library probably because Niccolai was relying on Ruediger (1896) as his source and had not visited the Munich library himself.

[22]The copy at Munich with the pages removed is catalogued as 2° L. impr.c.n.mass.81/1b.

[23]For example, Niccolai (1912, p. 228) pointed out ". . .in order to understand better and therefore, when necessary, to correct and illustrate the passages of the orators and of the ancient poets quoted as evidence by Aristotle, Victorius read a great many of them (Vict. Epp. IX.12)."

[24]Kassel (1971, p. 101): "But in the preparation of the text, however, Victorius had also left a lot undone that, with his resources, could easily have been set right. The basis for this failure lies in his enormous, frequently even debilitating care in being scrupulous that made him suspicious, not only in protecting himself against ticklish and unusual conjecture, but actually inclined him to set himself in general against major changes, even if they could be resolved by manuscript authority." Kassel (1976) has published his own edition of the Greek text.

[25]Victorius is not included as a sixth translator in this list because his 1579 translation, as influential as it was, was apparently only reprinted once during the period examined and his work was more of a scholarly nature than the five popular rhetoricians discussed here.

[26]For bibliographical details on the 19th and 20th century collations and a general oversight on Aristotelian research, see Grimaldi (1980, 357-362), Cooper (1932, 243-245), and Erickson (1975).

[27]In addition to the 50 sets of this work that contain the *Rhetoric*, a number of other incomplete sets that did not contain the *Rhetoric* were found at such locations as the University of Virginia, Boston Public, *Universitäts Bibliothek Göttingen*, and *Universitäts Bibliothek Heidelberg*.

[28]The editor of the 1584 edition, Frederick Sylburg, did not number his volumes but was content to list what he considered to be their order in the preface to volume one that appeared in 1587, three years after the first volume containing the *Rhetoric* had been issued. He therefore opened the door for librarians to establish their own order for his 10 volumes, causing problems in identifying the 1584 *Rhetoric* in a collection that does not index the holdings by volume, or that may not have identified the *Rhetoric* as belonging to the 10 volume series. Libraries with the set generally classify the *Rhetoric* as volume two to conform to the 1587 preface, but the *Bibliothèque Nationale* has the *Rhetoric* as volume nine, the Cambridge University Library as volume eight, Emmanuel College Library at Cambridge as volume five, and Northwestern University Library as volume one.

[29]Cranz (1971, viii) provided a table showing, in five year periods, the frequency of all Aristotelian publications between 1466 and 1600. The printings of the *Rhetoric* do not conform to the pattern of the Aristotle editions in general. The *Rhetoric* appeared in a much steadier stream than did Aristotle's overall publications and does not show the skewing toward the middle of the 16th century.

[30]Among those who have made contributions toward the exploration of the use to which the *Rhetoric* was put during the Renaissance are Herrick (1926), Hultzen (1932), Murphy (1960), and Weiss (1967).

References

American Library Association, Resources & Technical Services Division, Resources Section, Subcommittee on the National Union Catalogue. (1968-1980). *The national union catalogue: Pre-1956 imprints*. London: Mansell.

Boggess, W.F. (1971). Hermannus Alemannus's rhetorical translations. *Viator: Medieval and Renaissance Studies*, 2, 227-250.

Centro Nazionale per il Catalogo Unico della Biblioteche Italiane e per le Informazioni Bibliografiche. (1962-) *Primo catalogo collettiro delle biblioteche italiane*. Rome: Collegea Romano.

Cooper, L. (1932). *The Rhetoric of Aristotle*. New York: D. Appleton-Century Company.

Erickson, K.V. (1975). *Aristotle's Rhetoric: Five centuries of philological research*. Metuchen, NJ: Scarecrow Press.

Grimaldi, W. M.A. (1980). *Aristotle, rhetoric 1: A commentary*. New York: Fordham University Press.

Herrick, M. (1926). The early history of Aristotle's *Rhetoric* in England. *Philological Quarterly*, 5, 242-257.

Hultzen, L. (1932). Aristotle's *Rhetoric* in England to 1600. Unpublished doctoral dissertation, Department of Classics, Cornell University.

Index aureliensis catalogus librorum sedecimo saeculo impressorum. (1962-). Geneva: Foundation Index Aureliensis.

Jourdain, A. (1960). *Recherches critiques sur l'âge et l'origine des traductions latines d'Aristote*. New York: Burt Franklin. New edition edited by C. Jourdain.

Kassel, R. (Ed.). (1976). *Aristotelis ars rhetorica*. Berlin: Walter de Gruyter.

Kassel, R. (1971). *Der text der Aristotelischen rhetorik*. Berlin: Walter de Gruyter.

Kristeller, P.O. (1961). *Renaissance thought*. New York: Harper Torchbooks.

Lacombe G. (1939). *Aristoteles latinus. Pars prior*. Rome: La Libreria dello Stato.

Lacombe G. (1955). *Aristoteles latinus. Pars posterior*. Cambridge: Cambridge University Press.

Monfasani, J. (1976) *George of Trebizond*. Leiden: Brill.

Monfasani, J. (Ed.). (1984). *Collectanea Trapezuntiana: Texts, documents, and bibliographies of George of Trebizond*. Binghamton, NY: Medieval & Renaissance Texts & Studies.

Murphy, J. J. (1960). The earliest teaching of rhetoric at Oxford. *Speech Monographs*, 27, 345-347.

Murphy, J. J. (1969). The scholastic condemnation of rhetoric in the commentary of Giles of Rome on the *Rhetoric* of Aristotle. In *Arts Libéraux et Philosophie au Moyen Âge (Acts du Quatrième Congrès International de Philosophie Mediévale)*, 833-841. Montreal: Institut d'Études Mediévales.

Murphy, J.J. (1971). *Medieval rhetoric: a select bibliography*. Toronto: University of Toronto Press.

Niccolai, F. (1912). *Pier Vettori (1499-1589)*. Florence: Succ. B. Seeber.

Prussian Board of Education. (1931-1939). *Gesamtkatalog der Preussischen bibliotheken mit nachweis des Identischen Besitzes der Bayerischen Staatsbibliothek in München und der Nationalbibliothek in Wien*. Berlin: Preussische Druckerei- und verlags-aktiengesellschaftig. 14 Vols. Interrupted by World War II.

Prussian Board of Education. (1925-1940). *Gesamtkatalog der Wiegendrucke Herausgeben von der Kommission für den Gesamtkatalog der Wiegendrucke.* Leipzig: Karl W. Hiersemann. 8 Vols. Interrupted by World War II.

Ruediger, W. (1896). *Petrus Victorius aus Florenz; studien zu einem Lebensbilde.* Halle: M. Niemeyer.

Schneider, B. (1971). *Die mittelalterlichen griechisch-lateinischen übersetzungen der Aristotelischen Rhetorik.* Berlin: Walter de Gruyter.

Wartelle, A. (1963). *Inventaire des manuscrits Grecs d'Aristote et de ses commentateurs.* Paris: Belles Lettres.

Index